CONFOUNDING FATHER

JEFFERSONIAN AMERICA

Jan Ellen Lewis, Peter S. Onuf,
and Andrew O'Shaughnessy, Editors

CONFOUNDING FATHER

Thomas Jefferson's Image
in His Own Time

Robert M. S. McDonald

UNIVERSITY OF VIRGINIA PRESS

CHARLOTTESVILLE & LONDON

University of Virginia Press

© 2016 by the Rector and Visitors of the University of Virginia

Printed in the United States of America on acid-free paper

First published 2016

1 3 5 7 9 8 6 4 2

Library of Congress Cataloging-in-Publication Data
Names: McDonald, Robert M. S., 1970– author.
Title: Confounding father : Thomas Jefferson's image in his own time /
Robert M. S. McDonald.
Description: Charlottesville : University of Virginia Press, 2016. |
Series: Jeffersonian America | Includes bibliographical references and index.
Identifiers: LCCN 2016004208| ISBN 9780813938967 (cloth : alk. paper) |
ISBN 9780813938974 (ebook)
Subjects: LCSH: Jefferson, Thomas, 1743–1826 — Public opinion. |
Jefferson, Thomas, 1743–1826 — Influence. | Presidents — United States —
Public opinion — History. | Public opinion — United States —
History — 19th century.
Classification: LCC E332.2 .M419 2016 | DDC 973.4/6092 — dc23
LC record available at https://lccn.loc.gov/2016004208

Cover art: Portrait of Thomas Jefferson by Rembrandt Peale, ca. 1810s.
(Shutterstock, © Everett Historical)

For Christine

To glide unnoticed thro' a silent execution of duty,
is the only ambition which becomes me, and
it is the sincere desire of my heart.

———

Thomas Jefferson to John Paradise,
July 5, 1789

CONTENTS

ACKNOWLEDGMENTS

I HAVE BEEN WORKING on this book for a long time. I have not been working on it for even longer. I have many explanations but no real excuse. Certainly I cannot blame the numerous individuals who have patiently and generously contributed their assistance, advice, encouragement, and support.

I will begin at the beginning and thank my parents, to whom I owe nearly everything. My late father, Milton McDonald, and my mother, Barbara McDonald, demonstrated a commitment to my education that extended from family vacations in Williamsburg and Washington to rent checks during my first year of graduate school. Words cannot capture either all they did in my behalf or my gratitude for all their love.

My graduate mentor, the late Don Higginbotham, at the University of North Carolina at Chapel Hill steered the doctoral dissertation that, after significant rethinking, revision, expansion, and contraction, at long last emerges as this book. From my first meeting with Don he extended to me his generosity and true-blue goodness. He remains a real inspiration. North Carolina offered the gift of not only his tutelage but also the opportunity to learn from other members of its faculty, such as Harry Watson and Peter Coclanis, as well as fellow graduate students, most notably my friends Stuart Leibiger, H. R. McMaster, Steve Stebbins, and Brian Steele.

My debt to Don is equaled only by my debt to Peter Onuf, who has not been able to shake me since my days as an undergraduate at the University of Virginia. A mentor for more than half my life, it would be difficult to overstate the extent to which I have been the beneficiary of his wisdom, kindness, and patience. It would also be difficult to name all of the many fine people to whom he has introduced me. Two are Joanne Freeman and Frank Cogliano, formerly anonymous reviewers of this book whose critiques improved it considerably. Two others are my friends Richard Samuelson and Johann Neem. Another is Dick Holway, acquisitions editor at the University of Virginia Press, who in previous projects has acquainted me with Mark Mones, Raennah Mitchell, Angie Hogan, and Anna Kariel, all of whom, together with Margaret Hogan, an impressive historian as well as a most meticulous copyeditor, helped to move this book toward the finish line.

Don and Peter helped to connect me to the faculty at Oxford University. I left Chapel Hill for a year to earn a second master's there and drafted portions of this book while under the guidance of Peter Thompson, whose candid criticism helped me to improve my writing, and Bob Middlekauff, whose generous praise bolstered my confidence. Dan Howe, my adviser, very kindly did everything else.

Joe Ellis could not have been more busy but always found time to read and comment on several of my early chapter drafts. Others who also provided feedback on versions of this book's chapters, often as rushed and raw conference papers, include William Howard Adams, Joyce Appleby, Andy Burstein, Ted Crackel, Annette Gordon-Reed, James Lewis, Jan Lewis, David Mayer, Barbara Oberg, Jeff Pasley, Andy Robertson, Herb Sloan, Alan Taylor, David Waldstreicher, and Rosemarie Zagarri. Several of the chapters in this book have been revised and recast from previously published essays and journal articles. I am indebted to the editors and peer reviewers of "Thomas Jefferson's Changing Reputation as Author of the Declaration of Independence: The First Fifty Years," *Journal of the Early Republic* 19 (Summer 1999): 169–95; "The Hamiltonian Invention of Thomas Jefferson," in *The Many Faces of Alexander Hamilton: The Life and Legacy of America's Most Elusive Founding Father,* ed. Douglas Ambrose and Robert W. T. Martin (New York: New York University Press, 2006), 54–76; "Was There a Religious Revolution of 1800?" in *The Election of 1800: Democracy, Race, and the New Republic,* ed. Peter S. Onuf, Jan Lewis, and James Horn (Charlottesville: University of Virginia Press, 2002), 173–98; "Race, Sex, and Reputation: Thomas Jefferson and the Sally Hemings Story," *Southern Cultures* 4 (Summer 1998): 46–63; and "Thomas Jefferson and Historical Self-Construction: The Earth Belongs to the Living?" *The Historian* 61 (Winter 1999): 289–310.

My colleagues in the Department of History at the United States Military Academy, civilians as well as those in uniform, have been uniformly civil, supportive, and insightful. West Point's small classes require a large faculty, including army officers assigned for two- or three-year tours. In eighteen years I have been lucky enough to work with more than 250 fellow historians, many of whom, through their friendship and favors, supported this project in important ways. Attempting to name some would guarantee the inadvertent exclusion of others. Instead, I offer my sincere thanks to all. I am also grateful for the many cadets whose earnest effort and unrehearsed brilliance inspires and educates those of us on the faculty.

Then there are the friends—some of whom I have known since kinder-
garten—who cheered me on and offered not only welcome distractions from
research and writing but sometimes also pullout sofas not far from archives.
Those whom I cannot in good conscience fail to mention are Caleb Cage,
Scott and Kara Bowers, Charles Duncan, Nick Gardiner, Bill and Alison
Rausch, Dave Carpenter, Wade Carpenter, Ken Carpenter, and the late,
great, Jeff Carpenter. I also thank my friend Joe Dooley, former president
general of the National Society of the Sons of the American Revolution, an
organization that in recent years has done much to support scholarly projects,
including this one.

One of the greatest supporters of inquiry on topics related to early America
is the Thomas Jefferson Foundation, which owns and interprets Monticello. It
has bestowed on me many valuable gifts, including opportunities for research
and writing provided by its Robert H. Smith International Center for Jefferson Studies, where I have benefited from the expertise of Jim Horn, Andrew
O'Shaughnessy, Cinder Stanton, Jeff Looney, and especially Gaye Wilson,
who, beginning with my undergraduate thesis, has shared sources, advice, and
encouragement.

Yet the greatest gift I received from the Thomas Jefferson Foundation was
the opportunity to meet the former Christine Coalwell, then a research associate at the International Center, with whom I worked to clarify the origin
and provenance of a curious set of newspaper scrapbooks at the University of
Virginia Library. Christine uncovered much of the information featured in
this book's appendix, but this was only the beginning of our collaboration.
Now Christine McDonald, she is the co-author of our children, Jefferson and
Grace, and the love of my life.

O F ALL THE American Revolutionaries to whom successive generations affixed the appellation "founding father," during his lifetime
Thomas Jefferson loomed as the most controversial and confounding. Loved and hated, revered and reviled, for his contemporaries he served
as a lightning rod for dispute. Few major figures in American history provoked such a polarization of public opinion. John Beckley, one of his most
effective political allies, described him as the possessor of "a pure, ardent,
and unaffected piety; of sincere and genuine virtue; of an enlightened mind
and superior wisdom; the adorer of our God; the patriot of his country;
and the friend and benefactor of the whole human race." To the Marquis de
Lafayette he stood out as "everything that is good, upright, enlightened, and
clever," a man "respected and beloved by everyone that knows him." Martha
Washington disagreed. According to Reverend Manasseh Cutler, a Federalist
congressman, she proclaimed Jefferson "one of the most detestable of mankind." While Jefferson's supporters organized festivals in his honor where they
launched fireworks, marched in parades, and praised him in poem and song,
his opponents portrayed him as a dilettante and demagogue, double-faced
and dangerously radical, an atheist and "Anti-Christ" hostile to Christianity.
Yale president Timothy Dwight predicted that, if Jefferson won the nation's
highest office, "our sons" might "become the disciples of Voltaire, and . . . our
daughters the concubines of the Illuminati." Church services, transformed
"into a dance of Jacobin phrenzy," could feature "a strumpet [im]personating
a goddess on the altars of JEHOVAH." The charges inspired such fear that,
on the eve of his inauguration, pious New Englanders, fearing that the new
president would dispatch federal troops to seize their Bibles, reportedly hid
the books in locations where no one would think to look—such as the homes
of Jeffersonian Republicans.[1]

What made Jefferson, by nearly all accounts a man with a manner so mild
that some described it as meek, such a divisive figure? How did his image take

shape and develop? To what degree was his public persona a product of his own creation—and to what extent did it take shape in response to factors largely beyond his control? These are the central questions of this book, which traces the development of Jefferson's public reputation from 1776, when his authorship of the Declaration of Independence first placed him on the stage of national service, to 1826, when, after nearly five decades in the spotlight, he died at Monticello, the mountaintop home for which he had always claimed to yearn.

It is somewhat surprising that, after nearly two hundred years of sustained scholarship on Jefferson, this is the first extended analysis of the growth and development of his image among his contemporaries. Numerous books have examined public perceptions of other notable Americans, and many decades ago Merrill D. Peterson's *The Jefferson Image in the American Mind* traced the fascinating history of Jefferson's posthumous fame. "*The Jefferson image,*" Peterson wrote, "may be defined as the composite representation" of Jefferson "and of the ideas and ideals, policies and sentiments, habitually identified with him." Reflecting not only the reputation he had earned but also projections of "memory and hope" as well as "fact and myth," Peterson found Jefferson's posthumous image to be "highly complex, never uniform and never stationary." Jefferson's words, deeds, and name—whether appropriated by Jacksonian Democrats or Whigs, emancipationists and abolitionists or slavery's proponents, unionists or secessionists, agrarians or industrialists; whether evoked by populists and progressives, socialists and communists, or twentieth-century Republicans and Democrats—served as touchstones for generations of Americans advancing a diverse array of causes. Not all these groups always claimed his imprimatur or held him up as a hero, but his reputation, whether on the rise or on the wane, nevertheless always seemed to serve as "a sensitive reflector . . . of America's troubled search for the image of itself."[2]

While Franklin Roosevelt's 1943 dedication of the Jefferson Memorial marks the culmination of Peterson's account, it serves as a starting point of sorts for Francis D. Cogliano's more recent *Thomas Jefferson: Reputation and Legacy.* A meditation on how Jefferson's views on issues such as race, slavery, and America's place in the world have buffeted his popularity among historians, in some respects Cogliano's book focuses more narrowly than Peterson's. Yet it also looks back at Jefferson's earnest efforts to secure his place in history as a defender of liberty—to "stack the deck," according to Cogliano, by leaving a paper trail of letters and other documents for future generations to follow. This helps to explain Jefferson's enduring relevance as *Democracy's Muse,* as Andrew Burstein recently termed him. Americans continue to appeal to his authority because, from different political vantage points, this paper trail can seem to lead in different directions. Yet in an era of cynicism and irony, as Cogliano makes clear, a reputation embodying America's highest ideals and best aspirations can also carry a heavy burden and play a weak hand. By the dawn of the twenty-first century, scholars generally regarded with some skepticism the life and legacy of the third president, who, in the eyes of many, had come "to epitomize not America's promise but its limitations."[3]

Some of the most notable aspects of Jefferson's posthumous image also characterized perceptions of him before his death. Nearly all Americans, whether or not they supported him or agreed with what they perceived to be his vision, seemed to understand that Jefferson mattered and that the public's view of him had consequence. Like Andrew Jackson a generation later, Jefferson stood as a symbol for his age, a figure who, although hardly representative in terms of his background and attainments, nonetheless appeared to champion a future for which many hoped and that many others feared. His friends viewed him as a proponent of the Spirit of '76—freedom from distant authority, political as well as individual self-government, and the sort of commonsense, workaday egalitarianism that many read into the Declaration of Independence. His foes linked him instead with the French Revolution—the opening scenes of which he witnessed approvingly—and all of its excesses of democracy, anticlericalism, violence, and despotism. If for some the draftsman of the Declaration represented the quintessence of Americanism, for others he loomed as the un-American purveyor of philosophies both dangerously radical and fundamentally foreign.

Jefferson played no small role in inspiring and reinforcing these competing conceptions, in part because each, in many respects, constituted the mirror image of the other. When Charles Cornwallis surrendered at Yorktown, the British band probably did not, as is commonly believed, play a tune called "The World Turned Upside Down," but Jefferson's supporters hoped he would keep it upside down nonetheless. His detractors feared he would go too far, turning it inside out. These expectations served also as interpretive filters, causing partisans to dig in their heels when considering Jefferson's pronouncements, such as his declaration that "it does me no injury for my neighbour to say there are twenty gods, or no god. It neither picks my pocket nor breaks my leg." For Republicans a testimonial of tolerance and his understanding of government's rightful limits, the statement for Federalists served as proof of his disregard for Americans' souls and the soul of America. Jefferson had a knack for stepping on the tripwire stretching over the central tension of government. "Sometimes it is said that man cannot be trusted with the government of himself," he stated in his first inaugural address. "Can he then be trusted with the government of others? Or have we found angels, in the form of kings, to govern him? Let history answer this question." A rhetorical inversion of James Madison's earlier phrasing ("If men were angels, no government would be necessary. If angels were to govern men, neither external nor internal controls on government would be necessary"), it possessed a similar meaning but invited different interpretations. Some heard a call for liberty while others heard the voice of an anarchist.[4]

Jefferson had little doubt that human experience proved his intended point. Throughout the recorded past, he argued, men who gained power over others consolidated it with avarice and wielded it without mercy. Examples abounded. Greece had its Alexander and Rome its Caesar. Europe had suffered under a multitude of despots. Even at the dawn of the Enlightenment, and even in relatively enlightened lands such as England, usurpers such as Oliver Cromwell, James II, and George III abused and terrorized those they pretended to protect. The United States, Jefferson believed, had Alexander Hamilton, who, at a dinner party in Jefferson's presence, pronounced Julius Caesar "the greatest man . . . that ever lived."[5] Everywhere the story seemed the same. Government, which claimed to consolidate power for the common good, in reality worked for the good of the uncommonly powerful.

Jefferson stood at the threshold of a new age. Behind him languished the tired and tattered vestiges of aristocracy, an elitist system based on the premise that most men could not be trusted to rule themselves. Before him spanned a new, more democratic world, beguiling in its promises that the majority would select their rulers, that the rulers would represent the majority, and that all people—even those in the minority—would retain their individual rights. For some Hamiltonians, this constituted an impossible dream, a naive proposition likely to result in chaos and calamity. Popular politics, especially when decentralized, could give license to lesser characters all too willing to undermine the rights and republicanism for which the War for Independence had been fought. If, in hindsight, the contest between the ideas of Hamilton and Jefferson seems like the tension between the philosophies of Edmund Burke and Thomas Paine—two other men united in their sympathy for American Revolutionaries but divided on so much else—at the time it stood out as a competition to define the meaning of America. It is no exaggeration to note that the American leaders' differences, although exaggerated by their contemporaries, were nonetheless significant.

While Hamilton prized ordered liberty, Jefferson saw in America the promise of a new liberal order. While Hamilton looked east to England as a model for America, Jefferson saw America's future in the West. Hamilton sought to build an Anglicized empire featuring a powerful and centralized government, bustling cities, large-scale manufacturing, a robust navy shielding oceanic commerce, and a standing army ready for combat on distant battlefields. Jefferson, on the other hand, dreamed of small-town "ward republics" where men governed themselves, small-scale "manufactories" where free laborers enjoyed viable options for alternative employment, and plentiful land for independent farmers whose harvests so much filled the mouths of Europeans that they would never choke out words hostile to the United States. As if Hamilton's ambitions for an Old World future were not obvious enough, he once let slip his eastward orientation when, in a memorandum to George Washington, he positioned the United States with Canada on "our left" and Latin America on "our right." Jefferson, meanwhile, believed that the differences between American and European governments constituted "a comparison of heaven and hell" with that of England somewhere in the middle. He looked not across the Atlantic but beyond the Mississippi for "important aids to our treasury, an ample provision for our posterity, & a wide spread for the blessings of freedom and equal laws."[6]

Citizens forming opinions of Jefferson could contrast him with Hamilton in terms of style as well as substance. Hamilton, a transplant to New York, had been born poor to unmarried parents on Nevis, in the Caribbean's Leeward Islands. He nonetheless enjoyed numerous gifts. Perhaps most important among them, his confidence served first as the cause and then as the consequence of his unlikely rise. Impressing others as well as himself, his reputation became the prized possession for which he risked and lost his life. By comparison, Jefferson, the "Friend of the People," as supporters sometimes described him, began his life as the firstborn son of a father who owned the people who toiled for his comfort. His first real memory—as a two-year-old being carried on a pillow by one of his family's slaves—testified to his privilege. He demonstrated real ambivalence about his status as a member of the aristocracy, which later in life he would work to undermine. He never spurned the advantages it provided but felt some shame for being proud of ancestral accomplishments for which he could take no credit. Nothing better shows this

Jefferson's seal, ca. 1790.
(Albert and Shirley Small Special Collections Library,
University of Virginia)

ambivalence than the contrast between Jefferson's efforts in 1771 to confirm the authenticity of his family's coat of arms and his simultaneous assertion that "a coat of arms may be purchased as cheaply as any other coat." By 1790, in true Jeffersonian style, he had come to a compromise, designing for a stamp to seal his letters a personal coat of arms. The device, a second signature, included the exceedingly American motto: "Rebellion to Tyrants Is Obedience to God."[7]

This sort of self-definition helps to explain the deep division of opinion on Jefferson. To detractors convinced of his ambition and atheism, his personal seal would have smacked of self-serving self-aggrandizement bordering on blasphemy. To supporters the seal would have confirmed the depth of his commitment to liberty. The development of Jefferson's image, the result of issues and ideology, was also the product of the sometimes novel ways in which he presented himself and was perceived by others. Long before the emergence of modern identity politics, in the era of the early republic there existed a politics of identity.

If an increased understanding of the role of ideology in early American politics has proved to be historians' greatest insight of the past several decades, a not unrelated focus on the sometimes crucial roles of the various modes of "self" and self-presentation has also emerged as an important interpretive category. Even before Bernard Bailyn's *Ideological Origins of the American Revolution,* there was Charles S. Sydnor's *Gentlemen Freeholders,* an influential study paying close attention to the characteristics and behavior eighteenth-century voters sought from their leaders. These expectations, historians of republicanism later noted, resulted from ingrained presumptions about human nature and the dangers of concentrated power. In the transitional world of the American Revolutionary era, a period characterized by vestiges of aristocracy and portents of democracy, a decreasingly deferential public judged the fitness of its representatives on the basis of the virtue made possible by wealth and the disinterestedness made possible by virtue. Political power, not so much bestowed as entrusted, was rarely conferred on those who had not mastered the art of at least pretending to have no desire to govern.[8] Add other imperatives that have caught historians' attention—an emerging synthesis of the founding generation's understanding and expression of self that ranges from elite notions of honor and conceptions of character to the rise of oftentimes ritualized and increasingly issues-based conveyance of popular sentiment—and the result is the rediscovery of a fluid, unpredictable, deeply personal, and high-pitched political environment hinging on contingency and evolving rules of engagement.[9] No wonder opinions of Jefferson, who often appeared at the center of conflicts involving not only politics but also public culture, diverged so widely and divided so deeply.

To underscore this point, this book begins with a prologue describing how Jefferson's signature achievement, his "authorship" of the Declaration of Independence, for years remained unknown to most Americans. The document, of course, originated as a group statement issued by the Continental Congress—"The unanimous Declaration of the thirteen united States of America." Jefferson's anonymity as draftsman made sense, especially against the backdrop of Enlightenment print culture and the dictates of republican self-effacement. Eighteenth-century penmen refrained from attaching their names to printed arguments and sometimes freely appropriated the words and ideas of others because what gave a text authority was not the identity of its author or its originality as a composition but the persuasiveness of its argument. Within the full context of the development of Jefferson's image, subsequent chapters trace the rise of his reputation as the scribe of independence alongside the emergence of more modern conceptions of authorship, which, by the second decade of the nineteenth century, people had begun to conceive as an act of individual creation. Authors signed their works, claimed ownership of them, and imparted to their creations credibility derived from their own reputations. This characterized the development of Jefferson's fame as creator of the Declaration, a story of the shifting of attention away from its principles and toward the man who had inscribed them. By the end of Jefferson's life, the new understanding of authorship allowed some to regard him as a plagiarist of John Locke and other writers, whose ideas and phrasing Jefferson employed in the draft he composed for Congress. It made it possible for others, however, to extol him as the veritable inventor of America.

Jefferson began to gain widespread attention as the Declaration's draftsman in the 1790s, when political disputes brought about the invention of his public image. Amid controversies over the direction of American government, he drew fire on the pages of Federalist newspapers and pamphlets. As chapter 1 argues, during his service as George Washington's secretary of state Jefferson's political enemies inadvertently elevated him to prominence as the recognized leader of the Republican opposition, a position previously occupied by James Madison, his personal friend and political ally. Jefferson, ever careful not to appear to serve as an advocate for his own advancement, refused to pick up his pen in self-defense. This did not prevent him, however, from urging Madison and others to do so. Jefferson's allies rushed to vindicate his name, praising him in the public prints and laying the foundation of his image as a true republican and friend of liberty. Although Jefferson in 1793 resigned as secretary of state and returned to Monticello, his mountaintop home, the retirement that he claimed to be permanent proved short-lived.

Even in the relative seclusion of Monticello, Jefferson continued as titular head of the Republicans, who some now described as "Jeffersonians." Although he purported to maintain "a much loved ignorance" of public affairs, preoccupied instead with "the peaches, grapes and figs of my own garden," his distance from the controversies that consumed Washington's second term allowed him to cultivate not only tobacco, wheat, fruits, and vegetables but also his image as a disinterested patriot who stood aloof from impassioned partisanship.[10] He understood that supporters would advance him as a candidate to succeed Washington in the presidential election of 1796. If in this contest, the focus of chapter 2, Jefferson's primary role in the development of his reputation was to remain behind the scenes, others nonetheless did much to embellish and reinforce it—both to his benefit and detriment. Ultimately, two opposing images of Jefferson came into focus. His allies held him up as a friend of liberty, for example, while his adversaries decried his hostility to order. His friends responded to Federalist attempts to render his views as radical and French (and therefore un-American) by highlighting his role in crafting the Declaration, which justified America's independence and laid out its fundamental principles. They praised his stand in favor of religious freedom after Federalists accused him of aiming to undermine Christian thought and practice. Both sides characterized Jefferson simultaneously as a slaveholder and emancipationist—although each side divided its portrayal for targeted sectional audiences.

Jefferson, whose sixty-eight electoral votes fell short of John Adams's seventy-one, returned to Philadelphia in 1797 as vice president with less connection to the Federalist administration than the Senate, where he presided. If at first he considered his duties "honorable & easy" he soon could have appreciated his predecessor's later characterization of the vice presidency as a "nauseous fog."[11] In chapter 3, Jefferson returns to center stage in this analysis, for as vice president his efforts to protect his reputation by finessing the politics of self-effacement and self-presentation proved crucial. In situations ranging from the publication of a confidential letter to friend Philip Mazzei criticizing Washington and appearing to criticize the Constitution, to his anonymous authorship of an early version of the Kentucky Resolutions, to his high-stakes confrontation with Maryland Federalist Luther Martin over the accuracy of his 1785 *Notes on the State of Virginia,* Jefferson carefully navigated to preserve his status as both a man of honor and a man of the Enlightenment by presenting himself before the public as a man of principle.

While the late 1790s tested Jefferson's capacity to preserve his political viability, Adams shouldered even heavier burdens. The events of his presidency, which Jefferson described as a "reign of witches," confirmed Republicans' fears about the imperiled status of American liberty while simultaneously imperiling Adams's support from fellow Federalists, many of whom had come to view him as unreliable and capricious.[12] As chapter 4 points out, rather than highlighting Adams's public record or personal virtues, Federalists in the 1800 presidential campaign focused on painting a dark portrait of Jefferson's religious faith and intellectual habits. While Republicans defended Jefferson's character, their main effort aimed to emphasize his principles, which they said restored the promise of the American Revolution. Both sides seemed to sense that the election could prove pivotal for the future of the republic. Certainly they acted as if it did, ratcheting up their rhetoric and organizing their efforts in innovative ways. Compared to 1796, Jefferson's behind-the-scenes involvement also increased, although in public he projected an ambivalence that testified to his pretended lack of ambition. Only after an electoral college tie with Aaron Burr, the Republican vice presidential candidate, and the unlikely support of Hamilton did Jefferson, on the thirty-sixth ballot in the lame duck, Federalist-controlled House of Representatives, win the opportunity to stand before the public and, in his inaugural address, attempt to explain not only his goals but also himself.

Many Americans responded with enthusiasm, celebrating Jefferson's victory as if it heralded a new era of liberation. While Federalists tended to adhere to the notion that only men of virtue and substance stood fit to participate in politics, Republicans downplayed this presumption in order to embrace egalitarianism and democracy. Chapter 5 points out, however, that Jeffersonians, although exuberant in their assumption of power, nonetheless felt anxious about its potential to corrupt. Throughout the 1790s, when criticizing the courtly pomp of the Washington and Adams administrations, they had repeated as one of their slogans "principles and not men."[13] Just as Jefferson's initially anonymous authorship of the Declaration affirmed that the text's substance and not his identity as its author imparted its authority, Republicans, even after their man had taken the oath of office, insisted that their support hinged on his fidelity to principle. Federalists might have cared about the character of men who held office, but Jefferson's supporters vowed that their support stood contingent on the character of his measures. Promising vigilance and not confidence in their leaders, Jeffersonians undercut antique traditions of deference at the same time that they sought to inoculate themselves against the temptation to fall into the sort of personality cults that in revolutionary France and elsewhere had turned citizens into members of mobs.

Jefferson took note of demonstrations of support for his principles and policy; the several dozen newspapers to which he subscribed frequently contained accounts of Republicans' festivities on dates such as the Fourth of July and the Fourth of March (the latter marking the anniversary of his inauguration, which, like Federalists' celebration of Washington's birthday, had become a partisan holiday) as well as other indications of public sentiment that he clipped and then pasted onto the pages of scrapbooks. What an evocative picture this paints of a self-conscious man with deep regard for not only his reputation but also his conviction that nearly all Americans (except for the duped and the duplicitous) shared his core beliefs. While supporters watched him, he watched them, creating a continuous feedback loop between the represented and their representative.

For a while it seemed nearly impossible for the popular president to lose.

Not even renegade journalist James T. Callender's claims that Jefferson had fathered the children of Sally Hemings, an enslaved woman he had inherited from his father-in-law, resulted in a particularly bad outcome. As chapter 6 explains, Federalists welcomed this news as confirmation of their view of Jefferson's character. They mocked him in the North while in the South they leveraged the reports to allege that he had undermined racial distinctions essential to slavery's survival. Everywhere they called on him to either admit or disavow the truthfulness of the charges. Yet Jefferson exercised his right to remain silent, denying his detractors fresh news to exploit. Meanwhile, Jeffersonians took to the newspapers to reaffirm their longstanding position that the details of his private life had no bearing on their assessment of his official actions, which they found exemplary.

The Hemings controversy earned few mentions during Jefferson's triumphant reelection to the presidency in 1804. Chapter 7, which centers on this 162-to-14 electoral vote landslide, takes note of the importance of the Louisiana Purchase, seemingly cheered without reservation by nearly everyone except the most diehard Federalists and, in private when consulting his constitutional scruples, Jefferson himself. Federalist prophecies of widespread atheism and anarchy had proved false, and the country prospered. Taking into account Jefferson's success at eliminating internal taxes, slashing bureaucracy, and paying down the national debt, maybe the real wonder is that in 1804 he did not perform even better. This is especially true since the 12th Amendment, adopted just in time for the election, added clarity to the electoral process. Precluding a reenactment of an electoral college tie between Jefferson and his running mate (this time, conspicuously, not Burr but George Clinton), Federalists claimed that the measure revealed the president's ambition for power and the democratic populace's unthinking acquiescence to his retention of it. "I do not see any reason to suppose there will be any discontent from any violations of right or Constitution that the ruling faction many perpetuate," wrote former Massachusetts congressman Fisher Ames. "Any people will bear wrongs because they may be blinded by their authors."[14]

While Republicans in 1804 continued to repeat their mantra of "principles and not men," by the second half of Jefferson's second term it seemed that many only paid lip service to the concept. If the U.S. military's success on the shores of Tripoli buoyed Jefferson's confidence in the efficacy of armed force, he nevertheless hoped to avoid armed confrontation with major European powers. "Of all the enemies to public liberty," Secretary of State Madison had noted, "war is, perhaps, the most to be dreaded, because it comprises and develops the germ of every other," including "debts and taxes" as well as powerful armies, which throughout history had served as "the known instruments for bringing the many under the few."[15] Jefferson's response to British and French attacks on American shipping was to embargo all international trade. As chapter 8 suggests, although numerous principles substantiated Jefferson's decision to experiment with commercial coercion as an alternative to war, his supporters appeared to find it difficult to explain them. Rather than making principled defenses of the controversial embargo, a good number of Republican writers abandoned their old slogan and argued that the public should support the measure because it had been signed into law by Jefferson, a man who had earned their trust. While Federalists took note of this seemingly sudden and certainly opportunistic elevation of men over measures, few others appear to have objected, in part perhaps because it reflected larger trends in American culture. As the eighteenth century gave way to the nineteenth—as the Enlightenment gave way to the Romantic era—the dichotomy between principles and men began to give way to a new conception of heroic individualism celebrating men of principle. By this point Jefferson, author of the embargo, had become widely known not merely as the penman, compiler, or draftsman of the Declaration but as the author of independence.

During his final retirement at Monticello the former president labored to cement such connections. Chapter 9 surveys his numerous efforts to secure his place in history, memorializing himself as an enduring symbol of liberty. He worked with historians, artists, and educators, racing against time and struggling against setbacks to promote his principles and ensure that long after his death he would be remembered as their champion. Of all the acts that burnished Jefferson's reputation as the embodiment of independence none could match the impact of the final one. Jefferson died on the Fourth of July 1826, fifty years after the Continental Congress ratified his Declaration. That his name would resound through the ages was Jefferson's final wish, and now it was fulfilled.

Yet Jefferson's timely demise, which did much to bolster his fame, also marked the moment at which, despite his best efforts, he lost the power to influence his image. The epilogue, "The Apotheosis," pays homage through its title to Peterson's *Jefferson Image in the American Mind.* The eponymous prologue of Peterson's book begins the story where this one concludes. Somewhat different in focus, both share the same observation. Jefferson's image, together with his "ideas and ideals, his prophesies and legacies," as Peterson writes, would all remain "engaged in the great campaigns of history to come."[16]

Thomas Jefferson's Declaration of Virtue

MORE THAN a quarter century after 1776, Americans who applauded Thomas Jefferson as the author of the Declaration of Independence continued to confound John Adams. He, too, had sat on the committee assigned to compose the treasonous tract. The committee approved it, and then so did the Continental Congress, but only after subjecting it to "severe Criticism, and striking out several of the most oratorical Paragraphs." The Declaration was a group project and not, as Jefferson's admirers had come to claim, a solitary performance. "Was there ever a *coup de theatre* that had so great effect," Adams wondered in 1805, "as Jefferson's penmanship of the Declaration of Independence?" As the New Englander wrote six years later, "the Declaration of Independence I always considered as a theatrical show. Jefferson ran away with all the stage effect . . . and all the glory of it."[1]

Adams's resentment resulted from bewilderment as much as jealousy. Congress, not Jefferson, had authorized the Declaration. Few people had known that Jefferson drafted the document and even fewer people cared. Yet in the decades that followed, Jefferson gradually gained fame as the man responsible for the Declaration, which itself gained fame as Jeffersonian Republicans transformed it from the Continental Congress's press release on independence to the statement of purpose for the American nation. Adams still thought of Jefferson as the Declaration's penman, but Americans had come to exalt him as its author.

The first thing to know about the history of Jefferson's reputation is that, in the earliest days of United States, his contributions to the Declaration of Independence remained largely unknown. His initial anonymity as draftsman of the Declaration, which only recently has attracted the attention of scholars, helps to underscore not only the political culture of Revolutionary America but also Jefferson's eagerness, as a young man, to act in accordance with it.[2]

A product of the Enlightenment, the Declaration during the Revolution served as a statement of consensus, a unanimous assertion of "self-evident" "truths" designed to solidify Americans' support for independence, secure foreign assistance, and convey a reassuring message of political virtue. As such, Jefferson's authorship of the text remained unknown to all but a handful of citizens until 1783, when Yale president Ezra Stiles noted the Virginian's "signal act" in a sermon that subsequently appeared as a pamphlet.[3] Not until the 1790s, when memories of the War for Independence had receded, factionalism had intensified, and the Declaration had become a weapon of partisan warfare, did Jefferson's fame as its creator gradually take root. In response to Federalists, who cast Jefferson as a radical French revolutionary, Jeffersonian Republicans promoted his role in the creation of the Declaration as evidence that his political views helped establish the essence of Americanism. Eventually both factions linked the Declaration's authority to its author, a leader whom they sought to discredit or promote by situating his text within an increasingly modern conception of authorship stressing creative originality. Not for decades, however, would the Declaration achieve national, nonpartisan eminence as a hallowed relic of the Revolution, and not until the final year of his life did Jefferson, who earlier remained silent about his contribution, publicly embrace his status as the scribe of independence.[4]

WHEN JEFFERSON arrived at the Continental Congress he was neither famous nor obscure. Although most Americans outside of Virginia had never heard of him, in Philadelphia a few of his peers already knew his name, and on many he would soon make a lasting impression. The day after Jefferson joined Congress, Rhode Island representative Samuel Ward described him as "a very sensible spirited fine Fellow & by the Pamphlet which he wrote last Summer he certainly is one." The pamphlet was Jefferson's 1774 *Summary View of the Rights of British America,* an anonymously written tract that, after individuals in the Virginia legislature leaked their knowledge of his authorship, gained him notoriety as far away as London. James Duane of New York soon developed a high opinion of Jefferson, calling him "the greatest Rubber off of Dust" whom Duane had met, adding "that he has learned French, Italian, Spanish and wants to learn German." Jefferson distinguished himself on numerous committees, which often asked him to draft their reports. According to Adams, one of the prime movers for independence, Jefferson's "Reputation of a masterly pen" made him a logical choice to draft the Declaration.

While he gained a reputation as an ardent patriot and man of letters, how-ever, he rarely participated in debate. "During the whole Time I satt with him in Congress," Adams recalled in his autobiography, "I never heard him utter three Sentences together."[5]

But Jefferson's avoidance of conflict enhanced his credentials as a prospec-tive draftsman of a unifying proclamation of independence. After Richard Henry Lee on June 7, 1776, introduced the motion that "these United colonies are, and of right ought to be, free and independent States," Congress appointed a committee consisting of Adams, Jefferson, Benjamin Franklin, Roger Sher-man, and Robert R. Livingston to compose a formal declaration of indepen-dence. As Adams recollected nearly fifty years later, Jefferson called on him, as one of Congress's most vocal agitators for separation from Britain, to take the lead in writing it. It was a modest move on Jefferson's part, one nicely calibrated to stroke Adams's prickly ego. But Adams refused: "You can write ten times better than I can," he reported telling Jefferson. In addition, Adams said, "a Virginian ought to be at the head of this business." He understood that his status as a delegate from Massachusetts, which had borne the brunt of British sanctions and gunfire, together with his "early and constant Zeal in promot-ing" independence, would enable members of Congress to criticize anything he might write as the product of local interests and personal prejudice. Vir-ginia, the most populous of the colonies and the only southern one represented on the drafting committee, had sacrificed far fewer lives and fortunes to rebel-lion than Massachusetts; presumably, it could better elevate principle above interest. So could Jefferson who, unlike Adams, had not publicly committed himself to the idea of independence. As Adams remembered telling Jefferson, "I am obnoxious, suspected, and unpopular. You are very much otherwise."[6]

The independence of mind and means, the cultivated and recognized vir-tue, and the devotion to the good of society that Adams ascribed to Jefferson were modeled, in part, on the examples of elders who for decades had embraced the idea of selfless public service. George Washington also lived in accordance with this ethic, which Jefferson in 1793 described as "disinterestedness," a term encompassing the commander in chief's ability to resist "motives of interest or consanguinity, of friendship or hatred." Veteran statesman Edmund Pen-dleton, who wrote late in life that he had attained "without solicitation . . . the highest offices," suggested an important corollary: Virginia aristocrats could not openly seek political influence, for doing so would make them suspect of seeking office for private gain. The spirit of disinterestedness animated civic-minded Americans throughout the colonies. "The only principles of public

conduct that are worthy of a gentleman or a man," contended Massachusetts
native James Otis, Jr., "are to sacrifice estate, ease, health, and applause, and
even life, to the sacred calls of his country. These manly sentiments, in private
life, make the good citizen; in public life, the patriot and the hero."[7]

Jefferson also learned proper political behavior from the writings of John
Locke, the Baron de Montesquieu, and Algernon Sidney. Each man asserted
that leaders should bolster their virtue but not their earthly fortunes, that
they should pursue the common good but not chase after popular acclaim.
Locke found the roots of political corruption in the "Ambition and Luxury"
of lawmakers, "aided by Flattery" from an undiscerning public. Given the
opportunity, Locke wrote in 1689, rulers developed "distinct and separate Interests from their People." Montesquieu argued in his 1748 *Spirit of the Laws*
that only "the single desire, the single happiness, of rendering greater services
to one's homeland" should animate leaders. Similarly, in his 1698 *Discourses
concerning Government,* Sidney contended that a fit leader does not hold office
"for his own pleasure, glory or profit, but for the good of those that are under
him." In 1771, Jefferson endorsed these works as among "the best" on politics
available. It was Jefferson's reputation for disinterestedness, together with his
skill as a writer and status as a Virginian, that Adams hoped would help cement consensus for independence in Congress.[8]

Beyond this assemblage of statesmen, Jefferson's proclamation aimed to enhance the public's support for separation by asserting the working fiction that
nearly all Americans had already coalesced around the idea of independence.
Like all resolutions of Congress, the Declaration was a group statement. The
word "I" is entirely absent. "We" appears thirteen times in Jefferson's draft and
ten times in the Declaration as altered by Congress. As adopted on July 4, "A
Declaration by the representatives of the United states of America, in Congress assembled," it spoke "in the name and by the authority of the good people of these . . . free and independent states." After July 15, when the New York
delegation received instructions to vote for independence, Congress inserted
the word "unanimous" in the title and deleted the reference to state "representatives," strengthening the affirmation of consensus. Although the *Journals
of the Continental Congress* listed the members of the committee appointed
to prepare the Declaration, the records did not disclose Jefferson's particular
contribution, which likely seemed an irrelevant detail. More important than
the proclamation itself were the courageous assertions it made, which the
"unanimous" Declaration attributed to the "thirteen united States."[9]

In addition to the Declaration's status as a corporate document, there was another important cloak shielding Jefferson's identity as its author. The sublimation of self was a cornerstone of not only public service but also political texts. Writers endeavored to avoid suspicions that they sought popularity or fame either by writing anonymously or by employing pseudonyms. The trio of Alexander Hamilton, John Jay, and James Madison, for example, authored their *Federalist* essays as "Publius." Franklin also cloaked himself under fictive identities, appearing as "Poor Richard," "Silence Dogood," and "Richard Saunders." The Constitution claimed authorship by "We, the People." Philadelphia lawyer John Dickinson called himself a "Pennsylvania Farmer" and assured his audience that he was "contented" and "undisturbed by worldly hopes or fears"—in other words, that his public writings did not aim at private gain. Whether explicit or implied, for radical tracts such as the Declaration this promise mattered a great deal. The strategy shielded authors from charges of interestedness at the same time it empowered them to express subversive opinions without fear of censure.[10]

Not surprisingly, Jefferson's *Notes on the State of Virginia,* which criticized the slave system that brought wealth to his peers and himself, appeared under his name without his consent. He told Madison that, while he intended for the *Notes,* the bulk of which he wrote in 1780 and 1781 before revising and enlarging it for anonymous publication in 1785, to be circulated among a few friends, he did not want it "to go to the public at large." Only after he had learned that a French publisher intended to sell an unauthorized version did Jefferson arrange for the 1787 publication of his *Notes,* corrected and edited for general distribution with his name on the title page. As an appropriately pseudonymous "Epaminondas" wrote in the June 1775 *Pennsylvania Magazine,* "self-denial" in argument "is both more powerful and more safe" than "triumphant vanity." Similarly, as an anonymous writer contended in a 1776 pamphlet, "no man is a true republican, or worthy of that name, that will not give up his single voice to that of the public."[11]

Pseudonymity appealed to Americans for yet another reason. As pamphleteers' pen names suggest, even high-born writers could assume common personas. Radically egalitarian, the concealment of a writer's identity offered a level field to all literate citizens. At a time when British decrees established their authority in the name of the king, in the alternative tradition of the Enlightenment the "self-evident" nature of logical arguments enhanced the persuasiveness of texts. Thomas Paine titled his 1776 pamphlet *Common Sense.* He published it anonymously and, in response to speculation sparked by the success of its first printing, stipulated that "who the Author of this

Production is, is wholly unnecessary to the Public, as the Object for Attention
is the *Doctrine itself,* not *the Man.* Yet it may not be unnecessary to say, That
he is unconnected with any Party, and under no sort of Influence public or
private, but the influence of reason and principle." Thus, an anonymous Declaration, similarly elevated from complicating suspicions that its draftsman
sought to promote not only independence but also himself, according to the
standards of the time communicated sincerity.[12]

But the Declaration differed from other printed tracts in that Jefferson
wrote it to be read aloud. On one of his early drafts he appears to have placed
marks after words and phrases to indicate points of emphasis and places to
pause. He intended for the Declaration to be proclaimed in the form of an
emotionally evocative appeal. But while an oratorical Declaration stirred the
sentiments of citizens at readings throughout the colonies, by vesting its authority in the states represented at Philadelphia it averted alienating those who
suspected political speech-makers of rabble-rousing and self-promotion.[13] Unlike standard oratory, the Declaration took the form of a self-evident proof,
not a personal statement that relied for authority on a single man's credibility.
Jefferson himself distrusted orators, sharing a commonly held view of them as
disingenuous, self-interested demagogues. He recalled in 1808 that as a young
man he had asked himself "which of these kinds of reputations should I prefer? That of a horse jockey? a fox hunter? an orator? or the honest advocate of
my country's rights?" Resolved "to the prudent selection and steady pursuit of
what is right," Jefferson chose the final option.[14]

His Declaration's depersonalized voice enabled it to sound disinterested
at the same time that it aired the colonists' grievances. Since anonymity enhanced the authority of eighteenth-century political writing, signed political pamphlets and essays were rare. For Americans, a Declaration lacking a
readily identifiable author raised no eyebrows. For Jefferson, shy by nature,
an anonymous Declaration provided shelter from public exposure as well as
charges of self-promotion and demagoguery. As Montesquieu wrote, "Political virtue is a renunciation of oneself." Anonymity not only underscored the
Declaration's status as a group statement; it also drew a line between Jefferson's private interests and the public good, serving for him as a personal declaration of selflessness.[15]

Yet Jefferson rarely resisted taking credit for his modesty. His appetite for
having his cake and eating it too never matched the hunger of Paine, who, after
publishing *Common Sense* without his name attached, produced a new edition with a preface highlighting his anonymity but all the while, according to

the pamphlet's jilted first printer, bragged about his authorship "in every beer house" in Philadelphia.[16] Jefferson was never so crass, and later in life he recognized the Declaration as a collective statement, aiming neither "at originality of principle or sentiment" and repeating much that had already appeared in American newspapers, pamphlets, and broadsides—not to mention the writings of Locke and George Mason.[17] Immediately after its adoption, however, he wrote to Virginia's leading powerbrokers, calling attention to his accomplishment while claiming to wince at what the Continental Congress had done to his composition. He complained that, although he penned the text with great care, making repeated revisions and soliciting still others from Adams and Franklin, Congress altered sections of his draft and deleted others, such as his passage blaming the slave trade on the king. To Richard Henry Lee on July 8 he enclosed "a copy of the declaration of independence as agreed to by the House, and also, as originally framed." After Jefferson asked Lee to "judge whether it is better or worse for the Critics," Lee affirmed his wish "that the Manuscript had not been mangled as it is." Jefferson also sent a copy of his draft to Edmund Pendleton, who responded that Congress "altered it much for the worse." Jefferson may have been thin-skinned and shy, but early in his career he aimed to impress. As president his simple manners and simple attire would attract notice, but as a thirty-two year old arriving in Philadelphia, it was his four fine horses—and two enslaved attendants—that made an impression.[18]

THE EARLIEST KNOWN public reference to Jefferson's role as draftsman attributed the Declaration's sentiments neither to Jefferson nor to Congress but instead to all Americans. Ezra Stiles mentioned in a sermon delivered to the Connecticut General Assembly that it was "Jefferson, who poured the soul of the continent into the monumental act of independence."[19] Stiles's May 8, 1783, remarks constituted the first printed account of Jefferson's service as the framer of independence. With hundreds of copies sold in New England, Stiles's pronouncement about the origins of the Declaration resonated far beyond the walls of the Hartford statehouse.[20] A year later a Boston newspaper, noting Jefferson's arrival in town to embark on a diplomatic mission to France, observed that "the memorable declaration of American Independence is said to have been penned by him."[21]

The recording in print of Jefferson's contribution hastened the dispersal of the information, which formerly had passed through conversations. Stiles, for example, in 1777 recorded in his diary that he had "Dined in Company with

Col. [John] Langdon formerly of the Continental Congress. He says Mr. Jef-
fries of Virginia drafted the Declaration of Independency." Stiles's confusion
about Jefferson's name probably resulted from the fact that Langdon, too, was
a secondhand source. Although Langdon left the Congress prior to July 4, he
was a close friend of William Whipple, who had replaced him in the New
Hampshire delegation and signed the Declaration. Jefferson's authorship may
even have been known to most members of Connecticut's legislature. Stiles's
brief reference to "Jefferson, who poured the soul of the continent into" Congress's "monumental act," reads like a reminder, not an announcement. Besides Stiles, however, the small and slowly growing number of Americans who
knew of Jefferson's service had found no reason to consider it important.[22]

Jefferson's draftsmanship remained obscure during the Revolution and
throughout the 1780s. Americans who celebrated the Fourth of July as the
anniversary of independence paid scant attention to the Declaration and even
less to its writer. Dignitaries at a 1785 Independence Day dinner in New York,
for example, toasted George Washington, soldiers who had died in combat,
European allies, and "Liberty, peace and happiness to all mankind." But no
one raised a glass to Jefferson. The earliest chroniclers of the nation's history,
moreover, displayed similar indifference about the Declaration and its authorship. Philip Mazzei, Jefferson's longtime friend, mentioned only incidentally
in his 1788 history of American politics that the Virginian had served as the
scribe of independence. William Gordon's 1788 history of resistance and war
termed the Declaration an "act of separation from the crown of Great Britain" and identified Jefferson only as one member of the committee charged
with drafting the document. Similarly, David Ramsay's *History of the American Revolution,* published the following year, ignored Jefferson and dryly described the Declaration as the "act of the united colonies for separating themselves from the government of Great-Britain." It was a means to an end of
British rule, not a powerfully penned beginning of American government.[23]

Yet in the decades to follow, the Declaration rose to prominence as a means
to burnish Jefferson's fame and blunt the barbs of political enemies. Beginning
in the 1790s, detractors would question his patriotism, undermining his status
as an American Revolutionary by asserting his fidelity to the eventual violence
and radicalism of the French Revolution. What better defense against those
who questioned Jefferson's allegiance to the United States, who suggested that
his philosophies were not only dangerous but also un-American, than the fact
that he had written the declaration announcing America's birth, extolling its
purpose, and defining its best principles?

CHAPTER ONE

The Invention of Thomas Jefferson

B Y THE SPRING OF 1790, signs of division cracked the optimistic facade of the New World's newest government. A proposal that the nation absorb the states' Revolutionary War debts split the federal government into two camps. Secretary of the Treasury Alexander Hamilton, author and chief proponent of the measure, faced stiff resistance from officeholders who charged that it would favor some of the states at the others' expense and line the pockets of lawmakers and those who had purchased state-issued bonds.[1]

The faction that favored Hamilton's proposal blamed the impasse on a single man. Vice President John Adams granted that this individual was "a studious scholar," but "his Reputation as a man of Abilities is a Creature of French Puffs." Heaping on the vitriol, he added that "some of the worse Measures, some of the most stupid Motions stand on Record to his Infamy." Abigail Adams shared her husband's sentiments. "I have watch'd a certain character much celebrated," she wrote, but "I do not like his Politicks." Massachusetts Representative Theodore Sedgwick confided that "the leader of the opposition" had the character of "a very timid man" and wondered "whether he is actuated by the mean and base motive of acquiring popularity in his own state, . . . or whether he means to put himself at the head of the discontented in America." Artist John Trumbull linked this man's conduct "to motives of envy" against the treasury secretary. The Adamses, Sedgwick, and Trumbull referred to James Madison.[2]

Madison led the resistance to Hamilton's policies during the first half of George Washington's first term. In addition to organizing a coalition to oppose the assumption plan, a few months later the Virginia congressman railed against the treasury chief's proposal for a national bank and promoted a partisan press designed to rally the public behind the cause of republicanism.

Madison relied heavily on Thomas Jefferson, his friend and neighbor—and also Washington's secretary of state—for advice and support. But Madison, acknowledged as the leader of the opposition, steered the campaign. He also bore the brunt of public and private attacks from the group that took possession of the "Federalist" mantle, the bloc he had helped to lead through the constitutional ratification debates of the late 1780s.[3]

By the time Jefferson resigned his cabinet position on December 31, 1793, however, many Americans had changed their minds about the identity of the Republican faction's most prominent man, and some even described the opposition alliance as "Jeffersonian."[4] Citizens saw Madison less as a ringleader. Instead, he served as the "second in command" to Jefferson, whom one pamphlet writer described as the "Generalissimo."[5] Federalists maintained a vigorous assault on Jefferson's reputation, and Republicans began to circulate his name as a possible candidate in the 1796 presidential election.

Americans who kept abreast of newspapers could only conclude that Jefferson had replaced his younger colleague at the head of the Republican movement. But how and why did this change in public perceptions occur? What, moreover, were the roles of politicians, the press, and Jefferson himself in refocusing Americans' attention? A number of factors, including his own actions, contributed to his rise to national prominence, but the most important was the scorn of Hamilton who, tirelessly and almost single-handedly, savaged Jefferson's character in printed attacks. At Jefferson's urging, Madison and other Republicans penned vigorous responses that developed his reputation as a foe of aristocracy and a friend of the people. In short, Hamilton's eagerness to discredit the secretary of state brought about the invention of a public figure whose popular appeal would eventually contribute to the Federalist faction's demise.

JEFFERSON PORTRAYED himself as an unlikely candidate for either national prominence or contentious debate. Throughout his adult life, and most emphatically after his two turbulent terms as Revolutionary War governor of Virginia, he claimed to cringe at the thought of political controversy and the burdens of high office. "Public service and private misery," he contended, are "inseparably linked together." As the Old Dominion's chief executive, he had endured intense scrutiny. He made futile attempts to arm and feed the militia, make the government solvent, and repel British invasions. When Redcoats seized his mountaintop home at the end of his second term, forcing him to flee on horseback, his embarrassments were compounded. Some charged him with cowardice; critics in the legislature ordered an investigation into his performance and patriotism. Public service, moreover, endangered more than his reputation. He confessed that it required "constant sacrifice of time" as well as "labour, loss," and dereliction of "parental and friendly duties." It tore him from the company of his frail wife, who died fifteen months after his final term expired. It forced him to neglect his finances, which consequently fell "into great disorder and ruin." When James Monroe suggested in 1782 that he return to Richmond as a member of the House of Delegates, Jefferson replied that the idea left him "mortified."[6]

Despite his refusal to entertain Monroe's request, calls to public service continued, and Jefferson's sense of obligation made them difficult to resist. He served in the Confederation Congress in 1783 and 1784 before embarking for France, where he worked as a trade commissioner and then succeeded Benjamin Franklin as minister plenipotentiary. He described the demands of diplomatic office as more agreeable. "My little transactions are not made for public detail," he wrote in 1789. "They are best in the shade: the light of the picture is justly occupied by others. To glide unnoticed thro' a silent execution of duty, is the only ambition which becomes me, and it is the sincere desire of my heart."[7]

His subsequent rise to prominence might seem to cast doubt on his candor. So did his habit, shared by nearly all the young republic's leading lights, of disavowing any desire for positions likely to bring power or acclaim. While disinterested pronouncements coalesced nicely with the republican belief that public office was less a reward than a burden, they also made prospective officeholders seem worthy of holding office. The more they protested their desire for private life, the greater their apparent abhorrence of public posts, then the greater the confidence fellow citizens believed could be entrusted to them. Reluctance in the face of calls to public prominence signaled not only humility but also a lack of the dangerous ambition that, when possessed by leaders, could imperil a republic. Washington, the new president, had rendered himself the archetype of republican disinterestedness through his apparent reluctance to serve and eagerness to return to Mount Vernon. It was his resignation as commander of the Continental Army at the end of the War for Independence— at a time when the gratitude of his countrymen could have allowed him to augment his powers—that made him seem a safe choice to wield the executive authority laid out in the Constitution.[8]

Yet when Jefferson claimed to prefer "a silent execution of duty" over fame he really meant it. He was rarely averse to gaining influence, but he had discovered the perils of prominence. As he learned as governor, it could result in not only public praise but also scrutiny and scandal. He had no desire to return to high office. He furthermore saw little need. In Jefferson's eyes, in the final years of the 1780s all was well with the world. Freedom would be secured in America, where the Constitution fathered by his friend Madison promised just enough order to maximize liberty. In France, after Britain the world's second most powerful nation, freedom appeared to be on the march. As minister plenipotentiary he witnessed with optimism the first and most promising scenes of the French Revolution. Not even Shays's Rebellion, the armed uprising of western Massachusetts farmers seeking to avoid payment on debts to which they had freely agreed, could dampen his mood. At least the citizens there remembered how to fight perceived oppression. Their insurgency, although wrongheaded, gave them good exercise. "I like a little rebellion now and then," he told Abigail Adams. "The spirit of resistance to government is so valuable on certain occasions, that I wish it to be always kept alive."[9]

After five years abroad, Congress granted Jefferson's petition for a leave of absence and he sailed for home. After a few months, he planned to return to Paris to follow the course of the brewing revolution. He had already made clear his intentions to Madison, who, in consultation with Washington, asked him to consider appointment to a domestic post. In a letter consumed by news of French politics, Jefferson, almost as an afterthought, spurned the idea. He reminded his friend of "the circumstances which led me from retirement" and into diplomatic service. He made clear that upon the completion of his work abroad, "my object is a return to the same retirement." The fact that Jefferson left in Paris the bulk of his household goods underscores the sincerity of his intention to return. Meanwhile, the Senate confirmed Jefferson as secretary of state, and Washington's pleas to join his new administration grew more desperate. Jefferson accepted the appointment only after repeated protests and with what he described as "real regret." As William Short, Jefferson's secretary, predicted, such an offer from President Washington, who himself had sacrificed so much, proved difficult to refuse.[10]

Washington's powers of persuasion and Jefferson's sense of duty were perhaps not the only forces compelling acceptance of the new assignment. During Jefferson's years in Paris, political insiders and literati had showered him with accolades, including honorary law degrees from Harvard and Yale.[11] Madison, who knew his friend well, calculated that additional expressions of thanks might soften Jefferson's reluctance to assume a more onerous role. Probably at Madison's behest, a committee of Jefferson's neighbors sent to him an address that he received in January. The message communicated their gratitude for past services and desire for future ones. Even earlier, after the Virginia House of Delegates thanked him for his achievements in Europe, Jefferson basked in the glow of acclaim. "I shall hope to merit a continuance of their goodness," he wrote back to Richmond, "by obeying the impulse of a zeal of which public good is the first object, and public esteem the highest reward." If opportunities for praise rose with the relative importance of a particular post, then the "very dignified office" into which Washington pressed him promised many such chances.[12]

Another factor was equally ego-driven. Ever since the start of the American Revolution, Jefferson had understood Washington's seniority in terms of rank and prominence. His elder by eleven years, Washington possessed a résumé that bested his own in nearly every respect. In the House of Burgesses and the Continental Congress, Washington had served earlier and more famously. Although Jefferson had led a state while it suffered invasion by the British Army, Washington had led the Continental Army to victory. Jefferson, when his term of office expired, was called a coward. Washington, when taking leave of his command, was deemed a hero. Jefferson had chaired the committee charged with drafting the Declaration of Independence, a task for which, at the time, he received little notice. Washington, on the other hand, chaired the Constitutional Convention, a task for which he attracted much attention. Jefferson no doubt felt flattered to learn of Washington's repeated praise for his abilities and accomplishments. No doubt he grew fond of hearing of it.[13]

Although Jefferson accepted the post, the lure of continued commendation did not cause him to forget entirely the coupling of private misery and public service. He predicted ensuing events in his half-hearted acceptance letter to Washington. Maintaining that he possessed "no motive to public service but the public satisfaction," he shared with the president his "gloomy forebodings [of] the criticisms and censures of the public, just indeed in their intentions, but sometimes misinformed and misled." With remarkable foresight, he added that "I can not but foresee that this may end disagreeably for me."[14]

On a superficial level, Jefferson's note to Washington served as a somewhat formulaic reaffirmation of his republicanism. It reinforced his reputation for disinterestedness by forecasting that his new office offered meager prospects for public acclaim. His willingness to serve had little to do with its slender opportunities for any sort of reward. In the context of his earlier pronouncements about office-holding, however, Jefferson's acceptance letter suggested deeper meanings. Although he claimed not to seek praise, he admitted that he possessed a strong aversion to criticism. He desired to assist fellow citizens while also seeking to be shielded from their scorn. Although he committed himself to the personal sacrifices and public rewards of government service, he held out hope for success in his private pursuit of tranquility. He relished appointments that allowed him to work independently and creatively while also empowering him to control his appearance in the eyes of others. He had developed, moreover, a strong distaste for day-to-day politics and disputation, two certain characteristics of a cabinet post. In his new capacity as a member of Washington's administration, his dual desire to satisfy the public and yet "glide unnoticed thro' the silent execution of duty" almost guaranteed frustration.

IN MARCH 1790, when Jefferson arrived in New York City, the temporary American capital, his career as a diplomat had not yet ended. As secretary of state, of course, his responsibilities included the supervision of negotiations between representatives of the United States and foreign powers. But Jefferson also agreed to serve as a peacemaking intermediary between Alexander Hamilton and the loose band of congressional opponents who balked at his financial programs.

For more than two months the House of Representatives had been embroiled in controversy over the New Yorker's *First Report on the Public Credit,* which proposed measures such as the federal assumption of unpaid state Revolutionary War debts. Hamilton's supporters argued that the program would affirm American honor, establish American credit at home and abroad, and guarantee interest payments to patriots who bought bonds and lent credit when the new nation needed quick cash. Madison, however, organized a group of congressmen who believed that the plan would unfairly benefit investors who had purchased bond issues and other credit certificates from their original holders at significantly deflated prices. His coalition also argued that the measure would wrongfully increase the payment burden of citizens in states such as Virginia, which had already begun to pay its creditors, while diminishing the obligations of taxpayers in debt-ridden Massachusetts and South Carolina.[15]

The fight focused considerable attention on Madison. Newspapers such as Boston's *Massachusetts Centinel* praised him for defending the interests of the Revolutionary War veterans to whom the bonds and promissory notes had been issued. Other journals criticized him for a lack of public spiritedness.[16] Abigail Adams, herself an investor in government bonds, observed that he led his followers "like a flock of sheep." Also underscoring Madison's centrality in the conflict was a friend of Hamilton's who wished him luck in his efforts to "fend off the Maddisons of the South."[17]

Jefferson, meanwhile, worked behind the scenes to resolve the dispute between Hamilton and Madison. Emboldened by the belief that "men of sound heads and honest views" could compromise, in June he arranged to host a dinner for the adversaries. The three men deliberated, and days later Hamilton emerged victorious from the debt-funding debate. At the same time, Virginians received a congressional commitment to locate the nation's permanent capital on the Potomac.[18]

Any hopes that Jefferson may have harbored for permanent reconciliation collapsed the following year. At the end of April 1791, he helped to set off the opening salvo of an intensely public battle that would vault him to preeminence as opposition leader. Through Madison, Jefferson received John Beckley's copy of the first volume of Thomas Paine's *Rights of Man,* a barbed rejoinder to Edmund Burke's recently published condemnation of the revolution in France. Beckley, clerk of the House of Representatives, had already arranged for the first American printing of Paine's most recent work. He asked Jefferson to forward the pamphlet to a Philadelphia publisher, who would use it to set the type for the American edition. When Jefferson complied, he dashed off a letter that described how he had come into possession of the work. "To take off a little of the dryness of the note," as he later explained to Madison, he informed the printer that he was "extremely pleased to find that it will be re-printed here, and that something is at length to be publicly said against the political heresies which have sprung up among us." He followed this thinly veiled reference to a series of political essays ("Discourses on Davila") by John Adams in the *Gazette of the United States,* which Jefferson thought revealed the vice president's monarchical leanings, with the remark that he had "no doubt our citizens will rally a second time round the standard of Common sense." Seizing on Jefferson's personal communication as a public endorsement, the printer included it as a foreword to Paine's pamphlet, the American publication of which, the publisher implied in an editorial note, Jefferson himself had masterminded.[19]

THE DISCOVERY that his letter prefaced the *Rights of Man,* Jefferson told the offended vice president, left him "thunderstruck." To Madison he expressed "astonishment" and regret concerning both the pamphlet and the

publicity it had generated. "I tell [Adams] freely that he is a heretic," he asserted, "but certainly never meant to step into a public newspaper with that
in my mouth." Not only did the printer's indiscretion wound Adams's ego; it
also strained Jefferson's relationship with Hamilton. The treasury secretary,
Jefferson reported to Madison, stood "open mouthed against me."[20]

Although Adams and Hamilton seemed to suspect otherwise, Jefferson
maintained his innocence in the affair. Were his intentions really so pure?
Making the case that he actually meant to attach his name to a public endorsement of Paine's work (and a public rebuke of Adams's) requires the belief
that, even at this early stage, Jefferson possessed the cunning and foresight of
a political mastermind bent on his own aggrandizement at the expense of the
reputation of the man who, as vice president, seemed most likely to stand in
his way. Yet such a strategy hinged on the belief that the endorsement would
spark the sort of controversy and exposure that the thin-skinned, stage-shy,
and risk-averse Virginian claimed to abhor. To Washington he expressed frustration at having been "brought forward on the public stage, where to remain,
to advance or to retire, will be equally against my love of silence and quiet, and
my abhorrence of dispute."[21]

Whether or not he intended for his words to spawn a maelstrom of debate,
that was their effect. The *Rights of Man* controversy reverberated through the
public prints. Under the pseudonym "Publicola" in Boston's *Columbian Centinel,* John Quincy Adams, the vice president's son, led the attack on Jefferson
in eleven essays soon reprinted elsewhere. The young Adams's commentaries
were careful, reasoned, and predictable. Jefferson's "political heresies" remark
proved that he possessed little tolerance for differing opinions, according
to Publicola. Moreover, Paine had insisted that only "a general convention
elected for the purpose" could rightfully change a constitution; the secretary of state's apparent concurrence with this idea exposed his opposition to
America's founding charter, which granted amending powers to the Congress
and state legislatures. Jefferson was a subversive demagogue, suggested Publicola, who implored his readers to "remain immovably fixed at the banners of
our constitutional freedom, and not desert the impregnable fortress of our
liberties, for the insubstantial fabrick of visionary politicians."[22]

If claims about Jefferson's supposed hostility to the Constitution characterized Adams's attack on the surface, anxiety over the propriety of his behavior emanated from its core. As Jefferson himself observed, open battle
between two cabinet officers was an act of "indecency." It made the executive
branch appear weak and divided, as Washington noted when, a year after the

publication of the Publicola essays, he called for conciliation between the feuding members of his administration.[23] Still worse, Jefferson's endorsement of Paine's treatise brazenly dispensed with the customary cloak of pseudonymity behind which nearly every office-holding polemicist retreated. Although the rules of republican discourse permitted public servants to promote ideas, they spurned self-promotion. Charges of interestedness could fall on those who signed their names to political publications, the practice of which Jefferson seemed guilty. Nonetheless, as Madison pointed out to his friend, he had crossed no lines not already stepped on by John Adams himself. "Since he has been the 2d. Magistrate in the new Republic," Madison observed, "his pen has constantly been at work." Although Adams's "name has not been prefixed to his antirepublican discourses, the author has been as well known as if that formality had [not] been observed. Surely if it be innocent and decent in one servant of the public thus to write attacks against its Government," Madison maintained, "it can not be very criminal" to provide "a written defense of the principles on which that Government is founded."[24]

The emerging Federalist faction saw matters differently. Jefferson's repeated disavowals of any role in the appearance of his note failed to convince them. Jefferson knew exactly what he was doing, they thought. His endorsement represented political posturing, perhaps in preparation for a bid for higher office. "Mr. J[efferson] appears to have shown rather too much of a disposition to cultivate vulgar prejudices," sneered Oliver Wolcott; "accordingly he will become popular in ale houses, and will do much mischief to his country by exciting apprehensions" against the government. "It is thought rather early for Electioneering," John Adams dryly remarked to Secretary of War Henry Knox. A subsequent pamphlet made the same allegation: Jefferson, eager to succeed Washington as president, would trample the character not only of Adams but also of Hamilton to prevail. This sort of demagoguery could not be taken lightly, Jefferson's opponents agreed. As Adams asserted in his "Discourses," the darkest force confronting republicanism was "the *passion for distinction*"—the desire of men to climb the ladder of politics. Yet government, Adams contended, could "regulate this passion" and make it "an instrument of order and subordination." For Americans who agreed with the vice president, Jefferson's ambitions seemed to fly in the face of propriety.[25]

Jefferson attempted to console his critics, but only in ways that worked to his advantage. He recognized that "a host of writers" had rushed forward to defend him, so it cost him little to resolve "to be utterly silent" in the skirmish, "except so far as verbal explanations could be made." If anything, his silence before the public strengthened his hand. It confirmed the character that he had established for himself, bolstering his image as a shy, retiring, disinterested public servant who cared more about advancing principles than himself. By refusing to join the debate he made the notion that he ever intended to attach his name to a printed endorsement of Paine's work seem all the more unlikely. Privately, however, he offered the olive branch to Adams, assuring him that he still valued their friendship. He had played no part in having "our names thrown on the public stage as public antagonists," he assured Adams, issuing a similar assurance to the president. Yet still he revealed an opportunistic steak. His letter to Adams ignored his original allusion to the "Davila" essays and blamed "the writer of Publicola" for casting them as adversaries. His letter to Washington, however, swiped at Adams's fondness for "hereditary monarchy" and confirmed that, when he penned his note to the printer, "I had in my view the Discourses on Davila."[26]

Had his opponents seen his words, they would likely have found little connection with his deeds. At the same time as the *Rights of Man* controversy, Jefferson journeyed with Madison through New York and New England. The trip compounded suspicions that the two stood at the forefront of a partisan vanguard. While they characterized their expedition as a vacation, the emerging Federalist faction thought otherwise. Nathaniel Hazard, a New York City merchant, held that the two "scouted silently thro' the Country, shunning the Gentry, communing with & pitying the Shayites."[27]

The joint journey helped to underscore that Jefferson had not yet displaced Madison as the real or recognized leader of the opposition. During the latter half of 1791 and the spring of 1792, the two men appeared as more or less equal partners in a continuing battle against Hamilton's programs. Although some still singled out Madison for special vitriol, in the letters of their contemporaries, their names often appeared together. The usual formulation—"Jefferson & Madison"—gave precedence to the more established statesman.[28] While Columbia College president William Samuel Johnson reportedly praised Jefferson at a November 1791 dinner party, he said that Madison "ought not to be mentioned in the same Day" as Hamilton. The treasury secretary himself harbored deep resentment toward his former friend. As Beckley told Madison in September of 1792, "Mr. H[amilton] unequivocally declares, that yo. are his *personal & political* enemy."[29]

But Hamilton's hostility for Jefferson already exceeded his enmity for Madison, in no small part because he blamed Jefferson for his "personal & political" disillusionment with Madison, with whom he had enjoyed a healthy and lengthy relationship. Hamilton and Madison had collaborated in the constitutional ratification debate; they had also cooperated on public matters, such as debt funding and assumption, as their respective responsibilities within the new government began to crystallize. How could the treasury chief reconcile that he and his former ally, from whom he had expected support and with whom he shared political views that "had formerly so much the *same point of departure,* should now diverge so widely in our opinions"? Two explanations existed. He either had badly mistaken Madison's original intentions or Madison had now fallen prey to the pernicious spell of Jefferson, who had been absent during the springtime of their partnership but had since returned to break it apart. Hamilton gravitated toward the second possibility. Jefferson, the real leader of the faction opposed to him, had actively misled Madison, who "had always entertained an exalted opinion" of his neighbor's "talents, knowledge and virtues."[30]

Jefferson's unseemly involvement in a dubious endeavor with Philip Freneau, his political appointee, lent credence to Hamilton's theory. Like Jefferson's purportedly inadvertent public condemnation of Adams's "Davila" essays, his nearly simultaneous grant of a State Department post to Freneau, a Republican newspaperman, seemed to Hamilton a case of unpardonable partisanship. This action also provided ample justification for a flurry of anti-Jefferson opprobrium. If the first offense seemed merely improper, the second appeared corrupt and left the Virginian singularly exposed to criticism. Since November 1791, when a correspondent of Hamilton's unfurled a plan to target the secretary of state, Federalists had itched to attack the vice president's critic. The New Yorker waited, however, until May 1792. By then, he had suffered not only from Jefferson's influence over Madison but also from regular condemnation on the pages of the *National Gazette,* which Freneau edited. Enraged, bitter, and thoroughly convinced that Jefferson was the source of all his problems, Hamilton lashed back.[31]

In a letter to Edward Carrington, with whom he had fought during the siege of Yorktown, Hamilton drew up a list of charges that would color the image of his nemesis for decades. The secretary of state had long evinced hostility toward the Constitution, Hamilton said; he was also an ambitious demagogue, servile to France and subversive to the American government. Jefferson was a "visionary" philosopher and an atheist who duped his supporters with remarkable cunning and intentional deceit. His most "ardent desire," Hamilton speculated, was to win for himself "the Presidential Chair." Jefferson's "true colors," he concluded, must "be told."[32]

Seizing on Jefferson's support of Freneau to discredit him, in August Hamilton unleashed a series of essays in John Fenno's *Gazette of the United States* that soon reappeared in other journals. Reiterating the charges that he had first outlined to Carrington, Hamilton's torrent of animus provided a lexicon of anti-Jefferson invective. By then Hamilton's hostility toward Jefferson had turned into seething hatred. He had surmised that the secretary of state, in a letter to the president, had criticized his financial system as foolhardy, corrupt, and monarchical. But even as he worked to destroy Jefferson's reputation, he was promoting Jefferson's image as the opposition's chief leader and unintentionally stimulating the development of a Republican press that would rush to Jefferson's defense.[33]

COMPARED TO THE vicious mudslinging of 1792, previous partisan newspaper skirmishes must have seemed restrained. The year brought new methods of attack as criticism of Jefferson became increasingly frequent and remarkably personal. Federalist newspapers, led by Fenno's *Gazette of the United States,* assailed the secretary of state, charging that he had abused the powers of his office, conspired against the Constitution, and undermined Washington's government, deviously concealing his immoral ambitions as he kowtowed to the common man like a brazen sycophant. Playing on Revolutionary-era anxieties about corruption, interestedness, licentiousness, and demagoguery, Federalists employed the language of civic virtue to discredit Jefferson, defeat their opponents, and clear the pathway toward the consolidation of federal power.

Republicans, of course, did their part in promoting this frenzied press battle; through their establishment of a party newspaper, they helped to precipitate it. More than a year before Hamilton's entry into the anti-Jefferson press crusade, Jefferson had joined with Madison in a search for a popular and Republican alternative to Fenno's journal. At first, Jefferson assisted Benjamin Franklin Bache in his efforts to bolster the faltering *General Advertiser.* By the summer of 1791, however, the continued success of the *Gazette of the United States* and its sponsorship of Publicola caused him to seek a more effective alternative.[34]

Alongside Madison, he approached Revolutionary War poet Philip Freneau with the notion of establishing a national newspaper. After some indecision, Freneau agreed to set up shop in the temporary capital of Philadelphia and commence publication of the *National Gazette.* Believing that the monarchist threat loomed larger than ever, Jefferson provided Freneau with not only foreign intelligence and advertising revenue but also his personal assistance in enlisting subscribers and—to help put the enterprise on firm financial footing—a $250-a-year job as the State Department's clerk for foreign languages.[35]

While Jefferson refused to advertise his support for the *National Gazette,* Hamilton, cloaked under various pseudonyms, asserted that Jefferson's patronage of Freneau, as well as the contents of the paper, revealed Jefferson's corrupt nature.[36] While Jefferson was Hamilton's target, Madison stood in the crossfire. But because Hamilton failed to find firm evidence of the congressional leader's involvement in the affair, only Jefferson could be charged with violations of the public trust. "The late northern papers are replete with the abuse of Mr. Jefferson as the patron of Freneau's gazette," Henry Lee informed Madison. "You are introduced without being directly named."[37]

Writing as "An American" in Fenno's paper, Hamilton fumed that his cabinet rival kept Freneau under his employ. The "connection ... between the *editor of a newspaper* and the head of a department of government," he argued, "is *indelicate* and *unfit.*" He labeled Jefferson both a hypocrite and an influence peddler. The secretary of state was an American Walpole, Hamilton claimed, procuring Freneau's favors with the federal purse. Although Hamilton understood that Madison worked hand in hand with Jefferson to encourage the poet-turned-newspaperman, he could point to no similar financial relationship between Freneau and the Virginia representative. Accepting his own theory that Madison merely acted as Jefferson's disciple and hoping, no doubt, to wound all of his Republican opponents, Hamilton for the first time publicly labeled Jefferson as "the head of a party." The *National Gazette* amounted to a party organ, printed by Jefferson's State Department subordinate and bolstered by funds that flowed from the federal treasury. Freneau was Jefferson's "faithful and devoted servant," Hamilton asserted, and "the whole complexion of his paper is an exact copy of the politics of his employer." John Quincy Adams agreed. The secretary of state, Adams implied in a letter to his brother, was the "Great man." Freneau was "his parasite."[38]

Hamilton did not stop after charging Jefferson with corruption. He contended that Jefferson aimed to use his ill-gotten influence to subvert the government and malign its leaders. Although Madison's central role in the creation and ratification of the Constitution protected him from allegations of hostility to the federal form of government, Hamilton could more persuasively claim as "a fact that Mr. Jefferson was in the origin opposed to the present Constitution of the United States." Writing under the pseudonym

"Catullus," Hamilton reiterated that the secretary of state sought to undermine the Constitution, "which it is the evident object of the National Gazette to discredit." Worse yet, he charged, Jefferson sought to use the *National Gazette* to criticize the president. South Carolina congressman William Loughton Smith, a close ally of the treasury chief, wrote an anonymous pamphlet amplifying this accusation: Jefferson burned with "ambitious ardor to dislodge" Washington from the presidency and assume the office himself. If there lived any Americans not impressed by Hamilton's accusations of corruption, anti-constitutionalism, and impropriety, Jefferson's alleged support of attacks on Washington, whom citizens had elevated to demigod status, would have had an impact.[39]

Hamilton portrayed Jefferson's support of the *National Gazette* not only as corrupt and contemptuous of President Washington and the Constitution but also as atheistic. In Freneau's paper "the clergy of our country [are] vilified, and religion [is] constantly ridiculed," Hamilton charged. The publication "must afford a rich repair to Infidels and Free-thinkers." Here, as elsewhere, the Federalist chieftain cast widely his net of persuasion. He made the charge sufficiently vague so as to cultivate the concern of all Americans who considered themselves religious—no small number in the Revolutionary republic, especially in New England, where Hamilton might expect to consolidate alliances with pious, commercially connected citizens.[40]

But the virulence of Hamilton's critique reflected his anxiety about Jefferson's expanding popularity, a phenomenon that several of his essays addressed. One noted the "affected appeals" made by his opponents to the "great body of the yeomanry." Another bet that Americans had "too much discernment to be dupes of hollow and ostentatious pretensions," that they knew "how to distinguish the men who *serve* them, from those who merely *flatter* them." Perhaps the treasury secretary had in mind a *National Gazette* piece assuring readers that "Tom Jefferson" was unlike Federalists, "who say the people are not . . . fit to be trusted."[41]

Despite Hamilton's self-assured avowals that Americans would rebuff the Republicans, between the lines of his essays lurked fear over Jefferson's rising popularity in the eyes of his countrymen, especially the upstarts who, like the maid of Englishman Joseph Priestley, shocked this transplant to Pennsylvania by carrying herself "as stately and as proud as a queen" despite being "a poor, sickly girl, perfectly ignorant." By directing his appeals at the mass of the population, Hamilton assisted in the gradual creation of a more broadly based public discourse. A few years earlier, while penning *The Federalist* with John

Jay and Madison, Hamilton had joined with his partners to write as "Publius," a pseudonym that suggested singular authorship. But now he assumed at least four personas—T. L., Catullus, An American, and Metellus,—and worked in concert with Congressman Smith, who, writing as "Scourge," constituted a fifth, in an apparent effort to conjure an appearance of consensus.[42] With elections for the House and Senate fast approaching, this strategy seemed both logical and necessary. It did not, however, yield sufficient results. The votes of 1792, Jefferson gloated, produced "a decided majority in favor of the republican interest."[43]

UNLIKE HIS CABINET RIVAL, Jefferson refused to contribute to the polemics of 1792. While Hamilton, on the Federalist side, and Republicans such as Madison, Monroe, and Edmund Randolph authored pseudonymous polemics, the stage-shy Virginian held fast to his "resolution" to never "write in a public paper without subscribing my name, and to engage openly an adversary who does not let himself be seen." He claimed to feel revolted by "the indecency" of open "squabbling between two public ministers." The allegations against him were false, he contended, "and can be proved so; and perhaps will be one day." But he insisted that the defense of his character rest in the hands of others, not his own.[44]

Even so, Jefferson's loud refusal to fire the rhetorical cannons of the Republican press did not prevent him from quietly supplying his compatriots with ammunition and encouragement. In October, for example, he provided Madison and Monroe with notes concerning a 1786 letter he had written to Jay, knowing that the information would prove useful in their production of newspaper essays rebutting Hamilton's aspersions.[45] Madison and Monroe also published excerpts from a number of other letters that Jefferson sent to Madison in the late 1780s that, contrary to the treasury secretary's claims, affirmed his general support for ratification of the Constitution. In an unsigned note introducing these documents, Madison and Monroe insisted that Jefferson's permission to print them had "neither been asked nor attained." Similarly, the secretary of state reported to Washington that "not a word" of the enterprise "had ever been communicated to me."[46] At best, these statements stretched the truth, for the three men kept in close contact during the entire episode and Monroe, more than a week before Jefferson professed to the president his surprise on seeing his words in print, sent through Madison a packet of papers regarding the letters "to return" to their mutual friend.[47]

Jefferson's concern for what he viewed as the national welfare, which nearly always coalesced with his attentive regard for his own reputation, also moved him to prod Madison. In 1793, for example, when the treasury secretary, writing as "Pacificus," insisted on neutrality toward France, Jefferson asked Madison to retaliate. "For god's sake," he implored, "pick up your pen, select the most striking heresies, and cut him to pieces in the face of the public." Although Jefferson never lifted his pen for Freneau's paper, he aided Madison by circumnavigating his self-imposed rules, deleting words and phrases from the congressman's pieces prior to publication, and offering admission to his extensive library so that anti-Federalist articles might be fully grounded in republican texts.[48]

In this light, Jefferson's encouragement of the *National Gazette* can be viewed as self-defense by proxy. He maintained that his support for Freneau's paper stemmed merely from his early "desire of seeing a purely republican vehicle of news" and his insistence on a truthful reporting of events.[49] The *National Gazette,* however, propagated republicanism and truth as Jefferson and his allies saw them. The embattled secretary of state recognized that, in their version of reality, he was not a villain to be purged but a victim to be assisted.

Jefferson's avowals of innocence in the newspaper war seem no less disingenuous than his critics claimed, but they reflect nonetheless an earnest, if clumsy, attempt to adapt the traditional standards of civic virtue to the new dynamics of popular national politics.[50] He sought to model his conduct after that of men such as Washington, the paragon of republicanism whom contemporaries compared to Cincinnatus. Like that famed Roman patriot, the president had secured his reputation by answering his country's call to service and then, with victory in the Revolution secured, trading sword for plow and returning to Mount Vernon. Washington, moreover, accepted civilian posts with professions of reluctance, and only after he had received assurances that his nation could not succeed without him. He maintained a strict separation between his private finances and public duties. Throughout his long career, Washington assiduously avoided giving the impression that he wished to promote either his political or personal fortunes.[51]

Jefferson's attempt to secure for himself a reputation for disinterestedness proved less successful, if only because the position in which he found himself became more complicated. He saw the struggle against the Federalists as a reprise of the Revolution, a war to defend American liberty against British-style corruption and usurpation. But it was a guerrilla conflict with ill-defined battle lines, and it took place largely behind the scenes of American government. Jefferson understood that what he viewed as patriotic service could be taken by others as interestedness and factionalism. To defend himself—or to defend himself pseudonymously and risk being identified—might only provide his opponents with ammunition in their campaign to portray him as a self-promoter.[52] Given his sincere dislike of controversy and conflict, the decision to entrust his reputation to Madison, Monroe, and other friends came naturally.

It did not come without consequences, however, as he must have understood. Jefferson's continuing patronage of Freneau further entangled him in the partisan dispute, making him an easy target for the treasury secretary's vitriol. The *National Gazette,* like Jefferson, grew increasingly hostile to Washington and confirmed Hamilton's fears that the secretary of state wished to undermine the executive branch.[53] If, as Hamilton claimed, Jefferson hoped to be brought forward as a major figure in American politics, then he could only conclude that agitating the vociferous New Yorker, with whom he battled at cabinet meetings, would yield sure results.[54] Finally, Jefferson's resolve to let others uphold his honor—to lavish him with praise, describe his talents, and testify to his virtue—in no small way galvanized Republican opinion leaders around the notion that he personified their movement.

THERE EXISTED no shortage of writers willing to contradict Hamilton's aspersions against the secretary of state. Although Republican polemicists made scant reference to Jefferson during the first eight months of 1792, by September his name appeared frequently on the pages of the *National Gazette* and likeminded papers, where writers responded to the treasury secretary's election-season offensive. Even though he was not a candidate for office, steadfast assurances of Jefferson's virtue, genius, and sturdy record of service filled their essays. As a consequence, the five men nominated to challenge John Adams for the vice presidency—Madison among them—received little attention from newspapers, while Jefferson became the most heralded member of his fledgling faction. "The attacks which your enemies in [the] administration have made upon you," Robert R. Livingston assured his embattled friend, "have excited the public attention and served to convince those who were not acquaintd with your character of your attachment to the Liberties of your country."[55]

If an image of Jefferson as corrupt, subversive, irreligious, and crafty coalesced in the minds of his adversaries, patrons of Republican publications

viewed him quite differently. One *National Gazette* essay, appearing during
the second week of September, ridiculed the Hamiltonians' "shamefully
and glaringly false" charges and dubbed the secretary of state an "illustrious
Patriot, statesman, and Philosopher" who possessed "a virtuous and dignified conduct." Shortly thereafter, "A Republican" writing in the same paper
claimed that the "reputation of Mr. *Jefferson* [is] too well known to need any
panegyric, he having filled with honor, the most important public offices both
at home and abroad."[56]

Far from being a subversive, Jefferson espoused the defense and expansion
of Revolutionary liberty, Republican newspaper writers claimed. The Hamiltonians—not Jefferson—were corrupt, hostile to the Constitution, jealous of
the president, and motivated by mad ambition. They maligned Jefferson, one
of his allies contended, for his refusal to "sacrifice his judgment, his character,
his fidelity, his oath, to measures and views adopted by his colleagues." As
a result, his oppositional stance within the administration revealed not vice
but virtue, not political opportunism but steady attachment to principle. He
displayed a commendable "independence of character," according to an essay
in *Dunlap's American Daily Advertiser,* and held firm to the views "that he
possessed before he commenced the career of public trust." Jefferson's patriotism thus surpassed that of his cabinet colleagues. As one penman remarked,
"such an unfeigned and benevolent regard for mankind in all their classes;
such an anxious solicitude for their welfare, and vigilant attention to their
rights, are rarely to be found united in any one person." According to a writer
who called himself "Justice," in Jefferson "we see a mind highly illuminated by
the science of government, a heart warmly devoted to the liberty of mankind;
and a dutiful life to his country." Put simply, the secretary of state excelled
as the steadfast champion of liberty and all who aspired to it.[57] His opposition to Hamiltonian finance revealed his support of freedom, not faction; the
only interest that he advocated was that of the majority. "Mr. J[efferson] does
not suppress his dislike of any measures of the government," opined another
writer. "But does it follow that he is an enemy to the government? If it does,
then nine-tenths of the people are enemies."[58]

Republicans spurned Federalist attempts to marginalize Jefferson as eccen-
tric or extremist, and they considered absurd the implication that somehow
his views betrayed a lack of patriotism. Yet all but a single *National Gazette*
writer—who sought public support for "Tom Jefferson" by noting that "he
composed the Declaration of Independence" and claiming that he "moved for
it first in Congress"—failed to seize on the most obvious retort to allegations

that Jefferson's views placed him outside the political mainstream. Many remained unaware of his connection with the Declaration or, like the man who at a 1793 Fourth of July banquet offered a toast to "Jefferson, chairman of the committee that reported the declaration of American independence," remained unaware of the extent of his contribution. In addition, the political advantage provided by Jefferson's link with the Declaration, which itself had not yet realized its potential as a national icon, was not yet fully apparent. Certainly it failed to impress William Loughton Smith, a leader of the rival faction, for his 1792 pamphlet, *The Politicks and Views of a Certain Party, Displayed,* excoriated Jefferson but noted, in passing, that he had served as "Chairman of the Committee who drew up the Declaration of Independence."[59]

The Republican contention that Jefferson's political beliefs concurred with those held by the great mass of Americans facilitated an important phenomenon. Jefferson rose in the eyes of his countrymen not so much as the head of a faction but as a popular leader. "On the republican side," claimed a *National Gazette* contributor, "the superiority of numbers is so great, their sentiments are so decided, and the practice of making a common cause . . . is so well understood, that no temperate observer of human affairs will be surprised" if Hamiltonian policies "should be reversed, and the government be administered in the spirit and form approved by the great body of the people." Another writer argued that Federalist attacks on Jefferson displayed the "desperation of the Aristocratic junto" at the erosion of its public support. By the end of October, the *National Gazette* reported that "the publications against Mr. Jefferson . . . are more like the ravings of guilt in despair, than like the reasonings of a man in his sober senses."[60]

Yet Federalist barbs could not be taken lightly. To a large extent, Jefferson's reputation and the image of the Republican movement had merged together. "If a person of his note . . . could be destroyed in the public confidence," wrote Madison and Monroe in the first of their newspaper essays, "the cause would be humbled, and the friends of monarchy would triumph. An attack, therefore, upon this gentleman, must be deemed a direct but artful one upon principles, and in this view it becomes a matter of public concern, and merits particular attention."[61]

HAMILTON'S ATTEMPT to discredit Jefferson backfired. Instead, by criticizing Jefferson's conduct and character, Hamilton thrust him to the forefront of newspaper readers' political consciousness. By September 1792, less

A Peep into the Antifederal Club, 1793.
(American Antiquarian Society)

than a month after the secretary of the treasury commenced his "American" essays, Beckley noted that Americans regarded Jefferson "as the head of the republican party." Arch-Federalist Fisher Ames certainly did, bragging of his own "anti Jefferson principles," calling the chief Republican newspaper "Mr. Jefferson's Press," and criticizing the secretary of state for "the *factions* he has originated." Jefferson's new status even found expression in a 1793 etching by an unknown New York artist. Entitled *A Peep into the Antifederal Club,* it depicts him perched on a soapbox, surrounded by a dissolute gang of anarchists, Jacobins, and criminals as well as a black-faced "Citizen Mungo" (exclaiming "Our turn nex") and the devil himself. Wielding a gavel to bring order to the pandemonium, Jefferson declares his intention to "contrive some means of knocking down a Government and in its ruins raise myself to Eminence."[62]

Madison had been overshadowed, a fact he acknowledged. Loyal to his friend and their mutual convictions, the Virginia congressman had joined the small cadre of writers devoted to defending Jefferson's honor and promoting the party he had come to represent. "With respect to myself," Madison confessed, "the consequence in a public view is of little account."[63]

Like Hamilton's attempts to ruin Jefferson's image, his efforts to drive the secretary of state from office backfired. Concern for his reputation convinced Jefferson to delay his plans to retire at the conclusion of Washington's first term. His resignation was the aim of the Federalist press, as his friends pointed out and as he understood. "Retiring just when I had been attacked in the public papers, would injure me in the eyes of the public," Jefferson wrote to his daughter. Americans "would suppose I either withdrew from investigation, or had not the tone of mind sufficient to meet slander." Although concern for reputation was motivation enough to delay his retirement, it may be no coincidence that, just three days earlier, Congressman William Branch Giles introduced resolutions calling for an investigation into Hamilton's possible mishandling of public money. Backed by Jefferson, who offered covert encouragement and assistance, Giles's effort failed to force Hamilton from office. But this provided yet another reason for Jefferson to delay his departure since, as his friend Livingston argued, no one else in the cabinet could provide a "better check . . . on the encroachments of [the] administration." Jefferson, who professed to Washington an urgent desire to surround himself with people friendly to his views and to himself, as a member of the cabinet had "to move always exactly in the circle which I know to bear me peculiar hatred." He remained in office until the final day of 1793.[64]

His earlier decision to postpone retirement hinged on a desire not to harm his reputation, but now he seemed to sense that stepping down would help it by suggesting that the Federalists, who had cast him as an ambitious office-seeker, had been wrong. When Jefferson returned to his little mountain at the edge of the Blue Ridge, he claimed he would remain there for good. "The length of my tether is now fixed for life between Monticello and Richmond," he informed an ally. Neither business nor politics, "which I have ever hated both in theory and practice," could ever "call me elsewhere." But the sentiments that his stormy tenure as secretary of state had helped to stir conspired against his expressed intention. So did the message conveyed by his retirement—that he preferred private life to the political stage—which made him seem especially worthy of the public's trust. As one writer later maintained, "Mr. Jefferson cannot be denominated an ambitious character," for like "the renowned Cincinnatus" he retired "from public grandeur into the vale of obscurity." Even Congressman William Barry Grove, a Federalist, called Jefferson's retirement a "Melancholy thing" because it helped demonstrate his "Virtue" and support for "Rational Liberty & Equality."[65]

Others were less easily convinced. On first hearing of Jefferson's plans to step down, Oliver Wolcott reacted with skepticism: "Time will show whether this is a trick to gain a few compliments." Even after Jefferson's departure from Philadelphia, John Adams viewed his retirement as evidence for—and not against—the view that he lusted for power. "Jefferson thinks he shall by this step get a Reputation of a humble, modest, meek Man, wholly without ambition or Vanity," Adams informed his son. "But if a Prospect opens, The World will see and he will feel, that he is as ambitious as Oliver Cromwell."[66]

CHAPTER TWO

The Election of 1796

IS CLOTHES CLUNG too tightly to his lanky frame. Although he possessed an "Air of Stiffness" his posture seemed slovenly, for he sat lounging "on one hip, commonly, and with one of his shoulders elevated much above the other." His total "laxity of Manner" gave him "a loose shackling" appearance. His speech "partook of his personal demeanor. It was loose and rambling and yet he scattered information wherever he went, and some even brilliant Sentiments sparkled from him." So thought Pennsylvania senator William Maclay, whose first impression of Thomas Jefferson took shape as the secretary of state, afflicted with one of his chronic headaches, testified before a congressional committee. Maclay, who tended to agree with the Virginian's politics, felt disappointed that Jefferson lacked "that firm collected deportment which I expected would dignify the presence of a Secretary or Minister."[1]

As Maclay's surprise on his initial meeting with Jefferson indicates, few individuals possessed a clear picture of how the middle-aged master of Monticello looked or how he carried himself. This fact remained true through the first years of the eighteenth century's final decade, a time when the public learned of Jefferson's high-profile struggle against Alexander Hamilton. Although newspaper writers and pamphleteers did not focus on Jefferson's appearance, by the time of his retirement from office at the end of 1793, they had elevated him to leadership of the Republican faction and had provided two contrasting pictures of his political character. Jefferson's Federalist enemies depicted him as a dangerous opponent of government. His allies described him as a defender of liberty. At best, both sketches remained impressionistic.

During the autumn of 1796 the former secretary of state's bifurcated image gained greater clarity. Friends brought him forth as their candidate for the presidency and showered him with praise. Foes unleashed a torrent of abuse, indicting the Republican with a detailed account of his failures and weaknesses. What no American could dispute was that the image of Thomas Jefferson touched on nearly all issues, that it permeated the battle for the presidency on nearly every level. Federalists derided him as a Jacobin, an anarchist and atheist, a timid and sycophantic demagogue. Republicans trumpeted his enlightened concern for the common man, his love of liberty, his disinterested deference to the will of the people. They pushed him as their candidate because, as Madison believed, "Jefferson alone" could "be started with hope of success." Hamilton, on the other hand, focused his formidable talents on attacking the former secretary of state, explaining to a fellow Federalist that it mattered less who won the vote "than that it shall not be Jefferson."[2] As such, the contest represented more than a simple choice between the author of independence and Vice President John Adams, his primary rival in a field of nearly a dozen men likely to receive electoral votes. It was a referendum on the public's views of Jefferson himself.

His newly articulated reputation reflected recent politics more than his own actions and pronouncements. After his retirement he withdrew from the public eye and sheltered himself from controversy at Monticello. During the campaign, in which he took no part, he protested to correspondents that he wished to remain at home. Adding to these ironies, the electoral contest that forced his return to the national spotlight began under a shroud of darkness.

THE SKY ISSUED a black promise on the Fourth of July 1796. On this holiest holiday of the secular calendar, as citizens retreated to banquet halls, gathered for patriotic assemblies, or prepared for fireworks displays, they watched the moon trace a path in front of the sun and quickly extinguish the last light of day. The eclipse provided a spectacle both rare and troubling. "Is not this ominous?" asked Philadelphia's Republican *Aurora and General Advertiser*. Will it not be said "that the sun of our liberties sets eclipsed by the British Treaty?"[3]

Republicans could hardly stomach additional misfortune. Their alliance, loosely organized and out of favor with George Washington and his cabinet, had failed in its efforts to derail an agreement brokered by Chief Justice John Jay between the United States and Great Britain, which for three years had waged war on France. They criticized Jay's "British Treaty" for compromising America's neutral trading rights, endangering its sovereignty, failing to secure compensation for slaves carried off by British troops during the Revolution, and violating a 1778 commercial agreement with France. "Mr. Jay's treaty is almost universally condemned," said Unitarian theologian and English trans-plant Joseph Priestley in 1795; "many think the President will not ratify it." After Federalists in the Senate gave their assent, however, ratify it he did, and Republicans in the House of Representatives miscarried an attempt to pre-vent its implementation. By the end of April the contest over the Jay Treaty had been decided, and, Republicans feared, a trajectory had been set for dip-lomatic allegiance to the British monarchy.[4]

Federalists had problems of their own. For two years they had battled a growing spirit of popular unrest and civil disobedience. First, in 1794, west-ern Pennsylvanians took up arms to thwart collection of a federal excise tax on whiskey. That same year, residents of Kentucky hatched plans to secure unfettered access to the Mississippi, crucial to their commerce but controlled by Spain, which had recently allied itself with Great Britain. Some Kentucki-ans, itching for war with Madrid, whispered of secession should the national government lag in negotiations to secure their goals. The Jay Treaty provoked similar threats of insurrection. A writer for one Old Dominion newspaper claimed that its enactment would result in a petition to the Richmond legis-lature "praying" that the "state may recede from the Union, and be left under the government and protection of ONE HUNDRED THOUSAND FREE AND INDEPENDENT VIRGINIANS."[5]

Behind this mischief, Federalists believed, stood the Democratic-Republican societies intent on fomenting rebellion and undermining the Constitution. Scattered across the nation in cities such as Philadelphia, Bos-ton, New York, and Charleston, and in rural areas such as Wythe County, Virginia, these groups commanded indeterminate but much bragged-about bases of public support. Rankling Federalist leaders by eagerly imitating the customs and symbols of French Jacobinism, the groups' members addressed each other as "Citizen" and toasted the guillotine. They erected liberty poles, donned tricolored cockades, and compared the president's affinity for self-elevating ceremony to the courtly pomp of Louis XVI, who had recently lost his head before a cheering Parisian mob.[6]

The force that prevented Federalist fears from spiraling into hysteria was none other than Washington himself. Whatever the influence of the radical clubs on civic thought in the early republic, the commander in chief had more. He possessed a reputation so solid that the critics who bludgeoned his record made no appreciable dent in his popularity. Support for the whiskey rebels withered when the president marched with federalized militia toward western Pennsylvania; disdain for the Jay Treaty diminished after he gave it his assent.

His stern rebuke of the "self-created" Democratic-Republican societies soon left them humiliated before the public. As a Virginian, Washington's leadership forged a firm if fractious union of the northern-based Federalists, with whom he generally agreed, and Republicans, among whom he lived in their stronghold of the South.[7]

By the summer of 1796, however, the president's retirement at the conclusion of his second term seemed all but assured. Long a subject of anxious speculation, Washington's decision appeared certain both to Madison, chief coordinator of Republicans in Congress, and to Hamilton, who had recently resigned as secretary of the treasury but remained an important influence within Federalist circles.[8] For men of either political persuasion, the chief executive's imminent departure promised danger as well as opportunity. Although Washington, twice elected with little opposition, could claim to stand above faction, his successor would be a Federalist or Republican, a partisan with policies and programs amenable to one side but probably unacceptable to the other.

The presidential election of 1796 was thus a struggle between two competing visions of America's future. With so much ostensibly at stake, it occasioned more vitriol, vituperation, and frenzied maneuvering for advantage than any other voting contest in the new nation's brief history. In the two months between Washington's September 17 Farewell Address—which, as Congressman Fisher Ames predicted, served "as a signal, like dropping a hat, for party racers to start"—and the states' November elections, citizens witnessed an outpouring of debate over the fundamental character of American political culture.[9] Should the United States emulate Britain's tradition of aristocratic order or France's experiment with democratic liberty? What were the rightful roles of religion and region in politics? Should government officials lead the people or should they represent them? By no means did the results of the election fully answer these questions but, with more clarity than any event that had preceded it, this contest raised them in a heated debate that hinged on competing conceptions of Thomas Jefferson.

EVER SINCE HE HAD resigned from Washington's cabinet at the end of 1793, Jefferson had labored to remove himself from such controversies. Thin-skinned and shy, he recoiled in the face of criticism and, unlike John Adams, took care never to appear to pant after praise.[10] Jefferson claimed instead to seek "happiness in the lap and love of my family, in the society of my neighbors and my books, in the wholesome occupations of my farm and my affairs" at Monticello, "owing account to myself alone of my hours and actions." He maintained that he had little interest in political controversies and even less knowledge of them. He said that he refused to pick up a newspaper, relying instead on Madison and other friends for information on the progress of government.[11] He threw himself into agricultural pursuits, experimenting with crop rotation, uncommon varieties of clover, and his new design for a moldboard plow. He established a nail manufactory for supplemental income and supervised the firing of bricks for his planned renovation of Monticello. Not once during his three-year retirement did he venture more than seven miles from his mountaintop home.[12]

In an era when appearing eager for office could disqualify a candidate, Jefferson cast himself as an aloof and apolitical agrarian. He endeavored to convince his friends—and himself—that he was born for the role, mostly by reading from his script with a bit too much earnestness. The performance that resulted never seemed entirely true to life. He boasted about his supposed estrangement from national affairs. On a single day in September 1795, for example, he informed no fewer than three correspondents that he had little interest in the Jay Treaty debate. To one of them, his friend and former neighbor Philip Mazzei, he wrote that the treaty, which "is thought to have stipulated some things beyond the power of the President and the Senate," had "excited a more general disgust than any other public transaction" since the 1770s. Even so, he maintained, he would continue to "pursue my farm and my nailery, pay my taxes, and leave public measures to those who have longer to live under them." To another, Federalist diplomat Thomas Pinckney, Jefferson reported that the treaty had provided the "noise of the day in the political field. . . . But no body is so little able as myself to say what the public opinion is. I take no newspaper and by that device keep myself in a much loved ignorance." Did Jefferson protest too much? Despite these avowals of aloofness, which accompanied astute synopses of the controversy, one week later he thanked his former state department assistant for bound volumes of newspapers and wrote that he was "anxious" to receive more.[13]

While it is clear that Jefferson was faking his lack of interest in national affairs, it remains uncertain when he resolved to allow Republicans to rally around him as their 1796 candidate for the presidency. Since retiring as secretary of state he had been denying any desire for power, but such professions of disinterestedness were among the prerequisites for being entrusted with it. In a December 1794 letter, he initiated with Madison a convoluted yet carefully

worded conversation that boiled down to one simple question about the up-
coming election: will you be the candidate or will I? He told Madison that
he had long been waiting to broach the subject, but "double delicacies have
kept me silent." He implored Madison not to retire from Congress—unless
to the "more splendid and more efficacious post" of the presidency. "There,"
he wrote, "I should rejoice to see you." But then, backtracking, Jefferson asked
how he could possibly wish for someone "whose happiness I have as much at
heart as yours, to take the front of the battle"? Not missing the hint, Madison flatly rebuked the proposal that he stand for the presidency, intimating
instead that Jefferson should prepare for election to the office. "The question
is for ever closed with me," Jefferson replied, for he "would not give up my
own retirement for the empire of the Universe." Reminding Madison that
"my retirement from office had meant from all office high or low, without
exception," he insisted that the "little spice of ambition, which I had in my
younger days, has long since evaporated." In addition, a return to politics
would only confirm Federalists' "continual insinuations" during his stormy
tenure as a member of Washington's administration that he yearned to hold
the reigns of executive power. As a result, considerations of "reputation" and
"tranquility" ruled out a bid for office, and there existed no "opening for future discussion."[14]

But Madison could hardly have failed to recognize Jefferson's status as his
senior—and more recognizable—partner. He understood that ritualistic disavowals of desire for office frequently communicated a willingness to serve.
The congressman might also have dismissed Jefferson's profession that his fear
of confirming Federalists' charges of ambition outweighed his ambition to
prevent the elevation to the presidency of a Federalist. Maybe Madison believed that the real motivation for Jefferson's refusal was his desire to maintain
a reputation for disinterestedness with Madison and their circle of allies. It
is difficult to know with certainty, in part because Jefferson and Madison
communicated not only in writing but also through conversations that, when
not face to face, intermediaries facilitated. Their final meeting before the election took place at Monticello in October 1795. The result of their discussions
seems to have been Jefferson's acquiescence to election to the nation's highest
office. They next communicated in writing about the election in December
1796, when Madison told Jefferson that he should accept elevation not only
to the presidency but also to the vice presidency. The idea that the 1795 visit
resulted in an agreement between the men gains ground when their correspondence is surveyed. They raised the topic of the presidency repeatedly

before this visit. Afterward, they did not address the subject in nearly three dozen letters, all of which were written prior to May 1796, when—probably to insulate Jefferson from any suspicion of involvement in the campaign to elect him, which Madison helped mastermind—for six months their letter writing ceased entirely.[15]

Whenever Jefferson embraced the idea that he would be the Republican candidate for the presidency, throughout his retirement his behavior remained largely consistent. He was, as he informed Madison, committed to the preservation of his "reputation" and the careful observation of all necessary "delicacies." These included avoiding actions that made him seem ambitious for the presidency and creating the impression that he was uninterested in politics. His allies, who conceived of their mission as a struggle against the consolidation of power, must not be led to believe that a thirst for office or even "vanity" colored Jefferson's future plans. Thus Jefferson guarded with care even what he communicated to Madison, his most trusted ally, especially when he communicated in writing. An intercepted letter, an unfaithful messenger, the misguided publication of something expressed in confidence—all could aid enemies who "in the public papers" designed "to poison the public mind as to my motives" by portraying him as a conniving office-seeker.[16]

Whether or not, as detractors alleged, Jefferson's retirement as secretary of state and subsequent sequestration at Monticello aimed to bolster his reputation, a desire to boost his image at least partially influenced Jefferson's decision to keep a low profile. Referring to Washington, John Adams once marveled at how well "political Plants grow in the Shade." Since "continual Day light & sun shine, show our faults and record them," he believed that "the mode of becoming great is to retire."[17] In Jefferson's case, stepping down from office allowed him to avoid the potentially debilitating fights of Washington's second term at the same time that he burnished his credentials as a man hesitant to grasp the reins of power and focused instead on his farm and family. To whatever degree he was playing hard to get, the result was that his supporters' desire for him only seemed to increase.

"I BELIEVE all America looks up to yourself & our Friend Mr Jefferson," Reverend James Madison, president of the College of William and Mary, wrote to his cousin and namesake. "I hope he will feel, that there are Times when Retirement becomes almost criminal." While the scholar-preacher would have been satisfied to see Jefferson in the state legislature, New Yorker Robert R.

Livingston contended in late 1795 that the "public attention should as soon as possible be turned on Mr. Jefferson who will I hope have no reluctance in being brought forward" as a candidate for president. By the following April, a Maryland traveler reported home of gossip in Virginia that Jefferson "is to be the next President, the present one to resign." In June, a full three months prior to Washington's public announcement of his decision to step down, Jefferson had been entered into nomination in Massachusetts. Barring unlikely events, clerk of the House and Pennsylvania Republican John Beckley proclaimed it "morally certain" that Jefferson would win the election, in part because citizens viewed him as most qualified to smooth French-American relations, which had seemed dangerously bumpy since the ratification of the Jay Treaty. A few weeks later, Hubbard Taylor of Kentucky predicted that in his state "the vote will ... be unanimous for Mr. Jefferson as president."[18]

Such declarations revealed overconfidence, but they also suggested that partisan leaders in far-flung locales understood that Jefferson would be their man. Madison, from his perch in the House of Representatives, stood well-positioned to coordinate Republicans' national efforts. In addition, as Jefferson's closest confidant, Madison played a crucial role by keeping the disinclined standard-bearer at a distance. In September he provided James Monroe with gossip well worth sharing, for it spotlighted Jefferson's presumed reluctance: Madison had not only cut off his correspondence with Jefferson but also abstained throughout the year from making the short journey from his own Montpelier plantation to Monticello. "I have not seen Jefferson," he explained, "and have thought it best to present him no opportunity of protesting to his friend against being embarked in the contest."[19] Jefferson, however, was nobody's fool. In the final week of 1795, he sent payment to Philadelphia printer Benjamin Franklin Bache for a year's subscription to the Republican *Aurora*.[20] Fewer than ten days after Washington's official farewell, its pages reported news of what he claimed to fear most.

"It seems agreed on all hands that the contest will be between Mr. Jefferson and Mr. Adams," Albert Russel reminded his fellow Virginians in a letter that Bache's paper reprinted. Declaring himself a candidate for elector and pledging his support for Jefferson, Russel warned citizens of the vice president's "well known predilection for Monarchy." The retired secretary of state, however, possessed a "steady and firm attachment to republican government." Noted as "a friend to the adoption of the Federal constitution, and a zealous supporter of that constitution upon its true and genuine principles,"

Jefferson was "the only person who is considered as having a chance against Mr. Adams."[21]

The *Aurora* had hinted about a Jefferson candidacy as early as February, but Russel's appeal stood among the earliest published testimonials to address the matter without ambiguity.[22] Nor did it hedge on the theme repeated by the chorus of Republican polemicists during the campaign: while Adams favored aristocracy, support for Jefferson meant support for popular government. Of all the issues that would captivate public attention in the months leading up to the presidential contest, this, for Republicans, counted most. On July 4, for example, a large group of Philadelphians raised their glasses and drank to "The Election of 1796—May all the Officers of Government be cast in a pure Democratic Mould."[23]

Opponents of the Jay Treaty and Hamilton's financial system revolted at the prospect of a President Adams. They claimed that the vice president's forays into political philosophy, particularly his *Defence of the Constitutions of the United States* (1787) and "Discourses on Davila" (1790), displayed his elitism, affinity for hereditary ranks and titles, and fondness for the British constitution. They also elicited Republicans' scorn. One writer quoted Adams's own words so that voters could "judge whether a man who despises the people . . . and doubts the practicability of our elective republican constitutions, deserves to be placed at the head of the Federal Government."[24]

The vice president grabbed at power and prestige, writers charged. "He will likewise sue for the Presidential chair," contended one; another asserted that, if elected, Adams would use a standing army as "an instrument to exact obedience." According to a third report, his eagerness to establish titles resulted from his vain compulsion not to be ranked among the mob. "So desirous was he of distinctions, that he used to appear with a sword at his side, his hat under his arm," and his wig fashionably coiffed. Noting that "those who know Mr. Adams" will recall his "considerable sesquipedality of belly," the writer mentioned one senator who had suggested "his rotundity" as a title for the vice president.[25]

All jokes aside, these writers advanced a serious proposition. "Republicanism itself" was "menaced" and "everything dear to a freeman" hinged on the approaching election. Citizens' votes would decide "the future liberties and happiness of our country." The election would "determine whether we shall remain independent, or be colonized anew; whether we shall continue to enjoy a republican government, or be brought under the yoke of a master."[26]

People unsure about whom to support needed only to consult the candidates' résumés. Adams in the 1780s had taken up residence at the Court of St. James as American minister to Britain, where he "drank at the polluted fountain of political corruption" and "joined the gaudy group of sycophants" who kneeled "at the shrine of Majesty." He departed "dazzled with the splendor of royalty." Jefferson, on the other hand, had served during the same period as minister to France. Against the backdrop of a crumbling monarchy, buoyed by the promise of the brewing revolution, he preserved his "simplicity of manners" and remained "a *stern* republican." Freeholders "in favor of King, Lords, and *faithful Commons*," suggested "A Whig" in the *Aurora,* would champion Adams. Meanwhile, "the friends to our present constitution, will vote for no person as an elector who will not unequivocally pledge himself to vote for Mr. Jefferson."[27]

Jefferson's connection with the French Revolution, however, turned the stomachs of Federalists. While Republicans painted Adams as a British supplicant, their opponents could scarcely resist coming to the converse conclusion about Jefferson. He cheered the French Revolution, and this alone sufficed to make him unfit to lead America. "The revolution of France has been distinguished by many scenes of cruelty that shock humanity," noted one pro-Adams newspaperman, a fact that Federalists understood but some Republicans seemed to overlook. He reminded readers of the Jacobins' "sacrilegious attacks on popular religion, their violations of property, personal rights, and the fury of their political presentations." Blindly loyal to the land where he had once represented the United States, Jefferson, Federalists feared, would import disorder and ruin. Rather than place Jefferson in the presidential chair, a Federalist suggested, "we might as well elect [former French minister Edmond Charles] Genet President, and become a Colony of France at once."[28]

Judging from their panicked pronouncements, at least some of the Federalists viewed Jefferson's candidacy—along with the Whiskey Rebellion and the rise of Democratic-Republican societies—as evidence of a trans-Atlantic conspiracy to supplant constitutional order with anarchy. John Fenno's *Gazette of the United States* observed that "the 'excessive patriots' of Paris, the enemies of the French constitution, appear to be with the same cast with the enemies of the constitution of this country." A writer who called himself "Phocion," a man House of Representatives clerk John Beckley suspected to be Hamilton, claimed that "Mr. Jefferson foresaw the western insurrection" but did nothing to prevent it. "The democratic faction is wholly *foreign,*" asserted another penman. "Not a drop of American blood" pulsed in its leaders' veins, and "not a drop that is not degenerate."[29]

To favorably contrast Adams with Jefferson and his "species of fanaticism," Federalist candidates for elector stressed their commitment to "Order and good Government." Similarly, "A Farmer" who supported Adams held that the presidential contest pitted "the *'Friends'*" against "the *'Enemies'* of the government." Fenno, moreover, printed in his gazette an essay defending "the immortal principles contained" in the vice president's political writings. "If our republic is to stand," the author warned, "if those monsters, the jacobins," will be prevented from erecting "a murderous revolutionary empire," then Adams's dictums must become "the political creed of every friend of freedom."[30]

Republicans, however, insisted that, although Jefferson supported France's experiment with popular government, he did not condone the Jacobins' Reign of Terror. Tench Coxe, a former Federalist, contended in a November pamphlet that Jefferson's opponents wrongly accused him of being "so much disposed to justify the French Revolution, as to overlook all the excesses which that nation has committed." To the contrary, Jefferson stood alongside Washington in admiring the principles and promises of 1789 but "lamenting... their late stupendous despotism." Even so, given the uneasy state of French-American relations, Jefferson's election could work to the advantage of the United States. As one writer observed, "it will conciliate the people of France who have the idea that he has been leaning in their favor."[31]

In whatever direction Jefferson might lean, Republicans expressed no doubts that he stood firmly within the mainstream of American political thought. To make this point they now began to publicize his role as the penman of the Declaration of Independence. One newspaper, asserting that only the "purest motives" caused Jefferson to wish for the French Revolution's success, maintained that he was "wholly and truly an American." The Declaration, "written by Jefferson," placed him "above suspicion" because of the "energy and justice of its sentiments." Another writer maintained that Jefferson, "the principal personage" in the creation of the document, had earned a place "in the annals of fame, among the most distinguished patriots of America." Federalists, meanwhile, did their best to ignore his contributions to independence and thereby deny him the cover it provided against charges of anti-Americanism. One writer, never mentioning Jefferson, held that "it may truly be said that no one was more instrumental in the adoption" of the Declaration than John Adams. Another thought that credit should be shared:

"The names of Hancock and Adams will be remembered to the latest posterity, as two of the principal workmen in raising the glorious fabric of American
independence." People who took their news from Federalist papers, informed
of Jefferson's supposedly foreign philosophies, remained unaware that, twenty
years earlier, he had penned America's statement of purpose.[32]

The election of 1796, with all of its implications for international relations,
appeared to offer irreconcilable choices. How could Americans, with their
diametrically divergent outlooks, navigate the treacherous channel between a
British Scylla and a French Charybdis? For Republicans and Federalists alike,
the contest between Jefferson and Adams loomed as a defining moment for a
new nation still struggling to decide its role in world affairs.

THE ELECTION also exposed bitter feuds on the domestic front. It called on
citizens to confront cardinal questions about the nature of their polity. For
the most part, Federalists raised these points of contention as they aimed their
sights on Jefferson's character. They derided his religious beliefs and asked
voters if a man of such doubtful faith should lead their Christian nation.
They attacked his state and his status as a Virginian, and at the same time
they raised the issue of slavery in an attempt to exploit sectional rifts. Finally,
Federalists depicted Jefferson as an ambitious office-seeker, a panderer to the
people who, for victory, would sacrifice steady government to the whims of
the mob.

At least two factors, one foreign in origin and the other domestic, combined
to create an image of Jefferson as irreligious. The first was his association with
Thomas Paine, whose 1794 *Age of Reason,* according to one pamphleteer,
constituted a collection of "impious doctrines." Writing, significantly, from
France, Paine espoused the ideals of enlightenment Deism, attacked Christian dogma, and held that "I do not believe in the creed professed by . . . any
church that I know of. My own mind is my own church." Paine's pronouncements came on the heels of the Jacobins' campaign to secularize clergy and
de-Christianize their nation, which already had confiscated church-owned
property. Jefferson, in the eyes of Federalists, stood allied with both Paine and
the radical elements of the country in which Paine lived.[33]

As additional proof of his un-Christian principles, Jefferson's opponents
pointed to his bill to disestablish the Anglican church in Virginia. They ridiculed the "frivolous and impious passage" justifying the proposal in his *Notes
on the State of Virginia,* where he contended that "it does me no injury for

my neighbour to say there are twenty gods, or no god. It neither picks my pocket nor breaks my leg." "Good God!" exclaimed one indignant writer, "is this the man the *patriots* have cast their eyes on as successor to the *virtuous Washington,* who, in his farewell address, so warmly . . . recommends to his fellow citizens, the *cultivators of religion*"? America's status as a predominantly Christian country existed as one of the most important factors distinguishing it from the Gallic republic. "We are not Frenchmen," a Connecticut writer observed, "and until the Atheistical Philosophy of a certain great Virginian shall become the fashion (which God of his mercy forbid) we shall never be."[34]

Another writer tried to explain the sources and contours of Federalists' ruminations regarding Jefferson's religion. Britain and Spain worked to spread the belief that their French rivals were bent on "destroying" religion, the author observed, and "the writings of Thomas Paine have greatly contributed" to this opinion. "Having appeared as a conspicuous political writer, the moment he undertook to doubt" sectarian teachings "his opinions as to religion were supposed to be adopted by those who thought like him in politics." As a result, "to be a republican, or an admirer of the French revolution, was supposed to be synonymous" with being "an infidel, anxious to overthrow every vestige of the Christian system." Readers of this essay learned one thing more: not all Federalists condoned portrayals of Jefferson as an atheist. The writer's defense of Jefferson was implicit but clear, and it appeared, somewhat remarkably, in the New York *Minerva,* Noah Webster's Federalist sheet.[35]

Other essayists discussed religious freedom, a right that they traced to the foundations of American government. The *Aurora,* for example, quoted William Penn's writings on toleration to answer "an abuser of Thomas Jefferson." It also printed an amicable "Dialogue between an Aristocrat and a Republican." The aristocrat maintained that Jefferson "is not a friend to the old established religion of this country" and "does not hold that religious faith in which we have been brought up as a nation." The republican did not disagree but reminded his companion that "the religious sentiments of a man" remained a private matter. Individuals, he said, possessed "a right" to their beliefs in accordance with "the light of understanding which God has given to him." After all, he added, the Constitution "held sacred" the "freedom of conscience and religious sentiment." In regards to religion, "the ideas of a statesman, a Philosopher, or a gentlemen" could only be "determined to be of little consequence in public life."[36]

The Republicans' strategy probably did little to convince strict sectarians to toss aside Federalist charges. But it allowed them to avoid issuing a religious avowal in Jefferson's behalf, which, given his steady reticence regarding his faith, remained a problematic undertaking.[37] In an important way, however, their defense of Jefferson's right to religious freedom worked to their advantage. It gave them an opportunity to demonstrate the nature of their commitment to the Constitution. Unlike proponents of Adams, who saw it as an instrument of order, for Republicans America's charter stood as a guarantor of liberty. Jefferson, by implication, agreed.

If questions of faith and freedom could rally citizens from far-flung locales around a common cause, sectional hostility threatened to divide the United States into two distinct halves. Adams commanded a secure electoral base in New England. Jefferson's candidacy drew considerable strength from the South. The marriage of these disparate areas had always been an uneasy union, so regional enmity in the election came naturally. Partisans of Jefferson derided the "cunning Yankees," the "high-fliers of the East." Meanwhile, Adams's advocates spoke of "the pretensions of Virginia."[38] With support for the candidates on their home turf presumably so solid, the votes of the middle states—especially those of populous New York and Pennsylvania—appeared crucial. Here, Federalists exploited an entrenched emancipationist impulse in hopes of souring the public's opinion of Jefferson.

Led by the indefatigable "Phocion," they portrayed Jefferson as a racist who viewed African Americans as members of a species beneath whites but above orangutans. In addition, they charged, he was duplicitous concerning slavery, for he sought favor with slaveholders at the same time that he pursued "the plaudits of the abolition societies." Such reports helped to secure Adams's footing among Pennsylvania Quakers, many of whom had opposed slavery for decades and already leaned toward the Federalist side in their politics. More menacing to Jefferson's chances was the potential effect of such charges on the minds of his friends. Members of the middle states' Democratic-Republican clubs sometimes also belonged to local antislavery groups, and a few of the Jeffersonian organizations worked directly to redress racial injustice. In 1794, for example, New York's Tammany Society had demanded "speedy abolition of every species of slavery throughout America." The True Republican Society of Philadelphia even included as a member Cyrus Bustill, a free man of African descent ridiculed by some Federalists as "Citizen Sambo."[39]

But the former secretary of state enjoyed a longstanding reputation in mid-Atlantic Republican circles as a "firm and able asserter of the freedom of the blacks." As Tench Coxe noted, many understood "that Mr. Jefferson had proposed for consideration an un-adopted article in the declaration of independence censuring the kings of Great Britain for annulling the American laws to prohibit the slave trade," and that, in the Virginia legislature, he had advocated measures for gradual emancipation. Phocion, he concluded, labored "in vain" to marshal "the friends of the blacks" against Jefferson.[40]

Perhaps Phocion anticipated this result, for he endeavored simultaneously to fracture southern unity. In the same essay that blasted Jefferson as a pro-slavery slaveholder, he asserted that the Republican candidate had once designed an "extravagant project of *emancipating all the slaves* in Virginia." Another Federalist writer argued along the same lines. "For my part," he claimed, "were I a southern planter, owning negroes, I should be ten thousand times more alarmed at Mr. Jefferson's ardent wish for *emancipation,* than at any *fanciful* dangers from monarchy." This alternative strategy produced results as modest as those of the first. Congressman Robert Goodloe Harper, a South Carolina Federalist, informed Alexander Hamilton in November that southerners mentioned Jefferson's name in connection with the presidency more than any other.[41]

Whatever the influence of Federalist criticisms regarding Jefferson's views on religion and race, his detractors viewed him as alarmingly popular. His appeal seemed especially sinister because it waxed strong among the members of Democratic-Republican clubs, scorned by prominent Federalist editor William Cobbett as "poor rogues," rabble, and "the lowest order of mechanics, laborers and draymen." While in fact these societies often looked to attorneys and government officials for leadership, men of diverse occupations composed their rank and file, people characterized by New York sailmaker George Warner as "the industrious classes of society" who had once considered "themselves of TOO LITTLE CONSEQUENCE to the body politic." Now, however, they displayed political assertiveness, an awareness of power rooted in an economic reality that raised the eyebrows of even the most enlightened Old World transplants to America. "Here there is little difference between master and servant," complained Joseph Priestley. "Indeed," he said, "those terms are unknown." Even his "poor sickly" servant girl, although "perfectly ignorant," acted "as stately and proud as a queen." Whether members of organized groups or not, Americans who advanced Jefferson's candidacy tended to fit such descriptions, be they urban upstarts or middling yeomen, from the middle states or the South.[42]

Federalists accused Republicans of cultivating support through a campaign of misinformation. They cast "those who opposed them as monarchy men & Aristocrats," Maryland lawyer David Ross observed, and "alarm the People with apprehensions for their Government & liberties if they do not elect Mr Jefferson." Since "the great body of the People" possessed "no knowledge" of the presidential candidates, Ross lamented, and because Jefferson's supporters were generally "the most active" in electioneering, "I should not be surprised" if voters "should be imposed on to do what is so much against their own interest."[43]

Undoubtedly, Republicans pioneered campaign techniques never before used in a presidential election. In Pennsylvania, for instance, they publicized a "Jefferson ticket" of electors in order to prevent confusion with the pro-Adams "Federal and Republican ticket." A contributor to New York's *Minerva,* believing that citizens should defer selection of the president to the independent wisdom of electors, denounced this act of "impudence." He could not have been pleased when Beckley solicited volunteers in every county of his state to print, in their own handwriting, a total of thirty thousand ballots for the Jefferson slate—enough for one of every three Pennsylvanians eligible to vote, and two and a half times the number of citizens who actually turned out on election day.[44]

Why, inquired a Federalist newspaperman, was there such "extraordinary exertion in favor of Mr. Jefferson"? In 1795 "a conference was held at Mr. Jefferson's house," he reported, "at which all this business was preconcerted." Those gathered pursued corruption as well as power, the author suggested, for they aimed to place Republicans into positions "which honest and prudent men find unprofitable." Jefferson and his cohorts, he intimated, sought riches from mob rule. Borrowing words from Hamilton's third "Catullus" essay of 1792, another writer asserted that "Mr. Jefferson has been held up and characterized by his friends as 'the quiet, modest retiring philosopher—as the plain, simple, unambitious republican.'" But the one-time secretary of state could be understood as nothing less than "an intriguing incendiary" and "an aspiring turbulent competitor" for office. Despite Jefferson's claim that he had withdrawn from his post within the administration to tend to "philosophical pursuits," he devoted "his hours of retirement *to mature his schemes of concealed ambition.*"[45]

These Federalists levied heavy allegations, and Jefferson's partisans did not fail to respond. Coxe countered that his candidate "retired from public grandeur into a vale of obscurity" with the sort of "tranquility and complacence of mind which ever characterized true greatness. Like our beloved President, or the renowned Cincinnatus, he knows how to support the burden of high office with dignity, or to resign it without a sigh."[46]

These were the two men whom all elected officials in the early republic strived—or claimed—to emulate. Both Washington and his classical forbear had answered the calls of country in times of crisis and then, when all appeared safe, traded sword for plow and returned home. Because they had rejected the power and prestige of permanent government posts, because they had not needed salaries for sustenance, they had served only when patriotism required it and otherwise enjoyed independent, disinterested lives. While Republicans like Coxe responded to accusations that Jefferson worked as a demagogue to serve his own ends, only Jefferson's behavior could adequately answer such charges in the long run. To queries about his religion and racial views his silence prompted others to issue rebuttals. To charges that he sought profit from public service and schemed at self-promotion, however, his silence spoke volumes.

TWO HUNDRED MILES of uneven and sometimes impassible road separated Monticello from Philadelphia, the capital city, a staging area for public intrigue and the home of a crucial constituency of voters. Jefferson's subscription to the *Aurora*, however, caused news to traverse the distance and regularly arrive at his reading stand. The labors of Madison, Beckley, and other Republican leaders materialized regularly before Jefferson's eyes, even though he was not a party to their secret strategizing. The self-declared non-candidate became fully aware of his candidacy. By no means did he encourage attempts to elevate him to the presidential office but neither did he turn a deaf ear to his country's call.

On September 15, Jefferson received from Tennessee Republican William Cocke an indication of what the *Aurora* would report several days later. Cocke, who had first met Jefferson at the Continental Congress in 1776, announced "that the people of this State, of every description, express a wish that you should be the next President of the United States." Jefferson issued an interesting reply: "I always learn with great pleasure that I am recollected with approbation by those with whom I have served." But he did not want "the honorable office" even though, as he wrote, he lacked "the arrogance to say that I would refuse" it. As he informed Cocke, he could "say with truth that I had rather be thought worthy of it than to be appointed to it." His reservations about the presidency resulted, he maintained, from the knowledge "that no man will bring out of that office the reputation which carries him into it."[47]

Here he relaxed the posture he had assumed nineteen months earlier when Madison had suggested his possible candidacy and Jefferson had insisted that his concern for "reputation" prevented him from considering the presidency. In this earlier exchange, he had claimed to fear that making himself available for the post would tarnish his image by seeming to confirm his enemies' charges that ambition drove him to seek power. The situation would have changed, however, by the time that Cocke received his statement. The people would have made their choice. As a result, Jefferson's concerns about his reputation had less to do with his candidacy than the possibility of his victory. What if he won? Or what if he lost, finished second, and received his country's call to serve as vice president? Whatever the outcome, Jefferson would serve. He was too concerned about his reputation to make this fact known to even his closest confidants, but he was too concerned about his nation to do anything else. Madison, who had confided to Monroe his worry that Jefferson would mar his prospects by making a "*public* protest" against his nomination, could have rested easily. Jefferson's actions steered a middle course between a selfish pursuit of private leisure and power-hungry self-aggrandizement, one consistent with eighteenth-century notions of republican leadership and compatible with the most recent pronouncement of Washington, America's paragon of virtue.[48]

The president's Farewell Address warned against foreign alliance and sectional discord and served more than anything else as a guiding text of the election. Its accounting of why eight years earlier George Washington had accepted the executive chair, however, also described the force that drove even disinclined men into public life. He took the oath of office, he told his countrymen, "in deference of what appeared to be your desire" and in answer to the citizens "whose calls he has been ever accustomed to obey." With the United States prosperous and its people's liberties sufficiently safe, he decreed that his final tour of duty had ended. At last, he could "return to that retirement from which I had been reluctantly drawn." Washington assured Americans that his decision had not been made "without a strict regard to all the considerations appertaining to the relation" binding "a dutiful citizen to his country." In withdrawing from government life, he informed Americans, "I am influenced by no diminution of zeal for your future interest" nor any "deficiency of great respect for your past kindness."[49] Part explanation, part apology, the president's farewell underscored the imperative that true republicans abide by the will of the people. While they should not seek office, neither should they spurn it and place private interest above the good of their nation.

If they did, as Washington implied, they would suffer the scorn of those who solicited their talents.

Jefferson's performance in the election of 1796 conformed to these elevated standards of disinterestedness. True, when in 1795 he met with Madison he may have agreed to serve as the Republican candidate, but he took no active role in promoting his candidacy. (While drafting a letter to Edward Rutledge, a moderate South Carolina Republican and fellow signer of the Declaration, Jefferson wrote that his name was "brought forward, without consultation or expectation on my part." Then, to be more precise, he crossed out "consultation" and replaced it with "concert.") Not once during the campaign did he speak out in public to advance his own candidacy, and never did instructions to partisans pour from his pen. Such restraint, of course, was as much consistent with the actions of a man with political savvy as it was of a man with a distaste for politics. Jefferson, of course, was smart enough to know that, despite the stakes of the election and its unprecedented partisanship, aloofness remained the socially acceptable pose. As he informed Washington at the start of the summer, "political conversation I really dislike, and therefore avoid where I can without affectation."[50]

Yet even had he wished to do so, Jefferson could hardly have resisted the temptation to follow the news of the campaign. He cared deeply about his reputation not only among peers such as Rutledge and Washington but also in the eyes of the public. In the immediate aftermath of the election, he complained to Rutledge that "I did not know myself under the pens either of my friends or foes." The truth, he said, was that "unmerited abuse wounds, while unmerited praise has not the power to heal."[51]

This may have been the case, but Jefferson must not have minded that his friends, whatever their excesses, never missed a chance to do his reputation justice. At the height of the contest, when Federalists resurrected charges that, in the midst of the War for Independence, during his service as governor of Virginia, he snuck away from Monticello like a coward as British troops advanced, Virginia Republicans assembled a dossier of statements defending his actions. (At some point these documents were inserted into Jefferson's collection of letters and other papers, although when they were placed there— and by whom—remains unknown.)[52] Whether Jefferson had no knowledge of this effort or served as its silent mastermind, one reason he could remain silent in the press is that he never lacked for friends willing to defend him. The Federalist charge of cowardice provoked many responses, including retorts highlighting Jefferson's connection with the Declaration. "Did he display no firmness," one supporter asked, "when he stood forth [as] the ablest advocate of independence, of that bold measure which broke your chains, which rent asunder a vast empire, and which proclaimed in thunder to the world liberty and justice?" Jefferson's role in the 1796 election, of course, was not to thunder in support of liberty but instead to remain silent about his own desire for power. This confirmed for his allies his political purity, bolstering their enthusiasm for him and the cause they shared while making possible the decision of the Electoral College, which provided him with an opportunity to prove his patriotism through deeds instead of words.[53]

It called him to serve under John Adams as the new vice president. When electors' ballots were counted in February, the final tally awarded seventy-one votes to Adams, sixty-eight to Jefferson, and fifty-nine and thirty votes each to their respective running mates, South Carolina Federalist Thomas Pinckney and New York Republican Aaron Burr. As expected, Adams swept New England; support for Jefferson dominated the South and the new southwestern states of Kentucky and Tennessee. New York, New Jersey, and Delaware electors gave their assent to Adams while Beckley's efforts paid off for the Republicans in Pennsylvania.[54]

In December, Madison resumed his correspondence with his friend and informed him of the campaign's probable outcome. Although no letters had passed between them for half a year, the congressman had somehow come to understand that Jefferson "submitted to the election." Because you "made up your mind to obey the call of your Country," Madison reminded him, it "is expected" that "you will let it decide on the particular place where your services are to be rendered." As vice president, Madison maintained, Jefferson could influence the new Adams administration. "On the whole it seems *essential* that you should not refuse the station which is likely to be your lot."[55]

The former secretary of state needed little convincing. He had not really wanted the presidency, he explained. In fact, he had been prepared to cede the post to Adams in the case of a tie, as Adams had "always been my senior from the commencement of our public life." In addition, as Jefferson confessed to his son-in-law, Thomas Mann Randolph, "whether viewed with relation to interest, happiness, or reputation," it was smarter to come in second. Problems both foreign and domestic clouded the immediate future of the country, and, as he told Benjamin Rush, "the storm is about to burst."[56]

Once his position as Adams's vice president seemed set, Jefferson turned his attention toward his inauguration. Ever vigilant regarding his reputation, he deliberated over the means by which he would be admitted to office. At first he considered a simple oath-taking close to home, away from the nation's capital. Then he had second thoughts. "I shall come on the principle which had first determined me," he informed Madison: "respect to the public." Still, he hoped to "be made a part of no ceremony whatever." Aware of citizens' affection for his simple manners and their uneasiness with the Washington administration's courtly pomp, he determined "to escape into the city as covertly as possible."[57]

The citizens of Philadelphia foiled this plan. On the second of March, at the conclusion of a ten-day journey, he was met by a local militia company and welcomed with the firing of sixteen twelve-pound rounds from two cannons. Hoisted above the scene was a banner that heralded the arrival of "Jefferson the friend of the people."[58] Adams, whose position kept him stationed within the city, required no such welcome. Nor was he the center of attention in the celebrations that followed his oath of office. At the grand banquet celebrating his inauguration, President George Washington was the guest of honor. More than a week later, a newspaper from Adams's native state still referred to him and his predecessor as "the Vice-President and GEORGE WASHINGTON."[59]

THE CONTEST might have gone differently. Throughout the autumn, Hamilton had quietly schemed to place Thomas Pinckney in the presidential chair. Supposedly more susceptible than Adams to Hamilton's influence and apparently more amenable to his plans for a national bank, the South Carolinian had been the object of a surreptitious letter-writing campaign to relegate Adams to political irrelevancy. The original system for selecting executive officers made no distinction between nominees for the presidency and the vice presidency, calling on each elector to vote for two men. The highest office went to the individual accorded the greatest number of votes. Hamilton therefore urged solid support for both Federalist candidates in the northern states, reminding his correspondents "that the exclusion of Mr. Jefferson is far more important than any difference between Mr. Adams and Mr. Pinckney." He assumed that Pinckney would out-poll Adams in the South. As a result, if Federalists overpowered Republicans, Jefferson would finish third in the race. Adams would win the second-highest number of votes and remain as vice president. And Pinckney, predicted Hamilton ally Robert Troup, would be president and "completely within our power."[60]

While Adams, who years later described Hamilton as "a bastard Bratt of a Scotch Pedlar," succeeded in containing his outrage over Hamilton's ploy, he did so with difficulty. He quietly spurned Hamilton, creating a rift among the Federalists that deepened as Adams learned of Jefferson's willingness to stand in his shadow. This position was suggested by Jefferson's inaugural speech, which warmly referred to their "cordial and uninterrupted friendship" and glowingly described Adams's "talents and integrity." Hamilton was left to glower in the face of sweeping—often bipartisan—approval of Jefferson. "Our Jacobins say they are well pleased and that the *Lion* & the *Lamb* are to lie down together," he wrote after the election. "Mr. Adam's PERSONAL friends talk a little in the same way," stating that "Mr. *Jefferson* is not half so ill a man as we have been accustommed to think him. There is to be a united and a vigorous administration." Hamilton recognized, in other words, that Jefferson's practiced modesty and protests of disinterest in politics succeeded in securing for him greater power and greater popularity.[61]

Many Americans embraced the union of the men from Massachusetts and Virginia. Congressman William Barry Grove and his friend James Hogg, for example, were North Carolinians who fit neatly into neither of the two developing factions. As Grove informed Hogg, "Mr. Adams is Elected President & Mr. Jefferson Vice—this is as we both wished." He cheered Jefferson's acquiescence to the second post, as well as his magnanimous "satisfaction at the Election of Mr. A[dams], whose Character & Patriotism it seems he does and [has] respected." In Chester County, Pennsylvania, celebrants at a banquet honoring Washington toasted "Moderation" and raised their glasses to both "Adams and Jefferson" in hopes that "they, when at the head of the family of the United States, go hand in hand" in their duties. "There is no doubt they will act harmoniously together," wrote Joseph Priestley, "which shall greatly abate the animosity of both the parties."[62] Even the most virulent proponents of Jefferson and Adams hoped to cheer the fruits of their partnership.[63]

The detente between Federalists and Republicans did not last. Partisan conflict would flare in the near future, and polemicists on both sides would again resort to their lexicons of abuse and praise. The contest of 1796 failed to permanently resolve the questions that divided America, but it provided these issues with greater definition than had previously existed. It also positioned Jefferson in a post where, contrary to his hopes and despite his best efforts, he could not avoid public conflict. Revered by friends and reviled by foes, he represented, with more clarity than ever before, the aspirations and fears of his countrymen.

CHAPTER THREE

The "Nauseous Fog"

JOHN ADAMS described the vice presidency as a "nauseous fog." For a short while his successor disagreed. "The second office of this government is honorable & easy," Thomas Jefferson reported two months after his inauguration. He considered it "constitutionally confined to legislative functions," namely his role as the Senate's president and tie-breaker. "I could not take any part whatever in executive consultations, even were it proposed."[1]

It was not. Despite one Republican's assessment that Adams, "a small man," would "be led by others," and that "Jefferson bids fair to be his leader," the new president kept the vice president at a distance. Many of the members of Adams's cabinet, all of whom had held the same posts during George Washington's administration, maintained ties to Alexander Hamilton and antipathies toward Jefferson. Fisher Ames, whom Hamilton counted among his strongest allies, voiced fears typical of staunch Federalists when he said that Jefferson's perch would allow him to "go on affecting zeal for the people; combining the *antis,* and standing at the head, he will balance the power of the chief magistrate with his own. Two Presidents, like two suns in the meridian, could meet and jostle for four years, and then Vice would be first." If Adams, a fiercely independent man, was ever "led by others," he was led less by his rival than by this faction, and it is hard to imagine how its members, even under the best of circumstances, would have ever trusted Jefferson with a greater role.[2]

The circumstances for Jefferson, moreover, soon began a steady decline. The day after he pronounced the vice presidency "honorable & easy," Federalist newspapers published a private letter that he had written more than a year earlier to Philip Mazzei, a former Albemarle County neighbor who had returned to his native Italy, and used it in their continuing campaign to tarnish Jefferson's reputation. Subsequent months brought news of America's worsening relations with France, with which he had become associated in the public mind. As this "Quasi-War" unfolded, Hamilton and his allies fanned fears of French-backed domestic threats and pushed into law a package of national security legislation; one component, the 1798 Sedition Act, aimed to mute the Jeffersonian press.[3]

Excluded from Adams's administration by inclination and events, and dissuaded from open participation in public debate by inclination and law, Jefferson fought to preserve his faction and protect his public image through covert measures promising uncertain results. "I never deserted a friend for differences of opinion in politics," he said near the end of his term. "But great numbers have deserted me."[4] Although he had long since abandoned predictions of vice-presidential ease, his prudent handling of controversy helped him, at least, to avoid disaster.

As Jefferson struggled to salvage his reputation, however, he faced conflicting options, each promising its own special pain. This was his own "nauseous fog," and he emerged from it only after his tactics gained coherence and he, as a more experienced political combatant, gained a better understanding of how best to present himself. By pursuing a strategy of behind-the-scenes persuasion, Jefferson tried to diffuse the explosive controversies that surrounded his letter to Mazzei and underscored the more general concerns about his fitness as a leader. His tactics embraced his respect for precedent and his understanding of the power of symbolism. They also reflected a deeper need to compartmentalize, to distance himself from unsavory realities and connect, in different ways, with different audiences. In the company of peers, he whispered explanations of his conduct; before the public, however, he remained silent while constructing plans of self-defense based on the proposition that he, like the ideals he championed, could become self-evident. During this trying period Jefferson settled on a policy calculated to make himself appear as natural as the inherent, inalienable principles that he advocated. The course that he chose to pursue would not be easy, but, better than anything else he could imagine, it might reconcile the conflicting imperatives he faced: how could he simultaneously answer Federalists, who demanded leaders of virtuous character, and satisfy Republicans, who insisted on a character whom they could trust to safeguard principles greater than himself?

JEFFERSON'S LETTER, written in the midst of the Jay Treaty controversy in April 1796, warned Mazzei that Americans' "noble love of liberty and republican government" seemed imperiled. "An Anglican, monarchical and aristocratical party has sprung up, whose avowed object is to draw over us the substance as they have already done the forms of the British government." While most citizens still embraced the Revolution's principles, in the executive and judiciary branches lurked a dangerous clique of "timid men who prefer the calm of despotism to the boisterous sea of liberty. . . . It would give you a fever," he assured Mazzei, "were I to name to you the apostates who have gone over to these heresies, men who were Sampsons in the field and Solomons in the council, but who have had their heads shorn by the harlot England."[5]

Thanks to Mazzei's indiscretion, a translation of Jefferson's intemperate missive ended up in a Paris newspaper, which published it in French, omitted a reference to "the sound" parts of Britain's political system, and amplified Jefferson's disdain for that nation with a conclusion he did not write: "It suffices that we arrest the progress of that system of ingratitude and injustice towards France, from which [America's monarchists] would alienate us, to bring us under British influence." When Federalists learned of the letter, they seized on it as a damning confirmation of Jefferson's extremism. In May 1797, New York's *Minerva* printed its own translation of the French text, which other pro-administration prints quickly reprinted.[6]

This version of the letter not only included the French paper's embellishments but also garbled a key word. While Jefferson had written of "the *forms* of the British government" imported by members of the administration, such as the regal levees and birthday celebrations that marked Washington's presidency, the *Minerva* had him scorning "the *form* of the British government," which, the letter seemed to imply, the Constitution emulated. For years, Jefferson's opponents had blustered about his supposed hostility to the government's framing document, and now they could claim to prove their assertions with his own words. Few situations could have been more injurious to his reputation, especially since, as Joseph Priestley reported, politics constituted "the universal topic of all conversation."[7]

In John Fenno's *Gazette of the United States*, "A Native American" (whose pen name contrasted with Jefferson's supposedly foreign loyalties) told the vice president that his letter exposed his betrayal of the Constitution after "ambition threw you into the hands of a depraved faction, by whose means you expected, no doubt, to have filled the first office of our government." Writing in the same paper, "A Fellow Citizen" called the letter an "indecent libel against the government and character" of the United States. Even after three years had passed, the *Gazette of the United States* and the numerous likeminded papers that reprinted its articles would not allow readers to forget

"Mr. Jefferson's denunciation of the Federal constitution." While Federalists swiped at Jefferson's supposed reference to the monarchical "form" of the Constitution, they made it part of their more general practice of calling into question his patriotism. Jefferson, after all, had insulted even Washington, the Sampson who cavorted with a foreign "harlot." One writer, apparently fearful that readers would misread Jefferson's attack on Solomons and Sampsons, further misquoted the passage, claiming that it "falsely asserts, 'that Washington and the British faction ... had wished to impose on them the form of the British constitution.'"[8]

Impugning Jefferson's patriotism meshed nicely with another familiar charge: that his starry-eyed love for all things French blinded him to the interests of the United States. During the Adams administration especially, when outraged Americans read reports of Gallic warships raiding neutral American vessels delivering supplies to the British, with whom the French were at war, anything Federalists could do to deepen Jefferson's reputation as a Francophile could only diminish his popularity. So the vice president's opponents made the most of the episode, contending that the letter, well-known in Paris, invited France's "insults to our government, and the piracies committed on our commerce." As another penman noted, "its publication in a country, from whose government and citizens we have met with every kind of injury and insult, has a tendency to encourage a continuance of such conduct." To the editor of the *Minerva,* it seemed "hardly possible an American could be capable of writing such a letter." The New York *Herald* held that "when we see such abominable falsehoods as those contained in Mr. Jefferson's letter ... we are tempted to apologize for the resentment of a nation exposed to these deceptions. The evil is deep rooted among ourselves."[9]

The evil, Federalist papers repeatedly warned, was American jacobinism, a strain no less deadly than the French variety. The continuing influence of Jefferson, "the head of the democratic frenchified faction in this country," posed a serious threat to the nation's security. In a 1798 speech, Connecticut attorney Theodore Dwight told a Hartford crowd that when Jefferson wrote to Mazzei about a "sea of liberty," he envisioned "waves of blood," "ferocious monsters," and shores "white with the bones of millions." Jefferson and his faction would stop at nothing, a Boston paper exhorted, "to render our country subservient, if not tributary, to *France.*" The menace posed by "the grandest of all grand Villains" caused one citizen to dash off a note warning Adams to beware "that traitor to his country—the infernal Scoundrel Jefferson." Jefferson, meanwhile, despaired that "I have been for some time used as the property of the newspapers, a fair mark for every man's dirt."[10]

The Mazzei letter became even more of a liability after Adams, in April 1798, presented to Congress documents disclosing an attempt by French diplomats—identified only as X, Y, and Z—to extort from the United States a loan and bribe as preconditions for continuing negotiations. The proposed transaction wounded American pride, bolstered anti-French sentiments, and hobbled the Republicans, whose association with France Jefferson's letter had solidified. Moderate congressmen joined Federalist ranks in the House of Representatives, which later that year passed the Sedition Act. Citizens seemed to switch sides as well. As Abigail Adams reported, "the French Cockade so frequent in the streets" before the XYZ affair "is not now to be seen, and the Common People say if J[efferso]n had been our President... we should all have been sold to the French." Fenno's *Gazette* exulted that "Mazzei [i.e., Jefferson] may still remain Vice-President of the turbulent and factious," but now "he stands an awkward and misplaced Colossus," the leader of no one, for "the late French faction has died."[11]

The obituary was premature. Architect Benjamin Henry Latrobe, who traveled by stagecoach from Philadelphia to Richmond shortly after the president's disclosure of the XYZ incident, discovered that it actually heightened factionalism, infecting the countryside with "politicomania." He found "every place & every individual agitated" by politics. "What news? what news? what news? assailed me on every side," he reported. "XYZ... was my answer." The standard Republican response, he said, was "Shocking indeed! Who should have thought it of the virtuous French?" Federalists, on the other hand, sneered that "nothing else could be expected from the bloodsucking rascals." The Federalist position held sway near Philadelphia, but "in my progress Southward," he reported, "the opinions of those with whom I conversed grew gradually more unfettered by presidential veneration. On arriving in Virginia all our Passengers, except one Philadelphian, were exchanged for Democrats."[12]

WHILE THE VIRGINIANS whom Latrobe encountered refused to turn their backs on the Republican cause, Jefferson could not dismiss the fact that other people already had. How could he regain their support? The Sedition Act, which Adams signed into law in July, provided Jefferson with the opportunity he needed. The measure not only made it a crime for citizens to oppose or interfere with federal law or federal agents but also established punishments for anyone responsible for "any false, scandalous and malicious writing" against the president, the Congress, or the U.S. government that aimed to defame them or cultivate "the hatred of the good people of the United States." Obviously partisan, the act explicitly protected all government officials (except the vice president) by squelching dissent until March 3, 1801, the final day of Adams's term of office. Jefferson, who considered the sedition law the nadir of "the reign of witches," believed that, together with new alien laws empowering the president to deport foreign-born people whom he considered "dangerous," it constituted "an experiment on the American mind to see how far it will bear an avowed violation of the constitution." Confident that citizens, given proper encouragement, would share his view of the measures, Jefferson quietly drew up a set of resolutions opposing the laws and sent them to Wilson Cary Nicholas, who was to have them introduced—without Jefferson's name attached—in the North Carolina legislature. Nicholas altered the plan in consultation with John Breckinridge, a member of the Kentucky House of Representatives, who offered "Solemn assurances" to keep Jefferson's role in their creation a closely guarded secret and to sponsor them in his state's legislature. After cancelling a visit to Monticello (to avoid suspicion), Breckinridge returned home, and, in November, Kentucky adopted a slightly edited version of the resolutions as its own. A few weeks later Virginia's assembly passed another set of similar resolves, these secretly written by Madison. The effect was mixed. The measures rallied Republicans and, as Priestley reported, undermined the administration's position in Pennsylvania, where a "great majority of people" condemned its new laws, but they never seriously threatened to dethrone Federalism where its strength was greatest.[13]

Yet the Kentucky Resolutions put Federalists on the defensive. Meanwhile, Jefferson's efforts to conceal his part in their production hampered his opponents' search for an enemy to target. Even before passage of the sedition law, the Mazzei controversy had forced Jefferson to consider how best to defend himself. Could he reassure people who saw the letter as evidence that he lacked restraint? Could he disavow parts of it without disaffecting his most loyal supporters?

George Washington's recent behavior furnished one timely answer to such questions. Ever since 1777, when spurious letters attributed to him appeared first in London and then in America, he had been dogged by charges that he had warm feelings for Britain and never fully committed to American independence. Hostile presses had put into print falsified missives that, in the summer of 1776, he had purportedly sent to his wife, cousin, and stepson. The communiqués confessed his anticipation of "misfortune and disgrace" because "it is impossible we should succeed; and, I cannot with truth, say that I am sorry for it; because I am far from being sure that we deserve to succeed." They winced at his troops' "particularly hard" misfortune "to be deemed traitors to so good a King!" Forged, apparently, to embolden Britain's Parliament and reassure America's loyalists, two decades later the letters served as propaganda for opponents of the Jay Treaty, signed by Washington and scorned by many as soft on the British. When Republicans reprinted them in pamphlet form and later in Philadelphia's *Aurora,* the partisan journal of Benjamin Franklin Bache, Washington bristled with anger. The forgeries "attach principles to me which every action of my life have given lie to," he complained. "But *that* is no stumbling block with the Editors of these Papers and their supporters. And now, *perceiving* a disinclination on my part, perhaps *knowing,* that I had determined not to take notice of such attacks, they are pressing this matter upon the public mind with more avidity than usual; urging, that my silence, is a proof of their genuineness."[14]

To his peers, the former president's silence proved merely that he behaved in accordance with aristocratic ethics developed long before the advent of popular politics. While pre-Revolutionary Americans generally displayed a respectful deference to men of Washington's social and political rank, common people were becoming increasingly critical of their alleged "betters." Like Jefferson, who insisted that "the man who fears no truths has nothing to fear from lies," Washington refused to degrade his office or himself by openly responding to newspaper attacks, which would have implied that readers might take such charges seriously.[15] Most important, Washington knew that engaging people who sought political advantage would make him appear to seek it for himself.

On the final day of his presidency, however, Washington finally felt at liberty to set the record straight. He signed a rebuttal penned by Timothy Pickering, his secretary of state, and intended, ostensibly, for deposit in government archives "as a testimony of the truth to the present generation and to posterity." Pickering promptly forwarded the document, as well as his own cover letter asserting "the propriety of its being published," to the *Gazette of the United States.* There, for all Americans to read, appeared the hero of the Revolution's "solemn declaration, that the letters ... are a base forgery" alongside Pickering's request that the paper put it in print. The fact that

Washington's letter appeared after his retirement, along with the impression conveyed by Pickering's preface—that it came to light through the efforts of a second party—gave it a degree of credibility that an earlier, more direct refutation would have lacked. Returned to his farm, removed from politics, and with Pickering serving as a buffer between himself and the public prints, Washington could expect readers to view his statement less as an act of self-defense and more as a disinterested appeal to history.[16]

Like Washington, Jefferson understood the importance of carefully scripted political drama. Throughout his career he thought about the messages conveyed by public ceremonies, diplomatic etiquette, and the actions of officeholders. The turbulent factionalism of the 1790s, which convinced him that more than a few Federalists contemplated reshaping the republic along the lines of Britain's monarchy, caused him also to consider how the ruling party's affinity for pomp reflected its intentions. Only months before the passage of the sedition law, Jefferson took note of plans for lavish celebrations of Washington's birthday. Ironically, he found reason for optimism. Although he thought that the grand ball marking the occasion in the nation's capital was "very indelicate, & probably excites uneasy sensations in some," it caused him to hope that previous celebrations had meant to honor Washington the man, who had earned glory on the battlefield, but not the high office he had happened to hold. "To encourage the idea that the birthnights hitherto kept had been for the General & not the President," he reported to Madison, "and of course that time would bring an end to them," even some good Republicans had attended. Whether Jefferson masterminded this strategy remains uncertain, but he avoided alienating the orthodox of his constituency by refraining from doing so himself.[17]

Adams also declined to make an appearance at the birthday ball, but his justification underscored how differently from Jefferson he viewed his office. "How could the President appear at their ball and assembly but in a secondary character," asked Abigail Adams, echoing her husband's indignation; how could he "be held up in that light by all foreign nations?" He could never compromise his status by standing in the shadow of a mere citizen—"how ever Good, how ever great"—even if that citizen happened to be the father of his country. For Adams, rank commanded respect.[18]

No wonder John Adams's supporters objected to Jefferson's correspondence with Mazzei. While these Federalists exploited the letter for political purposes, they never would have thought to do so if it had not struck them as a crass violation of the deference that men should display toward Washington, his office, and the government over which he presided. Jefferson, however, disagreed. As he wrote in his draft of the Kentucky Resolutions opposing the Sedition Act, "confidence" in government "is every where the parent of despotism." The amount of criticism to which leaders should be subjected, he thought, rose in proportion to the power they commanded. The monarchies of Europe had already "divided their nations into two classes," he said: "wolves and sheep." If Americans became "inattentive to the public affairs," he once warned an office-holding friend, then "you and I, and Congress, and Assemblies, judges and governors shall become wolves." Even now, with public attention focusing on him, he considered harsh scrutiny "an injury to which duty requires every one to submit whom the public think proper to call into it's councils."[19] But the duty to endure criticism imposed no obligation to respond to it, as Washington's example of republican restraint suggested. Like the first president, Jefferson considered it best for his reputation to appear to suffer criticism in silence, responding selectively, at carefully chosen times, to specific audiences, and in ways calibrated to maximize benefits while minimizing costs.

IN APRIL 1796, a retired Jefferson relished his status as a private citizen and the opportunity for candor it afforded him. When he dashed off to Philip Mazzei his frank, impassioned note, he assumed the voice of his idealized American farmer, concerned with both God-given liberty and hard-earned happiness, mentioning not only his objections to the Federalist program but also his efforts to settle Mazzei's financial affairs in Virginia. Because the mood in Philadelphia had no bearing on Mazzei's business dealings, a disinterested officeholder or candidate for office would have understood that such an indiscriminate mixing of politics and money was bad form. Jefferson, however, cast himself as a reporter of, and not a participant in, public life. Years later, he rationalized that this "long letter of business" contained "a single paragraph only of political information" related so objectively that "there was not one word which would not have been ... approved by every republican in the United States."[20]

Fully aware of his presidential candidacy, Jefferson refused to yield the freedom that retirement afforded. He understood the likelihood of his return to office yet wrote to Mazzei with impolitic words destined to haunt his political future. George Washington had been much more careful. In 1797, both the Federalist *Minerva* and the Republican *Boston Gazette* agreed that "General

Washington did right in not denying" the spurious letters attributed to him
"until he retired from office." But why, asked the *Boston Gazette,* did he not
deny them in 1783, when he retired from the Continental Army? The answer,
the paper implied, was that Washington did not then intend a permanent
return to private life. He knew that people would view his disowning of the
letters as an attempt to clear his name in preparation for some future post, a
signal of continuing ambition that would undermine his image as a disinterested Cincinnatus and, along with it, his political prospects. Washington
had understood what Jefferson had refused to acknowledge: early retirement,
oftentimes temporary, required potential officeholders to avoid present-day
politics.[21]

Jefferson's ability to compartmentalize, his insistence on the perpetual viability of both his private and public selves, encouraged him to speak with the
freedom of a yeoman even though his pronouncements carried a statesman's
weight. With twenty-twenty hindsight, he later admitted his tendency to express "such sentiments too frankly both in private and public, often when
there is no necessity for it," but still he had let himself have it both ways. His
opponents, as they proved during the Mazzei controversy and in the years that
followed, would not.[22]

The Federalist papers not only republished Jefferson's private note to Mazzei. They also demanded that Jefferson issue a public statement on its authenticity. The *Minerva* portrayed its printing of the letter as "an opportunity" for
Jefferson "to disavow it." Other publications did not pretend such generosity.
John Fenno's "Fellow Citizen," for example, demanded "an explicit avowal or
disavowal of the . . . letter, which has been publicly ascribed to you in all our
newspapers, and which contains sentiments and principles too deeply affecting the interest, character and safety of America, to be passed by unnoticed."
Members of the public "have a right to know the real opinions" of holders of
high office, the author said. If Jefferson agreed with the letter attributed to
him, then it was his "duty . . . to come forward manfully" and explain himself.
Two weeks later, after Jefferson had said nothing, the writer informed him
and the rest of the nation that "your silence . . . is complete evidence of your
guilt."[23]

Even for Jefferson, who bragged about his insensitivity to anonymous critiques, words like these stung. When, as he told Madison, he first saw in print
the mistranslated Mazzei letter (and, undoubtedly, demands that he acknowledge it), he thought that he "must take the field of the public papers." Yet he
"could not disavow it wholly, because the greatest part was mine in substance

tho' not in form. I could not avow it as it stood because the form was not mine, and in one place the substance very materially falsified. This then would render explanations necessary; nay it would render proofs of the whole necessary, and draw me at length into a publication of all (even the secret) transactions" of Washington's administration during his tenure as secretary of state. In addition, it would "embroil me personally with every member of the Executive, with the Judiciary, and with others still." Worst of all, "it would be impossible for me to explain this publicly without bringing on a personal difference between Genl. Washington and myself" as well as "all those with whom his character is still popular"—a group amounting to "nine tenths of the people of the US." After deliberation tempered his anger, he said, "I soon decided in my own mind, to be entirely silent." Friends in the capital city agreed with his choice, "and some of them conjured me most earnestly" not to respond. But Federalists' continuing calls for an explanation still tempted. "Think for me," he begged Madison, "and advise me what to do, and confer with Colo. Monroe on the subject."[24]

Madison, who answered that he "viewed the subject pretty much in the light you do," warned that a reply "may bring on dilemmas, not to be particularly foreseen, of disagreeable explanations, or tacit confessions." Washington, after all, had remained "silent for many years as to the letters imputed to him, and it would seem" merely deposited his refutation of their authenticity in government files, which a zealous Pickering then "communicated to the public." When Adams found himself in a similar situation, he also held his tongue. It would be "a ticklish experiment to say publickly yes or no to the interrogatories of party spirit," Madison thought, "a gratification and triumph" for the Federalists who baited Jefferson, and a dangerous move likely to turn Washington's admirers against the Republican cause. Madison would confer with Monroe as requested, but already their friend had registered a different opinion: "that honest men would be encouraged by your owning and justifying the letter to Mazzei."[25]

Shortly before Jefferson had asked for his advice, Monroe had sent a note suggesting that the vice president acknowledge the letter to Mazzei, for "it was a private one and brought to public view without your knowledge or design." Jefferson, Monroe thought, should state "that the man to whom it was addressed had lived long as your neighbor & was now in Pisa" as well as the fact "that you do think that the principles of our Revolution and of Republican government have been substantially swerved from of late in many respects." Less cautious and more forthright than Madison, Monroe nevertheless urged

Jefferson to defend himself by emphasizing his status as a private citizen when he penned the letter. The public should know that you "have often express'd this sentiment," Monroe wrote, "which as a free man you had a right to express." Finally, he advised Jefferson to make clear that he had "declined saying any thing about it till you got home to examine how correct the letter was. This brings the question before the publick and raises the spirits of the honest part of the community."[26]

Although Monroe's opinion diverged from those of Jefferson and Madison, it accorded fully with a decision he had recently made for himself. In 1796, having lost the trust of the French government and the confidence of President Washington, Monroe was recalled from a diplomatic position in Paris. Embarrassed, indignant, and seething at the continuing criticisms of his performance coming from Adams, Monroe published *A View of the Conduct of the Executive, in the Foreign Affairs of the United States.* The tract, which bore his name on the title page, lashed out at Federalist diplomacy because it left "our national honor . . . in the dust." The administration had also impugned *his* honor, Monroe contended. Under different circumstances, he might not have mentioned his recall, "being in itself a circumstance too *trivial* to merit attention," but now he could not resist. To defend himself and denounce the claims of his foes, he appended to his sixty-seven-page essay more than four hundred pages of letters and memoranda. The book constituted a defense pamphlet; its mixing of personal assertion and documentary evidence made it part of a genre of political writing common at a time when individual honor intermingled with public discourse. Jefferson's explanation of the Mazzei letter, Monroe probably thought, should follow the same format.[27]

While Madison and Monroe both believed that their advice would lead Jefferson to minimize the potential for additional damage, Monroe saw more at stake than mere politics. The controversy involved Jefferson's personal, private conduct. In Monroe's eyes, it was an affair of honor. The inevitable calls for the vice president to own up to his letter and the subsequent inferences that his silence sprang from cowardice reflected a long-practiced Federalist tactic in disputes with Jefferson. By shifting attention from substantive issues to his motives and character, they put him on the defensive. He could choose, like Washington, to endure attacks in silence, fearful that citizens would view self-defense as self-promotion. If, however, he decided to "take the field" in print to explain his actions, it might, as Jefferson had told Madison, "embroil me personally" with a large number of high-profile figures in a high-stakes tit for tat—a duel of words. Although each option promised its own set of possible risks and rewards, Jefferson by far preferred the first. His enemies' barbs might sting, but he could rely on his performance as an officeholder to attest to the firmness of his character. His disregard of personal criticism would communicate that he discharged his duties with stoic selflessness. His unanswered detractors would soon run out of things to say, allowing the public to refocus on matters more advantageous to the Republican cause. All of this, however, assumed that his credibility outweighed that of his faceless attackers, who hardly ever signed their names to their polemics.[28]

His resolution to remain "entirely silent" in public left room, however, for the quiet encouragement of gossiping intermediaries. Even before he described his situation to Madison, or Monroe knew his story, Jefferson spoke to friends in Philadelphia. Only eleven days after Jefferson had first seen his letter in a newspaper, Connecticut congressman Chauncey Goodrich reported the hearsay that Jefferson admitted authorship of the note "but says it has been garbled in the translation."[29] The rumor could have only originated with Jefferson, the single individual in Philadelphia who could have known that the letter had been altered. Given his aversion to defending himself in print, where he could have better controlled his words and their reproduction, what explains his willingness to whisper explanations to one or more men whose imperfect memories might lead them to pass along unfaithful renderings of his account?

The greatest drawback of an oral defense was also its most obvious advantage. The inherent malleability of a rumor—the tendency of gossipers to forget details of stories at the same time that, intentionally or inadvertently, they embellished them—reduced Jefferson's liability for its content. While the mistranslated Mazzei letter, committed to print and apparently authorized by his signature, proved difficult to disown, he could plausibly deny rumors spread by word of mouth. Federalists, however, demanded a full, public, and personally humiliating explanation. They viewed his reticence as anything but honorable. To them, it revealed his role as an intriguer, a sly and cunning manipulator of the public mind. Their understanding of Jefferson was not altogether wrong, for not long after he seemed to have defended himself through rumor (as well as by providing his story to Madison and Monroe), he told a Virginia congressman that so many enemies had been "endeavoring to draw me into newspapers to harrass me personally, that I have found it necessary . . . to leave them in full possession of the field, and not to take the trouble of contradicting them even in private conversation." In other words, he portrayed himself as a victim of political combat but not as a participant. Federalists, on the other hand, portrayed him as a master strategist. Through ridicule and prosecution, they worked to neutralize James Duane, Benjamin Franklin Bache, James Callender, and other newspapermen who served as "Jeffersonian puppets," but they made clear that their real target was Jefferson himself. "The correspondent of *Mazzei* is in the centre of the circle," the *Columbian Centinel* warned in 1799. "His myrmidons, faithful to their duty, act as he directs and bellow as he prescribes." A few months later, the *Philadelphia Gazette* alleged that Jefferson had assumed "the entire management of the Jacobin puppets."[30]

THE MAZZEI LETTER was not the first of Jefferson's published writings to spark controversy, and it would not be the last. His endorsement of Thomas Paine's *Rights of Man,* excerpted from a private letter and printed on the title page of its first American edition, angered Federalists in 1792. Now, at the same time that newspapers made the most of his similarly private note to Mazzei, Luther Martin, Maryland's Federalist attorney general, took aim at Jefferson's description, in his *Notes on the State of Virginia,* of an oration reputed to have been delivered in 1774 by Mingo Indian chief John Logan. Jefferson's *Notes,* which attempted to disprove European claims that the New World's environment retarded the development of its flora, fauna, and people, highlighted Logan's poignant speech as an example of the "genius and mental powers" of Native Americans and, in particular, their "eminence in oratory." By way of introduction, Jefferson repeated the widely circulated account that Logan delivered the address shortly after Virginia militiamen led by Michael Cresap, "a man infamous for the many murders he had committed" against frontier Indians, had massacred Logan's family. In early 1797, when Philadelphia newspapers advertised dramatic performances of "The Story of Logan the Mingo Chief," Martin seized the opportunity to challenge Jefferson's account of the episode, dirtying the vice president's name and attempting to draw him into a public affair of honor.[31]

Cresap was Martin's father-in-law and, as Martin wrote in an open letter published in *Porcupine's Gazette,* another "worthy relation" bequeathed to Martin "as a sacred trust" the duty to "rescue his family from unmerited opprobrium." The charge against Cresap was "not founded in truth," Martin said, and he claimed that "no such specimen of Indian oratory was ever exhibited." By establishing his relationship with the man whom Jefferson had "calumniated" and then deriding the account of the speech's origin as "fiction," cobbled together from whatever testimony "came to his hands," Martin made clear his complaint against Jefferson and his right to prosecute it. In accordance with the custom followed by men who believed that their own or their family's honor had been questioned, Martin then baited Jefferson to respond by hurling insults. The *Notes on the State of Virginia,* Martin claimed, had been corrupted by its author's quest to prove his preconceived hypothesis about Native Americans' relative vigor; for Jefferson, the "trifles" that passed as evidence included measurements of penis size and body hair. While Cresap "was a man of undaunted resolution," Martin contended, "Mr. Jefferson is a philosopher" who, as Virginia's governor, flew "from the seat of government . . . when the British army invaded." In case anyone failed to regard his remarks as a public challenge using the ritualized language of honor to taunt and humiliate Jefferson, Martin affirmed his readiness "to enter the lists with the author of the Notes on Virginia."[32]

The "lists," like the "field," functioned as a metaphor for the physical or psychic space in which honorable warfare took place, be it a dueling ground or a printed page. Both words evoked an earlier, ostensibly more chivalrous era when knights faced off in battle.[33] Jefferson, who well understood the vocabulary of honor, in 1793 had urged Madison to "enter the lists" with Alexander Hamilton, whose pseudonymous newspaper writings had questioned Jefferson's fitness to serve as Washington's secretary of state. Ten years later, Jefferson employed the term again. When William Coleman's *New-York Evening Post* blasted his administration for purging Federalists from appointive office, an indignant Jefferson hazarded "a few lines for the press, altho' I have thro' life scrupulously refrained from it." He drafted an article, signed "Fair Play" and written "under the character of a Massachusetts citizen," and passed it on to a friend who would arrange for its publication but maintain "religious silence" about his identity as author. The essay rebuked Coleman's assertions and challenged him to "take the field for the state of New York, not doubting" that "some champion there," a person "able & ready to confront him with facts," would "enter the lists for the opposite interest." Jefferson would not, however, entertain the idea of openly defending himself. He had no desire "to enter the field in the newspapers with Mr. Martin." He said that, despite Martin's pretensions, politics and not family honor "divined the cause of his taking up the subject," for the Maryland lawyer had "never noticed" his account of the speech until "it became an object with a party to injure me in the eyes of my countrymen." A mere "cat's paw" of Federalist agitators who "served them with zeal," Martin's real gripe was political and not personal. He did not deserve the dignity of a response.[34]

Yet Martin, in what Jefferson described as "very abusive letters addressed to me in the publick papers," kept asking for one. In December 1797, six months after his initial attack, Martin informed Jefferson that his "obstinate, stubborn Silence" amounted to a confession of guilt. "Was I much more your Enemy than I am, I could not have wished you to have acted differently," he wrote, for Jefferson had played "precisely the part the least honorable to your head or to your heart." These were fighting words (a fact underscored by their publication in *Porcupine's Gazette*), but Jefferson refused to recognize them. "After the perusal of the first letter had shewn me what was to be the style of those subsequent," he claimed, "I have avoided reading a single one." Nonetheless, he gave Martin's challenge—and the impact it might have on his reputation—a good deal of thought, and ultimately decided that he would answer the attack, even if Martin's "object was not merely truth, but to gratify party passions." Some may have doubted that he had written the Mazzei letter, but he could not avoid defending the integrity of the *Notes,* of which his authorship was known to all. His credibility was at stake. But how could he protect his name without accepting Martin's dangerous invitation to offer a public explanation?[35]

The vice president settled on two responses, each focused on a different audience. First, as he reported a year after Martin made public his complaint, Jefferson took a letter that he had sent to Maryland governor John Henry, who "wished for a general explanation of the foundation of the case of Logan," and had "a few copies printed, to give to particular friends for their satisfaction." On these men, Jefferson said, he "could rely against the danger of it's being published." At the same time, he appealed to individuals with information about the Logan-Cresap affair to "communicate to me as fully as you can what you can recall." Although he did not "mean to notice mr Martin, or go into the newspapers on the subject," he wanted to learn more about the story and said that "if I find any thing wrong in it it shall be corrected, & what is right supported either in some new edition" of his *Notes* "or in an Appendix to it." This he did in 1800, when the book reappeared with several pages of letters testifying to the essential accuracy of his original account.[36]

His first tactic allowed him to affirm his honor among a strategically selected group of men. Maybe he believed that their confidence in him needed bolstering, or maybe he trusted them to tell others that they had seen proof of his innocence. Jefferson's note to Henry affirmed that if Martin had communicated his grievance directly and not through a newspaper, it would have been regarded as sincere and granted a reply. Jefferson insisted that he had "no reason to doubt" his original account, however, for it merely restated what everybody knew. In other words, politics motivated Martin more than honor, and his account contradicted conventional wisdom, placing the burden of proof on him, not Jefferson. The "particular friends" with whom Jefferson shared this statement did not in all likelihood include Madison, Monroe, or other constant allies; frequent conversations kept these men abreast of the scandal, and, more importantly, their intimate knowledge of the vice president's character precluded the need for such a formal means of "satisfaction." But Jefferson's "reserve on political issues" frustrated other "steadfast friends," as one such friend, *Aurora* publisher William Duane, later wrote.[37] To receive his explanation, Jefferson probably chose members of this secondary group of supporters, men whose positions as congressmen, polemicists, or, most strategically, Maryland partisans made their views especially important. It would reassure them of his honest intentions and, by demonstrating his willingness to defend himself, spur them to defend him as well. The printed explanation, moreover, conveyed a consistent story for these men to tell others. As in the Mazzei crisis, Jefferson relied for vindication on the whispering circles of the political elite.

His decision to substantiate the Logan-Cresap story in the next edition of his *Notes* revealed his attentiveness to a much larger audience, however. It also underscored that, although he refused to comment publicly about his mistranslated letter to Mazzei, he saw the propriety of printed rebuttals of Martin's aspersions. While the Mazzei controversy hinged on matters of opinion, he viewed Chief Logan's speech as a fact of history. His study of Virginia also differed from the Mazzei letter in that he had willingly, if at first begrudgingly, authorized the book's publication. He never chose to share with fellow citizens the thoughts communicated to Mazzei, but by volunteering his account of Logan he accepted responsibility for it. Despite some regret that he had published his *Notes,* which furnished his adversaries with "matter of abuse for want of something better" (he wished that an "enemy would write a book!"), he considered it his "duty" to answer Martin "by searching into the truth & publishing it to the world, whatever it should be."[38]

Like Benjamin Franklin, Timothy Dwight, and other men of the Enlightenment, Jefferson recognized the inability of duels—whether fought with words or bullets—to decide factual disputes. Inherently personal, they cast reason aside in favor of contests of courage and might. They also centered on character attacks and defenses. Martin could have challenged Jefferson's book's authority, but instead he lashed out at the character of the *Notes'* author. Jefferson, however, refused to take the bait. As an introduction to the 1800 appendix and its extensive documentation of the Logan story, he reprinted the 1797 letter to Governor Henry that explained his silence. "Had Mr. Martin thought proper" to communicate his concerns directly instead of stepping "at once into the newspapers," then he would have directly responded, Jefferson wrote. But while Martin's attacks "adopted a style which forbade the respect of an answer," Jefferson understood that "no act of his could absolve me from the justice due to others." His efforts to investigate more fully the circumstances of Logan's speech, he wanted it understood, had nothing to do with Martin's aspersions. In their duel of words, Jefferson sought to make clear, benevolence had caused him to hold his fire. He claimed to care only about historical justice, and in his appendix, a pseudo-defense pamphlet, he focused on facts.[39]

His facts, however, were hardly self-evident. In 1776, as the obscure and unknown draftsman of the Declaration of Independence, his assertion of "inherent" individual rights, such as life, liberty, and the pursuit of happiness, was a "truth" so fundamental to eighteenth-century views of human nature that he could appeal to the authority of "common sense." In 1800, well-known as the author of the *Notes on the State of Virginia,* his appendix on Logan vested authority in individuals who claimed intimate knowledge of the subject. Why did Jefferson reprint their signed testimonials, which merely confirmed the essential accuracy of his account, instead of saving space by revising his pages on the Logan affair to include some of the details that they added, or by leaving his story as it stood? As distasteful as it was for Jefferson to admit, he agreed with Martin's fundamental premise. By resting his case on the testimony of others, Jefferson admitted that his word as a scholar—and his honor as a gentleman—did not sufficiently substantiate his claims. Authority came from men as well as principle, Jefferson acknowledged; it emanated from authors as much as from the truths they held to be self-evident. But now, despite his pretensions of scholarship, Jefferson evasively and heavy-handedly separated truth from falsehood. He excluded from his appendix George Rogers Clark's response to his request for information on the Logan affair. It contradicted the other accounts by maintaining that Cresap took no part in the murder of Logan's family. It can be contended—and it has been—that Jefferson's suppression of Clark's testimony reflected a desire to spare the famous frontiersman the embarrassment of being mistaken. But self-interest may also have motivated the vice president, who stood to gain little through the admission of a reminiscence that undermined his argument. Even the testimonials that did appear in his appendix were edited to strike out contradictory details. The balance of the evidence justified Jefferson's portrayal of Logan's speech and its context, but Martin had a point when he said that "Mr. Jefferson is a philosopher" and "philosophers are pretty much the same" in their willingness to sacrifice mightily for a favorite hypothesis.[40]

Philosophy, however, was not Jefferson's primary concern at this time, and he refused to engage Martin as either a "gentlemen" or an honest scholar. Jefferson acted like neither for he responded like a politician. In 1800, when he re-released his *Notes,* he concentrated on the coming presidential election. He would not risk his personal honor by confronting Martin's attacks, and he would not risk his credibility by acknowledging his account's uncertainty as fact. Yet by presenting as self-evident firsthand accounts that he had sculpted to fit his narrative, he rested his arguments about Logan and Cresap on the partially redacted testimony of others.

Jefferson understood that his decision to substantiate his account of Logan's oration might blunt criticism, but it would not win over critics. After Monroe's publication of his *View of the Conduct of the Executive,* Jefferson assured his friend that his "narrative and letters wherever they are read produce irresistable conviction, and cannot be attacked but by a contradiction of facts." But even if the lengthy pamphlet made Monroe's diplomatic conduct "unassailable," as Jefferson believed, he warned Monroe that enemies had begun preparing for publication "a batch of small stuff, such as refusing to drink Genl. Washington's health," designed to whittle down Monroe's popularity. In other words, openly defending oneself, although not always ill-advised, often yielded limited results and sometimes gave adversaries "opportunities of slander, personal hatred, and injustice." Any man whose name was "the watchword of party" had better take care that it did not appear beneath any statement with the potential to spur further controversy. "It is really a most afflicting consideration," Jefferson consoled Monroe, "that it is impossible for a man to act in any office for the public without encountering a persecution which even his retirement will not withdraw him from."[41]

These timely words reached Monroe, who was contemplating a bid for office, while newspaper writers were criticizing his conduct overseas. "In order to replace yourself on the high ground you are entitled," Jefferson insisted, "it is absolutely necessary you should re-appear on the public theatre, & take an independent stand from which you can be seen & known to your fellow-citizens." Monroe should swallow his pride and stand for office, Jefferson suggested, because "no interval should be admitted between this last attack of enmity and your re-appearance with the approving voice of your constituents." For Jefferson, this was the best mode of self-defense. "Were I to undertake to answer the calumnies of newspapers," he informed newspaperman Samuel Smith a few months later, "it would be more than all my own time, & that of 20. aids could effect. For while I should be answering one, twenty new ones would be invented. I have thought it better to trust to the justice of my countrymen, that they would judge me by what they *see* of my conduct on the stage where they have placed me." He had numbed himself to the slanders of his critics but retained "all my sensibilities for the approbation of the good & just. That is indeed the chief consolation for the hatred of so many who, without the least personal knowledge, & on the sacred evidence of Porcupine and Fenno alone, cover me with their implacable hatred. The only return I will ever make them will be to do them all the good I can."[42]

THE CONTROVERSIES of Jefferson's vice presidency forced him to confront challenging questions about how best to defend his reputation and shape his image. As America's most visible Republican—as the man certain to be called forth to counter Federalism in the election of 1800—the stakes could not be higher. What to do—and what *not* to do—when his own words and the words of others prompted public scrutiny and scorn? While other men defended their honor by meeting challengers on "the field of the public papers," or even on the dueling field, Jefferson preferred to turn the other cheek. Why allow enemies to choose his battles? Why roll the dice in contests of private character when what mattered most was his performance as a defender of the public's liberty?

There were instances, such his confrontation with Luther Martin, in which his honor could be buttressed by presumptions of fact. But misrepresentations of his principles not only counted more but also could be even more complicated. In order to maintain his political viability, Jefferson whispered justifications, enlisted seconds to "take the field" in newspapers, and posed as a willing martyr to answer with stoic silence critics who questioned his inner virtue at the same time that he reassured friends who scrutinized his resolve to defend their rights and interests. He never lost faith that charges of hostility to the Constitution, unpatriotic attachment to France, and jacobinical radicalism would wither when contradicted by his lawfulness, patriotic neutrality, and humble republicanism. This enlightened strategy relied on the common sense of a reasonable audience as large as the republic itself. Like the "truths" that buttressed the Declaration of Independence, Jefferson thought himself to be self-evident. Years later, he told John Adams that "my mind has been long fixed to bow to the judgment of the world, who will judge me by my acts, and will never take counsel from me as to what that judgment shall be."[43]

CHAPTER FOUR

The Revolution of 1800

JEFFERSON—DEAD! The Republican *Baltimore American* broke the
news on June 30, 1800. Within days the story had spread as far as Boston,
and numerous Federalists could hardly contain their joy. "Exultation!
Exultation! All was glorious exultation!" among "the old Tories, Refugees
and haters of our independence," who greeted the intelligence with "snick-
ering and ogling," "nods of the head," and "winks of congratulation." The
Connecticut Courant noted the recent paucity of important developments and
wondered if "some *compassionate* being, in order to prevent starvation" among
the news-hungry, "has very humanely killed Mr. Jefferson." Thomas Boylston
Adams, the president's son, found that people regarded the report as "too good
to be true."[1]

Federalist enthusiasm for the false rumor of the vice president's demise
underscored the extent to which that faction's posturing prior to the election
of 1800 focused on Thomas Jefferson, the candidate most likely to unseat
John Adams. After fresh reports contradicted the erroneous ones and confirmed Jefferson's good health, the *Gazette of the United States* joked that
"the author of the report of Mr. Jefferson's death is chargeable with a gross
libel; that renowned Statesman being the man of the people, to accuse him
of being dead was no less than to accuse the people of being unmanned."
Sarcasm did not mask the statement's underlying assumption, the idea that
provided a foundation for the Federalists' 1800 campaign: Jefferson was the
head, heart, and face of Republicanism; he gave it its character; he was its
personal embodiment, and he embodied all of its faults. "The question is not
what he will *do*" as president, one of his opponents claimed, "but what he *is*."[2]

Republicans, as their own propaganda made clear, saw matters somewhat differently. Jefferson, they agreed, stood for their cause and the things
that made it right. But instead of doing the thinking of "the people," as his

opponents alleged, he did their bidding. Accordingly, in 1800 they battled not only to defend and advance Jefferson's reputation but also to defend and advance the principles that he—and they—held dear. Jefferson, meanwhile, kept a conspicuously low profile during the campaign. So, of course, did Adams, as well as virtually every other candidate for office during this era. But Jefferson engaged in a feverish behind-the-scenes effort to support Republican presses and, in contrast to his silence during the 1796 election, maintained an active correspondence with political friends. Emphasizing that his letters should not appear in print, he laid out the issues that his partisans, with remarkable fidelity, made the focus of their campaign. He maintained that principles should be the topic of debate and discouraged any personal attacks on Adams.[3]

This contest, like the election of 1796, exposed differing views of reality. Federalists mounted attacks on Jefferson's religion, character, intellectual habits, and other personal matters—sometimes to simultaneously score points on related public issues. Republicans defended Jefferson at the same time that they campaigned to associate him with issues of public importance. Not surprisingly, their reaction to the false reports of his death, which surfaced as the campaign for the states' electoral votes escalated, mixed sadness with outrage that their competitors "intended to damp the festivity of the 4th of July and prevent the author of the Declaration of Independence from being the universal toast" of the day. As noted physician Caspar Wistar recorded, no man would "be so greatly & sincerely missed by those who are of the same political sentiments." While Federalists focused on criticizing Jefferson's character, Republicans cheered him for his principles.[4]

THE FEDERALIST inclination to attack Jefferson's private life made sense for several reasons. First, doing so drew attention away from Adams, who, British minister Robert Liston was reported to have said, stood out as "the most passionate, intemperate man he ever had anything to do with." A treasury department official described him as "a man of jealous temper" who "has lately acted so strange . . . that many do not hesitate to assert that he is deranged in his intellect." Other Federalists also questioned his mental health.[5] A good many more complained about his efforts to improve relations with France, which minimized an issue that had boosted his popularity. As a result, according to Joseph Priestley, Adams "lost many friends" who viewed France as an enemy "with which they wish to be at war." John Marshall gossiped that the decision caused people in the Northeast to feel "very much dissatisfied with the President" and left some "strongly disposed to desert him & to push for some other candidate." The chief alternative was South Carolina's Charles Cotesworth Pinckney, who, although officially the Federalist vice-presidential contender, would win the top office if a few electors dropped support for Adams. Alexander Hamilton exposed the rift in Federalist circles by calling Adams to task in a published pamphlet, and some in 1800 so much doubted the president's scruples that they wondered aloud if he and Jefferson had "made a coalition." A sizeable part of Adams's own faction doubted his fitness to lead and had scant enthusiasm for promoting his candidacy.[6]

Federalists found themselves with neither an attractive leader nor a compelling agenda. For more than a decade they had controlled the capital; they had united around George Washington and centralized government as well as opposition to Jefferson and the changes for which they believed he stood. But for what did they stand? A New Jersey Federalist tried to lure voters with lukewarm assurances of "firm government" and "temperate liberty," promises that countless Americans viewed as threats. As New Yorker Robert Troup told diplomat Rufus King, "we have no rallying point."[7]

In addition to diverting attention from Adams and their own malaise, Federalists believed that targeting Jefferson verified their own self-image as virtuous and enlightened men, unselfish, disinterested, and independent—and differentiated them from the mobs of common folk who, they thought, answered Jefferson's siren song. The elitism of certain Federalists, a fundamental cause of their own undoing, permeated their political thought. Yale president Timothy Dwight, for example, while traveling through New England sneered at the "class of men" who lived along Vermont's frontier—the same sort who supported Jefferson. He considered them unfit for "regular society. They are too idle, too talkative, too passionate, too prodigal, & too shiftless to acquire property of character." Impatient with "restraints of Law, Religion, Morality & Public opinion," these frontiersmen grumbled "about the taxes by which rulers, ministers & school masters are supported." Even though they managed "their own concerns worse than any other men," Dwight found it shocking that they "feel perfectly satisfied that they could manage those of the nation." Other Federalists shared his disdain. Newspaperman John Fenno proposed dissolving the states; establishing ten to twenty districts commanded by presidential appointees; cutting off the franchise "from all paupers, vagabonds and outlaws"; and placing all legislation "in those hands to which it belongs, the proprietors of the country." Only "the best men"—"men of property, and of landed property, who must stand or fall with their country"—should rise to elective posts, a Rhode Islander claimed. "The intelligent and virtuous," asserted another anonymous Federalist, "have, at all times, been on the side of government." But Jefferson, like the people who supported him, apparently had neither quality, for he wanted to "crush the systems of *Washington* and *Adams,*" overturning the established order.[8]

Jefferson's enemies alleged that he not only opposed government. Ever since he presented his bill to disestablish the Anglican church in Virginia, and most especially when Republicans advanced him as Adams's challenger in the 1796 election, Federalists had characterized him as hostile to Christianity. Afterward, dire warnings continued to resonate from Congregational pulpits. In 1798, Dwight prophesied that a Republican ascendency might "change our holy worship into a dance of Jacobin phrenzy. . . . We may behold a strumpet [im]personating a Goddess on the altars of JEHOVAH." The Bible would be "cast into a bonfire, the vessels of the sacramental supper borne by an ass in public procession, and our children, either wheedled or terrified, uniting in . . . chanting mockeries against God." To the list of travesties he added "that we may see our wives and daughters the victims of legal prostitution."[9]

In 1800, attacks on the vice president's faith intensified. Henry William DeSaussure, a South Carolina pamphleteer, claimed that Jefferson "abhors the Christian system." Reverend John Mason called him "a confirmed infidel" known for "vilifying the divine word, and preaching insurrection against God." Thomas Robbins, a young Connecticut parson, called him a "howling atheist." The *Gazette of the United States* maintained that a voter need ask himself one easy question: "Shall I continue in allegiance to God—and a Religious President; Or impiously declare for Jefferson—and No God!!!"[10]

How did Federalists substantiate this view? The anonymous pamphlet of William Linn, pastor of Manhattan's Dutch Reformed church, constituted one of the most thorough attempts to prove Jefferson's "disbelief in the Holy Scriptures." It culled its evidence, Linn noted, "principally from Mr. Jefferson's own writings." As Mason boasted in his own tract, "the charge, unsupported by other proof, could hardly be pursued to conviction. Happily for truth and for us, Mr. Jefferson has *written;* he has *printed.*" While Jefferson's religious freedom bill first alerted the pious to his intentions, his enemies said, his *Notes on the State of Virginia* removed all doubts about Jefferson and his "fraternity of infidels."[11]

His heresies included doubting that fossilized shells found near mountaintops proved a universal deluge; he calculated that even if all the atmosphere turned to water and fell for forty days and nights, sea levels would rise less than fifty-three feet. His speculations about the world's languages and the time necessary for them to have become distinct—more "than many people give to the age of the earth"—demonstrated that he rejected the Bible's chronology of the history of mankind. By wondering if Africans constituted a distinct race, he degraded them, according to Linn, "from the rank which God hath given them" as descendants of Adam and Eve. Worse yet, he proposed that, instead of "putting the Bible and Testament into the hands of the children" of Virginia's schools "at an age when their judgments are not sufficiently matured for religious enquiries," they should read Greek, Roman, European, and American history. His remark that "it does me no injury for my neighbour to say there are twenty gods, or no god," revealed not tolerance but disregard for citizens' souls. "Ten thousand impieties and mischiefs" lurked within this sentiment, Mason warned. If all these blasphemies did not convince voters of his apostasy, they should consider his statement that farmers "are the chosen people of God, if ever he had a chosen people." This dumbfounded his critics: *if ever?*[12]

Jefferson proved his irreligion through deeds as well as words. He worked on Sundays, critics charged, and did not attend church. He neglected to show "so much as a decent external respect for the faith." The public also learned of a story, related by Linn and confirmed by Mason, that Jefferson's loose-lipped confidant Philip Mazzei supposedly told a respected Virginia divine. "Your great philosopher and statesman, Mr. Jefferson, is rather farther gone in infidelity than I am," Mazzei was said to have bragged to the clergyman. Once, as he and Jefferson rode through the countryside, he pointed to a decrepit church, shocked that parishioners would allow it to fall into such a condition. "It is good enough," Jefferson said, "for him that was borne in a manger!" That the vice president had made this "contemptuous fling at the blessed Jesus" Linn did not doubt, nor did he consider that Jefferson might have meant to praise Jesus's humility.[13]

The story of a Connecticut woman, while probably apocryphal, hardly exaggerates the sincerity with which some Federalists feared the implications of a Jefferson victory. Thinking that he might send troops to seize citizens' Bibles, she took hers to the only Republican in town. "My good woman," he said, "if all the Bibles are to be destroyed, what is the use of bringing yours to me?" Keep it, she insisted: "They'll never think of looking in the house of a Democrat for a Bible."[14]

Jefferson's supposed hostility to the first president constituted a secondary line of attack. Federalists noted that "since the adoption of the Federal

Constitution" Jefferson had opposed the agendas of Washington and Adams; the "insidious eloquence" of his 1796 letter to Mazzei, which surfaced a year later and now lingered as a campaign issue, proved his detachment from reality when it "designate[d] General Washington as a wicked party." The alleged libel touched especially raw nerves during the early part of 1800. As Theodore Dwight noted, the "afflicting event of Genl. Washington's death" in the waning days of 1799 now "entirely absorbed all other subjects of public consideration." Thus the editor of a Virginia newspaper scored points when he contended that "people cannot forget the author of that high wrought calumny on him who was their Samson in the field and their Solomon in council. Let every American citizen read it, and consider with himself, whether Thomas Jefferson is worthy succeeding to the office of PRESIDENT of a free, affectionate, and virtuous people."[15]

Using the letter also allowed Jefferson's foes to renew the old charge that he opposed the Constitution. The garbled version that Americans read in newspapers complained that the United States mimicked the "form" of British government. And if the Mazzei missive did not suffice as proof of the vice president's hostility to America's system of government, then there was also the "confidence reposed in Mr. Jefferson, and the anxiety for his election" displayed, as DeSaussure wrote, by "the most avowed enemies of the constitution." Voters must not ignore this "sure pledge that he is known . . . to retain his enmity to it."[16]

Besides his supposed hatred of God, Washington, and the Constitution, Jefferson's liabilities included his alleged timidity and his theoretical nature. DeSaussure found Jefferson "distinguished for shewy talents, for theoretic learning, and for the elegance of his *written style*," but said that he lacked essential qualities of leadership. During his governorship, Virginia "sustained immense losses," and he did little to help by fleeing on horseback from British troops as they advanced on his mountaintop home. Oliver Wolcott predicted that, once elected, "Mr. Jefferson's conduct would be frequently whimsical and undignified; that he would affect the character of a philosopher." Gouverneur Morris concurred, saying that the vice president, "a theoretic man," would return the national government to a loose confederacy of states. Fisher Ames believed that Jefferson, "like most men of genius," got "carried away by . . . the everlasting zeal to generalize, instead of proceeding, like common men of practical sense, on the low, but sure foundation of matter of fact."[17]

On the issue of race, Federalists struck opportunistic poses. In South Carolina, Jefferson earned criticism for carrying on a correspondence with black mathematician Benjamin Banneker. DeSaussure wrote that Jefferson's polite responses to Banneker's letters proved his hostility to slavery. A Virginia paper castigated Jefferson for seeking to broaden the franchise in that state; free blacks, it implied, would soon line up at ballot boxes. Northerners attacked the vice president from the opposite direction. The *Connecticut Courant* wondered how some Yankees could submit "to learn the principles of liberty" from Jefferson and other "slave-holders of Virginia." Newark's *Gazette* took a tongue-in-cheek approach. The "only *labourers in the earth of Virginia* are the Black People," it maintained. Yet the "labourers in the earth," according to Jefferson's *Notes,* were "the chosen people of God." There must be a contradiction, the paper contended, and it hoped that, in the future, "friends of Mr. Jefferson will be more explicit." Federalists themselves were not yet explicit about another charge, and although they did not put it into print in 1800, they appear to have whispered about "Mr. Jefferson's Congo Harem."[18]

If Jefferson was an atheist hostile to true patriots and orderly government, if he was a theorist and visionary lacking common sense and backbone, if he conflated emancipation with oppression and lived as a sexual libertine, then his character approximated that of a Jacobin. Federalists had earlier labored to link him with the excesses of revolutionary France, and in doing so had formulated their enduring view of the Republican leader. During the Quasi-War charges of Jacobinism had been especially damning, but now—thanks largely to the willingness of Adams to push for peace—they had lost some of their force. A 1799 assessment that New Englanders generally held "*friends of France* . . . in the greatest abhorrence" still retained its accuracy, but elsewhere Americans began to manifest a "general, conclusive and . . . fixed dislike of the English nation," which stood as France's archenemy. Thus Federalist contentions of Jefferson's Francophilia were more oblique in the election of 1800 than they had been in 1796, but they still existed. "Burleigh," a contributor to the *Connecticut Courant,* urged readers to view "every leading Jacobin as a ravening wolf, prepared to enter your peaceful fold, and glut his deadly appetite on the vitals of your country." "It was in France," as DeSaussure maintained, "that his disposition to theory, and his scepticism in religion, morals, and government, acquired full strength and vigor." Because he stood as "the favorite of a nation, which has heaped injuries on the head of his country, he is the last man to whom his fellow-citizens should entrust the government." He was a Jacobin and thus "destitute of morality and religion." More French than American, he would make a good Bonaparte, perhaps, but a terrible president of the United States.[19]

The Providential Detection, ca. 1797–1800.
(American Antiquarian Society)

An anonymous artist captured the totality of the Federalist image of Jefferson in a cartoon titled *The Providential Detection*. It depicts Jefferson prostrate before an "Altar of Gallic Despotism" on which the writings of Thomas Paine, Voltaire, and James "Munro" smolder alongside copies of Republican newspapers, attempting to destroy America's "Constitution & Independence." A serpent looks on, and so does Satan himself. But before Jefferson can sacrifice the country's government and autonomy as burnt offerings, an eagle, guided by the eye of God, snatches them from his reach. The Philip Mazzei letter, which reveals the conspiracy to destroy the United States, slips from the right hand of Jefferson, whose face betrays a look of utter horror.[20]

In sum, Federalists believed that the vice president possessed an un-American character and un-American opinions, making him entirely unsuitable for the nation's highest office. As DeSaussure predicted, the election of Jefferson would place the nation "nearly in a revolutionary state." If "unprincipled and abandoned Democrats" came to power, Noah Webster observed, "Deists, Atheists, Adulterers and profligate men" would take charge of the country. As Fenno wrote, a Jeffersonian victory promised to usher in "warfare of confusion against order." Another writer prophesied that a Republican victory might bring a "Civil War" during which "murder, robbery, rape, adultery, and incest will all be openly taught and practiced." In nearly all Federalist polemics, whether in newspapers or pamphlets, the message was clear: Jefferson must be stopped.[21]

BUT THE FEDERALISTS had cried wolf. As a North Carolina congressman later commented, the "sound of alarm" passed "with little more effect, than sound itself." A Rhode Islander, comparing the merits of Jefferson and Adams, took care to "preserve a distinction between the moral qualities which make a man amiable in private life, and those strong virtues which alone fit him for elevated public station. A very good man may indeed make a very bad President." Adams possessed an exemplary "private character," but his personal goodness would never compensate for his "political crimes" and "official deformities." The devil himself could serve the public with distinction, "provided that he disturbs not the public tranquility, nor abuses the high influence of his office." The very fact that the presidential election had aroused so much passion, another Republican said, exposed the extent to which Adams had placed power and glory in the hands of the executive and not the more representative Congress, where it belonged. The *National Intelligencer* of Washington, D.C., implied that Federalists' emphasis on character reflected their "servile spirit of adulation" for supposedly Great Men. "The enlightened friends of republicanism," it contended, should take care "to cling *exclusively to principle,* and to commend, not men but measures."[22]

Perhaps Federalist attacks provoked such assertions. Webster, for instance, had said that "no men fawn, cringe, and flatter, so much as democrats," who "extol Jefferson to the skies." But the power of denial can strongly shape one's view of oneself. That the vice president's opponents sensed that adoration of him eclipsed support for his ideas does not diminish the conviction with which Republicans regarded their stated agenda. Quite possibly, the Jeffersonians' desire to prove critics wrong caused them to convince themselves of what they told others: some people were "too apt to confound principles with men."[23]

Even so—and maybe not coincidentally—Jefferson had defenders who answered the attacks on his character. More than a few Republicans refused to sit silent while Federalists slung mud at the individual whom, as Priestley reported, they considered "the first man in this country." A writer calling himself "Marcus Brutus" described Jefferson's religious beliefs as "wholly unexceptional." He believed in a "superintending providence" and "is at least as good a christian as Mr. Adams, and in all probability a much better one." Another penman affirmed that Jefferson was no deist; even if he were, however, he would still make a better president than "secret friends to aristocracy or monarchy" like Adams and Pinckney. Jefferson was "superior" to all other contenders as a writer, negotiator, thinker, scholar, statesman, and scientist. He was an "invincible patriot" who embraced law, liberty, and "the original principles of our revolution." Despite assertions to the contrary, Jefferson was "not the man of France" but instead "the man of public liberty—the man of the people—the man of the constitution." Tench Coxe said that maybe Jefferson had not penned the infamous Mazzei letter but then asserted that, if he had, Adams's partisans had so altered its wording when they set it into print that it differed little "from a wicked and intentional *Forgery.*" Another writer lauded "Mr. Jefferson's good sense and moderation."[24]

Perhaps no one did as much to bolster the vice president's personal credibility as John Beckley, the Pennsylvania Republican and former clerk of the House of Representatives whose *Address to the People of the United States* described Jefferson as "a man of pure, ardent and unaffected piety; of sincere and genuine virtue; of an enlightened mind and superior wisdom; the adorer of our God; the patriot of his country; and the friend and benefactor of the whole human race." Beckley appended to the pamphlet a biographical "Epitome" of Jefferson's "public life and services." His work reached a wide audience. In 1800, no fewer than five printers in five cities issued a total of five thousand copies.[25]

Oftentimes, however, defenders focused less on praising Jefferson than on censuring those who made "the incomparable JEFFERSON," as a Delaware Republican described him, "the theme of incessant slander and abuse. The man who could pen the Declaration of Independence" had "no Sedition Law to protect him" against vicious calumniators—scandalmongers Beckley derided as "fanatics, bigots, and religious hypocrites." Connecticut's Abraham Bishop failed to mention Jefferson when noting that Federalists' "great art . . . has been to paint up a certain character in every deformity of vice" while they styled themselves as "men famous for piety, goodness and science." They even went so far, he said, as to claim "all holy men of every age as federalists."[26]

Perceptions of Federalist arrogance infuriated Republicans, who balked at the implication that, because Jefferson was allegedly so bad, Federalists should continue to legislate so much worse. "I am willing to be governed by men greater, wiser, and richer than myself," Bishop said, but he had no patience for "men so great that their altitude must be taken by a quadrant and their width by a four-rod chain."[27] Bishop's poke at "great" men spotlighted a central Republican criticism of their opponents. Jefferson's supporters reminded all who would listen that, when Federalists spoke of "character," they meant inherited wealth, a costly education, and birth into a family with pretensions of nobility.

It was actions that mattered among political leaders, Republicans countered—not "character." Bishop contended that "in a free government the rulers must resign their pride, vanity, and avarice." Even Beckley, whose pamphlet gushed so extravagantly about Jefferson the man, also gushed about Jefferson the doer. Made "illustrious by an active life" filled with "great and constant efforts to promote the universal establishment of republican liberty, . . . he will neither disappoint your hopes nor defeat your wishes," Beckley vowed. "Examine all his conduct, and if you can discover any apostasy, or the dereliction of one republican principle, then withhold from him your confidence and your suffrages." DeWitt Clinton maintained that Federalists resorted to slandering Jefferson's private life because they did not dare "attack him by a fare exposition of his political principles."[28]

He may well have been right. Federalists had steered the nation for twelve years, plenty of time to make mistakes and enemies. Untested Jeffersonians had no record to attack, but they did have their enemies' record, and they used it to their fullest advantage. "A Republican" writing in the *National Intelligencer* listed nearly all Federalist sins when he noted the assumption of state debts, the Jay Treaty, the Alien and Sedition Acts, an expensive and foreboding military establishment, the national debt, and "the mighty power of Presidential favor" for unqualified seekers of government jobs. These events demonstrated that the existing regime had erected a "government in which the will of one man is *every thing,* and the will of the people and their immediate representatives is *nothing.*"[29]

Jefferson and his supporters had many issues with which to win votes but, for the most part, they focused on four: the need for economy in government, the threat to free speech posed by the Alien and Sedition Acts, Federalists' apparent antipathy toward religious freedom, and—the great catch-all— the administration's hostility toward individual rights and affinity for monarchy. Adams's spending habits seemed to underscore his elitism and detachment. Bishop, for example, demonstrated that, during the reign of the Federalists, the American government had spent more than $83 million of Americans' money—about $20,000 a day. In 1800, the daily expenditure was more than double that figure: $40,800 a day, or $1,700 each hour! Where was it all going? A Delaware Republican railed at "the enormous increase of executive patronage by the multiplication of offices," a $5 million federal loan to be repaid at 8 percent interest, and "the establishment of a useless and expensive army." A New Yorker noted that a good part of citizens' tax dollars had gone to Adams himself; in 22 years of public service, he had earned $240,000. The time had come for Adams to retire with all of his "public honors and public money." Jefferson would tax less, spend less, and do less, leaving people freer to do for themselves.[30]

He would also allow them to speak for themselves. Like Stanford, who later described the Alien and Sedition Acts as "a complete system of national disgust," Jefferson opposed the bills, though few suspected that he had authored the Kentucky Resolutions. Nevertheless, his advocates knew to associate him with the "warmest opponents" of the laws, who "unanimously recommended legal obedience" to their strictures while arguing that the "pernicious effects" of the measures would cause free speech to wither. "An unequivocal majority of the citizens" had "become vigilant and animated" against "these obnoxious laws," a Republican newspaper contended. The need to squelch dissent merely proved Adams's malfeasance, another Jeffersonian said: "If the conduct of our leaders will bear the test of examination, why should it take shelter under Sedition laws?"[31]

The attacks on Jefferson's private faith, some suggested, also aimed to divert attention from the administration's record. It was a shoddy tactic according to a *National Intelligencer* penman; Federalists should not confuse personal and public concerns, and "religion ought to be kept distinct from politics." Shoemakers and tailors did not quarrel because they had made different personal choices, reasoned another writer, and neither should "men who entertain different moral principles." Bishop, moreover, asked how much religion had been advanced by the clerics who claimed that "Satan and Cain were jacobins?" Would the bishop of Ephesus leave "the care of soul to ascertain

the number of votes . . . his favorites could get for a seat in Congress? Would
Paul of Tarsus have preached to an anxious listening audience on the propriety of sending envoys?" Jefferson, conversely, had authored Virginia's religious
freedom law. It proved that he was a "truly religious man" because it assumed
"no dominion over the faith of others" and returned "the rites of religion"
to the realm of individual choice. According to "Timoleon," the vice president's tolerance for different sects flowed from an understanding that coercion
"never has been, and never will be of service to christianity." Persecution "may
generate and multiply hypocrites, but will never produce a single convert."[32]

Not surprisingly, Catholics, Baptists, Jews, and members of other minority
faiths generally concurred, and together they stood as an important source
of support for Jefferson. Perhaps they suspected that Federalists wanted to
establish a national church, or maybe they empathized with Benjamin Noves,
a veteran of the Revolution who wrote that "I am a *Jew* and . . . for that reason I am a *republican*." In monarchies Jews are "hunted from society," but in
"Republics we have *rights*."[33]

Jefferson supported freedom from overreaching government, freedom of
speech, and freedom of religion, according to Republicans. The liberty that
their candidate offered to Americans was what partisans of Adams, according to Bishop, had endeavored to take away by creating "great distinctions of
rank," suppressing "public opinion," and preaching "intolerance." That Adams's "writings, his speeches, and his actions" proved that "he is a monarchist"
was a point made by many Republicans, including one who said that Adams
had told senators that the presidency should be hereditary—and that the Senate "should be hereditary or for life." Federalists had focused on Jefferson's
1796 letter to Philip Mazzei in part because it seemed to smear Washington as
a clandestine royalist. Now, however, a pseudonymous "Washington" applied
the letter to Adams's administration. Its sedition bill, pomp, and grasping
executive authority presented "strong evidences of an anglo-mononarchic-
aristocratic faction in the United States, just as the much abused" piece of
correspondence had claimed. "Your rights and liberties have never been in as
great jeopardy as at the present moment," "A Voter" warned citizens. If people allow themselves to become distracted "by a jargon of nick-names and
nonsense, the time may soon come when . . . instead of manly and free discussion of the conduct of public servants, we shall see nothing but servile nods
of approbation." Principles mattered, and without them, people would soon
lose their liberties. Jefferson, however, would tolerate neither the ceremony

nor the substance of authoritarian government. Which system would govern America? "It is beyond the reach of faction or conspiracy to endanger your liberties," a Delaware writer informed his audience, "unless you surrender them yourselves."[34]

This voters refused to do. During the summer and autumn of 1800, enough people cast ballots for Jeffersonian electors to give the vice president a decisive victory over the Federalist ticket. Delaware, New Jersey, and the New England states, which threw their votes into the Federalist column, left the election in the hands of their legislatures and not in those of common citizens. Rhode Island, which Federalist electors swept in a statewide popular vote, proved the only exception. Jeffersonian electors triumphed in the general election of Virginia, winning nearly four-fifths of all votes. They also out-polled their Federalist counterparts in the district elections of Kentucky, North Carolina, and Tennessee, which apportioned electoral votes among regions. In Maryland, which followed a similar practice, Federalists and Republicans evenly divided the vote. Finally, the ticket of Jefferson and Aaron Burr, the Republican vice-presidential candidate, out-polled opponents in the state assemblies of New York, Pennsylvania, South Carolina, and Georgia. Since the rules of the electoral college required members to cast two votes—one each for presidential and vice-presidential candidates—but did not distinguish between the two, Adams received sixty-five votes (Pinckney won sixty-four and John Jay was given one) while Jefferson and Burr tied with seventy-three votes each. The current House of Representatives would break the tie, Republicans assumed, by withholding a vote or two from their choice for vice president. While the awkward and generally indirect system by which Americans chose a president in 1800 causes support for Jefferson to appear less than commanding elections for the seventh Congress tell a different story: the next House would include sixty-five Republicans and only forty-one Federalists.[35]

FEDERALISTS COULD hardly believe their eyes. "Great God! What a change," gasped one friend of the old order. "It appears certain that Adams is gone." Others threw up their hands as they confronted the people's "unaccountable infatuation for bad men." Thomas Robbins, the minister who had wished Jefferson dead, said that he had "never heard such bad tidings." Republicans, meanwhile, could hardly contain their enthusiasm. So resounding seemed the defeat that George Keatinge of Baltimore, publisher of *The Jefferson*

Almanac, offered purchasers of 1801 editions, whether "Tory or Jacobin—Federal or Republican," a free copy for 1802 if "Thomas Jefferson is not elected president."[36]

Such confidence was premature. Much effort was being thrown behind a campaign "to prevent a majority of the States from voting for Mr. Jefferson," a congressional insider confided, "and many of his Friends doubt of his success." Samuel Johnston, a North Carolina judge and former senator, vented typical Federalist worries when he wrote that Jefferson's election would bring about "a great change in our Constitution, and that we shall be roused from the *calm of Despotism* to bustle in the Hurricane of Republicanism, nearly allied to Anarchy." He wished to avoid "the troubled ocean of popular politics." So did Dartmouth student Daniel Webster, now in the middle of a Federalist phase, who could think of nothing nice to say about Jefferson's looming election except that there "is some consistency in the Jacobins raising Thomas to the Executive Chair; it is in conformity to their avowed principles." But why not elect Burr, who, as Jefferson's running mate, had an equal number of votes? Most Federalists had focused more on defeating Jefferson than preserving Adams or elevating Pinckney. As William Linn had written, "*who* ought to be President" mattered less than that Jefferson "ought not." The election would now be in the hands of the lame-duck Congress, where Federalists commanded nearly half of the states' delegations. Gouverneur Morris said that his friends considered Jefferson and Burr of nearly equal worth or, more accurately, "equally void of it." But to them Jefferson's "false Principles of Government," along with his "cold blooded Vices," seemed "particularly dangerous." Burr, however, possessed a "temper and disposition" promising "conduct hostile to the democratic spirit."[37]

Hamilton disagreed. Despite Federalists' misgivings about Jefferson's character and principles, Burr, he thought, had "no principle public or private." The New York Republican, the former treasury secretary wrote, "loves nothing but himself; thinks of nothing but his own aggrandizement, and will be content with nothing, short of permanent power in his own hands." In the past, Hamilton had stood as Jefferson's greatest enemy, but now he regarded Jefferson as the lesser of two evils. He implored his allies to put a halt to Burr's election. "For heaven's sake," he urged Theodore Sedgwick, "let not the Federal party be responsible for the elevation of the Man." To Federalist Congressman James A. Bayard, who, as Delaware's lone representative, could swing the vote of an entire state, Hamilton made a special plea. Even though Jefferson was fanatical, crafty, unscrupulous, "not very mindful of truth," and a "contemptible hypocrite," he at least was not "zealot enough to do anything in pursuance of his principles that will contravene his popularity, or his interest. He is as likely as any man I know to temporize—to calculate what will be likely to promote his own reputation." The deeply felt need for acclaim that Federalists had long maintained was one of Jefferson's most dangerous qualities Hamilton now cast as his saving grace. It would moderate his actions, leading him to preserve the "measures of our past administration."[38]

Meanwhile, as a Jefferson supporter confided, the House's indecision caused "great Anxiety" in the new capital, Washington, D.C. The stalling, maneuvering, and suspected deal-making was "universally condemned by even the Federalists." In late January, North Carolina Congressman Joseph Dickson reported that the impasse prevented all other business; even though greater "opposition cannot be Made than is now made" to Burr's election, his chances remained "equal to Mr. Jefferson's." Some whispered of a possible uprising should Jefferson's candidacy fail. Even though weapons of the Pennsylvania militia had "been taken by the federalists," John Beckley predicted that continued "opposition to the voice of the country" might make resistance "a duty and obedience a crime." That "prompt, energetic, and decisive measures shall be taken," he said, "is the sentiment of every man I see and converse with."[39]

Tensions ran high in the House of Representatives. For six days, ballot after ballot, the vote remained unchanged: eight states for Jefferson and six for Burr, with Maryland and Vermont evenly split. Since victory would go to the candidate who secured a majority of the delegations, the defection of a single man in either of the divided states would give Jefferson the presidency. "The poor fellows" in Congress, a Connecticut lawyer observed, "were together all the afternoon, evening, and night" as the proceedings dragged on. They drank "wine & porter in the course of the night" and eventually looked like a bunch of "stewed quakers." Even so, he said, "I am incapable of laughing" because the condition of the country remained "a serious one." Finally, on February 17, on the thirty-sixth ballot, Jefferson's opponents cracked. Vermont's Federalist representative withdrew from his seat; his Republican colleague moved the state into the Jeffersonian column, giving the vice president the nine states—a majority—needed to win. Maryland's Federalists cast blank ballots, allowing the delegation's Republicans to add a tenth state to the total. The Federalists of South Carolina abstained, as did Delaware's Bayard. He, in fact, had spurred the general change of heart when—either heeding Hamilton's advice or responding favorably to news that a President Jefferson would protect the jobs of friends in appointive office, and, maybe not coincidentally, his nomination on the same day as the new minister plenipotentiary to France—he announced his decision to drop his support for Burr and hand to Jefferson the victory. "Thus ended the fruitless contest," North Carolina's governor soon learned, "that has agitated the public mind & threatened the peace of these United States."[40]

A Republican representative's prediction that the outcome would "give very general satisfaction to the Southern & Middle States" proved correct. From the Mississippi frontier, Cato West reported that "news of Mr. Jeffersons Election was recd here with Joy by all the Republicans amongst us, & the drooping spirits of the people are refreshed, & elevated." Joseph Priestley, a trans-Atlantic radical who considered himself "the principle object with the promoters of the *Alien bill*," saw the Republican victory as a personal one: "congratulate me," he wrote to a friend. The decision, moreover, seemed to herald a conciliatory mood. Moderate Federalists such as Dickson, who had championed Jefferson in the contest with Burr, boasted that "Good Humour and friendship prevailed" in the House for a few days after Jefferson's victory, raising "great hopes" of more unanimity at the Capitol. Fellow Tar Heel David Stone was sanguine that the new administration would satisfy entirely "the Friends of our Constitution and Country."[41]

But those with a dimmer view of Jefferson cringed, foreseeing dark days for the republic. As West noted, "those who were friends to the late Administration are quite long fac'd." Parson Robbins viewed the election as a "great frown of Providence." A man in Deerfield, Massachusetts, who had started building a house during Adams's presidency, vowed not to complete it until the forces of order returned to power. It remained unfinished for decades. As the *National Intelligencer* observed, people viewed the election's "importance as little short of infinite."[42]

A FEW FEDERALISTS paid lip service to the republican mantra of "principles and not men." Linn, the anonymous author of one of the pamphlets damning Jefferson's religious views, contended that he refused to attach his name to the work not because he was "either afraid or ashamed" but because he wished it "to be fairly judged by its own merits." It troubled him little, however, that his highly personal attack—so personal that DeWitt Clinton responded with words that could have led to a duel—might discourage serious consideration of Jefferson's political agenda.[43]

Republicans, of course, were not entirely successful in their efforts to disentangle the politics of principle from the politics of personality. For much of the decade they had capitalized on Jefferson's authorship of the Declaration of Independence, seizing an almost irresistible opportunity to honor a single man for a statement of principles authorized by the entirety of the Continental Congress. One publication worried that "the frequent mention that Jefferson was the author of the Declaration of Independence" might lead "ignorant people . . . to doubt whether others, who were esteemed patriots, approved of the measure." Even before citizens had cast a single ballot, a disgusted Boston newspaper noted that if "a foreigner were to judge" the state of American politics on the basis of toasts made at Fourth of July banquets, "he would conclude that JEFFERSON was President." His association with the document had by then grown strong enough that, at a patriotic celebration in Philadelphia, two Federalist schoolmasters indignantly exited when one of their pupils rose to recite the Declaration. The "names of *Independence* and *Jefferson*," Beckley contended, together would remain "*forever* and *inseparable*." Jefferson, after all, had not only espoused republican principles but also acted in a manner that suggested a desire to embody them.[44]

In 1800, however, Jefferson's performance was imperfect—in part because the stakes were so high. He viewed Adams's presidency as a "reign of witches," as an extended moment of real peril for the republic. Although earlier Jefferson had disclaimed partisanship, as the election approached he asserted that "perhaps this party division is necessary." America's best hope was to induce Federalists and Republicans to "debate to the people" their records and philosophies so that citizens, "recovering their true sight," would "restore their government to it's true principles." While some called for rash measures, in 1798 Jefferson had urged "patience, till luck turns, & then we shall have an opportunity of winning back the *principles* we have lost." Yet he was not content to merely wait for a brighter day. Principles mattered, and Jefferson foresaw the election of 1800 as a contest "where principles are at stake."[45] The people would determine the philosophies of the young nation to which he had devoted his adult life and, because extraordinary times called for extraordinary measures, on several occasions Jefferson took an active role in the promotion of his cause through the promotion of himself. He sought to shape not only people's opinions about politics but also their opinions about his record as a man of state. Because republican means could not be upheld at the possible expense of republicanism itself, he violated the rule that good republicans never seek office and he blurred the line that disjoined principles from men.[46]

Beckley's *Address to the People of the United States* probably serves as one good example, in part because Jefferson likely assisted in its creation. An odd work, its publication suggests much about Jefferson's struggle to obey republican traditions while working to guarantee that America would enjoy a republican future. Half defense pamphlet and half biography, it focused almost entirely on Jefferson's official actions and political beliefs. It sought not only to clear Jefferson of the charges against him but also to tell the story of his public life. Signed "Americanus" and dated July 1800, the *Address* provided the first full account of Jefferson's career ever published. Beckley could not have cribbed his biography from some other printed source. His work was original, and it required original research. It was also mostly accurate and richly detailed. The biographical portion informed readers that Jefferson had been admitted to the Virginia bar in 1766, and that on August 4, 1775, he was elected to the Continental Congress. It described Jefferson's 1776 initiatives in the Virginia legislature and surveyed his efforts to shape his state's constitution. It noted his appointment on May 7, 1783, as minister plenipotentiary to France and provided a fulsome account of his accomplishments while overseas.[47]

There is no proof that Beckley consulted with Jefferson when putting together the *Address,* but there is a good amount of circumstantial evidence. Given Jefferson's lack of faith in the security of his mail and his reluctance to be seen as a willing participant in his own advancement, it is not surprising that no correspondence on the subject survives between the men. In addition, through the first half of May Jefferson remained in Philadelphia, where he could have met with Beckley and supplied him with key information or corrected a draft of the pamphlet. It is difficult to imagine that Beckley, a fiercely loyal Republican near the center of the campaign to unseat Adams, did not at least approach Jefferson to solicit his endorsement of the project. Why not also solicit information that might otherwise have to come from less authoritative sources? Certainly the project struck Beckley as important enough to complete with care. Once finished, he sent the work to correspondents and handed bundles of copies to friends traveling from Philadelphia to other cities where, for an ever-widening audience, it was reprinted in pamphlet form or excerpted in newspapers.[48] With the stakes so high and Beckley's efforts so intense, it seems unlikely that Jefferson was unaware of the project.

If he was involved, then his eagerness to save the nation from Adams's policies led him to break a rule that republicans standing for office took pains to uphold. Although frequently transgressed, the rule was that candidates did not engage in electioneering of any kind. True republicans bowed to fellow citizens who called them to public service, but they did so only out of a sense of duty. Their aim was not to gain power but instead to secure liberty. Although Jefferson's aim was liberty, he believed that, to secure it, he would first need to convince the public to entrust him with the most powerful office in the land.

And if he was, in fact, connected to the production of Beckley's pamphlet, then he sought to secure that trust in a manner that blurred a second rule. As his purposeful anonymity as author of the Declaration of Independence had exemplified, principles mattered more than men. In a perfect and perfectly "candid world," "truths" were "self-evident" and therefore discernable to all. Such was not the case in the imperfect environment of 1800, when Federalists targeted Jefferson's principles less than they did Jefferson's character. They succeeded in making the central issue of the campaign his private life and the way in which it colored his public conduct. Beckley's *Address* constituted a response. Although it provided a brief rebuttal to Federalist depictions of Jefferson's temperament (he was "mild" and not radical, "amiable" and not mean-spirited, "refined in manners" and not coarse), its main service was to lay out Jefferson's record as an officeholder, urging readers to "look into his past life" and "examine all his conduct" to see that he had never proven himself guilty of "the dereliction of republican principles." Had such been the case, citizens could justly withhold from him their "confidence" and votes. As Jefferson would write in 1816, he never wished "federal slanders" against him "to be answered" by anything except "the tenor of my life, half a century of which has been on a theatre at which the public have been spectators, and competent judges of it's merit." His actions, after all, were the measures that exemplified his principles—and it was his principles that were supposed to matter more than the testimonials of either his friends or his foes.[49]

In Richmond, however, when Meriwether Jones, publisher of a Republican newspaper called the *Examiner,* reprinted Beckley's *Address* and augmented it with a half-dozen testimonials of Jefferson's fitness as an officeholder, this rule was further bent. Jones's addendum to Beckley's pamphlet included letters signed specifically for the occasion by John Tyler, John Harvie, Daniel Hylton, Drury Ragsdale, and James Strange. All either refuted charges that Jefferson as governor had reacted as a coward during the Revolution, when British troops advanced on Richmond, or that Jefferson as a private citizen had opposed British rule because he owed large sums of money to British subjects. These letters based their authority on their authors' testimony. Although deeply personal, they were documentary evidence of Jefferson's character. They derived their strength from their authors' reputations and credibility. In short, they contradicted Republicans' frequently stated reliance on principles and not men.[50]

In the heated atmosphere of 1800, Jefferson also flirted with the idea of making direct personal appeals. Although he maintained that he continued to "dislike . . . being the Mannequin of a ceremony," in March he told Monroe, then governor of Virginia, of his plans in May to travel from Washington to Monticello. He would take a new route through parts of the state that he had never before traveled and pass near Richmond on his way home. "I say nothing of it to anybody," he wrote, "because I do not wish to beget ceremony anywhere." Even so, he confessed his belief that "sometimes it is useful to furnish occasions for the flame of public opinion to break out from time to time." Federalists, he noted, had "made powerful use of this." It might be better for Republicans "to rest solely on the slow but sure progress of good sense . . . and build our fabric on a basis which can never give way." Yet he was tempted by the prospect that seemingly spontaneous applause would follow him on his journey—that public displays of affection would broaden the Republican circle—and he admitted that he had "deliberated" on the matter.[51]

He considered the subject indelicate. He worded his letter to Monroe to read as if he had already dismissed the notion, but Monroe understood that if Jefferson had really decided against the idea he never would have raised it. As a result, Monroe responded by laying out a number of options. He offered to meet Jefferson at Virginia's border with a hundred members of the militia on horseback. This "military parade" would then conduct Jefferson either to Richmond or Monticello. If Jefferson preferred, the martial trappings could be dropped and instead a procession of civil officers, including Monroe and members of his governor's council, would provide the escort. Both ideas would make obvious Jefferson's complicity and would constitute displays far more ceremonious than Jefferson had seemed to suggest. These facts were likely not lost on Monroe, who aimed to discourage Jefferson from giving any more thought to the idea.[52]

The best option, Monroe wrote, was for Jefferson's journey to eschew pageantry and public notice altogether. When it came time to uphold the Republican mantra of "principles and *not* men," Monroe's faith was firm. "There can be no doubt," he maintained, that such ceremony "ought to be banished from

America." It tended to "raise a govt of influence at the expence of principle; to elevate individuals by depressing or degrading the Mass of the people." Better to allow "the enemies of free govt" to indulge in such displays "without counteracting" them than to elevate men acting "in defense of free govt & in support of the rights of the people."[53]

Although Monroe's strong words did not provoke Jefferson to deny that he had meant what he had written, they chastened him nonetheless. His own "letter had hardly gone out of my hand," he insisted, "before I convinced myself... to let things come to rights by the plain dictates of common sense." He had "never doubted the impropriety" of cultivating the practice "of pomp & fulsome attentions by our citizens to their functionaries," and he knew that "at any rate I ought not to take a part in them."[54]

This was the crux of the matter. To shape public opinion was one thing, especially for Republicans who viewed their actions, as Jefferson did, as the enlightenment of the uninformed or the aiding of "the sick who need medicine." It was another thing altogether for Jefferson, who stood to gain power from such actions, to be seen as having a hand in them. In 1799, he told Monroe, when passing along copies of a pamphlet defending his support for the Kentucky Resolutions for distribution "to the most influential characters" in Virginia, "do not let my name be connected with the business." His reputation as a humble and aloof republican, as a man who played by old rules in the new game of competitive national politics, constituted one of his most valuable and well-guarded assets.[55]

As such, his thoughts centered on strategy at least as much as on principle. In this he was not alone. Monroe, for example, frowned on Jefferson's proposal to make himself "the Mannequin of a ceremony" not only because such a spectacle might undermine Republican principles but also because "it might lay the foundation" for "a kind of competition" with other men. What if John Marshall, the Virginia Federalist whom Adams had recently appointed secretary of state, staged a similar parade and drew a greater number of supporters? Federalists, of course, had principles of their own, and their sense of proper political behavior differed little from that of Republicans. Even so, they too stood ready to make concessions in the interest of expediency. "In times like these in which we live," Hamilton wrote in 1800, "it will not do to be over-scrupulous. It is easy to sacrifice the substantial interests of society by a strict adherence to ordinary rules."[56]

THANKS IN PART to Hamilton's flexibility, the House declared Jefferson's victory. As a result, Jefferson had to stand before members of Congress and on the occasion of his inauguration deliver an address unlike any that he had previously given. In the past, his most important professions of political faith had been written rather than spoken, and most of the public ones he had written anonymously. Sometimes, as in the case of the Declaration of Independence, he wrote on behalf of groups of which he was a member, such as the Continental Congress. At other times, as in the case of the Kentucky Resolutions, he prepared words to represent the views of others. When he wrote to express only his own opinions he rarely intended to release his words to the public at large. His *Notes on the State of Virginia* and his 1796 letter to Philip Mazzei, both private documents intended for limited audiences, stand as two examples. And then there was the 1791 letter that helped to provoke the bickering that set the stage for the election of 1800, his note to the American publisher of Thomas Paine's *Rights of Man*. Had he intended the publication of his letter endorsing Paine and criticizing Adams? Jefferson denied that this was ever his plan; as he had told Adams, the appearance of the note with his name attached left him "thunderstruck."[57]

In all of these earlier pronouncements Jefferson crouched behind various sorts of authorial shelter. All of these statements were either written in the name of others, written anonymously, or written with his name attached but addressed to a private audience. In the case of his inaugural oration, however, he could sustain no such distance between his words and his identity. There could be no excuses and there was little room for error. Here, in full public view, Jefferson was crafting his own image for the nation.

His statement on his ascension to the presidency was the product of at least two drafts, each filled with insertions, deletions, and revisions. He wrote the speech with care, revised it with precision, and presented it only after pondering each phrase. His changes resulted in a pure, untainted, and republican presentation. In the opening line of his original draft he described himself as "called by the voice of our country to undertake the duties of it's first executive magistrate." This he pruned so that he could describe himself more modestly, undertaking "the duties of the first Executive office of our country." His enemies would not be reminded of the voice of the country, which had rebuked Adams, and his friends could think of him not as a magistrate but as an officeholder.

His words carefully chosen, he next ensured their faithful transcription. Early on the morning of his inauguration, Jefferson presented a copy of his final draft to Samuel Harrison Smith, editor of Washington's pro-administration *National Intelligencer*. Moments after Jefferson spoke on March 4, 1801, a crowd gathered at the offices of Smith's newspaper to purchase that day's edition, which contained the text of the speech. Within days, newspapers throughout the nation reprinted Smith's transcription.[58]

In addition to provoking anxiety, the transparency of the situation must have also struck Jefferson as liberating. No longer did his reputation rest in the hands of others bent either on praising his supposed virtues or damning his alleged flaws. No longer would his character be depicted solely by the writings and whispers of his friends and foes. No longer did he have to watch his every word or guard his every action in order to avoid suspicion that he was scheming for power. Now that the maneuvering was over, the power was finally his, and one of the greatest responsibilities that accompanied it was explaining to his fellow citizens how and why he intended to wield it. Now, finally, he could speak for himself.

His inaugural address aimed to reassure enemies and allies alike that he was neither a dangerous radical nor ready to relax his efforts to advance the cause of liberty. The part of his speech most remembered—and most commented on at the time—was his famous declaration that "we have called by different names brethren of the same principle. We are all republicans: we are all federalists." He offered other phrases to win the confidence of foes and friends. He heaped praise on George Washington, "our first and greatest revolutionary character," who in the Mazzei letter he had criticized. In one breath Jefferson combined "the rules of the Constitution" with the democratic "voice of the nation." In another he attached "the will of the law" to "the common good." He stood not for anarchy but for "harmony and affection without which liberty and even life itself are but dreary things." But he opposed "that religious intolerance under which mankind so long bled and suffered." Americans possessed "the strongest government on earth" because "every man, at the call of the law, would fly to the standard of the law, and would meet invasions of the public order as his own personal concern. Sometimes it is said that man can not be trusted with the government of himself. Can he, then, be trusted with the government of others?" The United States was a big country; it was removed from the influence and troubles of Europe, and it acknowledged and adored "an overruling providence." With these words the new president attempted to assuage the fears of Federalists, but with the next—and these tipped the scales—he elucidated the agenda of Republicans. "What more is necessary to make us a happy and a prosperous people? Still one thing more fellow citizens, a wise and frugal government, which shall restrain men from injuring one another, shall leave them otherwise free to regulate their own pursuits of industry and improvement, and shall not take from the mouth of labor the bread it has earned. This is the sum of good government."[59]

If these words gave Federalists no reason to fear his presidency, they nevertheless gave Republicans reason for hope, for they affirmed that he would pursue the agenda on which he had been elected. They also offered a deliberately drawn picture of Jefferson. He muted his status as a man with power by affirming his support for principles that empowered Americans. Unlike the ranting demagogue of Federalist propaganda, he delivered the address—as he did all his public utterances—in "almost femininely soft" tones, according to Margaret Bayard Smith, wife of the newspaper editor. Much like the "Man of the People" admired by Republicans, he dressed, as a Rhode Island newspaper reported, "as usual," like "a plain citizen, without any distinctive badge of office." Instead of riding from his boardinghouse to the Capitol in a liveried coach, which would have made his supporters cringe, he crossed the short distance on foot. But perhaps to disarm the critics who four years earlier said that he had diminished the dignity of office by receiving notice of his election to the vice presidency through the mail and not a special messenger, he walked not alone but in a "little parade" that included local militia officers, Republican congressmen, and—to underscore the peaceful transfer of power—two members of the outgoing cabinet. (Adams, grieving not only the loss of a job but also the loss of a son, had left town before dawn.) If Jefferson's acquiescence to this minor ceremony was a public nod toward the gravity of his new post, then on the eve of his inauguration, in the relative privacy of his boardinghouse, he took his usual seat far from the head of the dinner table. On this day, as he had long wanted to do, he had made himself self-evident. Neither jacobinical nor monarchical, serious but not self-aggrandizing, he made himself the embodiment of pure republicanism—and, he might have boasted, pure Americanism.[60]

Maybe he was not such a dangerous man, Federalists said, or maybe he was. By the day of his inauguration, "a number of *Priests*" who had earlier "sent their remonstrances, not only to their Parishes, but to Heaven, against the election of Jefferson, the deist," had begun "to speak of him, as *a pretty good sort of man!*" Maybe prudence warned them not to swim against a rising Jeffersonian tide. One Federalist bureaucrat, for example, wrote that however unfortunate the election had been for Adams, he considered himself "lucky in having escaped his favor" and "the disgrace which attended the last two months of his administration." Less opportunistic but greatly puzzled, William Barry Grove found the speech "as moderate as could be expected" but observed that it contrasted so much with the Mazzei letter and other writings attributed to Jefferson that he was either "a great hypocrite" or "his *notions* of our Constitution" had greatly changed. Whatever the case, the congressman believed, the address could not erase "the inconsistencies & evidences of Mr. Jefferson's arts, & machiavelian policy to get at the head of American affairs." Others, however, could not stand to hear good words spoken of the new president. Gouverneur Morris complained that Jefferson's speech was "too long by half," and Federalists in Staunton, Virginia, according to a Republican neighbor, even plotted an uprising to disrupt the harmony "which prevailed among us ever since Mr. Jefferson's speech."[61]

More than a few Americans tasted sour grapes. "Those who were disaffected to the revolution, & who only supported the constitution as a step stone to monarchy," claimed Massachusetts maverick Elbridge Gerry, now wished "to continue the schism" between themselves and "republican federalists." Scientist Benjamin Waterhouse averred that, despite the continued doubts of the president's detractors, Jefferson would be fair, prudent, and too protective of the nation's economic interests to allow any sort of "combination" with France.[62]

Only the future could determine which side was wrong and which was right. At the time, however, Federalists such as Theodore Sedgwick, an ardent Hamiltonian and the deposed speaker of the House of Representatives, wept that the "aristocracy of virtue is destroyed" and "personal influence is at an end." The same observations, however, gave Republicans who emphasized principles over personalities and measures over men cause for jubilation. As Jefferson said in his inaugural address, "I ask so much confidence only as may give firmness and effect to the legal administration of your affairs." Jefferson, of course, had an agenda, but his talent for presenting himself as the people's agent helped convince his followers—and also himself—that the direction in which he determined to lead was chosen by those who followed.[63]

CHAPTER FIVE

President of the People

THOMAS JEFFERSON stood at the doorway of the Executive Mansion to welcome Elder John Leland and his unusual, unwieldy gift. It was, the president and members of the press agreed, a "mammoth cheese." Measuring 4.5 feet in diameter and weighing 1,235 pounds, the cheese had accompanied its purveyor more than 400 miles from Cheshire, Massachusetts, a far-from-mammoth dairying community where the 900 cows that donated milk for the enterprise outnumbered the mostly Baptist citizens, who contributed funds for an oversized cheese vat, a good dose of Republican enthusiasm, and, no doubt at the urging of Leland, their prayers for its safe delivery.[1]

The preacher, who presented this "freewill-offering" to Jefferson on New Year's Day 1802, also conveyed to the president a message signed by his neighbors explaining their efforts. They tendered their "tribute of profound respect" alongside the cheese that stood as proof of their "love" for a man who was nothing short of heaven-sent: "We believe the Supreme Ruler of the Universe, who raises up men to achieve great events, has raised up a *Jefferson* at this critical day, to defend *Republicanism,* and to baffle the arts of *Aristocracy.*" The citizens also affirmed their support of the Constitution, which prohibited religious tests and established "free suffrage" to correct the "abuses" of officeholders. They considered it "a discription of those powers which the people have delegated to their Magistrates, to be exercised for definite purposes; and not as a charter of favor granted by a Sovereign to his subjects." As a result, they told Jefferson, they experienced the most "exquisite" joy on his election "to the first office in the nation."[2]

Proud of the gift and concurring with the political views it represented, the president gave Leland a message to bring back to Cheshire, where the number of Federalist voters could be counted on a hand missing both its thumb and forefinger.[3] Calling the cheese "extraordinary proof" of skill in "those

domestic arts which contribute so much to our daily comfort," Jefferson assured these "freeborn farmers" of his commitment to safeguard "the fruits
of their labour" from taxes and other forms of government interference; the
Constitution, he said, "is a Charter of authorities and duties, not a Charter of
rights to it's officers." Republican newspapers, which published the Cheshire
letter alongside Jefferson's reply, described the gift as "the greatest cheese in
America, for the greatest man in America."[4]

Visitors called on the president not long after Leland's arrival. Although he
spurned his predecessors' practice of greeting well-wishers at weekly levees,
which he described as "harbingers" of monarchical government, he bowed
to tradition on New Year's Day and the Fourth of July by throwing open the
doors of the President's House.[5] All sorts of people poured in, from common
merchants to foreign ministers, and even some Federalists. One of them, Con-
gregationalist minister and Massachusetts representative Manasseh Cutler,
reported that the "President invited us to 'Go into the mammoth room to see
the mammoth cheese.'" Cutler stepped into the East Room, where Jefferson
would later display not only the cheese but also his collection of mammoth
fossils, and witnessed the offering that had "on this morning, been presented
with all the parade of Democratic etiquette." Calling it a "monument to
human wickedness and folly," the congressman derided Leland, "the cheese-
monger," as a "poor, ignorant, illiterate, clownish preacher."[6]

News of the cheese provoked similar reactions from other Federalists,
whose sharp pronouncements mirrored the fervor with which Republicans
praised Leland's gesture. One writer, prior to the departure from Cheshire of
the "enormous" tribute, claimed to have witnessed in that town "a ludicrous
procession, in honor of a cheesen God." Leading the parade was a preacher,
"running and puffing" with a flag "to ornament and grace the idolatry." John
Davis, a British traveler whose visit in Baltimore coincided with Leland's arrival, fumed that "men, women, and children flocked to see the Mammoth
Cheese. The taverns were deserted; the gravy soup cooled on the table, and
the cats unrebuked revelled on the custards and cream. Even grey-bearded
shopkeepers neglected their counters, and participated in the Mammoth infatuation." Meanwhile, a printer ran off copies of a broadside entitled *Ode
to the Mammoth Cheese.* The "most excellent" present to the "man belov'd
by all" would evoke biting ridicule from some, it cautioned, but no matter:
"Do what they can—and say just what they please, RATS love to nibble at
good Cheshire Cheese." Sick of Republicans' raves over the "celebrated
MAMMOTH CHEESE," the *New-York Evening Post* complained that it "has

been toasted and re-toasted till it has become quite unpalatable." Tired of Federalists' sneers, a Jeffersonian paper, before even the delivery of Leland's gift, said that it had "probably drawn forth more *federal* objections against the New Administration" than almost anything else and wondered when the president's hyperbolic enemies would declare the cheese "a violation of the Constitution."[7]

The immensity of Leland's offering no doubt attracted the interest of many Americans. But it also loomed large as a political symbol, which explains the contentiousness of the discussion it inspired. Described by Jefferson as an "ebullition of the passion of republicanism," the cheese was also indicative of citizens' passion for him.[8] Not even George Washington received as many testimonials of praise and adoration, as seemingly spontaneous and as concentrated within the span of a few years, as did Jefferson during his presidency.

The outpouring of affection for the "Man of the People," as his supporters called him, in the eyes of Federalists confirmed terrible fears. Democracy could only unleash demagoguery, they thought, and give rise to a potentially despotic popular leader who roused the rabble through a cult of personality. Even more outrageous than the Cheshire cheese, Congressman Cutler thought, was Leland's sermon before the House and Senate—and the president—on January 3. "Such a performance I never heard before," Cutler reported, "and I hope never shall again. The text was, 'And behold a greater than Solomon is here.' The design of the preacher was principally to apply the allusion, not to the person intended in the text, but to *him* who was then present."[9]

Republicans also worried about despotism, but they considered aristocracy more prone to its production than democracy. Even so, for all their cheese-making, when Cheshire's citizens vowed their "love" to a god-sent Jefferson, they took care to emphasize that his status as their leader did not diminish their right to serve as their own rulers. The most prominent pro-administration print, moreover, made sure to note that Leland's journey was no odyssey of fawning servility. From the Berkshire hills all the way to Washington, it reported, citizens greeted the cheese with a "simple plainness" befitting the "dignity of republicanism."[10] What emboldened the widespread exaltation of Jefferson also made it possible. The self-effacing president eschewed courtly pomp and comported himself as a representative of the people who had elected him to serve. For the same reasons, he remained anathema to his shrinking circle of enemies.

WHEN THE people of Cheshire paid tribute to Jefferson, their voices joined a rousing chorus of adoration the likes of which Americans had never seen. At patriotic festivals and in the public prints, with poems, songs, sermons, and speeches, and through other, more private gestures, citizens from nearly all walks of life expressed reverence for their president. They lionized him as their savior, their deliverer from the dark specter of aristocracy. He championed freedom, they said in their various ways, and he restored hope.

Jefferson received not only a mammoth cheese but also a mammoth veal. It had arrived a few months earlier but not soon enough to forestall the effects of deterioration. To the German-born butchers who dispatched from Philadelphia the largest calf's rump they had ever seen, the president sent a letter of thanks containing a polite assurance that, although the veal could not be served to dinner guests, it still retained the original "beauty of it's appearance, it's fatness & enormous size." Like the members of Leland's congregation, these meat merchants, who described themselves as proud Republicans, considered the voluntary contribution of the bounties of their labor their highest tribute. While the persecuted Massachusetts Baptists appreciated Jefferson's firm support for religious freedom, the Pennsylvanians admired his rebuttal, in the *Notes on the State of Virginia,* of the European claim that American animals suffered from retarded growth. Such "successful examples of enlarging the animal volume," Jefferson modestly replied, disproved the foreign fallacy more effectively than mere words.[11]

Others honored the president with productions of a different sort. Shortly after his inauguration, a Charleston couple named their son Thomas Jefferson McBlair. At about the same time, a Newport woman gave birth to twins. One of them, Thomas Jefferson, later may have suffered the resentment of his brother, Aaron Burr. Rhode Island Republicans held both children aloft before a crowd celebrating the result of the recent election, and each benefited when someone passed a plate for money "to be applied to their future use."[12]

Such Jeffersonian gatherings were common immediately before and after the new chief executive's March 4 inauguration, but the elaborate Virginia pageant that dramatized his ascent to office was anything but typical. At center stage and dressed in "plain attire" appeared a "beautiful virgin" wearing a placard that identified her as "Liberty at the point of death!" Surrounding this weeping woman stood five menacing figures. From the first, crowned and wielding a scepter, hung a sign revealing his belief in "divine right." Tags similarly emblazoned the costumes of a fat bishop ("tythes"), a soldier with a bayonet ("I will stab my enemy"), and a politician grasping at a stack of legislation ("Energetic governments"). Rounding out the motley assemblage was a ranting orator, shouting "down with the antichrist" and calling on all "true Americans" to "destroy her, you wish to obtain wealth—establish good order—and recommend yourselves to God." More men then mounted the stage, bellowing in concurrence with the orator and holding in their hands commissions, diplomas, appointments, grants, contracts, and warrants. When all hope for Liberty seemed lost, a trumpet sounded. A courier rushed forward with an announcement that caused Liberty's enemies to cower: "Jefferson is President!"[13]

Equally indicative of citizens' affection for the commander in chief were the letters that arrived on his desk. Four days after Jefferson took office, a Quaker from southeastern Pennsylvania scribbled that "thy being Appoynted President is Caus of greate goy in oure part of the Cuntry." Months later, Willie Blount, a Tennessee man who in eight years would take office as his state's governor, counted himself among "those who admire your doings" and assured Jefferson of his desire "that you should continue to preside as President of the United States so long as you may feel disposed to act in that way." From the New York hamlet of Cazenovia, teenager Nehemiah W. Badger, a cabinetmaker's apprentice, sang the president's praises: "I sa[y] rejoice Columbia sons rejoice to tirents never bend thir nea but join in hart and sole and voice for Jefferson and leberty." Again displaying an affinity for rhyme, he closed by asking Jefferson to "overlock theas fue scrabblous lines, for my pen is por my inck is pail. My love for you shal never fail."[14]

Badger's memory surpassed his spelling. While his final lines were an original creation, he borrowed the verse that preceded them from the anthem "Jefferson and Liberty," frequently sung at festivals marking the anniversaries of independence and Jefferson's inauguration—the two most important days on the Republican calendar. Also popular were "Jefferson's March" and "Jefferson Columbia's Chief," which began

> HAIL Columbia! happy land,
> United forms a Patriot band;
>   For JEFFERSON is PRESIDENT,
>   For JEFFERSON is PRESIDENT.
> His Country's call he again obeys,
> Republicans their wish to please.
>   Our Constitution firm and just!
>   To JEFFERSON we freely trust:

> Then Heaven guide the rev'rend sage
> The admired Patriot of the age.

The chief executive inspired more than a half-dozen such tunes, which described him as "Liberty's darling son," "the People's friend," "America's choice," "hero, sage, and statesman," "Columbia's boast and pride," and "the firm friend of Freedom's cause." A Baltimore printer included a few of them in a pamphlet entitled *The Democratic Songster;* others appeared in Republican newspapers. People may not have reserved these serenades exclusively for special occasions. One featured a refrain revealing its status as a drinking song:

> Lo, *Jefferson* bright:
> Fill up bumpers—that's right—
> Here's his health; we'll support him—
>   if needful we'll fight.[15]

In a nation where printers circulated 250,000 newspapers, books, and pamphlets each week, as one observer estimated, there lived not a single citizen "who cannot have the requisite information to judge correctly of our national affairs." But not all Americans could read, and many who did possessed, like young Nehemiah Badger, only an imperfect command of the written word. For them popular music constituted a powerful, persuasive link between everyday experience and the political world.[16]

So did pictures, which provided the public with numerous images of Jefferson. During the first decade of the nineteenth century, printers issued copies of at least thirty separate engravings that, although often inspired by original portraits never seen by most citizens, ornamented the frontispieces of books and graced the walls of homes. His face—or faces purported to be his, for sometimes they bore no resemblance—even appeared on mugs and pitchers from which Americans drank their coffee and poured their tea.[17]

The sales strategies employed by distributors of such iconography testify to both the widespread demand for depictions of Jefferson and the competitiveness of early American enterprise. Philadelphia's George Helmbold, Jr., for example, offered to the public for twelve dollars a framed and glazed full-length portrait of "the man of the people." He assured potential buyers that "neatness and elegance" characterized the print, and extended to all subscribers a complementary biography "containing the most remarkable events of Mr. Jefferson's life" as well as a money-back guarantee should the work of art not meet with their satisfaction. The engraving, which showed the plainly dressed president surrounded by books and touching a globe, could be purchased not only at Helmbold's two Philadelphia shops but also through his distributors in sixteen other cities. A rival full-length engraving, ready for sale on July 4, 1801, was published by Augustus Day, another Philadelphian. Depicting a similarly attired Jefferson holding up a copy of the Declaration of Independence and situated between a bust of Benjamin Franklin and a static electric machine, this print rankled Helmbold but probably delighted Republicans with shallow pockets. He described it as "a very poor copy stolen from the original picture," but it sold for less than half the price.[18]

While entrepreneurs made Jefferson's image a commodity, others likened him to a deity. The biblical passage on which Leland based his sermon to Congress, "And behold a greater than Solomon is here," referred to Jesus. The Massachusetts Baptist, however, seemed to apply it to the president. In Connecticut, where Federalist clerics called Jefferson an infidel, Stanley Griswold found similarities between the friend of the people and "*Jesus,* the friend of the world," who hazarded traps "laid by a powerful hierarchy" that opposed his "liberal precepts" while the people "flocked in multitudes around him." Abraham Bishop, New Haven's most vociferous Republican, reminded his audience at a festival marking Jefferson's election that Jesus also "directed men to a better world. The chief priests and elders among the Jews, who arrogantly assumed to be exclusive friends of order and good government," exclaimed "What meaneth this blasphemer? he deceiveth the people, he soweth sedition." While those clergymen cheered Jesus's crucifixion, the ministers of Bishop's own time, he asserted, crucified Jefferson in print. Yet both Jesus and Jefferson triumphed. Compare, he said, "the illustrious chief who, once insulted, now presides over the union, with him who, once insulted, now presides over the universe." Hints of millennialism accompanied these figurative suggestions of a second coming. A Maryland printer, for example, dated a pamphlet "March 4, 1801: First Year of the Triumph of Republican Principles." Echoing this sentiment, a New York orator proclaimed that "a new order of things commences. A brighter era dawns upon our hopes—Liberty is triumphant . . . and our glorious Revolution established for ever." Make no mistake, he said: "The struggle is over."[19]

FEDERALISTS REFUSED to concede defeat, in no small part because, in their view, the president's burgeoning popularity threatened to undermine the republic that they had helped to establish. Over the course of twelve years,

Thomas Jefferson, President of the United States, 1801,
engraved by Cornelius Tiebout, published by Augustus Day.
(Prints and Photographs Division, Library of Congress)

Alexander Hamilton and his allies had labored to piece together a federal system uniting the interests of principled, propertied men. These individuals, Federalist leaders assured themselves, possessed the virtue required for enlightened public service. They also stood to lose the most if America, like France, sacrificed life, liberty, and property to predatory mobs and the demagogues who commanded them. At the forefront of Federalist fears loomed unrestrained democracy, the passionate, ignorant, and potentially devastating Goliath that, in the election of 1800, Republicans roused with promises of equality.[20] This worldview, combined with a good dose of snobbery, led Federalists to view adoration of Jefferson as a mammoth danger. Was it mere coincidence, some must have wondered, that Jean-Paul Marat, the infamously incendiary Jacobin journalist whose pen had portrayed the guillotine as a sacrificial altar of liberty, also rose to fame as the "friend of the people"?[21]

The conciliatory tone of the president's inaugural address, his assurance that "we are all republicans: we are all federalists," gave citizens no cause for celebration, one writer warned. Although Robespierre started as a "moderate reformer," he "advanced by regular gradations to the last extreme of democratic licentiousness." Jefferson was no less "ambitious and unprincipled." His removal of Federalists from appointive office soon after his speech revealed his insincerity, others suggested, and signaled a step toward despotism. Even Martha Washington felt fearful. The grieving widow and national matriarch was an ardent Federalist. As Congressman Cutler reported after a visit to Mount Vernon, she "spoke of the election of Mr. Jefferson, whom she considered as one of the most detestable of mankind, as the greatest misfortune this country had ever experienced."[22]

Jeffersonians' apparent solicitation of popular favor—for all of it could not, the president's opponents presumed, reflect candid sentiments—further confirmed Federalist prophecies. "Until very lately," the *Columbian Centinel* observed in June 1801, Republicans had "held that *Rulers* were 'Servants of the People,' and that the People ought to wait for evidence of faithful conduct before they rewarded them with their approbation." Now, with Jefferson as chief executive, they disregarded this principle. After all, another Federalist claimed, "no men are so fond of adulation as your self-stiled Republicans." Despite their "boasted love of simplicity, they hunger and thirst after applause with a most voracious appetite." They repaid the praise of even the most "humble" with "condescending and fulsome compliments." When flattery failed to call forth testimonials of support, men "deputed from the seat of government" shamelessly begged for them; when this tactic miscarried, the writer speculated, officials "manufactured at Washington" avowals of esteem, and then had them "transmitted for signatures." Either way, impressionable Americans would overestimate satisfaction with Jefferson's policies and, to cultivate their neighbors' goodwill, meekly concur with the supposed crowd.[23]

Federalists' jaws dropped as all around them this supposed strategy seemed to bear fruit. By 1802, even the Fourth of July portended frightful scenes of democratic disorder. Mobs marched through the streets, blustered about Jefferson's goodness, and then at banquets raised their glasses to the "Man of the People" until they could hardly stand. "On no occasion, since toasts came first into fashion," lamented the *New-York Evening Post,* "was ever composed so great a number of unmeaning, vapid, senseless stuff as the present anniversary has produced." This perhaps failed to shock many Federalists. "The drunken rabble," a Connecticut penman sniffed, "instinctively follow the standard of Jefferson."[24]

Instinctive or not, the impression remained strong among the president's critics that he and his allies actively cultivated public praise. "Mr. Jefferson's adherents very early tried to stick upon him the mountebank, imposter title of *The Man of the People,*" noted Fisher Ames, the former Massachusetts congressman; they then "had an easy access to the affections and confidence of the multitude." In order to win votes, Federalists frequently charged, the Republicans and their "crafty" chief, as Theodore Sedgwick described him, championed the elimination of most internal taxes and a reduction in defense expenditures. Very few of the president's actions, in fact, failed to strike his opponents as base electioneering. When early on summer mornings he ambled over to the Navy Yard and struck up conversations with shipwrights, his critics reportedly would whisper, "There! see the demagogue! There's Long Tom, sinking the dignity of his station, to get votes, and court the mob." When eschewing the liveried servants and gilded carriages of his predecessors, Jefferson rode unattended on his own horse to Capitol Hill and led it himself to the hitching post, New Hampshire Senator William Plumer wondered if this action signified some sort of "affectation." Whatever the case, he thought, it "ill accords with the dignity of the chief of a great nation."[25]

Even Jefferson's clothing raised suspicion. According to the *New-York Evening Post,* his attire not only revealed his "steady attachment to the filthy republicanism" of French revolutionists Marat, Danton, and Robespierre, who had dressed themselves "in the most dirty and disgusting manner possible," but it also seemed "well calculated to gain or prolong popularity." Visitors at the President's House, the paper reported, invariably encountered a shabby

man who they supposed worked in the stable. Hair unkempt and chin bris-
tling with stubble, "he is dressed in long boots with the tops pressed down
about his ankles like a Virginia buck" as well as "overalls of corduroy, faded
by frequent immersions in soap-suds from yellow to a dull white," and an
old, food-stained waistcoat. To visitors' "astonishment," he then introduced
himself as Thomas Jefferson. In sum, the president attempted to "approximate as near the ordinary dress, manners, and deportment, of his gardener
or coachman, as possible." Such costuming, the *Evening Post* concluded, was
"unquestionably the result of study and system." Federalists threw up their
hands in disgust. The Executive Mansion, bemoaned New York financier
Gouverneur Morris, harbored enough rudeness to "reduce even Greatness to
the Level of Vulgarity."[26]

While these accounts probably exaggerated Jefferson's informality, evidence abounds of his willingness to employ for political gain "mock-modesty,"
as he himself later described it. Accounts of his appearance varied so widely
that one wonders whether he sometimes dressed down to communicate a
common touch or sometimes dressed up to establish his respectability. Washington socialite Margaret Bayard Smith, the Federalist bride of Republican
newspaperman Samuel Harrison Smith, when first introduced to Jefferson
in 1800 found nothing about him that confirmed her "previously conceived
ideas of the coarseness and vulgarity of his appearance and manners." To the
contrary, she wrote that she encountered a man "whose deportment was so
dignified and gentlemanly, whose language was so refined, whose voice was
so gentle, and whose countenance was so benignant" that he "unlocked my
heart." Over the course of a long friendship, her opinion did not change. "If
his dress was plain, unstudied and sometimes old-fashioned in its form, it was
always of the finest materials," she later wrote, and he possessed "a natural and
quiet dignity" that "never degenerated into vulgarity."[27]

Ever-mounting evidence of citizens' devotion to this "Man of the People," combined with Jefferson's alleged kowtowing for applause, caused his
opponents to wonder where it would all lead. Hamilton in 1801 assured a
friend that, while Jefferson's "politics are tinctured with fanaticism," he was
not "zealot enough to do anything in pursuance of his principles which will
contravene his popularity." William Barry Grove, a Federalist congressman
from North Carolina, concurred, speculating that the "love of Popularity"
in the new administration would "bear down all other considerations." Several years later, Fisher Ames voiced a similar sentiment: "Mr. Jefferson only
takes care of his popularity, which forbids him to govern at all." But such

small consolations counted for little, Ames believed, because exalted demagogues quickly learned to behave like dictators. "The everlasting flattery of the people," he claimed, "has done almost all that is necessary to be done to make them slaves." Adoration could only "intoxicate" a leader with hubris and encourage a reckless abuse of power. "A despot," he insisted, "who is saluted as our multitude are [doing] from sunrise to sunset, with, O Great King, live forever, will think of nothing else."[28]

THE AMERICANS who extolled Jefferson, however, commended not their anointed king but their elected president. Their testimonials, which nearly always combined ringing praise with ardent affirmations of the philosophies he represented, made clear that honor paid to him remained inseparable from his duty to honor their collective authority and individual rights. As such, citizens' celebrations of Jefferson amounted to a much greater phenomenon: the celebration of themselves. More than merely their friend and their champion, they viewed the new president as their proxy, as the representative of common people's power.

As scripted in the Virginia pageant dramatizing the Republican ascendancy, the announcement of Jefferson's election saved Liberty from the clutches of aristocratic scoundrels. But the real turning point followed the audience's scripted pronouncement that "We are the votaries of Liberty and will destroy her enemies." Liberty admonished her attackers to "be content with equal rights" and then convinced the crowd to spare the erstwhile tyrants. These final events made clear the drama's message: principle would restrain the people, but in the new national order it was they who held the power. In another play, *Jefferson and Liberty,* the Republican leader owed thanks to citizens not only for his office but also for saving his life. After an actor portraying Jefferson proclaimed each individual to be "his own sovereign," a gang of gun-toting priests, printers, and lawyers mounted the stage. When all seemed lost, vigilant Republicans rushed forward, shouted "long live the friend of the people," and thwarted the assassins.[29]

Such loyalty, the *Aurora* insisted, could not be unconditional and would endure only so long as Jefferson maintained his commitment to the elimination of Federalist measures that intruded on people's lives and injured their rights. While his election provided citizens with "cause to exult," this leading Republican newspaper warned, "too great, too implicit confidence even in him, ought *rather* to be the result of long and actual experience" with his

administration "than lavished at the outset. It is the way by which the people have always duped themselves," and it might "tempt" and "lead astray"
the new president from "the virtuous principles upon which he has hitherto
acted." Similarly, on the day of Jefferson's inauguration, a group of New Jersey
Republicans reaffirmed their resolve to "keep a vigilant eye" on the "intrigues
and machinations" of elected officials. "Ignorance," they declared, "is the inlet
to error, undue confidence, and the desultory invasions and usurpations of
government." Others, although less cautious, nonetheless maintained that
their trust in Jefferson should not be construed as blind faith. As an orator
reminded individuals in Middlebury, Vermont, while the actions of Federalists made clear their "rebellion against the majesty of the people and the social
compact," Jefferson possessed a strong record of patriotism, and his "zeal in
the cause of man has merited our confidence."[30]

Among even the most ardent Jeffersonians, affection for the president remained subordinate to enthusiasm for the supremacy of popular will. Citizens at a Philadelphia banquet, for example, toasted "Thomas Jefferson—
The man whom the people delight to honor," but only after first raising their
glasses to "The People—The only legitimate source of all power." In Suffield,
Connecticut, 150 Republicans expressed this relationship in about the same
way. They toasted the people, the "best guardians of their own Liberty," and
then the Constitution. Jefferson, "First in the esteem of his Fellow-Citizens,"
received tertiary honors, and these, like those accorded in the City of Broth-
erly Love, implied fraternal respect but not filial devotion. At the Newport
festival where a crowd greeted Jefferson and Burr, the newborn twins, the
names of the president and vice president had also been affixed to two large
lanterns that adorned opposing sides of a triumphal arch erected for the occasion. A third lamp, "elevated a little above the others" and suspended from
the keystone, signified "The People." In Charleston, at a Republican banquet
attended by the governor and other dignitaries, organizers revealed a much
clumsier command of populist symbolism. They prominently displayed "an
elegant transparent portrait of Mr. Jefferson, as large as life." After guests
toasted the president, it was "immediately lighted, and drew a spontaneous
burst of applause." Practitioners of republican simplicity who witnessed this
display of idolatry probably cringed. An inscription above the portrait helped
to make amends, for it described Jefferson as "The Man of the People."[31]

If South Carolina's highest ranks failed to fully digest the new democratic
ethos, they paid it homage nonetheless. Jefferson's election inspired even the
patriarchs of this stratified society to accommodate the new wave of popular

enthusiasm. On March 4, 1801, Charleston's *City Gazette* proclaimed that the "voice of the people has prevailed." Contrary to Federalists' dire predictions, however, this voice did not demand the death of the Constitution or serve as a clarion call for "turbulent passions." Instead, it insisted on a minimalist government intent on "guarding the rights of freemen from invasion, and diffusing through all ranks the blessings of equal rights." These goals revealed that profound alterations in political culture had already taken place. The "exit of aristocracy to the tune of the rogue's march," as a Pennsylvanian described the Republican agenda, amounted to more than mere polemics. It constituted a disavowal of traditional forms of deference and, as the skeptical Republicans in New Jersey suggested, a repudiation of "improper reverence to the opinions of superiors or the dogmatical institutions of government." The new imperative demanded freedom "from these unnatural incumbrances" so that "the well-informed mind" could become "inspired with a consciousness of its own importance." As a result, "slavish feelings" would languish "excluded from the human breast." Most radical of all, these Republicans described their views as "Democratic."[32]

A decade earlier, only Federalists used the word "democrat," and then only as an epithet. But now people began to employ it proudly as a term of self-description. Individuals such as the compiler of *The Democratic Songster,* who brandished with pride the former slur, embraced the political egalitarianism expressed by the butchers who sent to Jefferson the mammoth veal. This gift, they told the president, represented their happiness at having "lived to see the time, when we may, with sentiments of respect & Veneration, subscribe ourselves without giving Offense, Your fellow Citizens." Much had changed since 1789, when Abigail Adams informed her husband that heads turned when congressmen addressed the commander in chief as an equal. Washington "was no more their fellow citizen whilst he was President of the united states," she said, paraphrasing the remarks of an acquaintance, than the British king "was fellow Subject to his people."[33]

The mammoth cheese, perhaps more conspicuously than anything else, exemplified the connection between Jefferson's popularity and the new wave of democratic self-assertion. The people of Cheshire tendered to the president their "love," but they also reminded him that their affection remained contingent on his adherence to a program of limited government, religious freedom, and civil equality. "The trust is great," read the message that accompanied the cheese, and "the task is arduous." It invoked the "infinite Being who governs the Universe" in a prayer "that your life and health may long be preserved—that your usefulness may be still continued—that your Administration may be no less pleasant to yourself than it is grateful to us." John Leland and his congregation demanded that Jefferson transform the ideals of the "revolution of 1800," as the president later described his election, into political fact. The cheese itself signaled their insistence on tangible action. It proved their affection, they said, "not by words alone, but in *deed and in truth.*"[34]

The cheese, together with the veal, stood as more implicit affirmations of yet another truth. With these gifts the Cheshire Baptists and Philadelphia butchers assured themselves, and communicated to their president, that humble productions of honest toil possessed a dignity worthy of even the most exalted of republicans. On this point, they understood, Jefferson required no convincing. The senders of the veal, for example, noted their familiarity with his *Notes on the State of Virginia,* by then widely circulated, which asserted that the moral benefits of independent yeomanry made farmers "the chosen people of God."[35] Although other officials might have taken offense to candid qualifications of public support, to either bold or implicit assertions of an elected official's usefulness as an instrument of popular will, for Jefferson the expression of sentiments like these could only confirm a dearly held image of self. "I should be unfaithful to my own feelings," he confessed in 1800, "were I not to say that it has been the greatest of all human consolations to me to be considered by the republican portion of my fellow citizens, as the safe depository of their rights."[36]

While John Adams lived in vain luxury, according to the *Aurora,* and as president had even ordered china enameled with his name, Jefferson remained "the rock of republicanism, unmoved by the storm of aristocracy." On the day of his inauguration, newspaper audiences read reports of a congressional debate on appropriations for furnishing the new President's House. One Republican managed to trim a proposed budget by declaring that "Mr. Jefferson did not want to plunge himself into extravagance, he did not wish to waste the public money on articles which would require an extraordinary number of servants, barely to keep them clean." Margaret Bayard Smith later described his furnishings in the federal city as "worn and faded" hand-me-downs from previous administrations or new pieces "plain and simple to excess." Additional evidence of the president's disdain for pretension emerged during the course of his administration. He once greeted a British diplomat while attired in a threadbare waistcoat and well-worn slippers. At public receptions, he eliminated the courtly bow and replaced it with the handshake. He shunned the practice of Washington and Adams, who issued dinner invitations from

"The President of the United States," and instead called people to his house with messages bearing the simpler inscription "Th: Jefferson." Once guests arrived, he had them seated around tables "pell-mell"—at random—and not by rank, which was the precedent set by his predecessors. He understood the value of such symbolism. A French traveler once asked him why, when reviewing troops, he wore civilian attire and not a military uniform befitting a commander in chief? "To show," Jefferson answered, "that the civil is superior to the military power." While some Federalists expressed their abhorrence of his unassuming, egalitarian displays, complaining that he comported himself as a common citizen, many Republicans cheered them for the same reason.[37]

Reports of Jefferson's manners, as well as the portraits displaying his face and the songs, speeches, festivals, and published writings invoking his name, provided only a few impressions about how he conducted himself in private life, about the traits that people now describe as "personality." A biography received by subscribers to Helmbold's print, for example, focused on Jefferson's public contributions but remained silent on all but the most basic matters relating to his family and upbringing. As a result, the most powerful images of Jefferson linked him with abstractions such as liberty and republicanism. This failed to bother Jeffersonians for, despite the aspersions of Federalists, what mattered to them most, they said, were "*Principles* and not *Men*." In their minds, Jefferson existed as an ideal as much as an individual. He represented simple manners, freedom from the constraints of aristocracy and political oppression, and the belief that independent citizens mastered their own destinies. In other words, he represented them.[38]

JEFFERSON AGREED that he represented the people—and in a manner much more fulsome than his predecessors, who seem to have considered themselves entrusted by the people to exercise their own independent judgment, notwithstanding the popular will. Before Jefferson's presidency, few leaders on the national level embraced the notion that officeholders should seek out expressions of public opinion and be mindful of citizens' views. Some even felt troubled by grassroots expressions of political opinion. George Washington, for example, disdained the "self-created" Democratic-Republican societies of the 1790s. Others frowned on vehicles of dissent—as did John Adams, who, at a time of crisis, signed the Sedition Act to clamp down on the opposition press. Even Benjamin Rush, who came to align himself with Jeffersonian Republicans, in 1787 insisted that political power, while "derived *from* the

people," should not be imagined to be "seated *in* the people," who "possess
it only on the days of their elections. After this, it is the property of their
rulers."[39]

Jefferson possessed a different philosophy, one that went beyond even James
Madison's pragmatic acceptance of public opinion as a force too powerful to
ignore. Jefferson took pleasure in indications that citizens approved of his
measures, winced when confronted with hostility to his actions, and, through
his voracious consumption of news, frequently took the pulse of the public
mood. It probably goes too far to suggest (as Hamilton did, when in 1801 he
argued that Jefferson's desire for popularity would moderate his "fanaticism")
that he allowed his countrymen's views to guide his actions, but he found it
difficult to imagine that the mass of the people—unless "hoodwinked from
their principles" by the "artifices" of those with "foreign views"—would ever
stand against him.[40]

Jefferson's attentiveness to the press is suggested by the frequency with
which he complained about the Federalist prints. In 1807, for example, he
wrote that "nothing can now be believed which is seen in a newspaper," for
even "truth itself becomes suspicious by being put into that polluted vehicle."
In 1808, he claimed that "the papers have lately advanced in boldness and fla-
gitiousness beyond even themselves." A few months later he told Madison
that newspapers issued correct accounts only "now and then like the drop
of water on the tongue of Dives."[41] This, however, did not prevent him from
subscribing to no fewer than fifty-five different periodicals during the course
his presidency. From the *Political Observatory* of Walpole, New Hampshire,
to Savannah's *Public Intelligencer,* he paid out of pocket for a wide array of
newspapers, some Federalist but most of them Republican, from every region
of the United States.[42]

His relationship with these manifestations of American thought was far
from passive. Reinforcing the case that Jefferson considered expressions of
public opinion with care are his four bound volumes of newspaper clippings.
Once attributed to members of his family, these scrapbooks' provenance, together with physical and documentary evidence, make clear their status as
Jefferson's own composition (see the appendix for a full discussion of their
attribution to Jefferson). Containing articles cut from newspapers during the
years of his presidency, these scrapbooks reflect the broad range of his interests and include items as varied as poems, essays, songs, and satire. Each volume contains pieces relating to American politics and representing viewpoints

both laudatory and censorious of Jefferson's service as chief executive. In the first of the four volumes (as numbered by the University of Virginia Library, where they reside), clippings relating to political topics stand out as especially dominant.

Although these compendia of newspaper clippings lack a formal title (an in-law, after exploring his library in 1826, referred to them simply as "Mr. Jefferson's scrap books"[43]), it seems most precise to describe them as Jefferson's newspaper commonplace scrapbooks, for "commonplacing," sometimes recommended by eighteenth-century educators, entailed excerpting into a notebook literary passages thought worthy of further contemplation. "Reflect, and remark on, and digest what you read," advised James Maury, one of Jefferson's earliest teachers. This Jefferson did, copying passages from authors ranging from Catullus and Cicero to William Shakespeare and Laurence Sterne as he compiled, in the decade prior to his thirtieth birthday, the bulk of his literary commonplace book. While in this earlier work he transcribed excerpts, in the newspaper commonplace scrapbooks, as in his contemporaneous scissor-edit of the Gospels known as "The Philosophy of Jesus," he pasted clippings onto sheets of paper later bound together. While such collections, anthologies of the thoughts of others, at first glance might not seem particularly revealing, they nonetheless represent the conscious selection of a handful of texts from a myriad of options. As a result, Jefferson's newspaper commonplace scrapbooks—like his literary commonplace books and Gospel extracts—stand out not only as deeply personal but also as deeply revealing. Unlike Jefferson's letters and other original creations, which he crafted with others in mind, for these scrapbooks his only immediate audience was himself.[44]

The "hard treatment" that Jefferson said he received from his critics is well-documented in the scrapbooks, but what emerges from their pages most clearly is his almost obsessive attentiveness to "the indulgent opinions" of his "fellow citizens." Many items stroked Jefferson's ego, providing evidence of widespread (and widening) support for him and his administration. The fourth volume includes lyrics to songs such as "Jefferson and Liberty" and "The People's Friend." In the first volume, about seventy pages of clippings relate to the Fourth of July, which celebrated not only the nation's birthday but also, when commandeered by Jefferson's allies, the Declaration of Independence and its author. Citizens in Litchfield, Connecticut, according to one clipping, trumpeted the "anniversary of the day, ever dear to true Republicans, when the Congress of the United Colonies, in the face of hostile fleets and armies, in defiance of the uplifted instruments of despotic vengeance, dared to declare what the soul of Jefferson had inspired."[45] (Escaping Jefferson's scissors was an 1802 *Virginia Gazette* article lamenting how Republicans used America's charter "as a weapon in favor of the election of a man to the first office of our government."[46]) Toasts, including ones in the president's honor, constitute the bulk of the accolades. People lauded him as a national savior, praised him for his restrained imperviousness to calumny, and credited him for the rise of Republicanism throughout America. In Newport, Rhode Island, he was known as the "favorite of his country" who was "meriting its favor." Massachusetts admirers noted that "he soars above defamation; 'tis the croaking of Crows against the Bird of Jove." Residents of the Connecticut towns of Fairfield, Stratford, Weston, Newtown, and Trumbull gathered to extol "THOMAS JEFFERSON, the man of the people," who was "above revenge, [for] he knows no way of *destroying* his enemies, but by converting them into friends." Their counterparts in Westmoreland, New Hampshire, noted "his fair fame," which the "envenomed fang of envy cannot wound." Bostonians gushed that "high above his enemies, he stands like a tower, unshaken and undisturbed by the malignant tempests, which howl around its summit."[47]

Jefferson's scrapbooks open a window into the mind of a man whose thoughts sometimes seem anything but transparent. Through his careful clipping and compiling of the testimonials of Americans—especially their expressions of approval for his conduct, measures, and principles—he reassured himself that he retained their support. The "itch for popularity" that John Quincy Adams thought afflicted him—the "mean thirst for popularity" that the elder John Adams believed Jefferson could never quench—was no figment of his critics' imaginations. But neither was it a personality defect, a necessarily nefarious outgrowth of inner insecurities. Instead, Jefferson's ambition for approval reflected his desire to lead. He had little desire to force. Government, he understood, marshaled a legal monopoly on coercion, on the ability to prohibit or compel. Yet the use of this authority, frequently within his reach as president, only rarely attracted his grasp. Far better, he thought, to allow statements of principle and the power of example to invite assent. The clippings collected in his newspaper commonplace scrapbooks provided proofs of the success of this strategy. The affinity of his scissors for expressions of support from New England, the traditional Federalist stronghold, confirmed in his mind his status as a man presiding over an ever-expanding "union of sentiment."[48]

THE ORATORS who compared Jefferson to Jesus might also have likened him to Moses, who led the Jews from slavery to freedom, but Americans had much earlier bestowed that honor on George Washington. It was just as well. The Mosaic mantle more readily accommodated Washington's persona, which took shape amid the uncertainty of the American Revolution. A stern Old Testament figure, the prophet not only led his people to freedom but also climbed the slopes of Mount Sinai and returned with laws to govern their conduct.[49] Jefferson's image, however, derived much of its luster from new testimonials of liberation, celebrations of humility, and the recognition that attempts to enforce faith corrupted earthly regimes. He amounted to a different sort of hero for a different sort of era.

Whether by design or by nature—or by both—Jefferson exhibited an accessibility that Washington lacked. Although the first president had paid careful attention to style when he clothed himself for his levees, Jefferson eschewed what he described as the "rags of royalty." While the first president had traveled in a spectacular cream-colored coach pulled by four white horses and steered by a liveried servant, the third president jaunted around town on horseback like a common citizen. As British diplomat Edward Thornton observed in 1792, Washington affected "a very *kingly* style" in his journeys. "I am informed that his Secretaries are not admitted into his carriage but stand with their horse's bridles in their hands, till he is seated, and then mount and ride before his carriage." One Pennsylvania farmer reportedly mistook Washington for Prince Edward, son of George III. A revealing legend holds that not even Gouverneur Morris, acting on a bet, could clasp his hand on the shoulder of the patriarch of Mount Vernon without suffering a frozen stare. Jefferson, according to a different legend, could engage in pleasant conversation with workers on a dock. Although Federalists held birthday fetes in honor of the former Continental Army leader, the author of the Declaration of Independence insisted that the only birthday he wished to celebrate was the Fourth of July. Washington won fame as the father of his country; Jefferson earned a reputation as a friend of its people.[50]

Few dared oppose Washington in public. Praise for him, in fact, was so nearly universal, so hackneyed and formalized with official pomp, and so "wound up," as Jefferson said, in "the ceremonials of government to a pitch of staleness," that it became unthinking.[51] Praise for Jefferson, on the other hand, amounted to a highly controversial political statement. It possessed freshness and potency precisely because it signaled involvement in an uncertain struggle on which so much seemed to hinge.

CHAPTER SIX

Race, Sex, and Reputation

I F BY AUGUST 1802 the image of Thomas Jefferson had not been carved in stone, it at least had been molded in wax. The likeness of the third president stood alongside twenty-four other famous figures in a traveling wax museum in Georgetown.[1] Had this exhibit been situated to the south in Richmond, the statue of Jefferson might have toppled. An earthquake rocked the Virginia capital; its noise, according to one published report, resembled "the roaring of a chimney on fire, or the rolling of a carriage on the pavement."[2]

Less than a month later, the Richmond *Recorder* created shock waves of its own. Threatening a similar potential to damage the president's image, these rumblings came in the form of charges levied by the newspaper against Jefferson's character. Around the environs of Monticello, the paper asserted, "it is well known that the man, *whom it delighteth the people to honor,* keeps, and for many years past has kept, as his concubine, one of his own slaves. Her name is SALLY." In the 1780s, according to the account, Sally (her surname was Hemings) had lived in her master's Parisian household during his diplomatic mission to France and gave birth to their first child within nine months of their return to America. "The name of her eldest son is TOM. His features are said to bear a striking, although sable resemblance to those of the President himself." Jefferson's "wench" had borne him "several children"—a later and more definitive report set the number at five—and "not an individual in the neighborhood of Charlottesville" did not "believe the story."[3]

Written by James Thomson Callender, a Scottish émigré and one-time Republican whom Jefferson had recently passed over for a federal job, the accusation reverberated through the Federalist press. "We have heard the same subject spoken of in Virginia, and by Virginia gentlemen," claimed the *Gazette of the United States.*[4] The *Connecticut Courant* held that Callender's "convincing" charges "startle the most impudent" and demonstrate "the villainy of the leader of the Jacobins." In addition, they confirmed the Federalists' opinion that Jefferson "is in every respect unfit to be the head of any people not lost to decency or given over to reprobation."[5] Soon, condemnations of the president's alleged affair appeared in poetic verse:

> Of all the damsels on the green
> On mountain or in valley,
> A lass so luscious ne'er was seen
> As Monticellian Sally.
> *Chorus:* Yankee Doodle, whose the noodle?
> What wife were half so handy?
> To breed a flock of slaves to stock,
> A blackamoors the dandy.[6]

On the issue of his reputed relationship with Hemings, as on other personal matters brought forth by detractors, Jefferson remained silent before the public. Only a few weeks after Callender published the allegations, Jefferson decried his opponents, whose "bitterness increases with their desperation," for "trying slanders now which nothing could prompt but a gall which blinds their judgments as well as their consciences." Yet he resolved to "take no other revenge than by a steady pursuit of economy, and peace, and by the establishment of republican principles in substance and in form, to sink federalism into an abyss from which there shall be no resurrection."[7]

Jefferson's strategy succeeded. His refusal to respond to the charges helped ensure that, like the Richmond earthquake, rumblings generated by the rumors neither lasted long nor caused much damage. By the end of 1802, after citizens bestowed on their president an overwhelming vote of confidence during midterm congressional elections by bolstering Republican majorities in both the House and the Senate, the Federalist outpouring of attacks on Jefferson's supposed amour had slowed to a trickle.[8] Little was said about Hemings, for example, in the months before the Republican's 1804 landslide reelection, and only infrequently during the remainder of Jefferson's lifetime did references to the alleged affair appear in print. By 1810, John Adams would characterize the rumors as "long forgotten anecdotes" best consigned to obscurity.[9]

Callender, as many historians now believe, was probably correct to claim that Jefferson and Sally Hemings engaged in a long-term relationship that yielded several children.[10] Yet Callender made clumsy use of race and sex as political issues. He indicted Jefferson for undermining the hegemony of white Americans, but he also overestimated his own credibility and misunderstood anxieties over miscegenation. In addition, he failed to perceive that some of his contemporaries would resist blurring the distinction between accusations of personal misdeeds and verified acts of official misconduct. As a result, the story that he hoped would serve as a funeral dirge for the president's political career merely produced a sour note. Even after widespread circulation of the Hemings allegations, Jefferson's image remained largely unscathed.

AS INTRODUCED by Callender and proffered by many Federalist prints, the Jefferson-Hemings story exploited racial anxieties, particularly fears of miscegenation. If the tale were true, the widower president would be a fornicator (if Hemings was willing) or a rapist (if she was not). His extramarital affair might have marred the morals of his white and black children, grandchildren, and other relatives, many of whom resided on Jefferson's mountaintop within earshot of his purportedly tempestuous bed. Finally, he would be guilty of fathering children out of wedlock. The Callender charges, however, did not address these crimes.[11] Instead, Jefferson stood accused of lusting after and loving a black woman and then impregnating her with children whose existence undermined rigid conceptions of race.

Lest anyone forget the heritage of the president's slave and supposed mistress, press pieces variously referred to her as an "African Venus" and a "black Venus," as "Dusky Sally," "Black Sal," "Sooty Sal," "a sooty daughter of Africa," "the copper coloured Sally," and the "mahogany colored charmer" who headed Jefferson's "Congo harem." In the *Boston Gazette* appeared a mock madrigal from Jefferson to his mistress. Here, as elsewhere, pigment preoccupied the author's attention:

> In glaring red, and chalky white,
>   Let others beauty see;
> Me no such tawdry tints delight—
>   No! *black's* the hue for me!
>
> Thick pouting lips! how sweet their grace!
>   When passion fires to kiss them!
> Wide spreading over half the face,
>   Impossible to miss them.
>
> Oh! Sally! hearken to my vows!
>   Yield up thy sooty charms—

My best belov'd! my more than spouse,
  Oh! take me to thy arms![12]

Similarly, articles reminded readers that the interracial union produced "a yellow son" and nearly half a dozen "mulatto children"—that Jefferson chose "an African stock where upon he was to graft his own descendants."[13]

The notoriously lascivious behavior of American slaveholders lent credence to Callender's charges. John Adams in 1810 repeated the claim of one southern woman that not a single Virginia planter "could not reckon among his slaves a number of his own children." Mary Boykin Chesnut later observed that husbands lived in the same house "with their wives and their concubines, and the mulattoes one sees in every family exactly resemble the white children." To live surrounded by slave women, she complained, is to "live surrounded by prostitutes." If unkind toward sexual chattel, Chesnut's description of the commerce between male masters and their female property possessed an element of truth. Slaveholders oftentimes purchased the compliance of slave women with small tokens of affection, such as jewelry and clothing, or offered them freedom from the lash. Less frequently, romantic attraction spurred white-black encounters; sometimes interracial plantation trysts were violent, coerced affairs. "A poor slave's wife can never be true to her husband contrary to the will of her master," former bondsman Henry Bibb explained in 1849. "She dare not refuse to be reduced to a state of adultery at the will of her master."[14]

Whatever the modes of suasion, white planters frequently brought slaves into their bedchambers. Noting that southern family trees oftentimes possessed both free and enslaved branches, Kentucky emancipationist David Rice claimed in 1792 that "men will humble their own sisters, or even their aunts, to gratify their lust." As a result, "fathers... have their own children for slaves, and leave them as an inheritance to their own [white] children." It was a "mathematical certainty," he held, "that if things go on in the present channel, the future inhabitants of America will inevitably be Mulattoes." At Monticello, twisted lineages reinforced Rice's remarks.[15]

Even before Jefferson's probable relationship with Hemings, race-mixing had affected his plantation family. Hemings and her enslaved siblings were noticeably light-skinned, and quite possibly they shared the same father as Jefferson's wife, who had died in 1782. If so, the president's inheritance from John Wayles, his father-in-law, included not only considerable wealth in land and slaves but also a biracial family.[16] Hemings and her siblings, then, were his own wife's half-brothers and half-sisters. No wonder he contended that miscegenation "has been observed by every one."[17]

Through his writings, Jefferson stood as a lifelong opponent of the inter-mingling of black and white blood. He recoiled at the notion of miscegena-tion in his *Notes on the State of Virginia,* for example, written only a few years before his intimacy with Hemings seems to have commenced. Suspicious that blacks were "inferior" to whites "in the endowments both of body and mind," he maintained that slaves, when emancipated, should be "removed beyond the reach of mixture" and colonized beyond the borders of the United States. He never revised these statements. Just months before his death in 1826, in fact, he informed William Short, who had served as his secretary in France, where his relationship with Hemings had reportedly begun, that America's slaves should be freed and then expatriated. This, he told Short, would prevent miscegenation, to which he claimed he had always possessed a "great aver-sion." Short would have been in a position to know—or at least think that he knew—whether the allegations concerning Hemings had been true. Should Jefferson's statement be taken at face value? Should it be seen as an attempt to convince Short that there had been no Hemings affair? Or was it a wink and nod to an intimate friend that amounted to an effort to plant for the eyes of posterity exculpatory evidence? Whatever the case—and whatever Jefferson's actual thoughts about interracial relationships—he understood that his ex-pressed opinion reflected prevailing sentiments.[18]

Racism, of course, was endemic throughout the United States even though slavery made many Americans uneasy. In the northern states especially, anti-slavery sentiment surged in the years following the Declaration of Indepen-dence. Pennsylvania passed a gradual emancipation bill in 1779. The territory of Vermont had banned involuntary servitude two years earlier in its bill of rights. Before the end of the 1780s, legislators ensured that slavery's days were numbered in Connecticut and Rhode Island, and judicial decisions in Mas-sachusetts and New Hampshire had abolished chattel servitude altogether. Support for emancipation, however, did not equal approval of miscegena-tion. Massachusetts governor and Jefferson ally James Sullivan, for example, proposed education and gradual emancipation for enslaved Americans. As he admitted in 1795, "there is an objection to this, which embraces all my feelings; that is, that it will tend to a mixture of blood, which I now abhor." With only a fraction of the number of African Americans as in the South, however, fears of race-mixing were much less acute in the northern states. "It is not to be doubted," Jonathan Edwards had written, "that the Negroes in these northern states also will, in time, mix with the common mass of the people. But we have this consolation, that they are so small a portion of the inhabitants, when mixed with the rest, they will not produce any very sensible diversity of colour."[19]

In the North, where people felt less anxious about blurring the color line, newspapers opted to capitalize on the scandal as an opportunity for mirth. Writers penned glib pieces that portrayed the president as a lusty philosopher-scientist, examining Hemings in an attempt to more fully discern the amorous capabilities of her race. After first mentioning the supposed Hemings romance and then describing Jefferson's low opinion of African Americans and of the mixing of black and white blood, Maryland's *Frederick-Town Herald* announced that "much matter of entertainment may now be connected." Perhaps, the paper speculated, the president's relationship with Hemings "has been merely a course of practical experiments, by the result of which Mr. Jefferson was afterwards moved to alter his first opinions." Callender's accusation gave northern Federalists yet another angle from which to portray the president as a hypocrite on issues of race. Even before his charges saw print, at least one editor had wondered aloud whether a statesman who relied for sustenance on "half-naked, ill-cared for slaves" could truly be "a mighty democrat—a warm stickler for the *rights* of man."[20]

Northerners may have joked about the rumors, but in the South interracial unions were seen as no laughing matter. In the first years of the nineteenth century, slave rebellions caused citizens to fear for their lives. Only months before the Callender story surfaced, five slaves swung from the gallows at Halifax, Virginia, sentenced to die for conspiring to revolt. In a nearby North Carolina town a similar scene took place a month later. Poorly organized and out-gunned by their white neighbors, participants in these uprisings never stood much chance of success. Many whites, however, assumed that the plots revealed only the tip of the iceberg and reeled in horror at the prospect of black revolution. Racist to the core and easily persuaded by conspiracy theories, Callender shared his fellow Virginians' sensibilities. It may be no coincidence that he chose to circulate rumors of Jefferson's reputed interracial relationship in September, when the Old Dominion marked the second anniversary of another set of executions. These had put to death twenty-seven perpetrators of Gabriel's Rebellion, an aborted revolt that involved blacks from no fewer than ten counties and came closer to toppling the Virginia slave system than any such uprising before or since.[21]

Slave insurrections made white southerners anxious, not only about the

138   CONFOUNDING FATHER

maintenance of their monopoly on power but also about the purity of their race. Many presumed that if African Americans craved whites' freedom, then they also craved white mates. The popular southern mentality held that those who engaged in interracial sex would also seek out other forms of intercourse. The dilution of white blood would compromise the existing political order; it would result in confusion, chaos, and eventually the diminution of white liberty.[22] This understood, the meaning of Callender's charges becomes clear. If Jefferson retired to his private chambers with Hemings, he did more than transgress the color line. He violated the promise of an all-white and entirely free America.

YET CALLENDER'S VOLLEY of opprobrium missed its mark. In October, at the same time that reports of "dusky Sally" filled Federalists papers, John Quincy Adams decried the president's "democratic popularity" and lamented that "the strength of the present administration is continually increasing."[23] Callender's efforts to impugn the president floundered both above and below the Mason-Dixon line, among Federalists and Republicans alike. His reputation as an erratic, spitfire polemicist curtailed his effectiveness with northerners, many of whom not only smirked at the journalist's depiction of Jefferson but also had difficulty regarding with seriousness anything that came from his pen. Federalist printers who wished to maintain their credibility could not embrace his account without equivocation. Not surprisingly, southerners also approached Callender's allegation with skepticism, for the behavior of the president, who stood accused of endangering white supremacy, confirmed that he did nothing to place it in jeopardy.

No matter how "convincing" printers of the *Connecticut Courant* claimed to find Callender's tale, the Richmond journalist had a reputation for scandal-mongering, and his record as a partisan hatchet man could have done little to persuade readers of his accusation's veracity. Under threat of arrest by British authorities for seditious libel, Callender had fled to America in 1793, where he soon took up his pen in opposition to what he viewed as Federalist corruption. He authored anti-Federalist pamphlets, wrote prolifically for Republican prints, and earned the scorn of prominent Hamiltonians such as Theodore Sedgwick, Samuel Dexter, Harrison Otis, Robert Goodloe Harper, and fellow newspaperman John Fenno, who described him in 1798 as a "wretch" entitled "to the benefit of the gallows." Stung by Callender's criticisms, voluminous and venomous, his enemies struck back. Judge Samuel Chase, an ardent

Federalist, fined and imprisoned him in 1800 for violation of the Adams administration's sedition law.[24]

For the president's opponents, to accept the Sally Hemings story as true meant endorsing the reliability of its source. Normally, the anti-Jefferson press gave scant scrutiny to charges that demeaned the chief executive; instead, it propagated them with haste. As Jefferson noted a few months prior to the appearance of Callender's accusations, Federalist editors habitually filled "their papers with falsehoods, calumnies & audacities."[25] But Callender's account raised problems for the president's detractors. For years, Federalists had smeared Callender's reputation and attacked his integrity. Now that he had switched sides in the political struggle, how could they best make use of his claims against Jefferson and still save face?

By the time the *Recorder* went to press with its report on misconduct at Monticello—complete with a James T. Callender byline—newspapers of the Federalist persuasion had already reprinted several installments of a *New-York Evening Post* series entitled "Jefferson & Callender." Damning the president for his contributions of money and advice to the polemicist, the series sought to cast doubt on Jefferson's patriotism by calling attention to claims made by Callender in his latest manifesto, *The Prospect before Us.*

The pamphlet, which Jefferson was said to have reviewed in its pre-publication form, contained "an open attack on the Federal constitution, and unqualified abuse of Gen. Washington, and of his [successor in] the Presidency, Mr. Adams, besides slander on other eminent and virtuous Federal characters." Quoting from the *Prospect,* the *Evening Post* spotlighted Callender's contention that the Constitution was shoved "down the gullet of *America,*" his belief that every "Virginian who values his freedom ... should perfect himself in the use of the musket" in preparation for battle with the federal army, and his disdain for the "Monarchs of Braintree and Mount Vernon." The *Columbian Centinel* printed a letter that called Callender's polemic an "*infamous* and *disgusting* publication." A few issues later the *Centinel*'s publisher quoted from Jefferson's correspondence with the Scotsman: "I thank you for the proof sheets you inclosed me, such papers cannot fail to produce the best effect." The Federalists scored points against Jefferson, to be sure, but they also savaged the reputation of the man who had now turned against him.[26]

Even if Federalists had not previously linked Callender with Jefferson, the journalist's decision to reveal himself as the author of the attack would have cast doubt on his credibility. Most penman of contentious tracts continued to sign them not with their own names but with pseudonyms; the substance of what they reported, they thought, possessed a self-evidence that required no readily identifiable author to substantiate their claims. There was nothing self-evident about Callender's depiction of Jefferson's interracial relationship unless, of course, Hemings's light-skinned children—whom few had actually seen—could count. In addition, the deeply engrained notion, common among consumers of early American print culture, that writers who took credit for their essays sought some sort of personal advantage, could not have helped Callender, who had every reason to bear a grudge against Jefferson. Thus the plausibility of the tale relied on the credibility of a man who behaved beyond the norms of the time and had much to gain—but little to lose—by telling a lie. "I believe nothing that Callender said, any more than if it had been said by an infernal spirit," John Adams wrote in 1810. "I would not convict a dog of killing a sheep upon the testimony of two such witnesses."[27]

Doubting Callender's credibility yet unwilling to ignore his assault on the president, Federalist newsmen seized on their one remaining alternative. They reprinted or repeated what Callender had written, sowing the seeds of scandal but at the same time saving face by reminding readers of his supposed penchant for fabrication. One *Gazette of the United States* writer, for example, reiterated the Hemings story but then piously maintained that "as we possess no positive vouchers for the truth of the narrative, we do not choose to admit it into the Gazette while there remains a possibility of its being a calumny." The *Connecticut Courant,* before reprinting the *Recorder*'s account, reported to readers that "J. T. Callender, who wrote and laboured to overthrow the administrations of Washington and Adams, has turned his artillery against Mr. Jefferson." The Federalist papers' duplicity regarding the contentious polemicist did not escape notice. As a delegate from Worcester noted several years later on the floor of the Massachusetts House of Representatives, "in one breath they call Callender the greatest liar that ever existed, and in the next produce him as their witness."[28]

The president's opponents circulated the allegations but failed to expand on them. Literary journals printed a few poetic and oftentimes satirical variations on the Hemings theme. So did some newspapers. The *Frederick-Town Herald,* for example, referred to Jefferson's remark in his *Notes on the State of Virginia* that primates preferred African women over their own species as prospective mates, and then sarcastically inquired if the president "might be making himself to be an Oranootan."[29] No amount of merriment, however, could make for more news. Callender ran out of rumors to repeat, and most Republican journals refused to respond to his charges. Federalists seized on the few replies to the Hemings story as opportunities to prolong the public's exposure to the issue. When one Jeffersonian penman angrily denounced Callender's "damnable lie" and warned that indignant citizens might reward the "outcast" with bodily harm, the *Recorder* reprinted the tirade in full. Anti-administration prints, in fact, tried to bait Jefferson's supporters. If the allegation against the commander in chief's character "is not true it will doubtless be contradicted by proper authority," averred one writer. Another pointed toward the "silent confession of the democratic prints." Callender himself goaded his former allies. "If the friends of Mr. Jefferson are convinced of his innocence, they will make an appeal of the same sort," he contended. "The allegation is of a nature too black to be suffered to remain in suspense." Yet only a few of the president's allies hazarded rebuttals.[30]

In the South, Republican reticence served not only to quiet the rumors but also to salve any anxieties that Callender's report provoked among the slaveholding elite. Although people who paid attention to the partisan press understood that he would go to great lengths—and perhaps even lie—to diminish his enemies in the eyes of the public, a good number of slaveholders, themselves experienced in interracial intimacies, must have found the idea of Jefferson acting in the same manner far from inconceivable. Any whites who questioned the president's chastity, however, could not have doubted his grace under pressure. He reacted to Callender's charges in full accordance with the standards of southern honor.

Ethics below the Mason-Dixon Line tolerated race-mixing under certain circumstances but rejected it in others. Whites found guilty of fornicating with free blacks often faced severe retribution. The child of a white man and a free black woman was, according to legal practices and social presumptions, a free black person—and, as many citizens thought, a likely recruit for dangerous revolutionaries such as Gabriel. Thus Callender printed one article in the series about "Sally, and President Tom" under the headline "Free Negroes." He failed to recognize, however, that planters could philander with slaves without fear of serious consequences because the child of a slave and her master was still only a slave. In the context of the antebellum South, this double standard made sense. So long as southerners abided by a certain set of unwritten rules, their actions did not imperil the balance of racial power.[31] If a tryst came under scrutiny, the only acceptable response was stoic and silent denial. In addition, the master had to be seen as sober and responsible. The enslaved woman had to be viewed as light-skinned and attractive.[32]

Callender and his journalist allies ineffectually accused the president of breaking this code of conduct. They laced with sarcasm their descriptions of Hemings, the "African Venus" and "copper coloured charmer" who supposedly caused Jefferson to abandon the anti-miscegenation arguments spelled out in his *Notes on the State of Virginia* and "to have laid aside all his fear about the 'beauty' of our race, suffering by a 'mixture' with the other." In addition, Callender claimed, Jefferson's "yellow son" did not know his place, for this "young MULATTO PRESIDENT" had begun "to give himself a great number of airs of importance in Charlottesville, and the neighborhood."[33]

Such reports smacked of satire. They could hardly rebut the testimony of Jefferson's own actions or cast doubt on the understanding that his behavior fully complied with the standards of his native South. If Jefferson lifted Hemings onto his bed, he did nothing to elevate her within society. Accused of miscegenation, the polymath master of Monticello could not be accused of indolence. His silence appeared to reflect a cool-headed disregard for the charges and indicated that he maintained firm control over his passions, his slaves, and himself.

Anxieties over intermixture in this era of black rebellion neither resulted from nor responded to the situation at Monticello. Since children born into slavery posed much less of a threat than free children produced by relationships between whites and free African Americans, even proven affairs between well-born men and their black paramours did little to damage planters' reputations. Master-slave adultery, in and of itself, was seldom grounds for divorce, and while white wives bemoaned the practice of plantation miscegenation, their husbands turned deaf ears.[34] Callender may have observed apprehensions over black uprisings, but he was blind to the subtleties of the southern psyche.

Callender blustered about the broad circulation of his "few entertaining facts" and their provocation of "copious commentaries" in the nation's journals, "the collected labour of a thousand intellects."[35] But those who supported the president stuck by him. Those who opposed Jefferson—by 1802 a diminished and dwindling number of individuals—continued to fight in vain against his burgeoning popularity. General satisfaction with his policies and programs accounts for much of this phenomenon, but so does Jefferson's refusal to fall into the trap that Callender laid before him. Because the president kept quiet his reactions to allegations concerning his behavior, the saga of "sooty Sal" remained a topic of suspect hearsay, ribald rumor, and, if true, a private affair of scant political consequence.

WHILE AN UNEVEN grasp of southern racial anxiety caused Callender to miss his target, his imperfect understanding of what Americans demanded from officeholders blunted his attack. Revelations of unseemly personal deeds among men in prominent posts titillated newspaper readers, but citizens of the early republic cared more that their leaders faithfully executed official duties. This fact Callender should have comprehended, for a recent controversy in which he had involved himself strongly suggested that revelations of private sins mattered less than public crimes.

Five years prior to the publication of the Hemings story and before the journalist had turned his back on the Republican cause, Callender printed rumors that Alexander Hamilton had abused his office, become involved with a reprobate character named James Reynolds, and joined him in a shady scheme involving the misuse of government funds. Hamilton, in turn, issued a printed response designed to show that he had violated his own marital vows but not the public's trust.

"The charge against me," Hamilton recounted in this infamous pamphlet, "is a connection with one James Reynolds for purposes of improper pecuniary speculation. My real crime is an amorous connection with his wife." In 1791, he confessed, while serving in Philadelphia as secretary of the treasury and during a period when his wife and children spent the summer in their native New York, he had "frequent meetings" with Maria Reynolds. Their first encounter took place in her bedroom; most subsequent rendezvous occurred at his own place of residence. "The intercourse with Mrs. Reynolds . . . continued," Hamilton admitted, even after it became apparent that her husband knew of their affair and would use it to blackmail him. James Reynolds initially sought compensation through appointment to office. But Hamilton, although thoroughly seduced by Maria's artful affections and "tender" love letters, could not bring himself to place "private gratification" above "the public interest." Instead of a job on the government payroll, he offered Reynolds one thousand dollars of his own money. This payment preceded a string of loans and contributions that for a few months bought Maria's services and her husband's silence.[36]

Hamilton's apologia admitted improprieties with Reynolds's wife but not with Reynolds himself. Contrary to the "vile" accusation of Callender, Hamilton countered, government funds had never entered into the sordid triangle of lust, seduction, and extortion. It was a personal affair of passion, not an official act of treachery.[37]

But it was also the wellspring of a rumor that placed Hamilton in a no-win situation. To ignore Callender's charge, the New Yorker thought, would leave allegations of official misdeeds unanswered. To hazard an honest response, however, would expose private infidelities by entering them into the public record. "Even at so great an expense," Hamilton wrote in his pamphlet, the "disagreeable embarrassments" that would surely result from his choice of the latter option seemed preferable because it promised to "wipe away a more serious stain."[38]

Hamilton's decision illuminates a salient fact that cannot be overlooked. In the early republic, marital malpractice was considered a crime far less serious than public wrongdoing. The political culture of the day accepted that officeholders might commit errors in their private lives; only in official capacities could mistakes justify widespread scorn and condemnation. Unsavory personal endeavors brought about ridicule to be sure. Republican papers merrily recounted Hamilton's extramarital relationship for more than a year. But even after public revelation of the Reynolds affair, he remained a viable and powerful public figure, humiliated personally but vindicated politically. His ability to act as a proper husband had little to do with his ability to husband a nation.[39]

The idea that private immorality did not constitute grounds for dismissal from office was nothing new. British statesmen Francis Hutcheson and Benjamin Hoadley had argued earlier in the eighteenth century that leaders' personal vices should not diminish their public authority. In America, Benjamin Franklin and George Washington survived accusations of improper sexual conduct. During a Pennsylvania Assembly election in 1764, Franklin stood accused of cavorting with his maid; during the Revolution, loyalists charged Washington with keeping a battlefield mistress. Franklin lost the election for numerous reasons, but, as was the case for Washington, allegations of immorality did not ruin his reputation.[40] Such was the same for Jefferson, who Callender alleged not only lusted after Hemings but also pursued the affections of a married white woman. While the accuracy of the first accusation is probable, the truthfulness of the second seems indisputable.

In 1768, a bachelor Jefferson had unsuccessfully sought the sexual charms of Betsey Walker, the wife of his friend and neighbor John Walker. By the 1790s, after politics drove a wedge between the two men, rumors of the attempted affair began to circulate. In 1802, they became public when Callender aired them shortly after he made his allegations concerning Hemings. Even before the journalist put details of the Walker involvement in print, others in the press alluded to Jefferson's clumsy venture into extramarital intrigue. In

September, a writer for the *Columbian Centinel* made note of Callender's tale of miscegenation at Monticello, but then added that there existed "a story, *the truth of which WE DO KNOW*, of a much more criminal and flagitious trans-action than the one of which the President is accused." Jefferson had once attempted adultery, the writer implied. After the discovery of this deceit, he had been "forced out" of the woman's house "with an insulted husband's foot at his crapper." A subsequent account of Betsey Walker's rebuff held that she herself had repulsed the would-be suitor, and not with a kick but with a pair of scissors.[41]

It made sense for contemporaries to brand Jefferson's youthful pursuit of his friend's wife "more criminal and flagitious" than his alleged relationship with an "African Venus." Betsey Walker belonged to another man, according to the ethic of the time, but "Black Sal" belonged to Jefferson. In attempting to seduce Walker, Jefferson endangered the sanctity of her legally recognized marriage. In addition, his behavior cast aside his own honor-bound friendship with her husband, with whom he shared memories of their years together as schoolboys and to whom he had pledged protection for Betsey, in 1768, when John Walker departed for distant Fort Stanwix to help negotiate a treaty with the Iroquois.[42] In the case of Hemings, however, given the de-humanizing views held of African Americans, to make her his mistress could be no less egregious than to indulge in a peculiar form of self-gratification. An affair with Hemings would be an unsavory but purely personal act.[43] Jeffer-son's attempted seduction of Betsey Walker revealed a more serious flaw in his character because it signified a disregard for fraternal loyalty and the rights of his peers.

Not surprisingly, Callender's charge regarding the Walker incident rever-berated more strongly than the Hemings story, and it more successfully goaded responses both from Jefferson's followers and from Jefferson himself. Early in 1805, the *New-England Palladium* repeated the Walker story in considerable detail and then made cursory reference to the "sable damsel" to whom Jeffer-son supposedly turned after receiving his friend's wife's rebuke. One of the newspaper's writers later noted the relative unimportance of the Hemings charge, explaining that "the person in question was a domestic, a part of his property." When Republicans in the Massachusetts House of Representatives advanced a resolution calling for their state to break a printing contract with the *Palladium*'s owners, they virtually ignored Hemings and, like the newspa-per, focused their attention on the publication of the Walker incident. They insisted that the sheet stepped out of bounds because it impugned an official

for an act of no public importance. Significantly, an opponent of the measure argued along similar lines. "Why," he asked, "should the House trouble
itself as to the [newspaper's] offence . . . against the *private* character of Mr.
Jefferson?" The charge against the president—acting improperly outside of
his official capacity and long before his term in office began—had no relevance to the public. As one Massachusetts legislator predicted, "whether the
resolution" against the *Palladium* "was approved, or negatived," the allegation
"would not hurt Mr. Jefferson's reputation."[44]

Jefferson was not so sure, although his response reveals concern over what
his peers, and not the public, would think. He did not concede, as John
Walker contended, that he had sustained the pursuit of his neighbor through
1779, seven years after he had married Martha Wayles Skelton. But in 1805,
to a small group of friends, he did "plead guilty to one of their charges, that
when young and single I offered love to a handsome lady. I acknolege its incorrectness." Already he had admitted as much to John Walker, seeking to make
amends for his mistake.[45]

Jefferson confessed to this impropriety through personal letters in which
he assumed the posture of a private citizen. Had he not been elected to the
presidency, the matter might not have been circulated so widely, but he likely
would have repented his misdeed nonetheless. Yet Hamilton thought that
Callender's maligning of his public behavior required a more open response.
He knew that such a reaction was bad form: "I owe perhaps to my friends
an apology for condescending to give a public explanation," he wrote in his
1797 confession of the Maria Reynolds affair. Still, he could not bring himself merely to answer accusations of bureaucratic malfeasance with "uniform
evidence of an upright character," precisely because extramarital excursions
possessed less potential for political damnation than public infidelities.[46]

A claim that Jefferson misused his presidential influence in order to suppress damaging testimony about his sexual past constituted the final, notable
aftershock of Callender's accusations. In 1806, the Republican-controlled
Connecticut circuit court indicted Reverend Azel Backus for seditious libel,
alleging that he had called Jefferson "a liar, whoremaster, debaucher, drunk-
ard, gambler, and infidel" who procured from his slaves "a wench as his whore."
The preacher subpoenaed a number of Virginians, including James Madison,
Henry Lee, and John Walker, apparently to bear witness that earlier in the
president's life he had, in fact, invited affection from Walker's wife. Not one
of these men wished to put this incident on the public record, and not one

made the long journey north to testify. Jefferson circulated word among this group of individuals that none of them could be compelled to answer the subpoenas since all lived outside of the court's jurisdiction. Through a friend in Connecticut, he also communicated to the court that "if the tenor of my life did not support my character, the verdict of a jury would hardly do it." Because, he claimed, of his sympathies for the feelings of the Walker family, he hoped for the case to be dropped. After some delay, the court acceded to his request. Although papers publicized the clergyman's alleged remarks, not a single direct reference to Hemings appeared in print during the episode. Even the *Connecticut Courant,* which a few years earlier had eagerly propagated Callender's rumor, now described Backus's charges against Jefferson as "unfounded."[47]

One Federalist pamphleteer calling himself "Hampden" learned of the president's involvement in the case's dismissal, however, and he argued that "the only opportunity that ever did, *or ever will occur,* of proving before a court and jury the *chaste* attempts of Mr. Jefferson upon the wife of his friend" had been "superseded *by Mr. Jefferson himself!*" He reminded the president that his oath of office bound him "to take care that the law be faithfully executed" and charged him with obstruction of justice. These serious allegations consumed the bulk of the broadside, and apparently the author saw neither a need nor felt an inclination to comment on the substance of Backus's remarks about Jefferson's "whore." Hampden's charges, although damning, appear to have gained no traction in the Federalist press. If Jefferson learned of them, he apparently saw neither a need nor felt an inclination to respond.[48]

It would be a mistake, however, to conclude that personal behavior counted for nothing. Jefferson, for example, believed that private virtue revealed a capacity for personal self-government, *especially* when no possibility existed for the public airing of misdeeds. "Whenever you are to do a thing, tho' it can only be known to yourself," he lectured his nephew Peter Carr in 1785, "ask yourself how you would act if all the world were looking at you and act accordingly." But sometimes fantasies of exposure proved insufficient to regulate conduct (as Jefferson knew from experience), a task that pious-sounding but opportunistic writers could gleefully claim to perform. The few Republican editors who responded to Callender's accusations against Jefferson, for example, lashed back by claiming that the journalist hired a black prostitute while in prison; one of them, suspecting that John Marshall provided the Sally Hemings story to Callender, hinted that the chief justice himself was "not invulnerable" to charges of miscegenation. They fought fire with fire, issuing personal attacks as a tactic that, among those who considered themselves gentlemen, sufficed when more abstract and principled (although usually no less heated) exchanges broke down.[49]

In most cases, however, public disagreements did not disrupt pretensions of amicability between opponents. After Massachusetts Congressman Thomas Dwight attended a reception for legislators at the Executive Mansion in 1803, he reminded his wife that "this is customary for all of our political sentiments excepting those only who have been or conceive themselves to be personally ill used." Then, in a quip that underscored the levity with which Jefferson's opponents regarded tales of Hemings, he reported, "If black Sal was in the house, she certainly did not appear in the drawing room or audience hall."[50]

Like others, Jefferson recognized the importance of the boundary between the public and the private. He treasured the small amount of privacy that a life in government service allowed, and he worked to maintain it. His autobiography, for example, reveals little about his personal history; so much did he identify his public work with what should interest posterity that, when his narrative reached his 1779 election as Virginia's governor, he claimed that "to write my own history during the two years of my administration, would be to write the public history of that portion of the revolution within this State. This has been done by others," and so he would not do it again. He allowed for the distinctness of the public and private even in the characters of his enemies. He described Hamilton as "disinterested, honest, and honorable in all private transactions . . . yet so bewitched & perverted by the British example, as to be under thoro' conviction that corruption was essential to the government of a nation." But, like the legislators who snubbed invitations to Jefferson's house because they believed themselves "personally ill used," he cut off—or at least minimized contact with—people who assailed him on personal matters. According to one congressman, Jefferson once attended a religious service given by a "parson Laury." Laury made his text the second epistle of Peter, which describes "false prophets among the people" who "bring in damnable heresies" and have "eyes full of adultery, and that cannot cease from sin." Laury so offended Jefferson, who apparently took this as an allusion to his religious and political beliefs, as well as a swipe at his interactions with Walker, Hemings, or both, that he "never spoke to him after." Even Callender recognized the difference between inner and outer worlds. Although he calculated that the Sally Hemings story would damage Jefferson's reputation, he admitted that the "world has no business" with the private element "of a public character, unless . . . it shall be connected with some interesting political truth."[51]

But some, like Callender, thought that Jefferson's private life revealed much about his public behavior. If Massachusetts assemblymen believed that the Walker and Hemings stories had little to do with his capacity to govern, others said that "the preservation of our Republican Constitutions, and the impartial and faithful administration of laws enacted in conformity to them, depend alone on the knowledge which the people may have of the *conduct, integrity and talents* of those . . . called to offices of trust and honour." Another writer held that a polity would go to ruin "if a sentiment should prevail, that public virtue and private vice are compatible qualities in the same character, [and] that licentiousness and profligacy are no objections in candidates for public office."[52]

The debate about the relative importance of private and public character, although sometimes tinged with political opportunism, reflected matters of principle. Since the earliest days of the imperial crisis, Americans had been grappling with the issue of how best to define sovereignty. Did it reside in the sovereign, a man or woman who served as the head of the body politic? Did it rest in the presumably able hands of an elite presumed to possess superior wisdom and virtue? Or did it reside with the people generally, whose wisdom enabled them to select as officeholders protectors of their rights and, on matters of public concern, representatives of their beliefs? Since the 1790s, Jefferson's faction had argued most forcefully for the latter option. What mattered most were principles and not men.[53] As the Hemings scandal's limited influence on Jefferson's reputation suggests, it was this philosophy that at the dawn of the nineteenth century seemed ascendant.

In the early republic's hierarchy of shame, abuse of office preceded violation of wedding vows. What Callender accused Hamilton of doing with the public purse had more gravity than what he accused Jefferson of attempting with a friend's wife. The president's rumored relationship with Sally Hemings weighed in last. Private in nature and, according to some, beyond the purview of polite attention, it occurred between two unmarried individuals with no preexisting attachments. This, however, for many people probably seemed a supercilious line of thought, for never in the public discussion did anyone really acknowledge Hemings's status as an individual human being. According to the prevailing logic, if Jefferson had slept with a slave, a member of a class of people systematically dehumanized as personal property, his actions affected him more than anyone else.

IF, AS SEEMS PROBABLE, Jefferson and Hemings had a long-term sexual relationship that resulted in the birth of Hemings's children, then Jefferson's actions affected many at Monticello, both black and white.[54] Only after Callender's exposure of the hidden elements of his domestic life, however, did Jefferson's actions pose a palpable threat to his public agenda. Out of all the factors that worked together to minimize the damage Callender hoped to inflict, Jefferson's silence seems most essential, but inaction was not the president's only response. Despite his supporters' insistence that an officeholder's public measures mattered and his personal life did not, Jefferson took no chances. Visiting Monticello when the story broke, he soon returned to Washington with his head held high. The presence of daughters Martha and Maria, who joined him a few weeks later, tamped down any gossip about a familial rift and acted as an implicit refutation that he was anything but the most chaste widower and conventional family man. All seemed normal except that Jefferson, daughters in tow, now never missed church services held for members of Congress at the Capitol. He also offered indirect denials to members of his administration. Alluding to Callender and his charges in letters to Attorney General Levi Lincoln and Robert R. Livingston, his minister to France, Jefferson decried the recent "slanders" and "filth" brought forth by "a lying renegado from republicanism."[55]

For obvious reasons, Jefferson had no desire to be seen as Callender had characterized him, and he welcomed indications of continuing public support. From newspapers he clipped at least a dozen accounts of festivals where citizens praised him in reassuring ways. In Huntington, Connecticut, for example, the locals who gathered on March 4, 1805, extolled him as "great, yet good. Slandered, ridiculed and buffeted by his political adversaries, yet like Noah's ark he rides above the waters." Similarly, at a Charlestown, Massachusetts, banquet celebrating Jefferson's second inauguration, a man toasted the president, "the *purity* of whose private character, adds *lustre* to his public virtues." A few months later, at a Philadelphia Fourth of July banquet, diners raised their glasses to Jefferson: "May his name hereafter be as a monument for public and private example." Jefferson must have been pleased to see so many supporters affirming their faith in the goodness of his personal conduct. On the other hand, he must have regretted the recognition among so many that the goodness of his personal conduct required affirmation.[56]

Of the hundreds of items relating to his public reputation that Jefferson clipped from newspapers, only one refers directly to Sally Hemings. A brief still animates it, be fanned by the standard of '75.

FEDERAL DICTIONARY.

SLANDER—whatever is said truly or falsely, against federalists.

TRUTH—*whatever* is said against democrats.

RELIGION—Tracy, Talmadge, Reeve, Dagger, parson Osgood, Joe Thomas.

GOOD ORDER—Frequent assaults upon neighbors with fists and whips, and way-laying them in dark nights—*and shooting them at Noon Day.*

LAW—Federal Lawyers.

HOLINESS—Moll Carey's songs, negro letters, *black Sal* stories.

GOSPEL MINISTERS—Those who seek to set one part of their congregation against the other, and the wife against the husband; who electioneer and vote for infidels, and harangue in freeman's meetings.

APOSTATE PRIESTS—Those who will not abuse democrats, and electioneer for federalists.

GOSPEL PREACHING—Calling Mr. Jefferson, in the pulpit, an *infidel*, a *debauchee* and a *liar*.

WASHINGTONIANS—men who propose a division of the states.

FELON—one who had rather lie in prison than cease doing what he believes to be his duty.

IMPARTIAL JUDGE—One who extols the men of one party—and denounces those of the other as "a stench in the nostrils of a holy God."

SENTIMENT—Hard names, and all kinds of abuse.

CHARITY—(obsolete.)

MEEKNESS—Interfering in a newspaper war, and claiming a thousand dollars of the enemy for being wounded.

CHRISTIANITY—a total want of charity and forbearance towards men of different opinions.

TAG-RAG—Farmers and Mechanics, and their wives and daughters.   [*Witness*

"Federal Dictionary," clipping in Thomas Jefferson's
Newspaper Commonplace Scrapbooks, ca. 1801–9.
(Albert and Shirley Small Special Collections Library,
University of Virginia)

bit of satire, titled the "Federal Dictionary," that he cut out of an August 1806 issue of a Boston paper, *The Democrat,* provided absurd definitions for words such as "slander" ("whatever is said truly or falsely, against federalists"), "truth" ("*whatever* is said against democrats"), "gospel preaching" ("Calling Mr. Jefferson, in the pulpit, an *infidel,* a *debauchee* and a *liar*"), and "Christianity" ("a total want of charity and forbearance towards men of different opinions"). It defined "holiness" as "Moll Carey's songs, negro letters, [and] *black Sal* stories."[57] The first two of these items reference racially charged attempts by Federalists (clergymen prominent among them) to undercut the respectability of nearly a thousand Republicans who gathered in New Haven to celebrate the second anniversary of Jefferson's inauguration. Set to the tune of "Jefferson and Liberty," "Moll Carey" took its name from an infamous brothel-keeper. Attributed to Theodore Dwight, future congressman and secretary of the Hartford Convention whose brother was president of Yale, the lyrics envisioned on New Haven Green a multiracial mob of "every shape, and hue" replete with "Drunkards, and whores" and "Rogues in scores."[58] Meanwhile, the "negro letters" might have been the notes ("written in negro dialect" by whites, as Hartford's *American Mercury* observed) printed in Connecticut papers encouraging African Americans to attend the celebration. One dangled before readers "a great feaste for all *de* friends to Liberte" and invited "all sort people and all Ladie, bose brack, white and brown" to attend.[59]

It is impossible to know what Jefferson was thinking when he decided to single out with his scissors the "Federal Dictionary" and its implicit condemnation of his enemies' lexicon of hypocrisy, although he usually gravitated toward items with which he agreed. For him, was the real meaning of "holiness" that Republicans should not stand accused of approving of the intermingling of black and white people? Or was it that relations between people with roots in Africa and others with roots in Europe should not be subject to mockery? The answer hinges on whether his thoughts coincided with the things that he wrote or the things that he appears to have done.

CHAPTER SEVEN

Triumphs

THE DAY STARTED at dawn, when sailors at the Washington Naval Yard greeted the twenty-seventh anniversary of American independence with an eighteen-gun salute. At noon, when they repeated this performance, the thunder of artillery punctuated conversations a mile and a half away at the President's House, where a crowd called on Thomas Jefferson. The well-wishers congratulated him on two distinct but equally momentous events. The first, of course, was independence. The second, news of which had arrived the night before, was a treaty signaling France's agreement to the American purchase of New Orleans, the Mississippi River Valley, and the vast entirety of Louisiana.[1]

"The Fourth of July was a proud day" for Jefferson, the *National Intelligencer* reported. "On that day in the year seventy-six, after having drawn the Declaration of Independence, with his illustrious co-patriots he pledged 'his life, his fortune, and his sacred honor' to support the independence of his country, and to maintain her liberties." What a stirring coincidence, the paper continued, that "on the same day in the year 1803 he reaped the merited reward of his labors in the wide spread joy of millions at an event which history will record among the most splendid in our annals." News of the pact, negotiated by Robert R. Livingston and James Monroe, spread throughout Washington and neighboring Georgetown. Before the conclusion of the various banquets that evening, the purchase of Louisiana and the presidency of Jefferson would be toasted in quick succession, and one celebrant, perhaps emboldened by drink but nonetheless inspired by patriotism, would rise from his table to pay tribute in song:

This day we find Munroe's success,
Is crown'd, and greets the nation

Without a blood stain'd deed, yea more
With increase to our station.
    Yankey doodle let us sing,
    Jefferson's the dandy.

That day the British representative in Washington observed that "there seems to be little which can affect the tranquility of the United States, or shake the firm footing which the President will have obtained, in the confidence of his countrymen."[2]

Americans heralded Jefferson as a hero. Although his administration's acquisition of Louisiana failed to satisfy Federalist critics, it succeeded in securing New Orleans, ensuring the flow of commerce on the Mississippi River, doubling the nation in size, and removing from the continent the threat of Napoleon Bonaparte's France, which would soon take possession of the territory from Spain. Concurrent news of the collapse of the peace of Amiens, which for a while had quieted the longstanding feud between Britain and France, made the treaty seem even more fortuitous. While the presence of France on the western frontier might have tempted Americans to enter the conflict, the United States now seemed better insulated from Europe's troubles than ever before.[3]

Disputes between Federalists and Republicans continued, however, despite the administration's success at accomplishing without bloodshed much more than what Federalists had been urging for months, even at the risk of war. Once eager to allocate 50,000 troops and $5 million for an invasion of New Orleans and all foreign-held lands east of the Mississippi—and critical of Jefferson, whose negotiations with France, in their eyes, could only amount to nothing—the president's opponents now recoiled at the acquisition of even more territory by peaceful means.[4] They predicted that the administration's victory would mean America's downfall. Republicans replied that Federalists would rather reverse their earlier arguments and lose Louisiana than approve a treaty that augmented Jefferson's increasing popularity.

Ironically, at this, the apex of his presidency, Jefferson revealed to a few close advisers a crisis of conscience. How could the national government annex Louisiana when the Constitution gave it no such authority? How could it administer the territory and naturalize its inhabitants? How would the example he set in this instance guide future leaders tempted to expand federal power? Never eager to wield powers not explicitly granted to the national government, he proceeded to draft a constitutional amendment sanctioning the treaty. Then, heeding his friends' fears that a public admission of his own doubts would prolong Congress's consideration of the pact and give France an excuse to withdraw from the agreement, he scuttled his plan in the hope that "the good sense of our country will correct the evil of construction when it shall produce ill effects." To an ally in the Senate, he sent a note discouraging any debate regarding "the constitutional difficulty." No doubt he realized that such a discussion would imperil not only the land deal but also his reputation for fidelity to the Constitution.[5]

Historians ever since have debated, discussed, and interpreted the third president's inner conflict, and a few have described his choice as hypocritical.[6] But rather than echoing the concerns of his contemporaries, these scholars have amplified them. The leaders of Jefferson's era had no access to his expressions of doubt and indecision. While a few Federalists in Congress and in private letters made pointed references to his apparent about-face, relatively few allegations of Jeffersonian inconsistency reached the public through the press.[7] Instead, the president's opponents focused on more pragmatic arguments against the purchase of Louisiana, claiming that it was an unnecessary, expensive, and dangerous folly, injurious to the health of the union and intended to benefit Jefferson's own political interests. At the same time, however, Republican printers produced voluminous critiques of the Federalists' assertions, contrasting the opposition's current stance with its earlier statements stressing the importance of the Mississippi region. Given most Americans' enthusiasm for doubling the nation's size and the inconsistencies of the Federalists' own statements, Jefferson's opponents faced a difficult battle in their attempt to defeat the treaty and discredit its public champion. In the end, the party of Alexander Hamilton lost. The president remained a hero in the eyes of his friends, and it was his enemies who looked like hypocrites.

Federalist opposition to the treaty emerged quickly. To each other, members of this faction confessed not only the desire to embarrass their nemesis but also some worries about how the admission of western states could diminish their influence, which centered in New England.[8] To the public they delivered lists of objections seeming only somewhat more disinterested. A writer calling himself "Fabricius," for example, derided Louisiana as a "great waste, a wilderness unpeopled with any beings except wolves and wandering Indians" that "may be cut up into States without number, but each with *two votes in the Senate.*" Their interests would coalesce with those of "imperial *Virginia*," which, as "arbitress of the whole," would spread her influence— and her slaves—across the continent. The nation would become so "unwieldy" and expansive that it would be impossible to collect taxes or maintain the order of "uncivilized" westerners. The proposed purchase signaled a "momentous crisis" that threatened to undermine the federal government and splinter the states.[9]

Federalists also criticized the president's Louisiana as "foolish," "dishonorable," and expensive. A penman described the territory's $15 million price as an "unconscionable bargain" by which "France is to be aided in her designs against Great Britain." Securing the vast territory, moreover, was impossible—or at least would require a "vast military establishment" diminishing Americans' freedom as well as their pocketbooks, "for it is impossible that any political system favorable to the rights of liberty and property could embrace so large a sphere." Meanwhile, Hamilton's *New-York Evening Post* wondered whether southern Republicans would convert the territory's forests into fields where slaves would toil and wondered if "FIFTEEN MILLIONS OF DOLLARS" for such a dubious enterprise could "be deemed a cheap purchase."[10]

Nothing, however, better underscored the opposition's contention that Jefferson had miscalculated the value of the boundless tract than his administration's publication of a pamphlet entitled *An Account of Louisiana*. The fifty-page treatise on the region's people, geography, flora, and fauna claimed that "about 1000 miles up the Missouri" stood a great "Salt Mountain!" About 180 miles long and 45 miles wide, it had been visited by "several respectable and enterprising traders," the report assured readers.[11] Federalists made the most of this intelligence. The *Gazette of the United States* joked that, had Napoleon known of the salt mountain, he would have doubled his price. Proud of their leader's sagacity, the paper continued, the "democrats . . . look upon Mr. Jefferson as a very cunning man." Another writer carried the lampoon further. He described individuals who "make haste to enter this land of promise, flowing with *salt punch and whiskey*." In Louisiana, "beasts and fowls are said to share in the honours and hospitalities done to strangers; inasmuch that pigs, geese and turkeys roast themselves with the utmost expedition, and then come and beg you to eat them. The strange and wonderful accounts which are daily arriving have so elevated the President," the writer continued, "that we are constantly looking out, expecting to see him on the top of his house to take an aeral flight to this region of felicity."[12]

Jefferson's supporters lashed back, answering the Federalists' charges not only with defenses of the value of Louisiana but also with a charge of their own. Federalists, they asserted, had let loose a flood of partisan bitterness

tainted by hypocrisy. In May 1804, as eighteen-year-old Samuel Brazer reminded a Massachusetts audience that gathered to celebrate the purchase,
prior to the treaty "the enemies of the government were loud in their assertions, that . . . no sacrifice would be too great" to secure America's interests
in the region. Of course, "they felt assured the Administration would incur
defeat, disgrace, and ruin" in the attempt. Federalists who formerly expressed
solidarity with their "Western-Brethren" now spoke of "Whiskey-Boys,"
"offscourings of the earth," and the "sweepings of creation." Jefferson's victory had transformed into a supposed wasteland an area that they once said
possessed "exuberant fertility of the soil."[13]

Joseph Priestley viewed the settlement as ideal. "We are happily at *peace*
here and without the most distant prospect of war," he wrote to a friend in
Britain. "The opposition was clamourous for taking possession of New Orleans by force," yet the purchase of all of Louisiana is "much more likely to be
permanent. Had it remained in the possession of France," it would "have been
taken from [them] by the English," who then "would have completely enclosed
all of the United States to the West."[14]

Other Republicans argued that buying Louisiana would prove far less
costly—in money as well as lives—than the sort of armed conflict that the
Federalists would have risked. As a writer who identified himself as "Curtius" told readers of the *National Intelligencer,* war with France had been the
opposition's aim all along. Brazer agreed, for only by war with France, a nation to which they linked Jefferson, and alliance with Britain, with which
they aligned themselves, "might they hope to regain their lost popularity."[15]
But the pact signified no such partnership with France, as some of its detractors charged. Instead, a Kentucky pamphleteer maintained, it prevented
Napoleon from marching troops across the Mississippi as he did the Rhine.
While a French presence in Louisiana would have required the maintenance
of a large standing army and a larger national debt, American ownership of
the tract promised so many economic benefits, a Virginian insisted, that the
purchase would quickly pay for itself.[16] And no cause existed for the fear that
an addition of new land to the union must lead to the disintegration of the
United States. Since the West's "rustic life" promoted "a heroic patriotism and
the most ardent devotions to liberty," one Republican claimed, under a truly
republican system the "extension of territory . . . could never produce any dangerous effect."[17]

What, asked William Duane's Philadelphia *Aurora,* prevented most Federalists from admitting these facts? After all, even Senator John Quincy Adams,

son of the former president, supported the treaty. The opposition's "pitiful attempt," as the *National Intelligencer* termed it, to cast a shadow over the administration's negotiations revealed its own inconsistency. Speaking to a Massachusetts crowd on Independence Day in 1804, William Charles White excoriated opponents of the treaty for lacking even a "semblance of sincerity." John Taylor agreed. The Federalists, he maintained, with "a temerity, unprecedented," had *"unsaid* all that they had a short time before so solemnly and eloquently affirmed."[18]

Admonished for inconsistency, the president's adversaries hastened to point out the incongruities of his own stance regarding Louisiana. But rather than criticize his apparent conversion from the doctrine of constitutional limits to the belief that the executive might do whatever he found necessary and proper, they devoted the bulk of their energy to the reloading of rhetorical guns that fired the familiar charge that Jefferson had always been hostile to the Constitution. This, they asserted, his administration's treaty proved. The pact that he had placed before Congress empowered him to "dispose of the lives, liberty and property of the inhabitants of New-Orleans and Louisiana" however he chose. The agreement would empower Jefferson as a despot who could govern the territory however he chose.[19]

But like the boy who cried wolf too many times, the Federalists, who had long insisted that Jefferson wished to undermine the foundation of American government, met with disbelieving ears. The president, whose conduct during his first years in office had cast doubt on earlier predictions of ruin, remained in the eyes of many citizens a hero. As Andrew Jackson informed Jefferson, the day would soon come "when all the western Hemisphere rejoices in the Joyfull news of the cession of Louisiana." Jefferson not only received congratulations but also read newspaper accounts of public support. Several of these he clipped for his scrapbooks, including a report of a gathering in Maryland to celebrate Louisiana's 1804 accession and an 1805 Fourth of July toast offered at Poultney, Vermont: "*Louisiana*—May the acquisition of that rich country, prove . . . a standing monument of the preference of negociation to war."[20]

The Federalists, however, did not stand alone among the partisans who sacrificed credibility at the altar of Louisiana. An addiction to kneejerk contrarianism so afflicted William Duane, editor of the Republican *Aurora,* that his initial reaction to the announcement of Jefferson's success was disbelief. The report constituted a trick, he warned readers, designed to lure good Republicans to the Federalists' faulty perspective. Louisiana, he said, was neither necessary nor desired, and the administration would never take an action sure to "diminish the price of our lands" and "disperse our population." The president's opponents gleefully publicized Duane's miscalculation. Meanwhile, as Republicans attempted to ignore his blunder, the embarrassed newspaperman experienced an abrupt change of heart.[21]

The episode reveals the lengths to which partisans of either political persuasion would go to prevent the other from gaining advantage. It also suggests something about Jefferson's character as an officeholder. His constitutional beliefs may have been quietly inconsistent with his policies, but the tension between competing principles caused him honest pain. While others issued strident statements that shifted and reversed in order to exploit circumstance for narrowly partisan purposes, the president maneuvered more nimbly. He steered a course designed to secure not only the public good but also his reputation as a man who was good for the public. In this he saw no duplicity and little need for balance or compromise. In his eyes, each one of these efforts served the other.

THE PURCHASE OF Louisiana marked the highpoint of Jefferson's presidency. Yet even at the midpoint it was but one of many triumphs. During his first term in office he had repealed all internal taxes, slashed the federal payroll, reduced the nation's debt, and brought to the fledgling capital city a new political culture that embraced equality, democracy, and republican simplicity. These accomplishments reinforced the popularity of not only Jefferson's principles but also Jefferson himself. This development, although flattering and not unwelcome, did, however, create circumstances providing the president with a conundrum. The imperative of American Revolutionary leadership was disinterestedness—the selfless notion that men should advance particular ideas but that ideas should never be used to advance particular men. This principle, which had inspired Jefferson to remain silent about his authorship of the Declaration of Independence, in 1804 moved him to intercede when men planned to honor him.

At issue was the reception of Jefferson's annual message, delivered by courier to Congress in November of that year. Unlike his predecessors, who had used speeches to joint sessions of the House and Senate to fulfill their constitutional obligation to "give to the Congress Information of the State of the Union," Jefferson since 1801 had submitted his messages in writing. This new practice, suggested shortly after his inauguration by Congressman Nathaniel Macon, a North Carolina Republican soon to be elected as speaker of the House,

represented not only a break with tradition but also a rebuke to the custom
of the British monarch, who with much pomp and circumstance delivered
from the throne an annual speech—known as "His Majesty's Most Gracious
Message"—to the Commons and Lords. Replacing monarchical ceremony
with republican simplicity, the new procedure highlighted the substance of the
president's message but not the president as its messenger.[22]

Federalists had long balked at such reforms, which, as displays of modesty,
they considered strangely ostentatious. While not surprising that the Federalist *United States Gazette* would discover irony (and opportunity for sarcasm)
in "the distant and dignified formality adopted by Mr. Jefferson, of sending
his mandates by the hand of one of his domesticks, to the representatives of
the American people to be registered by them in the form of laws," its report
of preparations made in advance of the arrival of Jefferson's 1804 written address gained enough notice to merit a Republican response. The Philadelphia
paper—the successor to the *Gazette of the United States* established by John
Fenno and continued by Joseph Dennie and others—revealed a startling ceremony to be "performed with all the solemn formality of the coronation of
Buonaparte." Its editor claimed firsthand knowledge "that for many days a flag
stood ready . . . in the capitol, with an officer attending for the purpose of displaying it on top of the building the moment the message should arrive. This
was to be a signal for a grand fire of artillery at the navy yard, where likewise
a number of officers and men were posted day after day, with their matches
lighted and every thing in exact preparation for announcing, in true republican style, his majesty's most gracious message." To the disappointment of "our
republican court, the senate did not form a quorum until near a fortnight after
the commencement of the session, by which time these preparations had excited so many sneers and sarcasms that the administration" called off the plans.
The Republican *Aurora* did not deny that these preparations had been made,
but it did dispute the *Gazette*'s account of who had been behind them. "Mr.
Jefferson never desired a flag to be raised, or a cannon to be fired, nor did any
of his friends," the paper reassured readers. The planned ceremony amounted
to "a *federal trick*" masterminded by Captain Thomas Tingey, commander of
the Washington Navy Yard, "a federalist" intent either on currying favor with
the president or exposing him to ridicule. Whatever Tingey's motive, when
"Mr. Jefferson was informed of the object of the flag and cannon, he ordered
the ceremony not to be performed, and censured those who had volunteered in
the business."[23]

Jefferson's intervention in this episode reflected his scruples as much as his penchant for political stagecraft. Sharing his sense of a cannon salute's impropriety were Connecticut Republicans. He later clipped for one of his scrapbooks an account of a dinner at which they made a toast to *"The Artillery of the United States*—Honored in proclaiming the triumph of *principles* over *men;* let it never be dishonored by proclaiming the triumph of *men* over *principles."* The cannon salute also would have violated Jefferson's sense that praise mattered most when it was spontaneous—or at least unscripted—and came from citizens rather than appointees. This kind of praise Jefferson had already received. Although not yet official, by the time Congress had reconvened he felt sure of his reelection. So certain seemed the outcome of the election that even the *National Intelligencer,* which had labored for months to energize the president's supporters, acknowledged it as one of those "events of great importance" that "do not command the attention to which their intrinsic merit entitles them." The confirmation of Jefferson as chief executive passed "without awakening either the rapturous exultation of his friends, or the angry passions of his enemies."[24]

The *National Intelligencer's* assessment was only partially true. While the outcome of the election appears to have surprised no one, a growing number of Americans praised the president. At an 1804 "Republican Festival" in Orange County, Virginia, for example, citizens lauded him as "the world's best hope" and a man "whose mind embraces the universe." Even in Connecticut, one of the few remaining Federalist strongholds, emboldened Republicans cheered him as a "truly great" and "truly good" man distinguished for his "love of peace" and "knowledge of Philosophy." Yet while the accomplishments of Jefferson's first term, together with his moderate tone and America's relative peace and prosperity, shrank the audience willing to believe his critics, the quantity of criticism generated by the Federalist press seems not to have diminished. In addition, there remained a number of Federalists—a small but "noisy band of royalists inhabiting the cities chiefly, & priests both of city & country," as Jefferson had described them in 1802—who were unmoved by his apparent successes and unwilling to imagine that his leadership would produce anything but calamity. Henry J. Knox, son of the former secretary of war, believed Republican rule to pose such a "great danger" to "the national character" that he welcomed "a civil war" as "the only alternative to save the Constitution."[25]

It comes as no surprise that Federalists in 1804 continued their assaults on Jefferson's character, religion, and private life. As in 1796 and 1800, questions about his faith provided fodder for those wishing to damn him. When H. Weld Fuller addressed the citizens of Augusta, Maine, on the Fourth of July 1804, he warned that "men *high in authority*" in America "cherished and supported" the dictums of French atheists. Left unchecked, their "*irreligion* and *infidelity*" would result in "our Religion and Government perishing together." A newspaper reported ominously that the president traveled on Sundays, and Reverend Clement Clarke Moore, best known in later years for his authorship of "The Night before Christmas," delivered to Jefferson a lump of coal titled *Observations upon Certain Passages in Mr. Jefferson's Notes on Virginia.* What bothered Moore was that even though Jefferson's *Notes on the State of Virginia* contained "so much infidelity, conveyed in so insidious a manner," its author continued to be "extolled by the majority of our people as a profound philosopher" and entrusted as "the guardian of our rights." As had earlier critics of Jefferson's treatise on Virginia's society, laws, and natural resources, Moore combed through its pages for evidence of atheism. He characterized as "an open denial of the universal deluge" Jefferson's calculations suggesting that the conversion to rain of all the atmosphere's water vapor would raise the sea level only about fifty-two feet. He pointed out that Jefferson's hypothesis concerning the time necessary for the development of North and South American Indian languages called into question the biblical account of the age of the earth. He used Jefferson's reference to Voltaire's observations on geology to help make the case that the *Notes* amounted to a work of "modern French philosophy." Taken as a whole, according to Moore, Jefferson's book could only be seen as the work of a man eager "to banish civilization from the earth," undermine people's faith in God, and "degrade us from the rank of angels" so that "we may complete the catalogue of brutes."[26]

While Moore sought to strengthen his case by linking Jefferson with Voltaire, others declared the president guilty by association with Thomas Paine, whose activities and pronouncements on behalf of the French Revolution had made him first an outlaw in his native Britain, then a prisoner of his adopted France, later Napoleon's disappointed sycophant, and finally—in the United States—a veritable pariah. In 1801, Jefferson took a drubbing in the Federalist press after revelations that he had offered safe passage to this trans-Atlantic radical, sparking criticisms that echoed in advance of the 1804 election. According to "Hume," the *Columbian Centinel*'s prolific essayist, the president's connection with Paine, who had issued sharp rebukes of the policies of George Washington, proved that Jefferson "has ever been hostile to this great and good

A Philosophic Cock, 1804, engraved by James Akin.
(American Antiquarian Society)

man." Likewise, Paine's "bold and acknowledged infidelity," his "bitter and un-
ceasing attacks on the principles of Christianity," and his contention in the
Age of Reason that "the Bible is a book of lies, wickedness, and blasphemy,"
furnished abundant evidence that Jefferson, his friend, "has secretly designed
the destruction of the national religion." Engraver James Akin's rendition of
Jefferson as *A Philosophic Cock* standing alongside Sally Hemings, his hen,
combined the critiques of Jefferson's supposed immorality with those of his
supposed radicalism. One of the campaign's relatively few references to the 1802
scandal, the illustration exemplified Federalists' penchant for satire by evoking
the multiple meanings of "cock." In addition to the literal depiction and crude
insinuation, the rooster was also a symbol of revolutionary France. Why not
synthesize Jefferson's public and private sins? Hume, who made no secret of his
belief that "a man's principles and feelings may be learned from a knowledge
of those . . . with whom he associates," connected personal views and private
relationships on the one hand with public policy on the other.[27]

In contrast—and as in the case of the Hemings scandal—many Republicans drew a bold line between Jefferson's private character and public accomplishments. More often than not, they ignored attacks on his personal life and highlighted instead his accomplishments while in office. This strategy offered the practical benefit of emphasizing the positive—of refusing to fan the flames of Federalists' sometimes incendiary charges by repeating and responding to them—and also reflected a central tenet of Jeffersonian philosophy. Since measures mattered more than men, the *Aurora,* looking back on the election, claimed that "the measures of his administration have been the only reply which he has offered to the unexpected abuse of his political opponents. . . . He has not been thus attacked because he is Thomas Jefferson, but because Thomas Jefferson is the ablest defender of the rights of the people, because his administration, more than any other, has proved not only the practibility but the superior excellence of our democratic representative form of government."[28]

Sometimes Jefferson's supporters defended his private character; sometimes they even extolled it. Yet the leading organs of the Jeffersonian press took care to remind citizens that "however just and striking the homage deservedly bestowed on the virtues of the *man,* it is the *cause* of liberty that excites the fullest devotion." As the *National Intelligencer* insisted, "principle, and principle only, should command the highest devotion of freemen; those whose lives are spent in its protection have the next claim to their respect and affection." Richmond Republicans had not misplaced their priorities when they gathered on March 4, 1804, to toast first the day, the people second, the Constitution third, and only fourth Jefferson, "the patriot who merits *public favor* by promoting the *public interest.*" So common had become the Republican "declaration that '*principles and not men are the objects of their contests*'" that a Federalist newspaper in Hudson, New York, claimed to "pass it over" as "just such stuff as we can always find in abundance."[29]

Although in certain respects the election of 1804 reprised the 1800 campaign, in other ways it inverted its charges and characterizations. To be sure, Federalist publications continued to swipe at Jefferson—the weak-willed philosopher and coward, the bon vivant dilettante who in 1781 took flight up Carter's Mountain to avoid Banastre Tarleton's cavalrymen—and Republican prints continued to defend him. Yet long gone were the days when commentators like Oliver Ellsworth, the Federalist senator-turned-Supreme Court chief justice, identified Jefferson's lack of leadership as his greatest weakness. "If he were President," Ellsworth reportedly had said in 1796, "he would take little or no responsibility on himself. The nation would be . . . without a head. Everything would be referred to Congress."[30] By 1804, Jefferson's detractors were portraying him as not too weak but too powerful, as not too philosophical but too Machiavellian.

One of the factors contributing to this new facet of Jefferson's image were his interventions in the federal court system, particularly his repeal of the 1801 Judiciary Act, an action that removed from the bench lower-court judges (none of them Republican) promised lifetime appointments, and his successful impeachment of district court judge John Pickering, a leading New Hampshire Federalist whose oftentimes inebriated pronouncements from the bench did not, according to Jefferson's critics, amount to the "high crimes and misdemeanors" necessary for his removal. The *Columbian Centinel,* which described the president as "the imitator of that miserable despot, BUONAPARTE," had no foreknowledge of Jefferson's unsuccessful impeachment later that year of Samuel Chase, associate justice of the Supreme Court, for a tangled web of alleged crimes that included the prosecution for seditious libel of James Callender, whose pen had savaged Hamilton, Washington, and Adams before turning against Jefferson. Even so, it predicted that when Jefferson's "party shall acquire new strength in Congress, the supreme court will be swept away" as an obstacle to "interest and ambition."[31]

The idea that Jefferson stood willing to rig in his favor the political process received reinforcement with the addition of the 12th Amendment. After two-thirds of both houses of Congress recommended it in December 1803, ratification by three-fourths of the states took only 189 days as Republicans raced to implement it prior to the presidential contest. The amendment, which provided for the casting of electoral votes for tickets containing designated presidential and vice-presidential candidates, offered conspicuous safeguards for Jefferson's reelection. Although Republicans such as John Taylor maintained that the amendment had neither been "officially suggested by him" nor "even in his individual character, recommended" by him (Jefferson, who considered the topic "of a nature which forbids my interference altogether," had nonetheless been aware of discussions about changing the electoral process since at least as early as September 1801), they recognized how the amendment could avert disasters like the 1800 electoral tie.[32]

That the framers of the Constitution gave to each elector two presidential votes was no accident. In 1787, no one predicted the increasingly organized partisanship that took root in the 1790s. If anything, the framers feared too little organization as electors forwarded the names of their home states' favorite sons. The requirement that an elector cast at least one of his two votes for an individual residing in a different state reflected a hope that, from among the many ballots reflecting parochial prejudices, at least a few men of national standing would emerge. More often than not, the framers assumed, the Electoral College would act merely as a filter, providing a list of five men—not one of whom received votes from a majority of electors—from which members of the House of Representatives, voting as state delegations, would select the chief executive. In instances in which one or two men received the support of a majority of electors, the individual with the greatest number of votes would be the president and the runner-up would be vice president. Although the framers believed that George Washington would assume the presidency under these circumstances, they assumed that such instances of consensus would be rare. A third scenario—the chances of which they considered remote but not impossible—was that two men would receive an equal number of votes from a majority of electors. Here, again, the choice would fall to the House of Representatives, where state delegations would decide between the two men.

This, of course, happened in the election of 1800, when Republican electors—voting at different places and times—exercised so much partisan discipline that, in their effort to ensure that the votes for Jefferson and Burr, their choice for vice president, eclipsed those cast for Adams and Charles Cotesworth Pinckney, they inadvertently gave to each of their candidates an equal number of votes. The 12th Amendment would prevent the repetition of such a mistake. It would also preclude yet another scenario.

What if a sufficient number of Federalist electors, conscious that their candidates would lose an election, decided instead to declare their support for the Republican vice presidential nominee, electing him president and turning upside down the Republican ticket? Had the 1804 Republican nominating caucus not determined to cast aside Burr, whose openness to such an inversion Jeffersonians did not doubt, he easily could have colluded with the administration's enemies to prompt such a result. Even after his exclusion, without the 12th Amendment there would still be room for confusion and intrigue. What if Federalists supported him in unison and some Republican electors ignored the caucus's instructions?

It was Jefferson's particular good fortune that actions helping to ensure his reelection also ensured a more reliable expression of the people's will. Even so, the proposed amendment emerged as one of 1804's chief issues. If Federalists felt hard-pressed to argue against its substance, they had no difficulty highlighting its presumed object—the perpetuation of Jefferson's presidency for at least another term.

Pointing toward the amendment as evidence of ambition possessed the potential to undermine Jefferson in more ways than one. Americans harbored not only a congenital suspicion of men who craved power but also a deep-rooted hostility toward hypocrites and frauds. Given Jefferson's calculated displays of modesty and often-stated preference for private pursuits over public service, in the 1804 campaign his supposed duplicity, which had long endured as one of his opponents' favorite themes, continued as a critique. The *Columbian Centinel,* for example, described him as a man determined "to preserve by DECEPTION, a popularity, which . . . he had obtained by DECEPTION." The *Port Folio,* meanwhile, published an "Ode to Popularity" reminding him that "Thou can'st affect humility, to hide / Some deep device of monstrous pride."[33]

His efforts to change presidential election procedures exposed still more "unblushing inconsistencies," according to the *Gazette of the United States,* which in 1804 continued the cherished tactic of using Jefferson's own words against him. The newspaper excerpted Jefferson's December 1787 letter to James Madison praising the recently drafted Constitution but objecting to the absence of term limits, "most particularly in the case of the President. Experience concurs with reason in concluding that the first magistrate will always be re-elected if the constitution permits it. He is then an officer for life." Since "the power of removing him every fourth year by the vote of the people is a power which will not be exercised," Jefferson suggested "an incapacity to be elected a second time" as the only sure means to prevent the presidency from devolving into an elective monarchy.[34]

Ultimately, in a letter to William Short, Jefferson suggested two four-year terms or a single seven-year term. But in 1804 this letter was unknown to the public. The missive to Madison, however, had been published as early 1792, when the *Gazette of the United States* first promoted the sentiments it expressed "as the free and spontaneous effusions of his heart." The letter, which Jefferson "could not have foreseen . . . would be laid before the public," remained as the only candid expression of Jefferson's original and, readers erroneously believed, longstanding view on the subject.[35] So far as Federalist writers surmised, his change of mind was abrupt and the reasons for it were no less obvious than obviously self-serving. While Jefferson possessed little confidence that others would volunteer to abdicate the presidency, they surmised, he retained a boundless faith in his own fitness to wield power indefinitely.

Even before the introduction of the 12th Amendment, the fact that power flowed from popularity provoked bitter references to "his majesty president Jef" and "King Jefferson," a high-and-mighty figure who was "beginning to ape the monarchs of Europe." After its passage, critics increased their jabs at "King Thomas" and "Thomas the King," for "a President for life" was "abhorrent to the genius of republican government." One writer noted that Washington and Adams had no desire for "visionary and fanciful amendments" to entrench them in power. Yet "no sooner do those who always have *republicanism* in their *mouths,* ascend the ladder of dominion, and possess themselves of un-controuled power," than they grasp for more. "We hope it is not yet treason to say . . . that the constitution was made for the *people* of the United States, and not for Mr. Jefferson or any other individual." Its purpose was not "to please him and support his re-election."[36]

These words stung, in part because they attempted to portray Republicans as apostates from time-worn beliefs such as the supremacy of the people over their leaders and the notion that principles mattered more than men. As one Boston paper intoned, "the democrats," having "inverted" their beliefs, seemed poised to begin "fighting for 'men, not measures.'" Not surprisingly, Republicans' response emphasized the amendment's purported purpose of expressing with clarity the people's will. "The feds pretend that the alteration in the con-stitution was made 'to secure the re-election of Mr. Jefferson,'" answered one of Jefferson's defenders, "and talk about the Democrats wanting 'a President for Life.'" The amendment, however, merely provided for the election of the winner of the necessary number of votes. "We believe the love, the respect, the gratitude, of the People of the United States towards Mr. Jefferson will 'secure his re-election,' as often as he will 'accept it,' provided he pursues the same line of conduct hereafter as heretofore." He could not be returned to office unless he was "the choice of a Majority of the People of the United States." Would "any Federalist have the hardihood to say" that he then "ought not to be re-elected?"[37]

The 12th Amendment, proposed to the states by Congress in December 1803 and ratified when the legislature of New Hampshire adopted the measure in June 1804, is often seen as an accommodation to the rise of national political parties. In actuality, however, it was a reflection of the rise of only one national political alliance, the Jeffersonian Republicans. By 1804, Federalism constituted a diminished and increasingly disjointed force in American government. Feder-alists held no national meetings, organized no committees of correspondence, and lacked sufficient numbers in Congress to conduct a national nominating caucus. In addition, while they coalesced around Charles Cotesworth Pinckney of South Carolina and Rufus King of New York as contenders for the first and second offices, one of their leading papers, Boston's *Columbian Centinel,* went so far as to declare "that the proper Personages to be voted for as President and Vice-President, will be the inquiry of the Electors after they are chosen." Since "Federal Republicans" (as some Federalists had rebranded themselves) selected as electors only "the wisest and most patriotic Citizens," it could be left "to them to ascertain who are the most suitable men in the United States to be honored with their suffrages." Republican electors, meanwhile, "have had their candidates imperiously prescribed to them." Republican electors—"the white *Virginians* of the North"—would no more "dare disobey the orders of their drivers" than enslaved "black *Virginians.*" They were "mere machines."[38]

It is difficult to imagine a Republican who, in a moment of candor, would dispute the *Centinel*'s second metaphor. The whole point of the 12th Amendment was to turn the Electoral College into a mechanism for conveying the intentions of the electorate. The paper's conception of it as an instrument to amalgamate the individual deliberations of "wise" and "independent men" casting "independent votes" for leaders possessing "ability" and "impartiality"— as a filter through which people presumed to possess less wisdom deferred to the judgment of others presumed to possess more—harkened back to not only a less partisan time but also a more aristocratic era. While this Federalist view of the Electoral College depended on voters' placing their trust in the judgment and character of the men who comprised it, the Republicans' amendment transformed it into a much more direct channel for the expression of voters' principles.[39]

The Republican nominating caucus, held in Washington on February 25, affirmed with unanimity its unsurprising confidence that Jefferson, the popular incumbent, as its designated presidential candidate could be counted on to represent Jeffersonian beliefs. More division marked the caucus's choice for vice president, but New York governor George Clinton, who received 67 out of 108 votes (more than three times the number of Kentucky senator John Breckinridge, who came in second), seemed not only reliably Jeffersonian but certain to win the support of his crucial state. Shortly after Clinton's nomination, an address signed by sixty-one New Yorkers praised his "inflexible integrity" and maintained that he possessed "the same unshaken attachment to principle" as well as "the same political virtues which have adorned the life and distinguished the administration of Mr. Jefferson." Detractors, meanwhile, pointed to Clinton's age as his most prized characteristic. At sixty-five, in four years' time he would likely be too old to impede the election to the presidency of James Madison, yet another Virginian.[40]

Receiving not a single vote at the Republican nominating caucus was the current vice president. Jefferson, who avowed that Aaron Burr had long "inspired me with distrust" and noted that "there never had been an intimacy between us, and but little association," held him at arm's length until the caucus cast him aside. Burr's subsequent willingness to collude with New York Federalists in order to pursue his election as that state's governor only reinforced the notion that advancing principles mattered less to him than advancing himself. Hamilton, as he had in 1801, interceded in opposition to Burr, and again Burr came up short. What infuriated Burr even more, however, was Hamilton's refusal to disavow remarks attributed to him in an Albany newspaper. Published at the height of the campaign, Hamilton was said not only to have declared Burr "a dangerous man, and one who ought not to be trusted with the reins of government," but also to have shared "a still more despicable opinion" that caution precluded committing to print. Viewing this as an affront to his personal honor, Burr ultimately challenged Hamilton to their July 1804 duel at Weehawken, New Jersey. When the vice president fired a one-ounce ball into the former treasury secretary's abdomen, he caused the death of not only his adversary but also his own political career. Jefferson, the only real victor in the duel, witnessed the demise of two rivals while being spared the grief-inspired scorn heaped on the vice president from whom he had been thoroughly disassociated. But the real irony is that Burr, who initiated this affair of honor to protect his reputation, as a result ruined it so completely.[41]

Jefferson cared about his reputation too, of course, but proved much more adept at choosing the battles on which he staked it. He identified concern for his public image when describing what motivated him to stand for reelection. "The unlimited calumnies of the federalists," he informed his daughter, "have obliged me to put myself on the trial of my country by standing another election. I have no fear as to their verdict; and that being secured for posterity, no consideration will induce me to continue beyond the term to which it will extend. My passions strengthen daily to quit political turmoil, and retire into the bosom of my family." Jefferson's statement, easily dismissible as just another example of disingenuous disinterestedness or telling a loved one what she presumably hoped to hear, helps nonetheless to underscore the degree to which he relied on the approbation of fellow citizens to refute what he viewed as Federalist lies. Maybe he believed, as an anti-dueling essay clipped for his scrapbooks argued, that "a man who calls me booby, who throws a glass in my face," or "who is mean enough to abuse me in a common newspaper" could do nothing to affect his character since "we are ourselves the source of our honor." Reputation, however, was a different thing, for it had less to do with one's character than others' perceptions of it. George Tucker, an acquaintance and early biographer, observed that Jefferson ardently wished for the support of "his countrymen. It may, indeed, be seen throughout his life that his desire of their esteem, for its own sake, was far stronger with him than for the power or any other benefits it could confer." Yet this is only half correct, for Jefferson recognized that public esteem provided him with more than reassurance. His conception of presidential leadership held that his authority came not only from the Constitution—amended to allow for the more faithful but still merely periodic expression of the popular will—but also from the popular will itself.[42]

Understanding that public opinion served as a source of power, Jefferson cultivated a much more direct relationship with the American people than his predecessors. His directed his first inaugural address not to members of Congress, as Washington had, but to his "Friends & Fellow Citizens" throughout the United States. The items that Jefferson clipped from newspapers demonstrate that he not only spoke to the American people; he also listened to them. Only occasionally did his scissors point toward Federalist critiques, for these he had already dismissed as not authentically American. No wonder that in this election and others, as he tried to convince Burr, he could claim a cheerful acquiescence to "my duty to be merely passive." He refused even to allow "any one to speak to me on the subject" of electoral politics, adding that he considered it "my duty to leave myself to the free discussion of the public."[43]

This, he had confidence, was a safe strategy. In 1811, he voiced his longstanding belief that it was "false and degrading" to describe those who avowed his principles as "our *party*." In truth, "the republicans are the *nation*." Opposed by a mere "faction" that, although well-heeled and British-backed, remained "weak in numbers," the mass of his countrymen could be counted on to make the right choices. His newspaper commonplace scrapbooks substantiated this theory. They not only muted the voice of Federalism but also celebrated the matrix of Republicanism. The first third of the first volume, which largely consists of accounts of celebrations of the Fourth of July and the Fourth of March, when citizens observed the anniversary of Jefferson's inauguration, makes clear the remarkable consistency of Jeffersonian ritual and the substance of Jeffersonian thought. Evidence abounds of the ways in which Republicans throughout the nation not only copied each others' words and ideas but also sometimes tailored these words and ideas to local circumstances. The same holds true for Republican songs, which populate the pages of the fourth volume of Jefferson's scrapbooks. An 1805 anthem, for example, written in advance of New Hampshire's gubernatorial election, adapted to the familiar tune of "Jefferson and Liberty" new lyrics promoting the candidacy of John Langdon. All of this helps to make sense of Jefferson's novel understanding of presidential leadership, which vested the executive with a new source of influence at the same time that it acknowledged the power of everyday citizens. With scissors and paste, he could ventriloquize Americans so that they said precisely what he wished to hear.[44]

Meanwhile, what Federalists heard sounded terrifying. Their dire prospects in 1804 led many to throw up their hands and lash out not only at Jefferson's supporters but also at America's increasingly democratized politics. The *Western Star* of Stockbridge, Massachusetts, exasperated by the "Democrats" who "consider the prevalence of their causes as a proof of the reasonableness of their principles," asserted that "the mere multitude is an idol, and a senseless idol too, on whose altar the incense of flattery forever smokes." The future looked bleak, since voters "will soon learn to prefer to office not him who will serve them best but him who will stoop to flatter most." The "wise and good," try as they might to stand as the flatterers' rivals, eventually would succumb as their victims. Eventually only "ONE who rose upon the shoulders of the rabble treads on their necks and reigns alone." Lest anyone forget Jefferson's supposed status as America's flatterer-in-chief, Joseph Dennie's *Port Folio* excerpted the account of a writer who claimed to have witnessed "the triumphs of democracy, on the scaffolds of Paris," and "thousands of headless human trunks, the victims of its fury." From France to Haiti to the depths of the ocean and finally "from the top of Monticello, by the side of the great Jefferson, I have watched its wild uproar, while we philosophised together on its sublime horrors."[45]

Somewhat obscured by such hyperventilation was the point, made more clearly by Fisher Ames, that "the people may be their own enemies." To believe otherwise an officeholder either "must be as ignorant as most of his constituents, or basely servile to their prejudices." The *Gazette of the United States,* which the likeminded *Port Folio* lauded for its "open, direct, decisive, and persevering hostility towards that democratic spirit which pervades this country," maintained "that no proofs of baseness or villainny will prevent the success of a candidate, where all the refuse of mankind collected from all nations, are admitted to the privilege of suffrage." Such lines vented frustration with the new nation's democratic direction, but they did not help to win elections.[46]

Or did they? The paradox of these Federalist critiques of mass politics was that they appeared in mass-circulation newspapers. The penmen who expressed skepticism about popular democracy believed that their missives possessed popular appeal. Maybe this should not surprise. Who would wish to hand the keys of government to the power-hungry, the ignorant, the duplicitous, the duped, or the desperate? Even Republicans, who believed they themselves fit within none of these categories, at their patriotic festivals drank toasts to "the Science of Government"—"may it engage the talents of the best and wisest of men." Yet a Federalist report, headlined "More Democratick Voters," noted that from a ship containing 400 Irish immigrants anchored in New York's East River, "upwards of 150 had jumped overboard and swum ashore" to cast their ballots.[47]

Although some Federalists regarded democratic politics with disdain, each party seemed to spur the other to intensify its efforts at electioneering. Congressman Samuel Thatcher, a Federalist from the Maine district of Massachusetts, urged another representative to act with "exertion" in "the approaching election" since there was "more than usual activity among the Jacobins," who were "employing every possible art to effect their purposes." Meanwhile, a Republican handbill sounded the alarm regarding Federalists' schemes for "hiring men to go" door to door "in search of electors to gain their votes." They were even "sending their lawyers in every direction," leaving "no stone unturned" in pursuit of victory at the ballot box. What a reflection of the times that, rather than condemning "such extraordinary and unparalleled exertions," Republicans were urged to "meet them on their own ground! Disperse yourselves through the wards, and bring up all your votes."[48]

This they did. In the end, Jefferson enjoyed one of the most lopsided victories in the history of U.S. presidential elections—a landslide that saw him win every state except Connecticut and Delaware. He earned all of the electoral votes of Massachusetts, the former Federalist stronghold, and all but two electors in Maryland. "The late grand Presidential election, is a declaration of the will of the people," proclaimed Congressman John Rhea of Tennessee. It offered "conclusive evidence of the public opinion," and "the sovereign people by a vote nearly unanimous, have pronounced the solemn sentence." Congressman Richard Stanford of North Carolina predicted that Jefferson's reelection "insured for four years to come" America's "peace, prosperity, and happiness" as "the freest and happiest nation under heaven."[49]

Jefferson himself avoided Stanford's rosy guarantees, but in his second inaugural address he echoed Rhea's words. Thanking his countrymen for their support, he assured them of "the zeal with which it inspires me . . . to conduct myself as may best satisfy their just expectations." He noted that, in his first inaugural, "I declared the principles on which I believed it my duty to administer the affairs of our commonwealth." Now, "my conscience tells me that I have, on every occasion, acted up to that declaration . . . to the understanding of every candid mind." The bulk of his address, a review of the policies of his first term, did not intend "to arrogate to myself the merit of the measures" undertaken, for what made these possible was "the weight of public opinion." In other words, principles and measures mattered more than any one man, and the "union of sentiment now manifested so generally" would only grow and "at length prevail" when "our doubting brethren" recognize "that the mass of their fellow citizens, with whom they cannot yet resolve to act, as to principles and measures, think as they think, and desire as they desire" for honest government, peace, "civil and religious liberty," "law and order," "equality of rights," and the protection of "property, equal or unequal, which results to every man from his own industry, or that of his fathers." If self-effacing, Jefferson's words were also self-serving. While he upheld the idea that fidelity to principles—and the measures necessary to effect them—mattered more than loyalty to any man, he likewise left no doubt that he was the man around whom Americans' dawning "union of opinion" would coalesce.[50]

JEFFERSON'S TRIUMPHS extended beyond the purchase of Louisiana and the election of 1804. In 1806, the Senate ratified a peace treaty with Tripoli, which in 1801 had declared war on the United States and unleashed privateers who seized American vessels in the Mediterranean and enslaved American citizens. The navy's 1804 bombardment of Tripoli's harbor, together with U.S. marines' 1805 capture of Derne, Tripoli's stronghold on the eastern edge of the Gulf of Sidra, caused the North African nation's dictator to sue for peace with the United States on terms more favorable than those endured by European nations, which bought safe passage for their vessels with higher annual tributes. Republicans hailed the treaty as a victory for strength and pragmatism. Federalists mocked it as evidence of the president's timidity and willingness to pant after praise.

By 1806, Jefferson—and Americans at large—had grown accustomed to such outpourings of reverence and revulsion. On balance, the president's encounter with the privateers seems to have burnished his reputation, which, Federalist efforts notwithstanding, appeared to gain strength each year he piloted the ship of state. His letters to political intimates revealed little concern at all regarding citizens' views of either his handling of the war or his pact for peace. Instead, Jefferson worried about how the nations of Europe perceived his actions.[51] Given the increasing threats to American commerce in the Atlantic, Britain and France, and not people at home, constituted his toughest audience.

CHAPTER EIGHT

"Dignified Retirement"

WRITING ANONYMOUSLY in the December 23, 1807, issue of the *National Intelligencer,* James Madison championed Thomas Jefferson's recent decision to pursue "a dignified retirement." He described it as "a demonstration to the world, that we possess a virtue and patriotism which can take any shape that will best suit the occasion."[1] Yet the president's decision to step down after two terms in office, announced to the public only thirteen days earlier, was not the "dignified retirement" that Madison applauded. Instead, the secretary of state referred to the almost simultaneous embargo of all foreign trade, which had begun on December 22. This "dignified retirement within ourselves," his own brainchild as much as Jefferson's, aimed initially to keep America's merchant fleet out of reach of the warring navies of Britain and France, each of which had pledged to seize commerce bound for ports of the other. Later, Madison and Jefferson would conceive of the embargo as an experiment in commercial coercion, an exercise in self-denial that would exhaust the material resources of the belligerent nations and bring one or both to recognize the right of Americans to cross the ocean unbothered. Then they would champion it as a development measure, one that—by cutting off the supply of foreign manufactured goods—would increase the demand for domestic products. Whether defensive, coercive, or developmental, the embargo aimed to steer the United States clear of war with the world's great powers, from which little could be gained and much—including lives, fortunes, and even independence—could be lost.[2]

Notwithstanding its noble purpose, the embargo and the measures enacted to enforce it constituted the most heavy-handed system of legislation ever envisioned by the federal government. There were precedents, to be sure. During the imperial crisis with Britain and then again in the 1790s Americans used as diplomatic tools restrictions on oceanic trade. These, however, were extra-legal, brief in duration, or both. Jefferson's embargo was neither, and thus its consequences were more profound. In his attempt to avoid war, he expanded the military and authorized it to aim its weapons at American civilians suspected of foreign commerce. Naval vessels scoured coastal areas and inland waterways for American ships with American crews, and the military assumed search-and-seizure powers that the 4th Amendment seemed to have reserved for law enforcement officers possessing court-issued warrants. As Jefferson explained in August 1808 to Albert Gallatin, his treasury secretary, "Congress should legalize all *means* which may be necessary to obtain it's *end*."[3]

This was hardly the Jefferson that his Republican contemporaries mythologized—the strict constructionist, the champion of principle and individual rights, the noble instrument of the people's will who elevated process above purpose. This was hardly the president who, in his first inaugural address, promised a government that, after restraining "men from injuring one another," would "leave them otherwise free to regulate their own pursuits of industry and improvement." If such a laissez-faire approach, as Jefferson had said, was "the sum of good government," then the embargo amounted to something altogether different.[4]

Also different were the ways in which Federalists criticized and Republicans justified this draconian measure, for the embargo not only transformed America's economy but also strained the Republic's partisan equilibrium. Republicans found the measure difficult to justify on the basis of their earlier principles of limited government. Federalists, who understood that the embargo hit hardest the same seafaring communities that constituted the cornerstone of their New England foothold, found themselves in the awkward position of opposing energetic government. Each of these political alliances adhered to a position on the embargo that undermined its philosophical foundation.

When Federalists employed their almost instinctive tactic of attacking Jefferson, characterizing the embargo as a manifestation of undesirable personality traits and dangerous ideological affinities, Republicans responded with more charitable assessments of his character. Trust in Jefferson, they argued, should yield acquiescence to his embargo. This for Jeffersonians marked a real departure, as throughout the 1790s and the first part of Jefferson's presidency they had done their best to appeal to the authority of principles and not men. As Jefferson had written in his draft of the Kentucky Resolutions of 1798, undue confidence in leaders "is every where the parent of despotism." Those who cherish liberty understand that "free government is founded in jealousy, and not in confidence" since "it is jealousy & not confidence which prescribes limited constitutions" that "bind down those whom we are obliged to trust with power."[5]

Republicans were not without principled reasons to promote the embargo as an alternative to war, which Madison described as "the most to be dreaded" of "all the enemies of public liberty" because it "comprises and develops the germ of every other." War was "the parent of armies," the expense of which yielded "debts and taxes" to fund these dangerous "instruments for bringing the many under the few."[6] In the aftermath of the HMS *Leopard*'s humiliating 1807 attack on the USS *Chesapeake,* however, antiwar appeals failed to satisfy. Far better to seek refuge in the authority of Jefferson, who had earned the people's trust.

The inconsistency of Republican rhetoric provided Federalists with an opening they were only too glad to exploit. Yet in chastising their adversaries' apparent hypocrisy, Federalists found it difficult to avoid casting doubt on their own fundamental presumptions. Their traditional emphasis on individual character originated in a more aristocratic, relatively closed, and localized political environment in which the natures of men could be known. In addition, the longstanding Republican insistence on principle, a product of the radical Enlightenment that gained adherents as an alternative to monarchy, served to broaden the political community by erecting a barrier between citizens and self-interested, self-promoting demagogues. The development, however, of cohesive, partisan alliances, each actively courting an expanding voting public, undermined both personal character and public principle as reliable indicators of merit. Either side, after all, could cast the motives of its own leaders as pure and those of the other's as corrupt. Likewise, competitive politics and electioneering subverted a system based on anonymous appeals to reason. Even when measures could not be attributed to a specific individual, almost always the discerning citizen could attribute them to a specific faction. Jefferson's embargo, more a catalyst for than a cause of this transformation in American political culture, muddied the choice between principles and men. As a growing number of citizens began to believe, there was a third way. Why settle for principles—or men—when instead it might be possible to elect to office men of principle? Why not insist that philosophy possess a face?

FIRST AMONG the victims of the embargo were the merchants and shipping interests whose property, Jefferson said, the embargo aimed to protect, as well as the seamen whose freedom from impressment the embargo claimed to preserve. Despite the president's good intentions, his policy had ruinous consequences for many Americans. Charleston's city council, for example, had to seek employment for displaced sailors and dockhands. Meanwhile, a Boston charity claimed to have found "useful work" for over one thousand citizens and relieved the "pressing want" of more than five thousand men, women, and children. In nearby Salem, a community almost entirely dependent on oceanic trade, the town baker distributed bread to the destitute and hundreds of families sought relief at a soup kitchen; according to the local paper, one-fifth of the population begged for food. A visitor to New York saw deserted streets that once had bustled with enterprise and witnessed grass growing on abandoned wharves. Massachusetts native John Park, whose 1808 pamphlet identified him only as a "Fellow Sufferer," charged that the embargo aimed not to safeguard America's trade but to destroy it. It "would fill a book," he contended, to provide a full account of the evidence that Jefferson and Madison "are, and have been, for twenty years, decided enemies of commerce."[7]

The embargo also hurt agriculture by depriving planters of overseas markets. As Benjamin Rush informed John Adams in July, among farmers "the Embargo becomes daily more and more unpopular." A Rhode Island resident predicted that a "remarkably prosperous" growing season would come to naught because "without commerce the surplus must rot on our land." Even Virginia Republican John Taylor worried that the continuance of the president's policy would "impoverish the agriculturalists." From Raleigh, North Carolina, came a report that "the Embargo has excited more dissatisfaction among the farmers . . . than any other measure done by Congress since the adoption of the constitution." Tobacco and cotton prices in Fayetteville had plummeted, and pork brought to market in Virginia found no buyers. People could not even use the meat to make bacon, for the cost of imported salt had skyrocketed.[8]

Not surprisingly, smuggling was rampant in some quarters, especially along the porous border of British Canada. In Utica, New York, for example, a British traveler witnessed wagons loaded with potash in procession along the road to Albany, where their cargoes would be sent up the Hudson. Later, he gloated in his diary that "with good malt liquor and excellent Port wine" newly prosperous Canadian traders now toasted "Thomas Jefferson & his Embargo" as often as they did the king. In just a few months, the burgeoning black market had "done more for Canada than fifty ordinary years would have effected." Already, detachments of militia had been sent from Rutland, Vermont, to Lake Champlain to crush what a Federalist paper dubbed "the *Potash and Lumber Rebellion.*" The enforcement efforts spurred ingenious tactics of evasion. At the crest of a hill straddling the Vermont-Canada border, smugglers reportedly erected a flimsy warehouse designed so that, "on the removal of a stone or a piece of wood, the whole edifice with its contents immediately falls on the British territory."⁹

While smuggling and gamesmanship represented the most common forms of resistance to the embargo, people worried that anger over the president's policy might escalate into armed revolt and even result in civil war. As early as January 1808, the *Connecticut Courant* voiced fears of mob violence by out-of-work seamen. Rosalie Stier Calvert, a Maryland Federalist who considered "Tommy Jeff" a "good-for-nothing President," eleven months later predicted that "if this embargo is not lifted soon, a civil war is inevitable." John Adams, although initially warm to Jefferson's trade stoppage, at this point also prophesied that "if the Embargo is not lightened," the United States might soon suffer "distraction and confusion, if not insurrections and civil war, and foreign war at the same time both with France and England."¹⁰

For months, northeastern states and towns had been issuing resolutions deploring the president's policies. Resistance reached an especially fevered pitch after Congress passed a fifth and final enforcing act in January 1809. The measure increased the cost of security bonds required for coastal trade, empowered revenue collectors to seize suspicious cargoes, and authorized Jefferson to use the navy, army, and militia against American citizens. The Connecticut General Assembly, employing the logic of Jefferson's Kentucky Resolutions, declared the law unconstitutional and asserted the "duty of the legislative and executive authorities" of the state "to withhold their aid and cooperation, from the execution of the act." Bostonians, as jurist Daniel Lyman reported, decreed "that any man who shall comply with its provisions [is] Infamous, and an Enemy to his Country." False rumors circulated that even Massachusetts governor Levi Lincoln, who had once served as Jefferson's attorney general, had resigned rather than execute the hated law—a course of action that several other New England officials did, in fact, take. To many the nation seemed on the edge of the abyss. Each step to tighten the embargo met with increased opposition, which in turn prompted the administration's friends to suggest increasingly draconian measures. "I do not certainly know the shape the opposition is to assume in the future," Lincoln informed Albert Gallatin at the end of January 1809, "but whatever it may be, it must be met, and the government supported at all events."[11]

FEAR OF ARMED REBELLION, if not entirely unwarranted, was certainly overwrought. Similarly, reports of contraband freely crossing borders and cascading down hillsides probably did not do justice to the government's success at enforcing the embargo.[12] In truth, the most widespread and powerful form of opposition to the administration and its policies remained the Federalist press. Always vigilant and ever eager to focus on Jefferson's supposed frailties, newspapermen and pamphleteers who opposed him made the most of the embargo as an occasion to reiterate themes that had long shaded their dark portraits of his character. He possessed, they said, a near-treasonous attachment to France, to which he stood ready to sacrifice American interests. He was an impractical theorist and an unrepentant atheist.

If during the French Revolution Federalists had linked Jefferson to France to underscore his radicalism, now that Napoleon ruled they depicted his attachment as the result of blind prejudice—or a love of power more than philosophy. Daniel Webster asserted that "the real cause of the Embargo" was Jefferson's wish "to FAVOUR FRANCE" in its war with Britain. "Great-Britain is a commercial Country," he explained, so it "feels the Embargo more." In addition, Webster maintained that Jefferson and his allies "are perpetually singing the praises of the French Emperour. They rejoice in his successes, and justify and applaud his most enormous acts of injustice and oppression." As another writer claimed, for "8 years he and his party have been truckling to France and abusing the British, and to crown all, they are ruining the country with their cursed Embargo." An Albany newspaper printed a letter speculating on the reasons for Jefferson's "partiality for France." Since nearly all of civilization kissed Napoleon's "iron sceptre," maybe the president aimed to betray his own nation in exchange for an appointment as "the second man in the mighty empire of the world."[13]

A pamphlet by "Civis" held that "in common with all philosophers, labouring under a constitutional timidity, or a blind attachment to French principles, French philosophy, and the French nation," Jefferson had long been known "for that weakness of nerve, imbecility, and indecision, which now mark his administration." A mocking nursery rhyme titled "Dignified Retirement" echoed this familiar theme when it described how the British lion "roared and frightened Thomas, the King," whom it also characterized as "the Priest, all shaven and shorn, / who fled to the mountain, all covered with scorn, / and studied philosophy evening and morn." Charles Brockden Brown, perhaps America's most luminous literary figure, opined that Jefferson had "also the misfortune to be a schemer, perpetually occupied with some strange out-of-the-way project.... He labours also under such defect of mental vision, that he seldom sees objects in their natural state and true position." Citizens in Springfield, Massachusetts, anticipating Jefferson's departure from office, offered a laconic toast to *"The President of the United States—* to ruin a country govern it by a French Philosopher—we hail the fourth of March, 1809."[14]

Jefferson's image as a partisan of France and an impractical philosopher coalesced nicely with his image as an atheist. Although writers never claimed that his religious beliefs had any direct bearing on his embargo policies, they nonetheless took the opportunity to remind the public of his alleged apostasy. Massachusetts minister Thomas Thacher, for example, said in a sermon that a man who was "intemperate and lewd, corrupt and unprincipled, profligate and impious, is an enemy to his country."[15]

All these aspersions, which sprang straight from the longstanding tradition of Federalist critique, focused squarely on Jefferson. That his adversaries often expressed skepticism about the efficacy of his policies comes as no surprise. More often than not, however, personal and not public character was the focus of the opposition. "I put it home to you," read a published letter signed by "Richard Saunders," a name that resonated as Benjamin Franklin's alter ego, "whether the men of the most respectable characters are not Federalists." Just "look round you," he suggested, "and see for yourself, if the religion, the honesty, and the good conduct in private life, of the federal leaders, is not at least equally good as their neighbors." Jefferson, however, paled in comparison. As Richard Saunders observed, "I don't like the man." That, he wrote, was the "end of it."[16]

NO MATTER its shortcomings, the embargo did yield some salutary effects. First—and as intended—it strained the resources of France and, most especially, Great Britain. The latter nation, which Napoleon had already excluded from many of the markets of continental Europe, relied heavily on American agriculture. A nearly 75 percent decline in imports from the United States helped to boost the prices that Britons paid for wheat, barley, oats, and particularly cotton. Even more important to the balance of power, Britain experienced greater difficulty replacing lost American produce than did the United States in finding domestic substitutes for British finished goods.[17]

This phenomenon points to a second, not as fully anticipated effect of the embargo: an increase in American manufacturing. Rising prices for imported products, the supply of which the embargo diminished, assured investors of the relative strength of consumer demand for things made in the United States. As a consequence, capital that had previously nurtured overseas trade now stimulated coastal commerce and production at home. Reports of advances in America's fledgling textile, shoe, glassware, iron, and paper industries promised greater economic independence. This, Jefferson said, gave him great solace. He had earlier criticized manufacturing, preferring a nation of self-sufficient farmers to one of dependent wage laborers. Now, however, the circumstances of the embargo accelerated his growing acceptance of light industry already spurred by the Louisiana Purchase, which supplied an abundance of cheap farmland for American laborers "to resort to . . . whenever it shall be attempted by the other classes to reduce them to the minimum of subsistence." Prospects for a new economic order also buoyed the spirits of many of the nation's entrepreneurs, especially in the mid-Atlantic states, where manufacturing growth was most robust. In June 1808, while citizens in some parts of the country faced poverty, Benjamin Rush marveled that the streets and parlors of Philadelphia "are constantly vocal with the language of a broker's office, and even at our convivial dinners 'Dollars' are a standing dish upon which all feed with rapacity and gluttony." Such was the passion for manufacturing that, just a few months later, at a banquet in Rush's city, revelers extolled Jefferson not only as their president but also as "the manufacturer of the Declaration of Independence."[18]

Falling short of describing him as "author," which would have implied innovation and authorization, this claim combined enthusiasm for industry with a relatively modest understanding of what Jefferson had achieved in 1776. Derived from Latin, "to manufacture" means to make by hand, to assemble parts to constitute a whole. Thus Jefferson's friends in Philadelphia paid him tribute as the man who had composed and compiled the Declaration, who had constructed an expression of the people's will. The dozens of wordsmiths who for more than a decade had been spreading news of Jefferson's contribution to independence revealed subtle differences in how they viewed his role. All agreed, of course, that Jefferson had performed the physical act of drafting the Declaration. Toasts at Fourth of July banquets in Washington,

D.C., for example, had described him as "the penman of the declaration of Independence" and noted that his was the "hand that drew the declaration of Independence." These printers not only signaled that Jefferson had assembled, rather than invented and approved, the document but also, through their frequent capitalization of "Independence" after their lowercasing of the word "declaration," provided evidence that, during the first decade of the nineteenth century, the Revolutionary idea of national autonomy could still remain above and apart from Jefferson's decree.[19]

In 1801, the pro-administration *National Intelligencer* had distinguished between Jefferson's singular action and the Continental Congress's shared assertion when it reported the "patriotic gratitude" that an enthusiastic Independence Day crowd showered upon the "first magistrate ... whose pen had traced, whose councils had recommended, and whose firmness and talents had co-operated to establish the declaration of Independence." Similarly, members of New York's zealously Republican Tammany Society had heard the 1800 Fourth of July address of Matthew Livingston Davis, who praised "the capacious mind and nervous pen of Jefferson," whose "Manly and energetic" text announced independence with a "Solemn and impressive ... sound." Davis pointed out, however, that Jefferson's words communicated "the voice of a free, united and indignant people." Hundreds of miles south, at St. Philip's Church in Charleston, orator John J. Pringle had extolled "JEFFERSON, in whose perspicuous and energetic language is expressed that sublime memorial of the rights, and the spirit of free-born Americans." James Kennedy, a year later at the same site (and displaying an uncommon spirit of nonpartisanship), had lauded "that celebrated declaration, penned by the enlightened, dignified and patriotic Jefferson, and advocated by the firm, honest and sagacious Adams." In sum, the young Virginian drew, penned, traced, and phrased the Declaration; the act of independence itself, however, required the cooperation, embodied the will, and depended on the advocacy of others.[20]

Not all Republicans drew such distinctions. An increasing number granted to Jefferson the much greater status of "author" and reified his text by conflating the Declaration as document, to which they imparted a more formalized title, with American autonomy as fact. At a July 4, 1805, Boston gathering of "Young Democratic Republicans," for example, Ebenezer French had praised the president as "the immortal author of the DECLARATION OF AMERICAN INDEPENDENCE." Twelve months later, he had focused the attention of an assembly of Maine Republicans on "the glorious instrument written by the illuminous JEFFERSON, called the '*Declaration of American Independence.*'"

Although other speechmakers merely credited Jefferson's hand for drawing up the document, these claimed that his thoughts had conceived it. In 1807, for example, Levi Lincoln, Jr., son of the former attorney general, applauded Jefferson, "the sublimity of whose mind first ken'd American Independence and whose pen impressed the solemn Declaration."[21]

Federalists continued their tactic of seldom mentioning Jefferson's name in connection with the Declaration, but for some the increasing stature of the document made his role difficult to ignore. If they acknowledged it, they did their best to diminish it. When Supreme Court chief justice John Marshall discussed proceedings at the Continental Congress in his 1805–7 biography of George Washington, he buried in a footnote a tepid recognition that "the draft reported by the committee has been generally attributed to Mr. Jefferson." Others, like the author of an 1802 newspaper essay, did their best to deny it. Despite "repeated and positive assertions to the contrary," the writer claimed, Jefferson "was not the draftsman of the declaration of American independence." Instead, the president had merely sat on a committee charged with composing the statement. After a proclamation "had been drawn by *the committee,* not by Mr. Jefferson," Congress made "essential alterations" of its language. Citing "the mouths of two of the venerable sages and patriots who composed that congress," this writer attributed the "elegant form" that the Declaration "at last assumed" to "the handsome amendments proposed by a gentleman who has since become the victim of jacobinical slanders" but not to "any brilliancy of talents on the part of Mr. Thomas Jefferson."[22]

Although this writer strived to deprive the president of any special claim to the Declaration's substance and style, his assertions confirmed that the Declaration as a text had begun to assume a position of importance rivaling that of Congress's collective declaration. Although a number of Republican statements already corroborated the accuracy of this implicit recognition, the 1806 murder of George Wythe, Jefferson's friend and mentor, set off a chain of events that attracted additional attention to the issue of authorship. Wythe, who drank the poison of an estranged grandnephew, left an estate including not only bank stock and a house but also a copy of the draft of the Declaration of Independence that Jefferson had apparently given him thirty years earlier.[23]

Thanks to the estate's executor and the editor of the *Richmond Enquirer,* Jefferson's *"original* Declaration of our Independence" gained a wide audience within the Old Dominion. The *National Intelligencer* reprinted it as well, adding its own recognition of the president as the "distinguished author" of this "splendid composition" to the *Enquirer'*s claim that

The federal assertion that Mr. Jefferson was not the author of this celebrated declaration, has long since been refuted or else these papers would
have furnished the most abundant refutation. What now will become
of the no less unfounded assertion, that this paper as it was adopted
by Congress, owes much of its beauty and its force to the committee
appointed to draft it? The world will see that not only were very few
additions made by the committee, but that they even struck out two of
the most forcible and striking passages in the whole composition.[24]

LIKE THE NEW CONCEPTION of Jefferson's "authorship" of the Declaration, the debate over the embargo also facilitated a new portrayal of Jefferson
as president. According to this understanding of his leadership, Jefferson was
not merely the agent of Republicanism. Instead, he was its embodiment. This
view of Jefferson's leadership—not novel to the embargo episode—coincided
with the start of his presidency and appeared in varying degrees of prevalence
ever since. As with his rising fame as "author" of the Declaration, here the
tides of cultural change oftentimes ebbed and flowed to coalesce with political
expediency.

Whatever the persuasive strength of principled justifications for the embargo laws, a number of Republicans seemed to sense that appeals to personal loyalty would work best to shore up support for the administration.
More than the embargo jeopardized Republican unity. In anticipation of the
presidential election of 1808, factions formed to promote the candidacies of
Secretary of State James Madison, Vice President George Clinton, and James
Monroe, who had recently returned from a disappointing diplomatic mission to Britain. William Duane, editor of Philadelphia's *Aurora,* understood
that these machinations not only threatened harmony among Republicans
but also distracted supporters of the administration from the embargo crisis.
"It is certainly not a period to bicker about men," he wrote, "and if we can
only ensure the pursuit of the same system of policy that has been pursued
under *Jefferson,*" the identity of his successor constituted "a very subordinate
consideration."[25]

The impending conclusion of Jefferson's presidency—together with his
imminent departure as America's leading Republican—worked to elevate
his symbolic importance as president and party leader. Later generations had
"lame ducks." Republicans, however, viewed Jefferson as an almost indispensable swan. The messiah of Republicanism, he had many apostles who

could serve as his successor but, to echo comments he made in France when elevated to Franklin's former role as minister plenipotentiary, not a single one who could satisfy all as his replacement. As early as 1806 Congressman Thomas Thompson, a New Hampshire Federalist who spread gossip about a third term for Jefferson, predicted "the impossibility" of Republicans uniting around "any other man." Josiah Quincy, Thompson's colleague from Massachusetts, surmised that neither "national honour" nor "national interest" mattered more than how "the people's passions be best arranged to secure the continuance of power in the present hands."[26]

More than a few Republicans seemed to call for trust in—and submission to—the chief executive. "Your government possesses better means of information than any printer of a newspaper," reasoned the Boston *Democrat,* "and will not conceal from you any information that is necessary to your good or prosperity." Pennsylvania legislators passed resolutions expressing "the fullest confidence in the wisdom, the patriotism, and the integrity of the administration." Similarly, the *National Intelligencer* reminded readers that the embargo had been "recommended by the President, who has the best means of knowing the policy of foreign governments." It maintained that "a people confiding in their government" should "rally round the measure ... by patiently and proudly submitting to every inconvenience" their government required. Later the paper held up the fact that "the embargo is the measure proposed by the executive"—"by Thomas Jefferson"—as one of the strongest reasons for citizens to lend it their support. "Has this man ever abused the confidence of his fellow-citizens? Has he ever crouched to foreign influence? Has he ever recommended a national measure, which has not promoted the public interest?" The newspaper claimed that "we are not the friends of blind confidence in any executive" but maintained nevertheless "that at a period like this ... confidence is the best of virtues," and one "a true republican will not blush to own."[27]

There existed no reason "to doubt the patriotism of our administration," according to a pamphlet published in Portsmouth, New Hampshire, and there existed no reason "to doubt its wisdom." The pamphlet mounted a defense of the embargo, in part by pointing to the success of Jefferson's previous record. He repealed internal taxes, dismissed overpaid tax collectors and judges, let lapse the sedition law, reduced by $30 million the national debt, and preserved America in peace. "Are not these measures the doings of a *Patriot?* Are they not the measures of wisdom?" Meanwhile, an 1809 Boston pamphlet seemed to argue for support of the embargo notwithstanding its wisdom as policy:

"A Government depending upon the confidence of the People to be enabled to do right, must have the power sometimes to do wrong." Citizens who bestowed on the president "a sincere approbation of wise measures" should also grant "a magnanimous indulgence for the errors which are incident to human nature. When the National Administration ceases to possess the confidence of the People, it will lose confidence in itself; and from the want of this will always follow a deficiency of energy and stability indispensable to its success."[28]

Such arguments displayed little fidelity to the traditional tenets of Jeffersonian Republicanism, which decried energetic government, favored political responsiveness over stability, and hitherto had valued principle over any one man. Now, however, Republicans called on citizens to submit to the authority of the embargo laws because Jefferson was their author. His endorsement of the embargo mattered more than its wisdom, which a surprising number of Republicans seemed happy to take for granted. Some even held up as evidence of the embargo's efficacy John Quincy Adams's early approbation of the measure. One writer cheered that Adams, a Federalist and a man "opposed in principle to the present administration," could be guided in this instance not by party but by "love of country." The writer never considered that Adams, in supporting the embargo's heavy-handed projection of government power, might have remained more firmly tethered to his Federalist principles than Republicans to theirs. Fourth of July celebrants in Philadelphia, for example, revised the traditional banquet toast to the people, who had previously been honored as the arbiters of law, by raising their glasses to "the people of the U.S.—May they ever submit with promptitude, to constitutional laws." As a writer who called himself "Livingston" opined, "all good men ought to be united in support of their government."[29]

It was not unthinkable in 1808 that Republicans, who once reminded the federal government that it served citizens, would now inform citizens that they had an obligation to serve their government. Nor was it improper for the men and women who attended the traditional New Year's Day open house at the Executive Mansion to shower Jefferson with praise. "It is no part of the character of a republican to be lavish of personal attentions on public men," the *National Intelligencer* maintained, "but on this occasion the spontaneous tribute of respect to a man whose whole life has been zealously devoted to the service of his country was no less honorable to those who paid than to him who received it." People attending an 1807 dinner in honor of James Monroe made a similarly awkward attempt to honor traditional Republican priorities while also extolling the president. After the last course, they offered toasts:

first, to the United States; second, to the people; and third, to Jefferson. But while the nation and its citizens each received three cheers, Jefferson, they thought, merited nine.[30]

Participants at an 1809 Fourth of March banquet near Richmond displayed a similar prejudice when they raised their glasses to Jefferson, who they said deserved "the confidence and approbation of his Country," only moments before lashing out at members of Congress, whose votes to repeal the embargo garnered the assemblage's scorn for "a timidity of conduct unworthy of our national character." Did these Republicans have so much confidence in Jefferson that they felt no need to inquire into his position on the bill to repeal the embargo? Were they blind to the fact that its passage required not only a majority in Congress but also Jefferson's signature?[31]

REPUBLICAN INCONSISTENCY flabbergasted Federalists. While their criticisms of the Republican leader's public policies and personal character continued, their critique of Republicans in general intensified. Given that Jefferson would soon retire, this development is not surprising. The personalized nature of their rhetoric, focused as it had been on the president, would do little for them once he departed—for good—to Monticello. Now, of course, they could aim at Madison, and they did. But Republican principles proved a more alluring if elusive target, for the alliance that had once championed "principles and *not* men" seemed now to have inverted its own motto.

Critics contended that Jefferson's star-struck supporters, so busy with their fawning adulation, had little time to examine his measures. One opponent of the embargo lashed out at the apparent "blind credulity in the infallibility of a political pontiff." Added another, "we have suffered ourselves to be led by the nose tamely and submissively, apparently satisfied with ruin, if we are only ruined by Mr. Jefferson." As republican thinkers had asserted since the days of Henry St. John, Viscount Bolingbroke, confidence in leaders could result in tyranny. "Like flammable air," warned a Massachusetts pamphlet, ambitious officials "expand and increase in power, the higher they ascend." As a "Citizen of Vermont" maintained, "our Rulers are responsible to the people, but, if the people refuse to call them to an account, all responsibility is at an end." The fact that several state legislatures had passed resolutions voicing their faith in Jefferson's measure disgusted another Federalist: "if Mr. Jefferson was to declare *himself King*," he insisted, "they would justify that also." A Maine writer advised his neighbors to guard "your Rights and Liberties, and despise the doctrine of *passive obedience,* which the friends of those who invade them, endeavor to inculcate." Voluntary submission to tyranny was worse than slavery. The *Connecticut Courant* minced no words making this point. "The negroes in Virginia," the paper pointed out, "submit to their drivers of necessity. A certain set of slaves submit to the same drivers of choice. Query—Which class of slaves are most despicable, the white or the black?"[32]

A Maryland writer went so far as to point toward people "who almost idolize our executive, who applaud all his opinions, and all his measures, who dissent in nothing even from his caprices, [and] who perceive in him only the purest virtue and the most sublime intelligence." South Carolina Federalist John Rutledge, Jr., threw up his hands at the "apathy & infatuation of our People" with "the tyranny & despotism," "misrule," and "follies" of Jefferson and his "quixotical Virginia cabinet." The existence of such "popular infatuation," as Rutledge described it, astounded Jefferson's critics at the same time that they exchanged knowing glances. On the one hand, the turnabout in Republican rhetoric caused whiplash. On the other, the self-described friends of order and good government had long been suspicious of Jeffersonians and the sycophants who courted their support. Sometimes these Federalists mixed their exasperation with contempt; sometimes they tempered it with condescension. A mocking poem called *The Times* exemplified the first combination:

> His Majesty, our royal sire,
> Hints his intention to retire.
> Stay, best of men, ah! stay thy hand,
> Still, still support, and save the land!
> This land, by thee alone sustained,
> About thy neck like mill-stone chained,
> And eke within thy bosom lies,
> Dear as the apple of thine eyes;
> And which, to compensate thy pains,
> Submits to infamy and chains—
> Our sorrowing eyes will never see
> Another President *like thee*—
> Like thee—to sing the honied song,
> And coax and cheat the gaping throng.

Another poem, dubbed *The Embargo* and written anonymously by William Cullen Bryant, a precocious thirteen year old, presented an even more scalding indictment of Jefferson's supporters. It lashed out less at their willingness to believe in the president's greatness than their own misplaced vanity. Bryant invited readers to imagine a scene of Jeffersonian electioneering:

> Enter, and view the thronging concourse there,
> Intent, with gaping mouth, and stupid stare,
> While in their midst their supple leader stands,
> Harangues aloud, and flourishes his hands;
> To adulation tunes his servile throat,
> And sues, successful, for each blockhead's vote.

These citizens reward the demagogue not only with election. They also make "their creed, his *dictum,* and their law, his will." (Bryant's composition appears in the third volume of Jefferson's newspaper commonplace scrapbooks. Another poem, pasted directly beneath the teenager's, is titled "Presumptuous Pride.")[33] Federalists also pitied the credulity of Republicans in Congress. "I believe them honest," a writer claimed shortly before the 1809 repeal of the embargo, "and I think they wish to get right; but from some cause or other, they still lend themselves to leaders, who are themselves led, and still listen to a person, whose system they no longer approve, and whose snares they perceive and resolve to shun, but do not manfully avoid."[34]

Federalists explained the embargo as the product of servility and Jefferson's unwillingness to allow people to make informed choices. Even before the embargo, John Adams, eager to vindicate himself against his erstwhile enemies and draw favorable distinctions between his presidency and that of Jefferson, informed Benjamin Rush that "our Monarchical, Anti-Republican administration conceal from us the People all that Information that I a zealous Republican was always prompt to communicate." Adams's comment amounted to sweet revenge against those who, in the 1790s, had criticized Federalists' refusal to disclose things such as the text of the Jay Treaty. Charles Brockden Brown stood as one of many who now charged Jefferson's administration with hypocrisy. "The gentlemen in power," he noted, "used formerly to insist that republics should have no state secrets. Times have changed," it seemed, and the Republicans, now in power, "have changed with the times. We have secrets in abundance. Indeed, we have little else." The *New-York Evening Post,* making the most of a Jeffersonian paper's reassurances that the embargo "was emphatically the PRESIDENT'S *measure,*" wondered if "the people will continue to *idolize* him when they find themselves without food or cloathing" as "he persists in concealing himself and his measures in the impenetrable secrecy which he is now pleased to observe." One *Connecticut Courant* writer reminded readers "how widely different Mr. Jefferson's *practice in power,* is, from his *professions* before he *obtained his power*." Another noted that, when Adams raised an army to bolster the nation's defenses during the Quasi-War with France, "the whole herd of democracy was let loose, to decry it; and the dangers to be apprehended from standing armies were pourtrayed in the strongest colours. But mark the consistency of the democrats!" Now Jefferson desired to raise an army—"and for what purposes nobody can tell, unless it is to carry into effect a ruinous embargo law"—and his supporters did not raise an eyebrow. "*The measure was recommended by Mr. Jefferson, and is therefore wise,* say the democrats. O! The consistency of democracy!"[35]

These remarks aimed to embarrass Republicans by exposing their contradictions. But Federalists seemed also to believe that their jibes could win over the president's supporters by forcing them to confront the disjunction between sincere pronouncements of the past and opportunistic poses of the present. New Hampshire senator Nicholas Gilman, a maverick Republican, reported in 1812 that "a very conspicuous Senator from one of our western states *who voted for the Embargo*" had recently reminded him that "not three members of the Senate . . . believed the measure to be a wise or proper one." Even so, they had deferred to their leader, for "to oppose the Executive, however erroneous his judgment may be . . . is to abandon party." As a result, "men are continually supporting pernicious measures, and we blunder on from bad to worse." Representative Barent Gardenier, a New York Federalist, also lashed out against presidential influence. "We sit here as mere automata," he said, for "we legislate without knowing, . . . without wishing to know, why or wherefore. We are told what we are to do."[36]

FEDERALISTS AND REPUBLICANS of the nineteenth century were not the Federalists and Republicans of the 1790s, when Republicans had aimed to restrain political power and Federalists had taken comfort in wielding it. During Jefferson's presidency, the turning of tables prompted a shift that had been noticed even before the embargo when, in 1806, Duane's *Aurora* featured an essay titled "Principles and Not Men—or, The Principles of the Old Republican Party." Jeffersonians merited "public contempt," it warned, if they denied "as indisputable truths" the "truths we held indisputable in 1797, and 1798, and 1799." (It is unclear whether Jefferson also noticed the shift. He noticed this essay, however, and he clipped it for inclusion in his scrapbooks.) Now, the growing inconsistency between earlier pronouncements and recent

behavior undermined the credibility of each of the factions. If "the absurdi-
ties and contradictions in principle and conduct of our two great parties," as
Rush wrote in 1808, were "laid out before the world in a candid and dispas-
sionate manner, we should be ashamed to call ourselves MEN." John Adams
agreed, characterizing the partisanship of 1808 as "squabbles of little girls"
fighting for dolls and "little boys" grabbing for "rattles and whistles." The
choice between factions, he said, amounted to "a mighty bustle about a mighty
bauble."[37]

Although Adams's statement minimized important and persistent distinctions, no one can deny that the embargo debate sometimes brought forth
instances of immaturity and examples of interchangeability. A silly song by
Henry Mellen, a Federalist attorney from New Hampshire, spawned silly Republican parodies. One of Mellen's verses held that

> Our ships all in motion,
> Once whiten'd the ocean,
> They sail'd and return'd with a Cargo;
> Now doom'd to decay,
> They have fallen prey,
> To Jefferson, worms and Embargo.

Mellen's lines inspired Jeffersonian retorts, including

> Tho' 'our ships all in motion once whiten'd the ocean,'
> 'And sail'd and return'd with a cargo;'
> Yet when foreign decrees so infest all our seas,
> We will preserve peace by 'Embargo.'

Jefferson, who pasted these and other lyrics in his newspaper scrapbooks,
arranged them together after Mellen's version. Maybe his object was simple
amusement. If this cluster instead represents an attempt to assemble and survey expressions of public opinion, his sampling skewed so heavily toward his
own partisans that, rather than truly listening to citizens, he only heard what
he wanted them to say. The parodies—reinforced by the appearance of other
lyrical expressions of support—had the effect of minimizing the critique.
Minimizing it further were arguments on both sides of the debate possessing
far more seriousness.[38]

The new Federalist emphasis on the politics of principle over the politics of
personality made sense given that the embargo, although unpopular in many
quarters, was not so unpopular as to erode significantly the affection with

which many Americans still regarded its author, whose actions while in office never came close to confirming their most dire assessments of his character. Yet their turn toward issues-based rhetoric amounted to more than the best of their remaining options. It also seemed to reflect a newfound sense of humility. Their nearly decade-long experience in the minority, combined with a dearth of men of national stature around whom they could rally, changed not only their circumstances but also, it seems, some of their most fundamental beliefs. The anti-Jefferson writer who signed himself "Richard Saunders" admitted that "all men have their faults, and the Federalists have talked too much about Mr. Jefferson's not believing in Religion, and about his black woman, and so on. I would not look at men," he wrote, "but at measures." It should not be overlooked that Richard Saunders, in dismissing discussion of Jefferson's supposed personal shortcomings, could not resist the urge to highlight two of them. Even so, his statement marked a significant shift.[39]

At a time when at least some Federalists demonstrated an increasing willingness to look beyond Jefferson, more and more Republicans seemed reluctant to let him go. For one thing, the recognition that his presidency would soon come to an end prompted a good deal of nostalgia. For another, his impending absence created a void in leadership. By whom should it be filled? A Virginia Republican, who described "the elevation of Jefferson to the presidential chair" as a "triumph of principle" over "folly and profusion," recalled that the "demon of faction had not *then* insinuated itself into the republican phalanx. We moved in one body.... *Principles,* not *men,* were the test of the patriots of 1800." Now, however, "jealousies and rivalships disturbed the harmony of the republican party." Not only "the intrigues of Burr" and the "ridiculous fulminations of John Randolph"—who marshaled support from Republican fundamentalists who viewed Jefferson, Madison, and their followers as apostates, trimmers, and sell-outs—testified to the new spirit of "ambition" but also "the present distraction" of whether Madison or Monroe would assume the presidency.[40]

The experience of the embargo had lasting implications for Republicans. It spurred them to base confidence in Jefferson's public measures on personal trust. But this development, in which they ascribed the authority of the embargo to its author, sprang from more than mere convenience, for it also reflected larger trends in American culture. The meaning of authorship was changing from the act of authorizing to the art of creating. Just as Jefferson received credit and blame for the embargo—envisioned and proposed by him but authorized by Congress—during the first decade of the nineteenth century, the Declaration of Independence, which had formerly derived its authority from its "self-evident" "truths," came to draw strength from an association with Jefferson, now less its penman than its "author."

Such relationships could cut both ways. While Jefferson's connection with the Declaration reinforced support for the document, its principles reinforced support for Jefferson. This, then, constituted a third conception of authority, more sophisticated than the simple choice of measures or men and more practicable for the expanding, expansive political community of an undeniably partisan democratic republic. The history of a man's actions revealed principles that citizens understood to foreshadow future proposals. As a group of Virginia Republicans proclaimed on the day of Madison's inauguration, the fourth president's "past services in the cause of his country" constituted "a sure pledge for his future conduct." Americans who once saw a choice between principles and men could now lionize men of principle.[41]

As a result, on July 4, 1807, capital city Republicans toasted the "*author of the declaration of independence*—May those who are enemies of his principles and the administration of them, obtain a personal exemption from the restraints of the embargo"—and then be sent overseas. An essay on the "False Colours" of individuals attempting "to hamper America's independence, divide its people, [and] repeal the embargo" attributed their failure "to the wisdom of the man who penned the declaration of independence." To Jefferson, it maintained, "we owe the assertion of the *principles* and policy now which squares and operates with the declaration." A caucus of Pennsylvania Republicans announced their nomination of Simon Snyder for governor by emphasizing that his "principles are consentaneous with those of Jefferson." In other words, Snyder devoted himself "to the principles of democratic representative government" and "the principles contained in the declaration of American independence." Annapolis Republicans also connected ideals with individuals. At a banquet honoring General James Wilkinson, an individual later revealed to possess few ideals and even less integrity, they drank to "the People—the only legitimate source of power," toasted "the Constitution of the United States—the palladium of our liberties," and raised their cups to "the President of the United States—the patriot who penned the declaration of independence—the honest guardian of the nation's rights, under whose banners we are prepared to conquer or die." Jefferson, these statements attested, served as the embodiment of Jeffersonian Republicanism.[42]

THE DIGNIFIED RETIREMENT for which Jefferson had hoped never fully materialized. To be sure, Republicans in Congress gave him the opportunity to sign the repeal of the embargo, which ended on March 4, 1809, the last day of his presidency. More important, Madison, his partner of two decades, had been elected to take from him the reins of government. Even so, as John Adams confided, "Mr. Jefferson has reason to reflect upon himself. How he will get rid of his remorse in his retirement, I know not. He must know that he leaves the government infinitely worse than he found it." While Adams's sour grapes salved his own punctured pride, his indictment of his successor—whom he described as a victim of either "error or ignorance"— also represented a mature assessment of Jefferson's desires for power and popularity. "If I have not mismeasured his ambition," Adams wrote, Jefferson would prove so dissatisfied with private life that his "sword will cut away the scabbard."[43]

Adams, of course, would be proven wrong—except for the fact that, in one sense, he turned out to be right. Never again would Jefferson hold public office. Never again would he collectivize and render into acts of coercion the decisions of individual voters, the minority of whom, as Adams knew better than anyone, could not have their way. After his presidency Jefferson kept a respectful distance from Madison, whom he wanted to leave free to make his own declarations of independence.[44] Nonetheless, he would continue to possess a degree of consequence that, upon his retirement from the presidency, reflected less the diminution of his actual powers than it did the magnification of his stature as a selfless servant of the people. Like Washington before him, Jefferson voluntarily left the presidency to return to his farm, his family, and his books. Also like Washington, Jefferson understood that giving up power served as the surest way to retain influence.

The National Intelligencer, for example, avowed that "this step was the dictate, not of necessity, but choice, and that it manifests the most illustrious homage which the mind of man can pay to principle." After all, had "Thomas Jefferson desired to retain power, there was no competitor," and his continuance in office would have been approved by "a vast majority." But the lessons of history had been learned by Jefferson, who understood that "the deadliest foe to liberty has ever been the permanent deposit of power in the hands of an individual," and recognized that "this last splendid act of his public life proves principle to have been his polar star."[45]

Such adulation, the Republican paper reasoned, "cannot be mistaken for flattery, or be ascribed to impure motives." Now that Jefferson had retired, in other words, praise for him required no restraint. Similarly, the *Baltimore American* published a laudatory address to Jefferson that had for months been withheld for fear that it might have seemed inappropriate. What better time to print it than "the moment of Mr. Jefferson's leaving power," when no one would been seen as guilty of "crouching flattery" in tendering their sincere "gratitude and affection"? Meanwhile, members of the legislature of South Carolina refused to applaud the president for his decision to step down. Unable to "suppress the strong desire" that Jefferson "should consent again to serve as our chief magistrate," they voted sixty-seven to twenty-two in favor of a resolution requesting that he agree to stand for a third term. (A separate proclamation, passed eighty-six to six, merely praised him for the successes of his presidency.) North Carolina's general assembly, taking note of his "uniformity of conduct" and "firmness of character"—of how in him "the statesman, philosopher and patriot are so happily and conspicuously united"—likewise petitioned Jefferson not to deny Americans "the pleasure of again selecting you for the discharge of those important duties, for the performance of which you appear so eminently qualified."[46]

But the enemies who had long painted Jefferson's actions with the darkest possible gloss did not now change. Some characterized his retirement not as an example of selflessness but instead as proof of his lack of resolve. "You have announced your determination to abandon the presidency," wrote "Junius" on the pages of Albany's *Republican Crisis*. "Those of us who are best acquainted with your inordinate love of power," he contended, understood that "you have not the courage and magnanimity . . . to stand forth and take the consequences of your ruinous measures." Others, such as Richard Saunders, appeared skeptical that Jefferson would ever actually step down. "Power, if long in one hand, is not easily given up," he wrote, "and the longer we possess power the more power we covet. Bonaparte was first consul, and France was a republic. What is France and Bonaparte now?"[47]

As much as Federalists had started to sound like 1790s Republicans, and as much as Republicans had started to sound like 1790s Federalists, the degrees to which these groups stood willing to accept at face value Jefferson's actions still seemed fixed. Federalists continued to divine ulterior motives behind his nearly every move. So did John Lambert, the British traveler who noted that, "in the plainest garb," the president, when in Washington, "would ride up to his splendid mansion, tie his horse to the paling, and immediately receive the visits of foreign ministers and others who had business to transact with him." But Jefferson's "republican simplicity," which encompassed his practice of assuming "the outward air of an unassuming patriot, was secretly employed in promoting his own aggrandizement."[48]

Maybe so, but Jefferson could not have failed to understand that retiring American merchant vessels to their own sheltered ports could do little to enhance his popularity. Some saw the move as too passive. Others viewed it as too provocative. Even one of his closest confidants, Treasury Secretary Gallatin, saw it as an unwise, unjust, and unseemly imposition on a freedom-loving people. "Government prohibitions," Gallatin warned, "do always more mischief than had been calculated; and it is not without much hesitation that a statesman should hazard to regulate the concerns of individuals as if he could do it better than themselves."[49] It is difficult to imagine how Jefferson could have failed to recognize the merit of any of these objections. Yet conciliation with either Britain or France in 1807 would have compromised the new nation's honor. War with one or both of these nations would have risked lives and fortunes. Either alternative could have sabotaged America's fledgling independence. It is nearly impossible to imagine that Jefferson could have conceived of more promising alternatives to the embargo and not have embraced them. His supporters understood the difficulty of his options, and many of them applauded his willingness to make a tough choice with tough personal consequences. Maybe the embargo, which under any other circumstances would have stained its author as an apostate to Republicanism, in this instance marked him as its defender. Those who objected to its effects on them needed only to survey its effects on him. It may have been his chosen policy, but it was not chosen to augment his renown.

Witness the spectacle that took place on the eve of Jefferson's departure from office. In the "Republican Square," in front of the tavern where New York City's Tammany Society regularly gathered, a disgruntled mariner scaled the liberty pole that stood as a representation of Republican rule. He suspended at the top a pair of red knee breeches stuffed with straw. Long associated with Jefferson's supposedly shabby attire, the trousers served as an abbreviated effigy. Here, on a monument that the sailor had slathered with grease, the pants dangled ignobly before the members of the group that had recently and extravagantly exalted the retiring president. This brilliant example of political graffiti not only encapsulated the disdain with which a good number of Americans regarded Jefferson at the time of his departure but also testified to his enduring importance as the living symbol of the Republican cause.[50]

CHAPTER NINE

Light, Liberty, and Posterity

A CLERGYMAN SAT in Flood's tavern, an inn on the roadside in Buckingham County, Virginia. When a stranger entered the room, the clergyman, making conversation, began a discussion about some new mechanical contrivance. The stranger demonstrated real knowledge of the topic, causing the cleric to assume he was an engineer. The discussion turned to agriculture, a subject about which the stranger seemed equally well-informed. The clergyman soon changed his mind: he must be a planter. When the topic shifted to religion, the parson strongly suspected that his companion was another man of the cloth, although of which faith he could not discern. He would have liked to ask, but the stranger seemed to value his privacy so he decided not to pry. When the stranger excused himself and retired to his room, the clergyman found the inn's proprietor and asked to whom he had been speaking. "Don't you know the Squire?" answered the innkeeper. "That was Mr. Jefferson."[1]

Now a private citizen, Jefferson was making his way between Monticello and Poplar Forest, his retirement retreat near Lynchburg. Construction commenced on this second house in 1806. He first stayed there three years later, soon after workmen raised the walls. For the former president, who always felt most comfortable in small, intimate groups, the house's completion could not come soon enough. Since his departure from office, Monticello frequently overflowed with visitors.[2] Margaret Bayard Smith, one of the earliest and most welcome, arrived during the summer of 1809 with her husband, the editor of Washington's *National Intelligencer*. Like the clergyman, she marveled at her host's expansive conversational range. "Frank and communicative," Jefferson "would talk of any thing and every thing that interested th[o]se around him," most especially matters other than politics. "In this *home-circle*," she said, "Mr. Jefferson appeared to the greatest advantage as a man. Public station and public cares were equally laid aside, while the father of the family, the friend, the companion, the man of letters, the philosopher, charmed all who were thus admitted to his private society."³

This was the life for which Jefferson had always claimed to yearn. Even back in 1775, fresh on the scene at the Continental Congress, he wrote that "consistently with duty, I may withdraw totally from the public stage." But duty kept beckoning him from the "retirement to which I am drawn by my nature with a propensity almost irresistible." Finally, after a forty-year political career and two terms as president, its calls fell silent. "My occupations are now in quite a different line," he wrote in 1811, "more suited to my age, my interests and inclinations. Having served my tour of duty, I leave public cares to younger and more vigorous minds, and repose my personal well being under their guardianship, in perfect confidence of it's safety." With Madison, his longtime partner, at the helm of the federal government, this confidence came easily.⁴

As the years passed, however, new threats to their vision of limited government emerged, and Jefferson's sense of certainty began to wane. "Federalism has changed its name and hidden itself among us," he told Albert Gallatin in 1823. Retreating from the plan "to monarchise this nation," for several years its proponents had aimed "to consolidate it into one government," which they considered "the next best thing." Worst of all, "young men are more easily seduced into this principle than the old one of monarchy." This "Era of Good Feelings," as a newspaper described it, struck Jefferson as a bad omen. With "the parties . . . all amalgamated," he confided, "the wolf now dwells with the lamb."⁵

If advancing age did not prevent him from taking a public stand against the troubling erosion of his party's ideals, then his sense of the impropriety of an old man meddling in the affairs of the young did. In 1789, he had told Madison that "the earth belongs in usufruct to the living," and during this period he voiced the sentiment many times again. "Our children are born free," he reminded his son-in-law in 1813; "that freedom is the gift of nature, and not of him who begot them." Three years later he said that the "globe, and every thing upon it, belongs to it's present . . . inhabitants, during their generation." Three years after that he expressed a wish to "withdraw from all contests of opinion, and resign everything cheerfully to the generation now in place." In 1824, he maintained that "the present generation has the same right to self-government which the past one has exercised for itself."⁶ But Jefferson refused to yield ownership of history, which he hoped would instruct the young, or of his reputation, which during his retirement he regarded with more solicitous care than ever, because he hoped it would inspire them. In this final struggle of his life—a battle for posterity—he used the knowledge that experience had taught him: nothing influenced American opinion more than words.

THIS CAME AS a hard lesson. A career in the spotlight made him understand that what he wrote and what he said could degrade his image as much as they could enhance it. Particularly trying ordeals, such as the Hemings controversy and the negative reaction to his embargo, put him on the defensive and pushed him back to the safer position offered by reticence. Here he sheltered himself immediately after his retirement, still stinging from the wounds inflicted by critics during the inglorious last years of his presidency. In 1808, when Americans cried out against the prohibition of foreign trade, he told his grandson that "I am glad you are so determined to be on the reserve on political subjects. The more you feel yourself piqued to express an opinion at what is perhaps said at you, the more the occasion is to be seized for persevering in silence." The practice, he advised, greatly enhanced "tranquility of mind."[7]

His return to Monticello did not immediately blunt the barbs of adversaries. Pockets of hostility persisted, even in Virginia. In 1810, when a friendly toast to Jefferson (that "Posterity will do him that Justice . . . which has been denied by his contemporaries") appeared in Staunton's *Republican Farmer,* one reader shot back with invective. He suggested to the editor "the erection of a monument to perpetuate to the latest ages" Jefferson's "Illustrious Services," which included "an empty treasury, Commerce destroyed," and "agriculture and the arts enfeebled." The memorial would consist of a pedestal "erected by fraud and supported by folly" on which "Mr. Jefferson is seated in a dreaming posture" holding in one hand a saw labeled "embargo" and in the other "a scorpion on which is inscribed . . . 'for the Chastisement of Haughty Britons.'" It would have been an ingenious creation, if for no other reason than that it would have incorporated so much of the opprobrium directed at Jefferson during his eight-year administration. It did not, however, assert that ambition drove him to seek and hold office, a formerly common charge that diminished after his voluntary departure from the nation's capital.[8] The former president, in fact, acknowledged no ambition even to influence his successor, to whom he avoided offering advice.[9]

Jefferson's vows to abstain from politics reflected not only his personal desire for tranquility but also the political culture in which he had been raised.

The tradition of disinterestedness—the custom that men forswear positions of power unless their peers press them into service—had long marked American politics. But members of the rising generation were gradually eroding this old ethic, either by refusing their country's call and staying at home or by actively seeking office, promoting themselves in ways that their elders considered vulgar.[10] Andrew Jackson epitomized the latter breed, and Jefferson lobbed against him the same charges of demagoguery and power-mongering that Federalist critics had long used in their attacks against Jefferson himself.

The retired president despised Jackson. In 1815, "Old Hickory" won acclaim as the hero of the Battle of New Orleans, where his outnumbered troops defeated a superior British force in the War of 1812's epilogue. But then he suspended civil law and jailed a legislator and a judge who questioned his authority. In 1818, Jackson gained additional popularity but inspired the disapproval of civilian authorities when he overstepped his orders, chased recalcitrant Seminoles into Spanish Florida, and hanged two British men whom he believed had incited them. By the 1820s, many viewed him as a coarse, unlettered pretender to the nation's most exalted post—a "jackass" who wooed Jefferson's Republican alliance and established the Democratic Party as a cult of personality. "I feel much alarmed at the prospect of seeing General Jackson, President," Jefferson told Daniel Webster in 1824. "He has very little respect for Laws or Constitutions," Jefferson said, for he impulsively sacrificed means to ends. All things considered, Jackson was "a *dangerous man*."[11]

Jefferson's and Jackson's early encounters took place on the Senate floor in 1797, where Vice President Jefferson presided and the frontier politician represented Tennessee. There, Jefferson recalled, Jackson's "terrible" passions caused him to "choak with rage." In 1804, when Jackson wanted Jefferson to name him governor of the new Louisiana Territory, he encouraged friends to send the president petitions and letters of recommendation. He even traveled to Washington, intending to make a direct appeal. He had second thoughts, however, because such a meeting "might be construed into the conduct of a courteor" bowing like a sycophant "to obtain a favour." As matters already stood, his ambition for office must have been obvious to Jefferson, who appointed someone else. During the autumn of 1815, the two men met in Lynchburg. Cheered by throngs of well-wishers, the general rode into town, enjoying all of the pomp that characterized George Washington's controversial parades. Afterward, about three hundred male citizens held a wine-soaked feast in Jackson's honor before turning up at a grand ball. "The majority of the Gentlemen were rather too much elated on the occasion," a local lady confided. "Mr. Jefferson," she reported, "said it was the most extravagant dinner ever he saw"—faint praise from this proponent of republican simplicity. As the former president made a speedy exit, the woman enjoyed the first dance of the evening in Jackson's arms, enchanted by the charismatic general and the "elegant" music of a twenty-piece band. Jefferson had not attended such a large event since Madison's inaugural reception, a much more sober affair where the newly retired statesman smiled, shook hands, and lingered to have a conversation with Margaret Bayard Smith. "You have now resigned a heavy burden," she said. "Yes indeed," he replied, "and am much happier at this moment than my friend."[12]

Jefferson, of course, was well-practiced in expressing aversion to the burdens of public life. Even before his presidency, he grumbled about the pressures of politics, particularly since they deprived him, as he told daughter Martha, of the "ineffable pleasures" of domestic life, the loss of which made him "more and more disgusted with the jealousies, the hatred, and the rancorous and malignant passions of this scene." He added that "I lament my having ever again been drawn into public view." While avowals of disinterestedness were expected from officeholders, Jefferson seems to have convinced not only others of his sincerity but also himself. In 1805, only a few months after his second inauguration, he clipped for one of his scrapbooks a poem containing the following lines:

> While he, beneath the proudest dome,
> Would languish for his native home. . . .
> While pomp & pride & pow'r appear
>   At best the glitt'ring plagues of men.

Jefferson either possessed a sincere desire for the life of a private citizen or a sincere desire to convince himself that he yearned for such a life. In the fourth of his scrapbooks appears a cluster of poems relating to retirement. The titles include "The Happy Fire-Side," "Home," "The Pleasure of Retirement," and "The Wish," which begins

> Give me, ye gods, a calm retreat,
> Far from the bustle of the great,
>   From empty pomp and noise;
> Where envy weaves destructive toils,
> Where malice basks in dimpling smiles,
>   And smiling—most destroys.[13]

Unlike his predecessor, Jackson seldom disclaimed an ambition for office, especially after the supposedly "corrupt bargain" that denied him the presidency. Even before the 1824 election, people said he craved glory and power. His actions revealed a tendency to place ego before principle. Henry Clay compared him to Greece's Alexander, England's Oliver Cromwell, and France's Napoleon Bonaparte, a man for whom Jackson expressed admiration tempered only by disappointment that he did not destroy the enemies who eventually stripped him of power. At the Lynchburg banquet, a number of men offered toasts to Jackson. Jefferson did not. Instead, he raised his glass and called for "gratitude to those who have filled the measure of their country's honor."[14]

To whatever extent the former president felt jilted by the attention paid to Jackson, the pain caused by a newfound sensation of irrelevance stung even more. This he had brought on himself. By sitting out controversies, Jefferson was earning the status not only of a beloved American elder but also of a tourist attraction incarnate, a national relic to be seen but not to be listened to or reflected on. In 1816, a rumor of his demise caused St. George Tucker, a noted jurist, to lament "the death of the greatest man Virginia had left to boast of." Given the frail state of some of the principles by which he had lived, reports of his passing seemed only slightly exaggerated. He could trust Madison with America's future, for his longtime ally shared his republican views, but he regarded Jackson with deep suspicion. Meanwhile, he thought, the "decided ascendancy" of Republicanism that left Federalism in a state of "silent, but unresisting anguish" could not be taken for granted. "Nature," he wrote, "made some men monarchists and tories by their constitution." Even well-meaning men who called themselves Republicans now championed federal spending on internal improvements that, although not necessarily harmful themselves, exceeded the original intent of the framers, many of them long dead and unable to sound the alarm. Ensnared within a present that offered equally unattractive alternatives, committed to political inaction by his own pronouncements, and weighed down by a heartfelt predilection to avoid the public gaze, Jefferson concentrated his energies on shaping the future by rescuing the past.[15]

THIS WAS SERIOUS BUSINESS. If the public record fell into the wrong hands, Jefferson thought, the people would forget the lessons that their forefathers had learned, sometimes painfully, over the course of millennia.

"History," he believed, "by appraising them of the past will enable them to judge the future. . . . It will qualify them as judges of the actions and designs of men; it will enable them to know ambition under every disguise it may assume; and knowing it, to defeat its views." Times changed but human nature did not. Unless Americans understood the age-old patterns of behavior that characterized usurpers of liberty from Julius Caesar to Alexander Hamilton, the past would repeat itself. "Enlighten the people generally," however, "and tyranny and oppressions of body and mind will vanish like evil spirits at the dawn of the day."[16] Yet recounting the past was also very personal business, for Jefferson had been an actor on the public stage since the nation's inception. America's history, more fully perhaps than for any other figure, paralleled the history of his life.

Ever since the 1807 completion of John Marshall's five-volume *Life of George Washington,* Jefferson fretted over the future view of the Revolutionary era. Marshall's work, which covered political events through the 1790s, characterized Federalists as a noble group who "contemplated America as a nation, and laboured incessantly to invest the federal head with powers competent to its preservation of the union." Jefferson's alliance "attached itself to the state authorities, viewed all powers of congress with jealousy, and assented reluctantly to measures which would enable the head to act, in any respect, independently of the members." The first group won the approbation of men with "enlarged and liberal minds," while the second courted the rabble.[17]

The chief justice's account amounted to a "party diatribe," Jefferson insisted. He had expected as much from the man whose unrepentant Federalism and "censorable" judicial opinions stuck as thorns in his side throughout his presidency. Even before the publication of Marshall's first volume, Jefferson had urged Joel Barlow to undertake a history of his own, an antidote to a work he assumed would disseminate Federalist half-truths. To Barlow he promised access to his books, letters, and recollections of things "not on paper," a treasure trove of evidence that the writer might arrange in "the most judicious form to convey useful information to the nation & to posterity." In 1811, however, Barlow suspended the project when President Madison dispatched him on a fruitless mission to wrestle trade concessions from Napoleon. The writer-turned-diplomat chased the French emperor through the frigid battlefields of Poland only to die of exposure on Christmas Eve 1812.[18]

Jefferson encouraged other historians, but for several years his luck—and theirs—could not have encouraged him. He loaned his collection of antique newspapers and legal documents to John Daly Burk, who published three

volumes of his *History of Virginia* but in 1808 fell in a duel. The important
task of narrating the Old Dominion's Revolutionary period passed on to Skelton Jones, who also benefited from Jefferson's counsel but in a duel four years
later suffered the same fate as his predecessor. Finally, Louis Girardin, an Albemarle County neighbor and the one-time teacher of Jefferson's grandson,
made the former president's myriad books, letters, and gubernatorial memoranda the basis of a fourth volume, which appeared in 1816. But Jefferson did
more than act as Girardin's bibliographer. For the sections that related to his
own role in the struggle for independence, he served as editor, shuffling the
order of the narrative and striking out statements that conflicted with his
recollections. For the appendix he contributed a careful revision of his diary
of Benedict Arnold's invasion of 1780–81, an episode that made his conduct
as governor the target of criticism then and ever since. Jefferson later described
Girardin's account as the definitive chronicle of Virginia's Revolutionary past.
It provided, Jefferson wrote without the slightest sense of irony, "as faithful an
account as I could myself."[19]

As much as Jefferson looked to Girardin to correct the "nonsense" circu-
lating about his early career, the provincial and chronological scope of his
neighbor's work made it no match for Marshall's broadly focused biography
of Washington. After Madison left office in 1817, Jefferson pressed him to
apply his "retirement to the best use possible, to a work which we have both
long wished to see well done." The papers on file at Monticello "are very voluminous, very full, and shall be entirely at your command." It would have
been like the old days, when an embattled Jefferson silently supplied his junior partner with facts and observations to arrange and publish as spirited
counterattacks. But this time Madison declined.[20] More than half a decade
passed before Jefferson believed he had found an equal to Marshall: Supreme
Court Justice William Johnson, Jefferson's first appointment to the highest
bench and an oftentimes lonely dissenter to the chief justice's opinions. The
South Carolina jurist, whose 1822 biography of General Nathanael Greene
concurred with Girardin's account of Jefferson as governor, now envisioned
a history of American parties. The prospect gave the former president "great
pleasure." "Our opponents are far ahead of us in preparations for placing their
cause favorably before posterity," Jefferson said, singling out as their fundamental error the charge that he had led "an opposition party, not on principle, but merely seeking for office." In reality, Federalists' "genuine monar-
chism" forced the bitter feuds of the 1790s. "The cherishment of the people,"
he maintained, "was our principle, the fear and distrust of them, that of the

other party." The accounts fabricated by "the high priests of federalism," who "garbled" evidence to suit their views, would collapse someday when more historical documents came to light. Until then, however, "history may distort truth ... by the superior efforts at justification of those who are conscious of needing it most."[21]

Jefferson believed he need not slant reality to justify his political past; he did, however, need history to secure his reputation. Around the time that Madison turned down his request to rebut Marshall's biography, Jefferson set to work compiling a three-volume anthology of public correspondence and private memoranda collected during his controversial tenure as a member of Washington's cabinet. This "Anas," as some historians have dubbed it, included Jefferson's notes recording his assistance to the ever-popular president, as well his experiences with Hamilton and the gossip received from others that led him to suspect a monarchical conspiracy to subvert the Revolution. The result was a paper trail for subsequent generations to follow—a portrayal of himself as a defender of liberty that possessed a freshness and veracity exceeding mere secondhand accounts. Even Jefferson's silence regarding the dates of his editorial craftsmanship underscores its purpose as a tale of truth transcending the changing contexts of time.[22]

A few years later, he penned the history of his life up until his service as secretary of state. He intended his autobiography, he claimed, "for my own more ready reference & for the information of my family." But the fact that he made this claim at all suggests an assumption—probably, a hope—that a larger audience might someday read his account and impute to it the authority of a private document intended for relatives who presumably knew him best. It contained none of the private reminiscences that he liked to share with loved ones, none of the tales of friendship and family devotion that his granddaughter Sarah Randolph later weaved into her 1871 *Domestic Life of Thomas Jefferson*. Beyond a few paragraphs of genealogical information, it constituted an account of his public career as he saw it and wanted it remembered.[23]

He refused to discuss his governorship. "This has been done by others," he said, "and particularly by Mr. Girardin.... For this portion therefore of my own life, I refer altogether to his history." He recounted his service as minister to France and his witnessing of the French Revolution's first phases with a "minuteness" of detail "disproportioned to the general scale of my narrative." He said he felt "justified by the interest which the whole world must take in this revolution." He might also have felt justified by the interest that Federalists had taken in his role in developments there, for they had sometimes linked the eventual carnage of Robespierre to the alleged radicalism of Jefferson and his *philosophe* friends. In truth, he now wrote, he had enjoyed the confidence of the moderates—"the leading patriots, & more than all of the Marquis Fayette, their head and Atlas, who had no secrets from me." The Marquis de Lafayette enjoyed immense popularity in America not only because of his leadership in the War for Independence but also as a result of his imprisonment under the Reign of Terror, and Jefferson managed to seal their very real attachment with symbolism. In 1824, after Lafayette's triumphant return to the United States and during the goodwill tour that followed, the two men embraced in front of three hundred spectators on the lawn of Monticello.[24]

Three years earlier, Jefferson had helped to cement another connection, in the process emphasizing not only his republicanism but also his friendship for the common man. When faculty and cadets of the United States Military Academy, which Jefferson had established in 1802, commissioned Thomas Sully to paint a portrait of their institution's founder, the artist spent over a week at Monticello. How he might best depict Jefferson appears to have been among their topics of conversation. Certainly Sully's portrayal reflected Jefferson's self-image. Simple but dignified, the former president's attire reinforced his connection to the people no less than the column next to which Sully imagined him. It bears no resemblance to those at Monticello, the Executive Mansion, or the Senate chamber, where, as vice president, he held the gavel. Instead, it matches those of the House of Representatives, the chamber most directly expressing the popular will. James Fenimore Cooper—novelist and inveterate Federalist—viewed the portrait during an 1823 visit to West Point. The slovenly demagogue he had long imagined was nowhere to be seen. Instead, Cooper gushed, "I saw nothing but . . . a gentleman, appearing in all republican simplicity, with a grace and ease on the canvas, that to me seemed unrivalled." Art so compelling, he thought, could not be artifice: "It has really shaken my opinion of Jefferson."[25]

Of all the things for which Jefferson wished to be remembered, he viewed as most important his drafting of the Declaration of Independence, which figured prominently in his autobiography. By the 1820s, to many his fame as penman seemed well established. But Jefferson knew of efforts to rob him of preeminence among the patriots of '76. Others besides Marshall worked to diminish his role as author. There was John Adams, who in 1822 described the Declaration as a "hackneyed" echo of words spoken by members of Congress, and Timothy Pickering, who (not intending irony) echoed Adams's account.

Thomas Jefferson, 1822, by Thomas Sully.
(West Point Museum Collection, United States Military Academy)

There was also Richard Henry Lee, who had charged that the document was "copied" from Locke. There was even the probably spurious Mecklenburg Declaration of Independence, essentially unheard of until 1819, when people suddenly held it up as an authentic document that scooped, by nearly a year, elements of the Declaration's wording and meaning.[26]

Jefferson, who said he consulted neither this nor any other text while writing the Declaration, nonetheless never claimed any originality. A work of synthesis, his draft neither aimed at nor purported to represent novelty. He intended merely to summarize Americans' thoughts. This was the task handed to him in 1776 when, as a member of the committee appointed by the Continental Congress to "prepare a declaration of independence," his fellow committee members called on him to compose the draft. "It was accordingly done, and being approved by them," he submitted it to Congress. Since "erroneous statements" appeared "before the public in latter times," he emphasized that his lengthy description of the Declaration's development came from notes taken on the spot. Because "the sentiments of men are known not only by what they receive, but what they reject also," Jefferson included in his autobiography not only the draft approved by Congress but also "the parts struck out" by its members "& those inserted by them." Jefferson's fixation on his role in writing the Declaration suggests not only his belief in the document's importance but also his understanding of its importance to his place in history.[27]

On one matter, neither his notes nor his recollections were perfect. He insisted that July 4 marked not only the date of the Declaration's ratification but also of its signing. In actuality, members of the Continental Congress did not inscribe their names on the document until August. His error makes sense in the context of the public's widespread confusion about the matter; most Americans already mythologized July 4 as the date of the signing, a phenomenon not unrelated to the growing reluctance of people to separate direct individual action (affixing one's signature) from indirect authorization (approval by representatives in Congress). The men who in 1776 signed the document did so for symbolic more than legal reasons, for it was "The Unanimous Declaration of the thirteen united States of America." Now, however, people honored not the state assemblies that directed the representatives but the representatives themselves. Charles Goodrich, for example, in 1829 would publish his *Lives of the Signers of the Declaration of Independence* as a tribute to their heroism.[28]

As author, Jefferson stood highest among this group—so high, in fact, that when admirers in Washington, D.C., inquired about the date of his birth so that they could plan a celebration in his honor, he could tell them to celebrate the birthday of the nation instead. This quintessential act of Jeffersonian self-effacement embraced both his posturing as a simple republican and his more complicated self-image as oracle of the American idea. On one hand, he eschewed an opportunity for individual glory, garnering enhanced standing as a selfless patriot. On the other, he redirected an impulse to praise him into an event that, given the predilections of its organizers, would reinforce his status as author of the Declaration and bolster the Fourth of July as America's most important secular holiday. "No occasion," he wrote in 1823, could arouse "higher excitement to my feelings." He hoped for "a repitition of these rejoicings thro' long ages to come, and that the spirit of the day which gave them birth, may continue pure, strong and imperishable." Here, as in his "Anas" and autobiography, Jefferson cast himself as modest, mild, shy, and retiring—as a reluctant Revolutionary who had no reluctance explaining and defending the principles of the Revolution.[29]

AT THE SAME TIME that he emphasized his struggles in behalf of liberty, Jefferson led a drive to establish an institution designed to diffuse light. He envisioned the University of Virginia, as he named it, as the "bulwark of the human mind" in the western hemisphere, and it would serve as an enduring and personal legacy. "I am closing the last scenes of life," he wrote, "by fashioning and fostering an establishment for the instruction of those who are to come after us. I hope its influence on their virtue, freedom, fame and happiness, will be salutary and permanent." Jefferson successfully lobbied to locate it near Charlottesville, within view of Monticello. He designed the buildings, planned the curriculum, hired the faculty, selected books for the library, and created what came to be called an "ever-lengthening shadow" of his own ideals. The professors would run their own affairs, according to his plan, and the students would govern themselves. As a state-supported university, it would have no religious affiliation; Jefferson, in fact, proscribed the teaching of theology altogether. "Here we are not afraid to follow truth wherever it may lead," he boasted, "nor to tolerate any error so long as reason is left free to combat it." He hoped, however, that the students would view the "truth" as he did. Until Madison dissuaded him, he planned for law and government classes a specified list of properly republican—and required—readings. If, in this instance, Jefferson's proposal seemed inconsistent with his plans for open-minded education, it nonetheless reflected his hope that future leaders would call the school their alma mater. "Mr. Jefferson is entirely absorbed in it," reported Harvard professor George Ticknor after a visit to Monticello, "and its success would make a *beau finale* indeed to his life."[30]

Even the ground plan evoked the Jeffersonian system. At the eastern edge of the university towered the Rotunda, modeled after the Roman Pantheon and containing the library, a focal point and secular temple of truth. Projecting from the Rotunda on either side of the central lawn, colonnaded rows of student rooms connected pavilions, which housed professors and their classrooms. Rather than closing off the three-sided complex, Jefferson left it open, providing seemingly infinite space for westward expansion along the paths laid out and preserving an unhindered view of the Blue Ridge Mountains. The result was an "academical village," as Jefferson described it, a coherent and cohesive community devoted to the pursuit of knowledge. When Ticknor visited the construction site in 1824, he imagined "a mass of buildings more beautiful than anything architectural in New England, and more appropriate to an university than can be found, perhaps, in the world." He might have also imagined the complex as the physical manifestation of the Jeffersonian information network. Jefferson, like the library, stood at the center to provide texts for discovery and dissemination.[31]

Yet the university emerged from oftentimes ugly legislative proceedings. This "strenuous labor," which Jefferson called "the greatest" of all his services, made him feel like "a physician pouring medicine down the throat of a patient insensible of needing it." The proposed institution drew fire from supporters of the College of William and Mary, who sensed a scheme to supplant their school, as well as certain religious leaders who opposed the university's suspected anticlericalism. The latter group proved particularly nettlesome. The tirades of John Rice, a Presbyterian clergyman, threatened the life of the university. In 1820, when Rice got wind of the theological skepticism of Thomas Cooper, whom Jefferson had selected as professor of chemistry, mineralogy, and natural philosophy, Rice lashed out in his *Virginia Evangelical and Literary Magazine*. He portrayed Cooper as either a Unitarian or an atheist (there was little difference, he thought) and hinted that such heresies undergirded the entire enterprise. He forced on Jefferson the old dilemma of either professing his own religious beliefs or silently enduring a time-worn charge that had always endangered his reputation but now also injured his plans for higher education. Even before the Rice episode, Jefferson understood that smoldering suspicions about his views on God and man ignited criticisms of his university. "There are fanatics in both religion and politics," he wrote two years earlier, "who, without knowing me personally, have long been taught to consider me as a raw head and bloody bones." This time he decided on a middle course and accepted Cooper's resignation. In private correspondence he scorned "the priests of the different religious sects," particularly the Presbyterian ones, the "loudest" and "most intolerant," whose "spells on the human mind" cast doubt on "its improvement." Even so, he said, rather than fight back, "it might be better to relieve Dr. Cooper, ourselves and the institution from this crusade."[32]

On his general vision for the University of Virginia, however, Jefferson refused to compromise. He threw the full weight of his reputation behind the endeavor and courted the support of other luminaries. For the 1817 groundbreaking ceremony, he arranged the attendance of not only James Madison but also President James Monroe, who laid the cornerstone. Some legislators balked as Jefferson kept revising upward his estimates of building expenses, but each year he succeeded in squeezing a bit more money out of the legislature. He shored up support by picking up his pen. In the aftermath of the Missouri Crisis, for example, he exploited sectional hostilities for the university's benefit. When Joseph C. Cabell, a key ally in the House of Delegates, suggested that he address a letter about the proposed school to James Breckenridge, a seemingly more neutral legislator, Jefferson complied, understanding that the recipient would circulate it as "thought expedient." In some of his writings during this period Jefferson looked back on the Missouri affair with serenity, but with Breckenridge he warned of a tornado on the horizon. "The line of division lately marked out, between different portions of our confederacy," he said, "will never, I fear, be obliterated. And we are now trusting to those who are against us in position and principle, to fashion to their own form the minds & affections of our youth." He estimated that Virginians spent $300,000 a year to send their sons to Harvard, Yale, and Princeton, "the Northern seminaries" where they imbibed opinions "in discord with those of their own country." Why not save money by converting a recent $60,000 loan to the university into an outright grant? This the legislature did, convinced, apparently, that Virginia's sectional interests coalesced with Jefferson's educational desires. But he did not want this letter copied or published, he told Cabell; he did not want his loyalty to the nation questioned. Others might not understand that his patriotism not only coexisted with but also required his resistance to the federal consolidation of power.[33]

Students arrived at the University of Virginia early in 1825. Workmen, still racing to complete the Rotunda and medical building, disturbed students with their hammering, but for the most part all was ready. Jefferson seemed pleased with his creation. It was, he said, "the last of my mortal cares, and the last service I can render my country." As Madison noted, "it bears the stamp of his genius, and will be a noble monument of his fame. His general view was to make it a nursery of Republican patriots as well as genuine scholars."[34]

Jefferson, however, could leave no such legacy to his family. To them he would bequeath little more than debt. The precariousness of his finances resulted from decades of unprofitable harvests, bad investments, and high living; the constant flow of visitors, reportedly as many as fifty on some nights, also strained his wallet with their hearty appetites and expensive thirsts. The 1819 default by Wilson Cary Nicholas, his grandson's father-in-law, on a loan that Jefferson had endorsed drove the former president toward bankruptcy. For a man who had honed the ability to wish away truths he wanted to be false, keeping up appearances was easier than keeping up with bills. By 1826 Jefferson could not even afford the interest on his debts. The situation forced him to contradict an earlier promise to make legislative fundraising for his university "the last object for which I shall obtrude myself on the public observation," for in the spring he dispatched his grandson to Richmond. Thomas Jefferson Randolph appealed to the House of Delegates and state senate for permission to offer up in a lottery the family's mill and one thousand acres of its land. These, according to the plan, would pass to a single winner; the cash received, which they expected to exceed considerably the value of the properties, would pay off Jefferson's obligations.[35]

Virginia law forbade such lotteries, and Jefferson recognized that he was pleading a "special case." So did legislators, many of them "ardent admirers" who thought it would cause "great injury" to his reputation. Never before had he asked personal favors from elected officials. The lower house rejected the petition by a single vote. Desperate, he applied the tactic employed during the struggle for increased state patronage of the university, penning to his grandson a plaintive letter intended for circulation among selected representatives. "It had great effect," an in-law reported, and brought tears to the eyes of at least two politicians. One of them "threw it down" half read, then "covered his face with his hands and blubbered like a baby." Direct to the legislature, Jefferson sent a detailed history of lotteries allowed in the past, to which he added a list of all the offices that kept him "far distant" from his farms and "unable to pay attention" to their management. He recalled how he "saved our country" from Federalists' "usurpations and violations of the Constitution," enduring "brow-beatings and insults" in the process. Did he now ask for compensation? "Not a cent," for he merely wished to solicit from others voluntary wagers for a piece of his property. Would the state's assent to his request set a precedent for approvals of future pleas by others? Not likely. He had given "sixty years' service" to the public, and since "no other instance of it has yet occurred in our country, so it probably never may again." In this extraordinary moment of weakness, Jefferson cashed in his modesty and put his reputation on the auction block. He did it to save his family from ruin, but he hated it just the same.[36]

The lower house reconsidered his case and modified the earlier plan for the lottery. The value of the tickets could not exceed the market value of whatever property he chose to award the winner, virtually guaranteeing the loss of Monticello in order to cover all debts. The measure sailed through both branches of the legislature. Jefferson "turned quite white" on hearing the news, one relative said, and he directed his grandson to follow an alternative, more agreeable course. He determined "to give the People an opportunity to raise the money" through donations. He slated April 13, the birthday that he had formerly kept private, for the commencement of the campaign; July 4 would mark the close. Randolph described this plan as "more flattering to his grandfather as it would show the feelings" of a grateful nation. Hat in hand, the grandson set off on a journey up the East Coast. Nothing came of the timetable, and the pledges—raised by citizens of New York, Philadelphia, Baltimore, and other communities—only sufficed to stave off creditors until after Jefferson's death.[37]

The knowledge that misfortune had led him into appeals for special favors amplified the painful fact that he could no longer provide for his family. The last-ditch efforts contradicted the reputation for disinterestedness—for giving but never taking—that Jefferson had cultivated for decades. As he wrote to Madison, the situation "cost me much mortification." He apologized to his friend for burdening him with the story but excused himself with the recognition that Madison had always acted as "a pillar of support." It gave him "great solace" to think that one day he would leave the University of Virginia under Madison's care, as well as the task of "vindicating to posterity the course" pursued by them throughout their careers. Then he added a final request: "Take care of me when dead."[38]

Years later, one of the university's professors expressed satisfaction after seeing these words in print. "It is somewhat singular," he said, "that at about the very time this letter must have been penned, Mr. Jefferson should have declared at table in my presence, that he had no desire for posthumous reputation, nor could he understand how any one could be anxious for it." The wish to transmit "a good name to posterity," the professor believed, served as a timeless incentive for proper behavior on the part of all good men, "and such could scarcely fail to have been the feeling of Mr. Jefferson." He could only conclude that "some paradox may have been involved in the remark which is not easy to unravel."[39] The record, however, of Jefferson's retirement—indeed, of his whole life—provides an answer to the puzzle. He played so great a part in the struggle to preserve liberty, as he saw it, that opinions of the struggle necessarily reflected opinions of him. As a result, he worked hard to improve and protect his image, and he understood that assuming the role of disinterested statesman, always solicitous of the common good and ever oblivious to his own cares, constituted the best way to do it. As a government figure he strove to appear to reject power, to disseminate it instead among the people, to spurn glory and welcome selfless service. He tried to embody the antithesis of his conception of government itself. If with Madison he leapt out of character, in the presence of guests at his dining table he remained on stage. Such self-effacement amounted to a heavy burden, but his reputation—and therefore the nation—required it. No wonder Jefferson felt most comfortable working behind the scenes. No wonder people whom he did not know well enough to trust frequently described him as shy. No wonder his debt and the lengths to which it drove him resulted in so much grief.

DURING THE summer of 1825, Jefferson quipped that he had one foot in the grave and the other uplifted to follow. For several years, he had suffered from chronic diarrhea; now, he experienced difficulties urinating, a condition that Dr. Robley Dunglison, the university's medical professor and its rector's physician, tried to ameliorate through regular catheterization. "My rides to the University have brought on me great sufferings," Jefferson confided to Madison. "This is a good index of the changes occurring." In March of the following year he drew up his will. But by May, he found that his "health, altho not restored, is greatly better," and in the second week of June made a final descent from the mountain. The circus had come to Charlottesville, and Jefferson joined the cheering audience of students, professors, and townspeople, a demonstration of resilience that one young scholar described as "a wonder." Within a few days, however, his symptoms reappeared, this time with such a force that, on June 24, he dispatched a note to Dunglison "begging of me," as the doctor remembered, "to visit him."[40]

Jefferson's life approached conclusion, a fact that he seemed to understand. Even so, the desperation marking his plea to the physician was nowhere to be found in the other letter that he wrote that day, a response to the invitation of Washington mayor Roger C. Weightman to join in that city's celebration of the fiftieth anniversary of American independence. His inability to attend the festivities added "sensibly to the sufferings of sickness," Jefferson explained, because he would have welcomed the opportunity to exchange congratulations "with the small band, the remnant of that host of worthies," who half a century earlier had joined with him "in the bold and doubtful election we were to make for our country, between submission or the sword." History had proven them right, he wrote, and to the future they had bequeathed through the Declaration of Independence a legacy of liberty.[41]

This letter, nearly the last one he would live to write, was Jefferson's valedictory, a literary triumph designed to hail America's destiny while also consecrating his pivotal role in the Revolution. By 1826, his fame as author of the Declaration, if still not completely uncontested, had become widespread. As Italian count Carlo Vidua noted after touring America a year earlier, "the document has become a national memorial which is publicly read each year," its "framed *facsimile* is found in almost every home," and its "author is regarded as the living *Patriarch* of the American Republic." Thus in Jefferson's letter to Weightman, when he portrayed the proclamation that "all men are created equal" with "certain inalienable rights" as the definitive break with the past and the start of the future, he scripted for himself the dual roles of national prophet and global messiah.[42] Already Jefferson had hinted of his desire to assume a high place in America's civil religion. In 1825, when he gave the lap desk upon which he had drafted the Declaration to his grandson-in-law, he emphasized "the part it has *borne* in history" and predicted that, in "another half century, he may yet see it carried in the procession of our nation's birthday, as the relics of the saints are in those of the church."[43]

At some point during his final year, Jefferson wondered if the dead could "feel any interest in Monuments or other remembrances of them." For the moment, however, he remained alive, and he took care to ensure that his services would not be forgotten. He laid onto paper instructions for his tombstone and epitaph, a monument that to him would be "the most gratifying." For the grave he prescribed "a plain die or cube . . . surmounted by an Obelisk" bearing "the following inscription, & not a word more":

Here was buried
Thomas Jefferson
Author of the Declaration of American Independence
of the Statute of Virginia for religious freedom
& Father of the University of Virginia.

He affirmed that "by these, as testimonials that I have lived, I wish most to be remembered."[44] The Declaration of Independence topped the list—the first and only recorded time when he explicitly claimed the title "Author." The fact that the epitaph conspicuously ignored his service as legislator, governor, minister to France, secretary of state, vice president, and president made it all the more impressive. To the very end Jefferson strove to exemplify the self-effacement that characterized disinterested leadership. A liberator of body, soul, and mind, Jefferson wanted posterity to understand what really mattered. His greatness resulted not from the power that men had given to him but from the powers that he had helped restore to mankind.[45]

While the text of the epitaph evoked his lifelong struggle for liberty, the obelisk on which he wanted it inscribed—a literal subtext—denoted light. (It was a fitting combination of concepts. As he once remarked, "light and liberty go together."[46]) Herodotus's *History,* frequently recommended by Jefferson, associates obelisks with the sun. So does the elder Pliny's *Natural History,* which Jefferson kept in his library. It describes the obelisk as a form developed by the ancient Egyptians symbolizing "the Sun's rays" and oftentimes bearing hieroglyphic accounts "of natural science according to the theories of the Egyptian sages." Jefferson also owned a copy of Vivant Denon's *Travels in Upper and Lower Egypt,* which suggests that rulers of the region's lost civilization used obelisks as signposts "to make certain things known to their subjects for their common good."[47] In the seventeenth and eighteenth centuries, members of the Anglo-Palladian architectural movement, from which Jefferson drew inspiration, regarded these totems as manifestations of divine wisdom and employed them in plans for buildings and landscapes. Englishman William Kent, for example, helped design not only Richard Boyle, the 3rd Earl of Burlington's Chiswick house but also the obelisk adorning its grounds. More than mere ornament, it promised enlightenment, for Kent spent long evenings meditating in its shadow.[48] Jefferson also harbored the belief that the antiquities of Egypt revealed timeless genius. "Learning and civilization will gain," he maintained, if men subjected the relics of the pharaohs to proper study.[49]

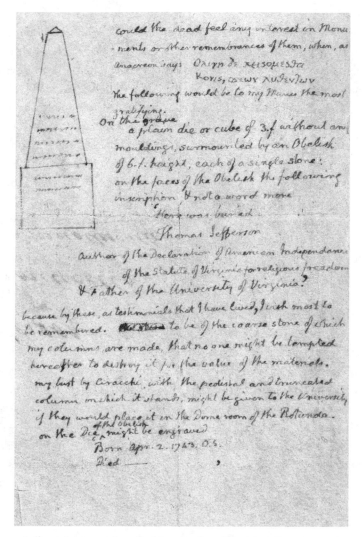

Jefferson's instructions for his epitaph and burial marker, ca. 1826.
(Manuscript Division, Library of Congress)

For Jefferson and the people of his era, who envisioned obelisks defiantly presiding over scenes of ruin, these stone spires linked light with time, endurance, and, for some, liberty.[50] At the foot of his bed Jefferson installed a clock, constructed according to his specifications, which featured a face and pendulum suspended between a pair of obelisks. Each morning he rose with the sun, Webster reported after visiting Monticello, as soon as its rays made visible the hands of this timepiece.[51] Obelisks had already emerged as popular funerary monuments, symbolizing the departed's permanence in memory. But Jefferson led fashion more often than he followed it.[52] The grave marker not only suggested the resilience of his legacy through metaphor; he designed it to make permanent the burial site itself. Crafted of "coarse stone" so "that no one might be tempted hereafter to destroy it for the value of the materials," the obelisk would slope to a point six feet above its cubic three-foot base. Its volume would thus approximate that of the cube, making the monument more balanced, with a lower center of gravity, than its slender Egyptian predecessors or the towering memorial obelisks soon to sprout from America's Revolutionary War battlefields, town greens, and the Mall of its capital city, all of which soared skyward to salute the lofty ideals of either the nation or George Washington, who led the fight for its independence.[53]

Jefferson's relatively squat monument offered little in the way of grandeur, but calculated humility had long characterized his manner of self-presentation. The conspicuous absence from his epitaph of the offices he had held deepened the understatement. Even his insistence on rough materials for the gravestone, since more expensive ones might tempt scavengers, colored with modesty a wish that, for a man on the brink of bankruptcy, coincided with financial necessity. In the years following his death, not scavengers but admirers chipped fragments from the obelisk. By 1882 these souvenir-seekers had so disfigured the monument that Congress commissioned a replacement twice the size of the original.[54]

Jefferson might have criticized the allocation of public funds for a private memorial, but he would have found the gesture gratifying nonetheless. The only thing that surpassed his desire to secure the permanence of his name and ideals was his insistence that accolades must seem to come from others and not from himself. Onto the same sheet of paper that he inscribed his epitaph, he also wrote, almost as an afterthought, that "my bust by Ciracchi, with the pedestal and truncated column on which it stands, might be given to the University if they would place it in the Dome room of the Rotunda." This secondary memorial, which owed its existence to friends, possessed none of the modesty of his tombstone. Giuseppe Ceracchi's larger-than-life marble bust portrayed a Romanized, toga-clad Jefferson. On its pedestal a Latin inscription commemorated its dedication "to the Supreme Ruler of the Universe, under whose watchful care the liberties of N. America were finally achieved, and under whose tutelage the name of Thomas Jefferson will descend forever blessed to posterity."[55]

Visitors to Monticello found the bust, column, and pedestal in the entrance hall, where they observed it towering over a much smaller sculpture of Alexander Hamilton. "Opposed in death as in life," their host would remark.[56] After his own demise, however, Jefferson wanted his bust to preside over the most important room of the most important building of the University of Virginia. The Rotunda's dome sheltered the library and, had crushing debt not forced his family to sell the sculpture, through a crowning glass oculus sunbeams would have shone down on this depiction of Jefferson, removed from his nemesis, a triumphant and solitary symbol of liberty—a somewhat ironic icon of a man who had always claimed to prefer the shadows of privacy to the incandescent public stage. Here it would have stood among the thousands of carefully selected books, a fitting representation of the statesman who could hardly resist propagating his version of truth, yet who also considered it somehow self-evident. Give light, he thought, and the people would find their own way. Here these untidy insistences would merge into one. He could be the light, but he could preserve his practiced diffidence, for the brilliance of the image reflected the glowing—and unsolicited—admiration of others.[57]

Of the multitudes who flocked to Monticello to pay homage to its patriarch, however, the final pilgrim harbored feelings of ambivalence. When young Henry Lee arrived on June 28, he surely saw the busts of Jefferson and Hamilton, but his mind focused on his host's entanglements with a less celebrated opponent, his father. General Henry ("Light-Horse Harry") Lee hated Jefferson, on whose embargo he blamed the financial ruin that in 1809 landed him in debtor's prison. When he died, he left to his son the rights to his 1812 *Memoirs of the War in the Southern Department of the United States,* which made Jefferson's supposed "timidity and impotence" as Revolutionary War governor of Virginia a case study in the supposed need for a bold, powerful government. Jefferson had derided the tract as "a tissue of errors from beginning to end," a "parody" based on "rumors" so "ridiculous that it is almost ridiculous seriously to notice it." But it prompted him to sort through his writings from that period, which he then supplied to Louis Girardin. Now, as the junior Lee prepared a revision of his father's book, Jefferson extended an invitation to "examine these papers at your ease." The manuscripts bore "an internal evidence of fidelity which must carry conviction to every one who sees them," their author claimed. "All should be laid open to you without reserve—for there is not a truth existing which I fear, or would wish unknown to the whole world."[58]

Lee sighed with disappointment when Martha Jefferson Randolph greeted him with the information that, although her father had anticipated seeing him, "he was then too unwell to receive any one." But soon she returned from the sickroom and said that the ailing statesman insisted on entertaining his guest. "My emotions at approaching *Jefferson's dying bed*, I cannot describe," Lee later recalled. "There he was extended—feeble, prostrate; but the fine and clear expression of his countenance not at all obscured. At the first glance he recognised me, and his hand and voice at once saluted me. The energy of his grasp, and the spirit of his conversation, were such as to make me hope he would yet rally—and that the superiority of mind over matter in his composition, would preserve him yet longer." He "regretted that I should find him so helpless" and "said if he got well, I should see all the papers he had promised." The two men talked about recent flooding on the James River, and Jefferson bragged about the new university. "At this time he became so cheerful as to smile, even to laughing, at a remark I made." The eighty-three-year-old never recovered, however, and the young visitor never did see his papers. But Lee departed with a changed heart. When he revised his father's *Memoirs* he not only softened the most damning passages but also reprinted a letter that Jefferson had written to him. After British troops captured Richmond in 1781, Jefferson recounted, he rode his horse through the countryside in tireless pursuit of recruits for the militia. The weary animal collapsed beneath him, so he walked with the saddle on his shoulders to a nearby farm, where he borrowed an unbroken colt and continued the journey.[59]

Not until the end did Jefferson cease his efforts to embellish his reputation. As the days passed and his condition worsened, he repeatedly expressed the hope that he might live to see the fiftieth anniversary of his Declaration of Independence.[60] Until the first of the month he remained lucid, but already Dr. Dunglison had confessed his fear that this latest illness "would prove fatal," an opinion that his patient shared. After several spells of unconsciousness and fits of nausea, Jefferson awoke on July 3 to find at his bedside his doctor, his grandson, and Nicholas Trist, the husband of his granddaughter Virginia. "This is the Fourth of July," the old man gasped. "It soon will be," Dunglison replied. Confused, Jefferson turned to Trist. "This is the Fourth?" he asked. "Thus pressed," Trist reported, "repugnant as it was to me to deceive him, I nodded assent. 'Ah,' he murmured, as an expression came over his countenance, which said, 'just as I wished.'" About two hours later, Dunglison roused the dying man for a dose of medication. Assured that the anniversary had arrived, Jefferson whispered "no, Doctor, nothing more."[61]

He slept restlessly. Imagination transported him back to the War for Independence. At one point during the night he sat up, scribbled into the air an urgent message, and called on the men to warn the Revolutionary Committee of Safety. As the sun rose over a land celebrating half a century of liberty, his pulse slowed and his life waned. Fifty minutes after noon, as canons, orators, and church bells tolled America's jubilee, Jefferson passed from the earth, his final wish fulfilled.[62]

EPILOGUE

The Apotheosis

WHEN JOSEPH CABELL, just hours after Jefferson's death, observed that, at no other time could the author of the Declaration "depart more happily for his own reputation," he knew as much as University of Virginia student Henry Horace Worthington, who asked "is there not something very impressive in the circumstances of his dying on the 50th anniversary?" In a letter to a friend about the "remarkable coincidence," Worthington noted that, at the university, it "filled us all with gloom," and he predicted it would "excite the grief of a whole nation. The illustrious Jefferson is no more! He departed this life on the *Fourth* of *July*."[1] But Cabell and Worthington had heard only half the story. What neither man at that point knew, but what all Americans would soon learn, was that Jefferson did not die alone on the day of America's jubilee. Ninety-year-old John Adams, hundreds of miles to the north and several hours after his successor in the presidency, also died on July 4, 1826.

Citizens looked skyward in wonderment as they learned that not just one but both of these sages, statesmen, and founding fathers—Jefferson the author of the Declaration of Independence and Adams its champion—died exactly fifty years after they and their colleagues in the Continental Congress proclaimed an autonomous America. In New York, where news of Jefferson's passing arrived soon after citizens learned of Adams's death, "it roused the attention of every individual," a local paper reported. "Nothing was heard after the first silent emotions of astonishment, but 'how strange! how singular! what a coincidence!'" Many viewed the timing of the deaths as a sign of divine intervention, as evidence that America enjoyed the sanction of Heaven. As one newspaper writer exclaimed, "Great God! Thy ways are inscrutable!"[2]

Fifty years earlier, news of the Declaration of Independence had arrived in Boston on horseback. Now, a steamboat brought word of its author's departure. The flags that a few days before had been lowered in homage to Adams once again descended their staffs. Church bells rang out in tribute as the militia issued a twenty-one-gun salute. On the other side of the Charles River a resident of Cambridge toasted the departed patriarchs as "the greatest men of the age." Similar scenes occurred in other cities. Mourners in Salem staged a mock funeral; in New Orleans the parade of black-creped citizens stretched for several blocks. Washingtonians who answered their mayor's call donned dark armbands for thirty days. The people of Nashville trudged through torrential rain to hear a eulogy in a church too small to accommodate them. Even in Hawaii, an independent nation, when the news arrived in December, flags fell and people assembled for the memorial sermon of missionary Hiram Bingham. All across America, newspapers bordered their pages in black. "Never, never has an event occurred," Sheldon Smith assured mourners in Buffalo, "which called more loudly for the emotion of the heart to break forth, in public demonstrations of mingled grief and gratitude."[3]

The event seemed to wash away doubts about America's destiny. What remained was a faith that some things surpassed rational explanation. "Let no cold calculating philosophy," Smith added, "attempt to ascribe such an unheard of coincidence to natural causes."[4] Such remonstrances actually may have inspired mathematician Nathaniel Bowditch, who demonstrated that, given the ages of Adams and Jefferson in 1776, the chance of both living for another fifty years and then both dying on the Fourth of July stood at "only one in *twelve hundred millions.*" (Five years later, young statisticians at the University of Virginia challenged Bowditch's figures, tabulating instead that "the odds were more than 1721 millions to 1 against the occurrence of both the events; or that a bet against it . . . should have been more than 17 millions of dollars to a cent.")[5]

These calculations, of course, suggested that mere chance could not explain such an event—that the logic of reason failed to make it intelligible. "There is language in this spectacle," Governor John Tyler proclaimed in Richmond, "which speaks more eloquence than the tongue can utter." In Providence, J. L. Tillinghast confessed that "amazement—solemnity—almost superstition —seem to lock up the sources of thought, and deny to the tongue its office." Robert Little, a clergyman at Washington's First Unitarian Church, declared that a "man's heart must be bad, or his reasonings unsound, who knows what has come to pass . . . and does not say, 'This is the finger of God!'"[6] Whether divine providence or astonishing coincidence, the double departure did much to sanctify Jefferson's reputation, first as a leader for all the nation and finally, through his authorship of the Declaration, as the man who gave voice to America at its defining moment.

THE VIRTUE of reconciliation, many eulogists informed their audiences, stood first among Jefferson's and Adams's teachings. Although the two men had once sat together on the committee charged with drafting the Declaration, more recently Adams had distinguished himself as the signer of the Alien and Sedition Acts, to which Jefferson had responded with his Kentucky Resolutions. Twice their allies had advanced them as presidential opponents, and twice their enemies had caricatured them in polar opposition. Adams, Republicans charged, concealed monarchical ambitions and stood as a traitor to the Revolution. Jefferson, Federalists asserted, revealed himself to be an atheist, demagogue, and Jacobin whose revolutionary ideals sprung not from America but France. After they retired from public life, however, the hostility of their detractors began to moderate. In 1812 the two men cast aside their differences and, as one memorialist said, "conspired to sacrifice their mutual resentments to their mutual admiration of each other's character." As they resumed a warm friendship that defied sometimes divergent sectional interests, embarking on a correspondence in which their once-discordant perspectives now brought them together in harmony, their names became intertwined with the nation's "Era of Good Feelings."[7]

"What a sublime lesson to rival partizans!" exclaimed Joseph E. Sprague before a crowd of mourners in Salem. "Between them all rivalry had ceased, and given place to the purest friendship." Everywhere the message remained the same. "The death of Jefferson and Adams is a lesson to our countrymen to cherish a spirit of mutual love and friendship," insisted Boston's *Independent Chronicle*. Their "bright example" stood as a reminder "to maintain inviolate that UNION, which is the foundation of our present prosperity, the assurance of all our future hopes." Others went further, suggesting that their renewed partnership and charmed departure had already consecrated a new era in national solidarity. Their deaths gave rise to "only one generous and general feeling," reported *Niles' Weekly Register*. "In their own reconciliation were harmonized the discordant feelings of their countrymen," a eulogist claimed, for "they cemented the friendship of all in their own union."[8]

Jefferson and Adams, partners in life, now shared a death that bonded the

nation in sorrow and joy. "They have died, together," Daniel Webster told
a crowd of mourners at Boston's Faneuil Hall: "They took their flight, together." The two "Holy Patriarchs of the Revolution," Samuel Smith said,
ascended like holy spirits to the heavens, where they were "seated on the left
hand of the father of his country."[9] Their differences melted in the glow of
apotheosis. "I know these great men, not as opponents, but as friends to each
other," Edward Everett, a Massachusetts congressman, told a South Carolina
audience. "The principles on which they contended are settled," he said, "some
in favor of one and some in favor of the other." To many it seemed as if their
coinciding deaths represented a conspiracy between the patriots and their
maker, as if finally, and with help from God, they had found a way, as Adams
once proposed to Jefferson, to "conjure down this damnable Rivalry between
Virginia, and Massachusetts."[10]

The rivalry, of course, had not ceased entirely, and while the hostility had
thinned it had also broadened. While most speakers seized the occasion as
an opportunity to urge conciliation, a few took sides by elevating one man at
the expense of the other. A Pennsylvania audience, for example, learned that,
although Jefferson's current "stature is greater," his "fame is less fitted to endure the burden of time." Citizens in Salem heard that "we owe our Independence more to John Adams than to any other created being, and that he was
the GREAT LEADER of the American Revolution." Meanwhile, speakers in
New York, Richmond, Charleston, and Fayetteville, North Carolina, like the
student orator at Washington's Columbian College, said little, if anything,
about Adams at all. One of Jefferson's Albemarle County neighbors, seething
with sectional suspicion, spurned reports of the second president's demise as
"a damn'd Yankee trick."[11]

Of all the questions that divided the nation, slavery predominated. Here
too eulogists looked to the founders for lessons, and it was Jefferson, in particular, whom several held up for emulation. One northern speaker claimed,
for example, that "the emancipation of slaves" constituted his "noblest effort."
Jefferson, he said, had called for "the abolition of this standing reproach to our
country and human nature. Had his measures been successful," the orator asserted, "instead of numbering slaves by millions, they would now be reduced
to a few thousands." Jefferson had only proposed *gradual* emancipation—
and only for Virginia—but this exaggeration echoed in Portland, where attorney Charles Daveis mentioned that Jefferson, "the enemy of oppression in
all forms," championed people of "all shades." He had "raised his voice for the
African and the Aboriginal" populations, and he "interested himself with all

his heart for the relief of one unfortunate race, and the redemption of the other." Jefferson, Daveis reminded his audience, held that Native Americans could successfully adapt to white society; in addition, he had provided moral leadership for advocates of colonization, the process by which slaves would be freed and relocated to Africa. Maine congressman Peleg Sprague applauded Jefferson for including in his draft of the Declaration of Independence "eloquent and impressive invective against the king," who, among other alleged crimes, "introduced negro slavery into the Colonies." While "Mr. Jefferson's friends" from the South struck his high-minded statement from the document, "they could not deprive him of the honor of having proposed it."[12]

Such accolades might have seemed strange to people with long memories, for during his presidency Jefferson's opponents sometimes criticized him as a slaveholder. They derided him as a hypocrite, questioning how such a proponent of the rights of man could own other men.[13] To make matters worse, they noted, the new era of liberty that the master of Monticello's election supposedly brought forth owed its existence to electoral votes made possible by the counting of slaves, whose numbers under the three-fifths clause of the Constitution augmented the strength of southern states. Jefferson's enemies sent mixed signals, however, for occasionally they publicized his antislavery pronouncements in attempts to frighten southern planters away from the Republican fold. Even in the North, where they had sometimes characterized him as a whip-wielding tyrant, more Federalists behaved like opportunists than abolitionists, taking care not to alienate audiences through calls for general emancipation.[14]

Even so, their charges of hypocrisy had the ring of truth. On this issue, Jefferson's actions seldom matched the energy of words, and his record was mixed. Of the six hundred slaves that he owned during the course of his lifetime, he freed only seven, all of them members of the Hemings family whose lineage—through his father-in-law and through himself—was probably tied to his own. All had marketable skills as well as skin that might allow them to pass for white. In 1820, he justified admission of Missouri as a slave state with the theory that extending the "peculiar institution" across the continent would dilute its influence. He had, however, spoken out against slavery as "a perpetual exercise of the most boisterous passions, the most unremitting despotism on the one part, and degrading submissions on the other." As a young Virginia legislator, he risked his reputation by sponsoring an unpopular bill to allow masters to liberate their human property. In 1784, in contrast to the position he would later take regarding Missouri, he stood virtually alone among southerners by voting for a ban on slavery west of the Appalachians. As a New York mentioned in a memorial oration, as president in 1808, his "humane and just principles" moved him to champion the "measure prohibiting the importation of slaves."[15]

Despite his inconsistencies, Jefferson had the scruples to sense the essential incorrectness of slavery, as well as the vision to imagine an America from which it had been eradicated. Abolitionist William Halsey, who on the anniversary of independence reminded a Newark audience that slaves that day could feel only "bitterness," maintained that for Jefferson they should feel only gratitude. "The friend of American liberty," after all, "was the friend too of thee, degraded, oppressed, enslaved, bleeding *Africa*," he said. Her "sable children" should "weep over his urn" and mourn the death of a man whose "tongue . . . boldly pleaded for the emancipation of her sons and daughters."[16]

Although advancing age cooled the ardor of Jefferson's resistance to slavery, when younger he hazarded criticism by seeking relief for these "unhappy human beings." Late in life, he increasingly despaired of ever himself devising a workable escape from "this evil," but to others in the crusade he offered "all my prayers, and they are the only weapons of an old man." Adams, however, throughout his career abstained from involving himself in the matter, trusting that slaveholders would resolve the problem on their own. "I constantly said in former times to the Southern Gentlemen," he had informed Jefferson, that "I cannot comprehend the object; I must leave it to you. I will vote for forcing no measure against your judgments." For a generation of emancipationists eager to find a patron saint among the founders, Jefferson, who offered their cause stirring words and a handful of positive deeds, easily surpassed Adams, who, although he owned no slaves and despised the institution of slavery, seemed to offer little.[17]

WHAT MADE JEFFERSON most attractive to opponents of slavery, of course, was his overarching image as a liberator—as a friend of the oppressed and a champion of freedom—and the most stirring words he ever penned, nearly all agreed, leaped from the seminal text of American liberation. As one eulogist remarked, he "wrote in letters of fire." Had Jefferson "left no other evidence of his talents," he said, "the Declaration of Independence alone would serve to immortalize his reputation." Similarly, in New York an orator reflected that, if Jefferson had died after "the production of that imperishable instrument," he still would have "secured for himself immortality—for wherever light and liberty shall drive ignorance and superstition before them, the name of Jefferson will be known as the benefactor of the human race." Chester Wright, a Vermont clergyman, agreed. "When we consider . . . its bearing on the present and future condition, not of this country only, but of the great family of mankind," he asked, "who will hesitate to pronounce that its author merits a rank among the greatest benefactors of the world?"[18]

As Henry Potter said of Jefferson, "above all, he was the author of the *Declaration of Independence.*" This contribution to the cause of liberty constituted the highpoint of his illustrious career, the North Carolinian maintained, for "all his other deeds merged into this colossal act." In the minds of eulogists, his creation of the University of Virginia seemed to stand tallest among these secondary services. Although this seminary of learning had only recently come into existence, Potter predicted that it "might one day vie with a Cambridge or an Oxford." Samuel Smith dubbed it "an imperishable monument to his own glory" and "a lasting benefit" to his country. For Governor Tyler, it promised to function as "the perpetual nursery" of its founder's "great principles."[19] Commentators also stressed Jefferson's authorship of Virginia's statute for religious freedom, which in 1786 disestablished the Anglican church and protected minority sects from persecution. New Yorker John Stanford, who ministered to the hospitalized residents of Bellevue, thanked Jefferson and his cohorts for ensuring that "the Church stands free and independent from the State." Potter enthused that his legislation "laid the foundation for religious toleration throughout Christendom." In the hamlet of Belfast, Maine, Alfred Johnson, Jr., praised the former president for finishing the work of Martin Luther and John Calvin, and for preventing "protestants from exercising upon others much of the authority which they had themselves denounced in the see of Rome." Jefferson's plan "was a bold one," he admitted, exposing "him to much theological hatred." But shrill reactions should have surprised no one, he maintained, for Jefferson "pushed doctrines of liberty and equality further than any of his predecessors or contemporaries."[20]

Fewer people mentioned Jefferson's record as president. Those who did cheered his purchase of Louisiana while ignoring his embargo. Most, like Pittsburgh's William Wilkins, simply glazed over "forty years of active service to his country."[21] Jefferson's reputation seldom derived strength from the vicissitudes of politics. Among supporters his image reflected the brilliance of self-evident truths and inalienable rights.

This dismayed his political opponents. Nearly a year before Adams and Jefferson reconciled, Adams still licked the wounds of his ego. What, Adams

asked, accounted for Jefferson's popularity? At this point in their history, one
answer stood out: the Declaration of Independence. Jefferson drafted the document, but on the floor of the Continental Congress it was Adams, as one
memorial noted, who served as its "eloquent advocate." Of all the eulogists,
however, Alfred Johnson of Maine came closest to appreciating the twist of
fate that vexed Adams. Because the Revolution had "begun in Massachusetts,"
and because "she needed that the other colonies should be brought into it as
allies," its leaders adopted "the policy of enlisting the pride of the 'ancient dominion'" and agreed "that Virginia should seem to take the lead" in asserting
independence. Here one found "the reason, if it were not merely accidental,
that Mr. Jefferson was made chairman of the committee appointed to draft"
the Declaration.[22]

Johnson's minimization of Jefferson's role amounted to more than sectional
sour grapes. It represented the residue of an earlier period when attribution of
the Declaration remained a hotly contested issue. Federalists had long labored
to ignore his authorship of the famous tract; a few had even endeavored to
deny it. Others, resigned to the fact that citizens connected the man with the
document, aimed to minimize his glory by overstating the extent that it was
revised ("improved," they claimed) by the Continental Congress. Thus one
eulogist felt compelled to affirm that "the Declaration is his draft, without
material alteration." Daniel Webster said the same thing, insisting that as "a
composition, the Declaration is Mr. Jefferson's. It is the production of his
mind, and the high honor of it belongs to him, clearly and absolutely."[23]

Certainly Roger Weightman, the Washington mayor who had invited Jefferson to participate in the capital city's celebration of the fiftieth anniversary
of independence, harbored no doubts about the connection between the Declaration and Jefferson, a dying man whose response soared like the fireworks
marking the day: "May it be to the world, what I believe it will be, (to some
parts sooner, to others later, but finally to all,) the signal of arousing men to
burst the chains under which monkish ignorance and superstition had persuaded them to bind themselves, and to assume the blessings and security of
self-government." The Declaration had raised the floodgates of progress, for
"all eyes are opened or opening to the rights of man. The general spread of the
light of science has already laid open to every view the palpable truth, that the
mass of mankind has not been born with saddles on their backs, nor a favored
few, booted and spurred, ready to ride them legitimately, by the grace of God."
The author of independence implored the young republic to carry forward

the cause. "Let the annual return of this day forever refresh our recollections of these rights," Jefferson wrote, "and an undiminished devotion to them."[24]

The Declaration's liberating philosophy, Jefferson believed, amounted to his greatest and most enduring legacy. In the fifty years since independence he not only had advanced his vision but also, in his eyes as well as the eyes of his countrymen, emerged as its embodiment. The current president, John Quincy Adams, while not present to hear his father's last words, recorded in his diary what he had been told. John Adams, at the end, whispered "Thomas Jefferson survives."[25] In one sense, of course, Adams was wrong. Jefferson had died hours earlier. Yet if Jefferson could endure through the perpetuation of his principles, no one more than Jefferson hoped that Adams was right.

Jefferson's Newspaper Commonplace Scrapbooks

NEARLY FOURTEEN YEARS after her 1809 visit to Monticello, Margaret Bayard Smith remembered Thomas Jefferson's private suite of rooms—the office, library, and bedchamber that she called his "sanctum sanctorum"—as "the most interesting spot in the house." Jefferson had filled his sanctuary with art, scientific instruments, useful gadgets, and the largest private collection of books in the United States. Amid this plenty, Smith recollected, a "co[a]rse looking volume attracted my notice." She flipped through its pages and "found it to consist of pieces cut out of newspapers, and pasted on the blank leaves of the book." Smith, a friend of the former president and wife of the editor of Washington, D.C.'s *National Intelligencer,* had stumbled across one of Jefferson's newspaper commonplace scrapbooks.[1]

Four such volumes of newspaper articles—carefully clipped, arranged, and pasted onto sheets of scrap paper by Jefferson during his presidency—for decades rested in a vault at the University of Virginia's library, safeguarded but virtually ignored.[2] Their obscurity, which resulted from uncertainty about their status as authentic Jefferson documents, precluded scholars from examining the multitudinous ways in which they shed light on the mind of their creator.[3] Since news of their "discovery," however, interest in the scrapbooks has increased.[4] Even so, this appendix constitutes the first sustained attempt to provide evidence for Jefferson's handiwork in the creation of this encyclopedic collection of clippings on politics, poetry, architecture, agriculture, education, exploration, marriage, morality, mortality, and myriad other topics. Among the many things these scrapbooks suggest about Jefferson is that, during his presidency, he harbored a keen interest in the public's perception of his performance in office.

A number of factors justify attribution to Jefferson of the four leatherbound octavo volumes. The first is the provenances of the volumes, all of which passed at various points through the hands of Jefferson's relatives. The second category of evidence is the nature of the composition of the scrapbooks, which is consistent with established practices and works of Jefferson. A third, especially compelling consideration is that the scrapbooks contain pagination and notations in Jefferson's handwriting. Finally, correspondence between Jefferson and John Adams—inspired by the publication of Smith's account of the volume in Jefferson's library—must be considered. Her somewhat muddled memoir, further confused by Adams, called forth from Jefferson a pronouncement that at first glance seems to cast doubt on his creation of the scrapbooks. A close reading of Jefferson's statement, however, along with an understanding of the uncomfortable situation in which Smith's account placed him, makes sense of his deflection of Adams's inquiry.

The four newspaper commonplace scrapbooks resemble each other in appearance, construction, and general content, even though they arrived at the University of Virginia from two distinct sources. The first contributor, A. T. Laird of Staunton, Virginia, donated in 1851 what the library currently catalogs as volume 4. A letter from Laird, now tucked inside the front cover of the volume, states that

> Mr. Jefferson left in his library two scrap books, which it is said were compiled by his own hands during the term of his political administration. One of these antique volumes was presented to Mr. Ewd: R. Chambers of Mecklenburg Va, and by him to me . . . [in 1844]. I propose to place the same at the disposal of the proper authorities of the University Library. If in this judgement it shall be deemed worthy [of] a position among the relicks of its supposed author, I shall be glad at its acceptance.

Laird, who relayed his understanding that Jefferson had compiled the newspaper anthologies, nevertheless expressed no doubt that they had once been in Jefferson's possession. This assurance, apparently conveyed to Laird by Edward Chambers, his father-in-law and a distant relative of Jefferson, probably originated with the unnamed individual who had given to Chambers the volume that, through Laird, became the property of the University of Virginia. The whereabouts of the second volume, like the identity of the person who possessed it, remains unknown.[5]

The remaining scrapbooks, which the University of Virginia Library catalogs as volumes 1–3, arrived more than a hundred years later, when in 1958 Monticello curator James Bear deposited them for Agnes Dillon Randolph Hill. On the first page of the first of these books appears the following inscription:

Bought at the sale of
the library of John Randolph
of Roanoke by Wm H. Clark
of Halifax Co: Va
and presented by
Mr. Clark to
Miss Sarah Randolph
   of
Edge Hill[6]

How John Randolph acquired the scrapbooks remains a mystery. His uneven relationship with Jefferson is well known, but in 1826 he bestowed on his cousin a gesture of generosity, offering to spend five hundred dollars in a lottery designed to save Monticello from Jefferson's creditors. Perhaps Jefferson's heirs gave the scrapbooks to Randolph as a token of appreciation. Certainly the volumes might interest him, for as a man of state he witnessed events and controversies referred to in some of the clippings, three of which mention his name.[7] After Randolph's 1833 death, William H. Clark, a close friend and neighbor, purchased the scrapbooks and, as his inscription attests, later gave them to Sarah Randolph, Jefferson's great-granddaughter and author of *The Domestic Life of Thomas Jefferson*.[8] An unmarried woman who lacked children of her own, she apparently passed the scrapbooks to either Margaret Smith Randolph, her niece, or nephew Thomas Jefferson Randolph, Jr. Hill, from whom the University of Virginia acquired the three scrapbooks, was a direct descendent of both of these individuals, for her parents were cousins.[9]

A consideration of the newspaper commonplace scrapbooks as physical evidence also helps to confirm their status as authentic Jefferson documents. The paper onto which Jefferson pasted newspaper articles includes not only blank scraps and pages from unidentified French- and English-language texts but also sheets of paper (folded and sealed with wax to serve as envelopes) addressed to Jefferson, Secretary of the Treasury Albert Gallatin, and Secretary of State James Madison. As the careful custodian of his own correspondence and an examiner of cabinet members' official letters, Jefferson had access to all of this paper. He made similar use of unfolded envelopes when assembling his "Anas." Thomas Jefferson Randolph, the grandson who served as the first editor of his papers, observed that this compendium of political gossip, dating mostly from the 1790s, consists of notes handwritten "often on the back of letters, addressed to him" and "stiched in with others." (Jefferson described the process in 1818: "I made memorandums on loose scraps of paper, taken out of my pocket in the moment, and laid by to be copied fair at leisure, which, however, they hardly ever were. These scraps, therefore, rugged, rubbed, and scribbled as they were, I had bound.")[10] Grandson-in-law Nicholas P. Trist pointed out another use to which Jefferson put the sheets that covered incoming correspondence. "It was his practice to separate the blank leaf of every letter received by him," Trist remembered. "These leaves were put under press, and served to write rough drafts upon."[11] He occasionally used them to make copies of his outgoing correspondence as well.[12] Eight newspaper clippings pasted on similarly addressed unfolded envelopes, filed alongside 121 loose newspaper clippings in the Jefferson Papers at the Library of Congress, provide yet another example of his reuse of the sheets that had once contained incoming correspondence.[13]

The mounted newspaper articles serve not only to verify Jefferson's recycling of these sheets but also his practice of extracting passages from printed documents and securing them to pieces of paper that for future reference he either filed away or had bound together. His scissor extracts from the New Testament also exemplify this practice. Jefferson cut out Greek, Latin, French, and English translations of Gospel verses and then pasted them side by side to create a compilation that he entitled "The Life and Morals of Jesus of Nazareth." Although he assembled this anthology during his retirement, he seems to have conceived of it soon after his reelection to the presidency.[14] While the planning of this work coincided with the creation of the newspaper scrapbooks, Jefferson may have honed his skills at cutting and pasting even earlier. As Douglas Wilson has pointed out, Jefferson's literary commonplace book includes not only transcriptions from published works but also a "newspaper clipping that may have been placed . . . by Jefferson himself." The item, an unsigned elegy, is similar to the more than twenty elegies that appear in the third volume of the scrapbooks.[15]

Consistencies between the newspaper commonplace scrapbooks and recognized Jefferson documents go beyond the use of envelope paper and the inclusion of items cut from printed sources. Handwritten notations within the scrapbooks match samples of Jefferson's penmanship. While arranging pages in the scrapbooks in preparation for binding, Jefferson marked many of them with Arabic numerals. Here, for example, his compressed twin-circle eights and triangle-topped fours are virtually indistinguishable from the handwritten numerals that appear in his "Life and Morals of Jesus."[16] In addition, penned or penciled notations appear occasionally on the pages or intrude into the texts of articles. Most of the handwriting resembles accepted examples of Jefferson's cursive style during his presidency.[17] One notation, however, does not; it seems instead to be in the hand of Martha Jefferson Randolph, the daughter whose writing appears also within Jefferson's literary commonplace book.[18]

One final piece of evidence linking the scrapbooks to Jefferson, Smith's memoir of her 1809 visit to Monticello, also helps to confirm his status as their creator. Yet her account called forth pronouncements by John Adams and Jefferson that led historians astray from the attribution. Soon after her 1823 account of her 1809 visit to Monticello first appeared in the *Richmond Enquirer,* Massachusetts's *Salem Gazette* reprinted it. When Adams, who was nearly blind, had a relative read to him Smith's description of the "coarse looking volume" that, as she remembered, "was entitled *Libels,* and contained all that has so lavishly, during the *war* of political parties, been written against" Jefferson, he sent a note to his old friend. Since quivering fingers prevented him from writing much more than his signature, Adams dictated the message. "This Lady," he wrote, "says she saw in your sanctum sanctorum a large folio Volume on which was written libels, on opening which she found it was a Magazine of Slips of newspapers, and pamphlets, vilifying, calumniating and defaming you." Too bad, he told Jefferson, that neither he nor his family had ever "thought to make a similar collection. If we had I am confident I could have produced a more splendid Mass than yours."[19]

Jefferson responded by casting doubt on the accuracy of Smith's memory. The passing of time had "occasioned some lapses of recollection, and a confusion of some things in the mind of our friend," he wrote, for "I never had such a volume. Indeed I rarely thought those libels worth reading, much less preserving and remembering." Jefferson explained, however, that each year he

sorted all my pamphlets, and had them bound according to their subjects. One of these volumes consisted of personal altercations between individuals, and calumnies on each other. This was lettered on the back "Personalities," and is now in the library of Congress. I was in the habit also, while living apart from my family, of cutting out of newspapers such morsels of poetry, or tales as I thought would please, and of sending them to my grand-children who pasted them on leaves of blank paper and formed them into a book. These two volumes have been confounded into one in the recollection of our friend.[20]

Jefferson was right to question Smith's recollections. Not one of the newspaper scrapbooks, which appear never to have been rebound, is labeled "Libels," nor is any one of them devoted exclusively to printed abuse of the third
president. But all four contain sharply critical items, such as volume 3, which
includes, for example, pieces blasting his 1807–9 embargo and a hostile poem
by a writer who identifies himself as "No Jeffersonian."[21] That the appearance
of such material in one of these scrapbooks should have attracted Smith's
notice and stuck in her mind is hardly surprising, for she began her account of
Jefferson's peaceful retirement by contrasting it with "the tempestuous sea of
political life," a theme to which she repeatedly returned. Jefferson, she wrote,
"has been enveloped in the clouds of calumny, and the storms of faction; assailed by foreign and domestic foes; and often threatened with a wreck of
happiness and fame. But these things," she maintained, "have now all passed
away." Smith's erroneous statement about the scrapbook's title and contents,
although possibly the result of having merely glanced through the volume
nearly fourteen years earlier, might also be attributed to a selective memory.
What is certain is that Smith's notes, which her grandson later published,
make no reference to the "co[a]rse looking volume" that she mentioned in the
newspaper account. She relied solely on her unwritten recollections.[22]

Smith, however, was not the only one confusing facts, for when Adams
relayed to Jefferson her description of the book he embellished it with details
that further muddled her memoir. After having heard Smith's account read
aloud as many as three days earlier, Adams dictated his letter to Jefferson.
He described the scrapbook as containing "pamphlets" and as "a large folio
Volume"—two particulars that Smith's account did not contain. Jefferson,
who held Adams's muddled characterization of the book in front of him but
had a looser grip on his memory of Smith's somewhat less confused account
from five weeks earlier, replied that she had conflated the bound pamphlets
labeled "Personalities" with a collection of clippings sent to his grandchildren.
The book of pamphlets, which today remains at the Library of Congress,
rebound and cataloged as "Political Pamphlets vol. 105," is octavo-sized.[23] Perhaps the grandchildren's scrapbook, which has not been located, conformed
to Adams's description of a large volume the size of a folio. Whatever the
case, Jefferson's 1823 statement about what a friend may have seen at his house
nearly fourteen years earlier may well represent an attempt to make sense of
Adams's confused recollection of a relative's reading of a newspaper essay
based on Smith's obscured or selective memory.

Even so, the possibility remains that Jefferson might have moved beyond Adams's muddled description to consider that Smith had handled one of his newspaper commonplace scrapbooks. Although not one of them had ever been entitled "Libels" and all contained articles that did not attack him, all of the scrapbooks also included criticisms of his administration, and all are otherwise consistent with the volume described by Smith. If Jefferson recognized these facts, why did he not mention them to Adams? The best explanation is that Jefferson wanted to change the subject. Adams, after all, had not only inquired about Jefferson's book of libels but also expressed regret that he had never thought "to make a similar collection," which "could have enumerated Alexander Hamilton, and Thomas Paine."[24]

These were fighting words. Although Adams and Jefferson had both opposed Hamilton, Jefferson's support for Paine had long been a source of friction. Adams's twenty-year estrangement from Jefferson, which ended in 1812 thanks to the tireless diplomacy of mutual friend Benjamin Rush, had been spurred by Jefferson's endorsement of Paine's 1791 *Rights of Man* as a remedy for "the political heresies which have sprung up among us"—an allusion to a controversial series of newspaper essays by Adams entitled "Discourses on Davila."[25] To make matters worse, shortly after assuming the presidency Jefferson had granted asylum in America to Paine, a refugee of the revolution in France that his own writings had helped to inflame. In a letter to Paine that appeared first in Paris newspapers and then in American ones, Jefferson had even endorsed and encouraged his "useful labours."[26] Not long after returning to the United States, Paine lashed out at Adams in the pages of the *National Intelligencer,* where he described the former president as an arrogant, self-aggrandizing hypocrite; as "a man of paradoxical heresies" with "a bewildered mind"; and as a monarchist whose "head was as full of kings, queens and knaves, as a pack of cards."[27] Jefferson's apparent sponsorship of Paine, as well as James Callender and other anti-Adams writers, inflicted wounds on Adams's ego that still had not healed. No wonder that, when correcting Adams's mistaken assumption that the report of the visit to Monticello had been authored by a Virginian, Jefferson referred obliquely to the "visitant from another state" as "our friend." Margaret Bayard Smith was not Adams's friend; she was the wife of the editor who had printed Paine's poison words. No wonder Jefferson suggested to Adams that Smith had examined his grandchildren's scrapbooks, which contained "morsels of poetry" and stories he "thought would please," but admitted neither the existence of nor the possibility that she had seen his own collection of newspaper extracts, which contained political essays that surely would not please Adams—such as Paine's scathing assault on him.[28] Jefferson's response to Adams can thus be read as an attempt to extricate himself from a potentially perilous discussion of newspaper politics and political newspaper clippings. The maneuver was fully in keeping with his long-practiced ability to choose words that told an audience what it wanted to hear while simultaneously, although sometimes selectively, telling the truth. It also reflected his habitual avoidance of open conflict with friends, Adams especially. Dropping the subject, Jefferson turned Adams's attention toward a new book on Napoleon, a much safer topic providing far more room for agreement.

NOTES

Abbreviations

AHP   Harold C. Syrett and Jacob E. Cooke, eds. *The Papers of Alexander Hamilton.* 27 vols. New York, 1961–87.

AJL   Lester J. Cappon, ed. *The Adams-Jefferson Letters: The Complete Correspondence between Thomas Jefferson and Abigail and John Adams.* 2 vols. Chapel Hill, N.C., 1959.

Ford   Paul Leicester Ford, ed. *The Writings of Thomas Jefferson.* 10 vols. New York, 1892–99.

JAH   *Journal of American History*

JER   *Journal of the Early Republic*

JMP   William T. Hutchinson et al., eds. *The Papers of James Madison: Congressional Series.* 17 vols. Chicago and Charlottesville, Va., 1962–91.

JSH   *Journal of Southern History*

L&B   Andrew A. Lipscomb and Albert Ellery Bergh, eds. *The Writings of Thomas Jefferson.* 20 vols. Washington, D.C., 1903–4.

Lib. Cong.   Library of Congress, Washington, D.C.

Malone   Dumas Malone. *Jefferson and His Time.* 6 vols. Boston, 1948–81.

TJ   Thomas Jefferson

TJP   Julian P. Boyd et al., eds. *The Papers of Thomas Jefferson.* 41 vols. to date. Princeton, N.J., 1950–.

TJP:RS   J. Jefferson Looney, ed. *The Papers of Thomas Jefferson: Retirement Series.* 11 vols. to date. Princeton, N.J., 2004–.

TJW   Merrill D. Peterson, ed. *Thomas Jefferson: Writings.* New York, 1984.

VMHB   *Virginia Magazine of History and Biography*

WMQ   *William and Mary Quarterly*

Introduction

1. Americanus [John Beckley], *Address to the People of the United States: With an Epitome and Vindication of the Public Life and Character of Thomas Jefferson* (Philadelphia, 1800), 32; Marquis de Lafayette to James McHenry, 3 December 1785, in Stanley J. Idzerda et al., eds., *Lafayette in the Age of the American Revolution: Selected Letters and Papers, 1776–1790,* 5 vols. (Ithaca, N.Y., 1977–83), 5:355; William Parker Cutler and Julia Perkins Cutler, comps., *Life, Journals, and Correspondence of Rev. Manasseh Cutler,* 2 vols. (Cincinnati, 1888), 2:56; Malone, 3:481; Timothy Dwight, *The Duty of Americans, at the Present Crisis, Illustrated in a Discourse, Preached on the Fourth of July, 1798* (New Haven, Conn., 1798), 20, 21; Paul F. Boller, Jr., *Presidential Campaigns* (New York, 1984), 17–18.

2. Merrill D. Peterson, *The Jefferson Image in the American Mind* (New York, 1960), vii. Other notable studies of the public reputations of historical figures include John William Ward, *Andrew Jackson: Symbol for an Age* (New York, 1955); Garry Wills, *Cincinnatus: George Washington and the Enlightenment* (Garden City, N.Y., 1984); Barry Schwartz, *George Washington: The Making of an American Symbol* (New York, 1987); Paul K. Longmore, *The Invention of George Washington* (Berkeley, Calif., 1988); Merrill D. Peterson, *Lincoln in American Memory* (New York, 1994); Stephen F. Knott, *Alexander Hamilton and the Persistence of Myth* (Lawrence, Kans., 2002); and Merrill D. Peterson, *John Brown: The Legend Revisited* (Charlottesville, Va., 2002).

3. Francis D. Cogliano, *Thomas Jefferson: Reputation and Legacy* (Charlottesville, Va., 2006), 9, 263; Andrew Burstein, *Democracy's Muse: How Thomas Jefferson Became an FDR Liberal, a Reagan Republican, and a Tea Party Fanatic, All the While Being Dead* (Charlottesville, Va., 2015). Other works analyzing the recent development of Jefferson's reputation are Scot A. French and Edward L. Ayers, "The Strange Career of Thomas Jefferson: Race and Slavery in American Memory, 1943–1993," in *Jeffersonian Legacies*, ed. Peter S. Onuf (Charlottesville, Va., 1993), 418–56, and Brian Steele, *Thomas Jefferson and American Nationhood* (New York, 2012), 291–314.

4. Andrew Jackson O'Shaughnessy, *The Men Who Lost America: British Leadership, the American Revolution, and the Fate of the Empire* (New Haven, Conn., 2013), 281; TJ, *Notes on the State of Virginia*, ed. William Peden (1787; Chapel Hill, N.C., 1954), 159; TJ, First Inaugural Address, 4 March 1801, *TJP*, 33:150; James Madison, Federalist No. 51, in Alexander Hamilton, James Madison, and John Jay, *The Federalist Papers*, ed. Clinton Rossiter (New York, 1961), 290.

5. TJ to Benjamin Rush, 16 January 1811, *TJP:RS*, 3:305.

6. Alexander Hamilton to George Washington, 15 September 1790 (enclosure), *AHP*, 7:52–53; TJ to Joseph Jones, 14 August 1787, *TJP*, 12:34; TJ, Annual Message to Congress, 17 October 1803, *TJP*, 41:535.

7. Joanne B. Freeman, *Affairs of Honor: National Politics in the New Republic* (New Haven, Conn., 2001), 160–61; Henry S. Randall, *The Life of Thomas Jefferson,* 3 vols. (New York, 1858), 1:11; TJ to Thomas Adams, 20 February 1771, *TJP*, 1:62; "Bradshaw's Epitaph," *TJP*, 1:677–79; Jefferson's Seal, *TJP*, 16: xxxii.

8. Bernard Bailyn, *The Ideological Origins of the American Revolution* (Cambridge, Mass., 1967); Charles S. Sydnor, *Gentlemen Freeholders: Political Practices in Washington's Virginia* (Chapel Hill, N.C., 1952). The historiography of the ideology of republicanism and republican leadership is broad and detailed. For a birth announcement of republicanism as an interpretive framework, see Robert E. Shalhope, "Toward a Republican Synthesis: The Emergence of an Understanding of Republicanism in American Historiography," *WMQ*, 3rd ser., 29 (1972): 49–80; for a premature obituary, see Daniel T. Rodgers, "Republicanism: The Career of a Concept," *JAH* 79 (1992): 11–38. For two essays that clarify key concepts, credit earlier seminal works, and make their own important contributions, see Gordon S. Wood, "Interests and Disinterestedness in the Making of the Constitution," in *Beyond Confederation: Origins of the Constitution and American National Identity,* ed. Richard R. Beeman, Stephen Botein, and Edward Carter II

(Chapel Hill, N.C., 1987), 69–109, and Richard R. Beeman, "Deference, Republicanism, and the Emergence of Popular Politics in Eighteenth-Century America," *WMQ,* 3rd ser., 49 (1992): 401–30.

9. A new generation of historians awaits its Shalhope. For now, an abbreviated list of studies informing this book's discussions of personal honor and personal and authorial character includes Andrew Burstein, *The Inner Jefferson: Portrait of a Grieving Optimist* (Charlottesville, Va., 1995); Joseph J. Ellis, *American Sphinx: The Character of Thomas Jefferson* (New York, 1997); Jay Fliegelman, *Declaring Independence: Jefferson, Natural Language, and the Culture of Performance* (Stanford, Calif., 1993); Freeman, *Affairs of Honor*; and Andrew S. Trees, *The Founding Fathers and the Politics of Character* (Princeton, N.J., 2004). Important books on the expression or reception of popular sentiment include Jeremy D. Bailey, *Thomas Jefferson and Executive Power* (New York, 2007); Simon P. Newman, *Parades and the Politics of the Street: Festive Culture in the Early American Republic* (Philadelphia, 1997); Jeffrey L. Pasley, Andrew W. Robertson, and David Waldstreicher, eds., *Beyond the Founders: New Approaches to the Political History of the Early American Republic* (Chapel Hill, N.C., 2004); Peter Thompson, *Rum Punch and Revolution: Taverngoing and Public Life in Eighteenth-Century Philadelphia* (Philadelphia, 1999); Len Travers, *Celebrating the Fourth: Independence Day and the Rites of Nationalism in the Early Republic* (Amherst, Mass., 1997); and David Waldstreicher, *In the Midst of Perpetual Fetes: The Making of American Nationalism, 1776–1820* (Chapel Hill, N.C., 1997).

10. TJ to Thomas Pinckney, 8 September 1795, *TJP,* 28:458; TJ to Maria Cosway, 8 September 179[5], *TJP,* 28:455.

11. TJ to Elbridge Gerry, 13 May 1797, *TJP,* 29:362; John Adams to Benjamin Rush, 4 January 1813, in John A. Schutz and Douglass Adair, eds., *The Spur of Fame: Dialogues of John Adams and Benjamin Rush, 1805–1813* (San Marino, Calif., 1966), 263.

12. TJ to John Taylor, 4 June 1798, *TJP,* 30:389.

13. Here and elsewhere, I am deeply indebted to Simon P. Newman's "Principles or Men? George Washington and the Political Culture of National Leadership, 1776–1801," *JER* 12 (1992): 477–507.

14. Fisher Ames to Colonel Dwight, 10 January 1805, in *Works of Fisher Ames,* ed. W. B. Allen, 2 vols. (Indianapolis, 1983), 2:1479.

15. Madison, *Political Observations,* 20 April 1795, *JMP,* 15:518.

16. Peterson, *The Jefferson Image in the American Mind,* 14.

Prologue

1. John Adams, Autobiography, 5 October 1802[–ca. 7 June 1805], in L. H. Butterfield et al., eds., *Diary and Autobiography of John Adams,* 4 vols. (Cambridge, Mass., 1961), 3:337; Adams to Benjamin Rush, 30 September 1805, 21 June 1811, in Schutz and Adair, eds., *Spur of Fame,* 43, 182.

2. Robert M. S. McDonald, "Thomas Jefferson's Changing Reputation as Author of the Declaration of Independence: The First Fifty Years," *JER* 19 (1999): 169–95. See

also Pauline Maier, *American Scripture: Making the Declaration of Independence* (New York, 1997), which notes that Jefferson's "authorship was not yet common knowledge" even in the 1780s (162) and includes a final chapter that updates and expands on the notable article by Philip F. Detweiler, "The Changing Reputation of the Declaration of Independence: The First Fifty Years," *WMQ*, 3rd ser., 19 (1962): 557–74; and Fliegelman, *Declaring Independence*, which incorporates ideas from Jacques Derrida's paper on the Declaration's "authority," delivered in 1976 at the University of Virginia and published in English as "Declarations of Independence," trans. Tom Keenan and Tom Pepper, *New Political Science* 15 (Summer 1986): 7–17. For other acknowledgments of Jefferson's initial obscurity as the Declaration's author, see Detweiler, "The Changing Reputation of the Declaration of Independence," 560; *TJP*, 15:241n; Ellis, *American Sphinx*, 243; and Willard Sterne Randall, *Thomas Jefferson: A Life* (New York, 1993), 272, 279, which correctly observes that "it was years [after 1776] before most people knew Thomas Jefferson wrote the Declaration of Independence" but erroneously dates the first public revelation of his authorship to 1800—seventeen years too late.

3. Ezra Stiles, *The United States Elevated to Glory and Honor: A Sermon Preached before His Excellency Jonathan Trumbull, . . . and the Honorable General Assembly of the State of Connecticut . . . May 8th, 1783* (New Haven, Conn., 1783), 46. See also the second printing, Worcester, Mass., 1785, 79.

4. McDonald, "Thomas Jefferson's Changing Reputation as Author of the Declaration of Independence," 179–95; Travers, *Celebrating the Fourth*, esp. chaps. 3–6; Maier, *American Scripture*, esp. 170–89; Detweiler, "The Changing Reputation of the Declaration of Independence," 565–74.

5. Samuel Ward to Henry Ward, 22 June 1775, in Paul H. Smith et al., eds., *Letters of Delegates to Congress, 1774–1789*, 25 vols. (Washington, D.C., 1976–2000), 1:535; Malone, 1:204; Adams, Autobiography, in Butterfield et al., eds., *Diary and Autobiography of John Adams*, 3:335; Adams, diary entry for 25 October 1775, in Butterfield et al., eds., *Diary and Autobiography of John Adams*, 2:218. Jefferson was identified as the author of *Summary View* in a 28 November 1774 dispatch from London printed in Alexander Purdie's *Virginia Gazette* (Williamsburg), 17 February 1775.

6. "Resolution of Independence," 7 June 1776, *TJP*, 1:298; Malone, 1:219–20; John Adams to Timothy Pickering, 6 August 1822, in Charles Francis Adams, ed., *The Works of John Adams, Second President of the United States,* 10 vols. (Boston, 1850–56), 2:514; Adams, Autobiography, in Butterfield et al., eds., *Diary and Autobiography of John Adams*, 3:336. While Adams maintained that the committee appointed Jefferson and him to draft a declaration, Jefferson recollected that the committee "unanimously pressed on myself alone to undertake the draught." See TJ to James Madison, 30 August 1823, in James Morton Smith, ed., *The Republic of Letters: The Correspondence between Thomas Jefferson and James Madison, 1776–1826,* 3 vols. (New York, 1995), 3:1875.

7. TJ to James Madison, 9 June 1793, *JMP*, 15:27; TJ to Walter Jones, 2 January 1814, *TJP:RS*, 7:101; Edmund Pendleton, "Autobiography," 20 July 1793, in David John Mays, ed., *The Letters and Papers of Edmund Pendleton, 1734–1803,* 2 vols. (Charlottesville, Va., 1967), 2:606; "Appendix," in Adams, ed., *Works of John Adams*, 2:524. On disinterested

leadership in late eighteenth-century America, see Jack P. Greene, "Character, Persona, and Authority: A Study of Alternative Styles of Political Leadership in Revolutionary Virginia," in *The Revolutionary War in the South: Power, Conflict, and Leadership*, ed. W. Robert Higgins (Durham, N.C., 1979), 3–42; Gordon S. Wood, *The Radicalism of the American Revolution* (New York, 1992), 204–12, 247; and Wood, "Interests and Disinterestedness in the Making of the Constitution," 83–93, 96, 99–104.

8. John Locke, *Two Treatises of Government: A Critical Edition with an Introduction and Apparatus Criticus,* ed. Peter Laslett (1689; New York, 1967), 361; Baron de Montesquieu, *The Spirit of the Laws*, ed. and trans. Anne M. Cohler et al. (1748; New York, 1989), 43, 67; Algernon Sidney, *Discourses concerning Government*, ed. Thomas G. West (1698; Indianapolis, 1990), 85; TJ to Robert Skipwith, with a List of Books for a Private Library, 3 August 1771, *TJP*, 1:77, 79.

9. "Notes of Proceedings of the Continental Congress," [7 June–1 August 1776], *TJP*, 1:315–19; Derrida, "Declarations of Independence," 9–10; Malone, 1:229–30; Worthington Chauncey Ford, ed., *Journals of the Continental Congress, 1774–1789,* 34 vols. (Washington, D.C., 1904–37), 5:431, 590–91.

10. Michael Warner, *The Letters of the Republic: Publication and the Public Sphere in Eighteenth-Century America* (Cambridge, Mass., 1990), 42–43, 66, 84–85, 96, 113; Fliegelman, *Declaring Independence*, 104–6, 150–51, 160–61; John Dickinson, *Letters of a Pennsylvania Farmer*, as quoted in Wood, *Radicalism of the American Revolution*, 210.

11. TJ, *Notes on the State of Virginia*, ed. Peden, xi–xxv; Douglas L. Wilson, "The Evolution of Jefferson's *Notes on the State of Virginia*," *VMHB* 112 (2004): 98–133; TJ to James Madison, 11 May 1785, *TJP*, 8:229; Epaminondas [John Witherspoon], *Pennsylvania Magazine; or, American Monthly Museum* (Philadelphia), June 1775, 263; *Four Letters on Interesting Subjects* (Philadelphia, 1776), 20.

12. [Thomas Paine], *Common Sense: Addressed to the Inhabitants of America* (Philadelphia, 1776), 5; Jürgen Habermas, *The Structural Transformation of the Public Sphere: An Inquiry into a Category of Bourgeois Society*, trans. Thomas Burger with Frederick Lawrence (Cambridge, Mass., 1989), 53–57.

13. Fliegelman, *Declaring Independence,* 3–15, 20–26, 50–52, 94–101.

14. Ibid., 52, 64–65, 94–95; John Adams to Benjamin Rush, 12 December 1811, in Schutz and Adair, eds., *Spur of Fame,* 201–2; TJ to Thomas Jefferson Randolph, 24 November 1808, Ford, 9:231.

15. Warner, *Letters of the Republic,* 40; Montesquieu, *Spirit of the Laws*, 35.

16. [Robert Bell], "To Mr. Anonymous," *Dunlap's Pennsylvania Packet; or, The General Advertiser* (Philadelphia), 5 February 1776; John Keane, *Tom Paine: A Political Life* (Boston, 1995), 108–9.

17. Maier, *American Scripture,* 115–16, 124–28, 133–39, 165–67, 268n62; TJ to Henry Lee, 8 May 1825, Ford, 10:343.

18. Malone, 1:221–23, 202; TJ to Richard Henry Lee, 8 July 1776, *TJP,* 1:455–56; Lee to TJ, 21 July 1776, *TJP*, 1:471; Edmund Pendleton to TJ, 10 August 1776, *TJP*, 1:488.

19. Stiles, *The United States Elevated to Glory and Honor* (New Haven, Conn., 1783), 46.

20. Previous investigations have also failed to uncover an earlier public reference to Jefferson as author of the Declaration. See Detweiler, "The Changing Reputation of the Declaration of Independence," 560, and *TJP,* 15:241n.

21. *Massachusetts Centinel and the Republican Journal* (Boston), June 30, 1784. See also Merrill D. Peterson, *Thomas Jefferson and the New Nation: A Biography* (New York, 1970), 294–95, which quotes the *Centinel* tribute and notes that it "suggests Jefferson's rising fame as the author of the Declaration of Independence as well as his reputation, even before the publication of the *Notes on the State of Virginia,* for philosophy."

22. Franklin Bowditch Dexter, ed., *The Literary Diary of Ezra Stiles,* 3 vols. (New York, 1901), 2:155; William A. Robinson, "William Whipple," in Dumas Malone, ed., *The Dictionary of American Biography,* 18 vols. (New York, 1928–88), 10, part 2:71.

23. *Connecticut Courant* (Hartford), 11 July 1785; Philip Mazzei, *Researches on the United States,* ed. and trans. Constance D. Sherman (1788; Charlottesville, Va., 1976), 157; William Gordon, *The History of the Rise, Progress, and Establishment of the Independence of the United States of America,* 4 vols. (London, 1788), 2:295, 276; David Ramsay, *The History of the American Revolution,* 2 vols. (Philadelphia, 1789), 1:340–41. On the unimportance of the Declaration during this period, see Maier, *American Scripture,* 154, 160, 168–69. On the early historiography of the Declaration, see Detweiler, "The Changing Reputation of the Declaration of Independence," 563–66.

1. The Invention of Thomas Jefferson

1. Accounts of the funding-assumption debate appear in Lance Banning, *The Jeffersonian Persuasion: Evolution of a Party Ideology* (Ithaca, N.Y., 1978), 139–47; Richard Buel, Jr., *Securing the Revolution: Ideology in American Politics, 1789–1815* (Ithaca, N.Y., 1972), 2, 8–18, 21, 23–24; Noble E. Cunningham, Jr., *The Jeffersonian Republicans: The Formation of a Party Organization, 1789–1801* (Chapel Hill, N.C., 1957), 4–7, 9; Stanley Elkins and Eric McKitrick, *The Age of Federalism: The Early American Republic, 1788–1800* (New York, 1993), 136–53; and James Roger Sharp, *American Politics in the Early Republic: The New Nation in Crisis* (New Haven, Conn., 1993), 34–38.

2. John Adams to John Trumbull, April 1790, Adams Family Papers, microfilm reel 373, Massachusetts Historical Society, Boston; Abigail Adams to John Adams, 26 May 1789, in L. H. Butterfield et al., eds., *Adams Family Correspondence,* 12 vols. to date (Cambridge, Mass., 1963–), 8:360; Theodore Sedgwick to Pamela Dwight Sedgwick, 4 March 1790, quoted in Ralph Ketcham, *James Madison: A Biography* (New York, 1971), 311; Trumbull to John Adams, 30 March 1790, Adams Family Papers, microfilm reel 373, Massachusetts Historical Society.

3. Peterson, *Thomas Jefferson and the New Nation,* 437; Cunningham, *The Jeffersonian Republicans,* 9; Ketcham, *James Madison,* 332; Malone, 2:423. The etymology of factional names is discussed in Joyce Appleby, *Capitalism and a New Social Order: The Republican Vision of the 1790s* (New York, 1984), 62–63.

4. The word was in use by 1793, although the term "Madisonian" had been coined as well. See "Madison in the Third Congress," 2 December 1793–3 March 1795 [editorial note], *JMP,* 15:152.

5. [William Loughton Smith], *The Politicks and Views of a Certain Party, Displayed* (N.p., 1792), 22.

6. Malone, 1:314–16, 319–22, 349–51, 353, 361–66, 394–96; TJ to James Monroe, 20 May 1782, *TJP*, 6:184–86.

7. TJ to John Paradise, 5 July 1789, *TJP*, 15:242. See also TJ to Alexander Donald, 2 February 1788, *TJP*, 12:572.

8. See Wills, *Cincinnatus*.

9. TJ to Abigail Adams, 22 February 1787, *TJP*, 11:174.

10. Stuart Leibiger, *Founding Friendship: George Washington, James Madison, and the Creation of the American Republic* (Charlottesville, Va., 1999), 114, 116–17; James Madison to TJ, 27 May 1789, *TJP*, 15:153–54; TJ to Madison, 28 August 1789, *TJP*, 15:369; TJ, Autobiography, *TJW*, 98–99; William Short to TJ, 30 November 1789, *TJP*, 15:563; Malone, 2:203, 205, 207, 229.

11. Ezra Stiles to TJ, 14 September 1786, *TJP*, 10:385–86; Joseph Willard to TJ, 24 September 1788, *TJP*, 13:637–38.

12. Address of Welcome by the Citizens of Albemarle, [prior to 16 January 1790], *TJP*, 16:178; TJ's Reply to the Address of Welcome of the Virginia House of Delegates, [November 1789], *TJP*, 16:11; TJ to George Washington, 15 December 1789, *TJP*, 16:34.

13. Leibiger, *Founding Friendship*, 117.

14. TJ to George Washington, 15 December 1789, *TJP*, 16:34.

15. Malone, 2:292–94. See also Charles Carroll to Mary Caton, 14 April 1790, Charles Carroll Papers, microfilm reel 2, Maryland Historical Society, Baltimore.

16. "A War-Worn Soldier," *Massachusetts Centinel*, 24 February 1790; "A Real Soldier," *Massachusetts Centinel*, 20 March 1790; "A Citizen," *Independent Chronicle* (Boston), 15 April 1790; *Gazette of the United States* (Philadelphia), 17 April 1790.

17. Woody Holton, "Abigail Adams, Bond Speculator," *WMQ*, 3rd ser., 64 (2007): 821–38; Abigail Adams to Cotton Tufts, 30 May 1790, in Butterfield et al., eds., *Adams Family Correspondence*, 9:64; James Tillary to Alexander Hamilton, [January 1791], *AHP*, 7:616.

18. Cunningham, *The Jeffersonian Republicans*, 4–5; TJ's Account of the Bargain on the Assumption and Residence Bills, [1792?], *TJP*, 17:206; Herbert E. Sloan, *Principle and Interest: Thomas Jefferson and the Problem of Debt* (New York, 1995), 148–50.

19. TJ to James Madison, 9 May 1791, *TJP*, 20:293; TJ to Jonathan B. Smith, 26 April 1791, *TJP*, 20:290. See "*Rights of Man*: The 'Contest of Burke and Paine . . . in America'" [editorial note], *TJP*, 20:268–73.

20. TJ to John Adams, 17 July 1791, *TJP*, 20:302; TJ to James Madison, 9 May 1791, *TJP*, 20:293–94. On Adams's sensitivity, see Peter Shaw, *The Character of John Adams* (Chapel Hill, N.C., 1976), esp. 240–44.

21. TJ to George Washington, 8 May 1791, *TJP*, 20:291. Most scholars have taken at face value Jefferson's claims. A notable exception is C. Bradley Thompson, *John Adams and the Spirit of Liberty* (Lawrence, Kans., 1998), 269–73.

22. Publicola, as quoted in "*Rights of Man*" [editorial note], *TJP*, 20:280–82. Most people at the time thought that Publicola's words had sprung from the pen of John Quincy Adams's father.

23. TJ to Edmund Randolph, 17 September 1792, *TJP*, 24:387; George Washington to Alexander Hamilton, 29 July, 6 August 1792, *AHP*, 12:129–34, 276–77; Washington to TJ, 23 August 1792, *TJP*, 24:317.

24. James Madison to TJ, 12 May 1791, *TJP*, 20:294. On the use of pseudonyms in political writing, see Warner, *Letters of the Republic*, 42–43, 66, 84–85, 96, 113, and Fliegelman, *Declaring Independence*, 104–6, 150–51, 160–61.

25. Oliver Wolcott, Jr., to Oliver Wolcott, Sr., 14 February 1792, in George Gibbs, ed., *Memoirs of the Administrations of Washington and John Adams, Edited from the Papers of Oliver Wolcott, Secretary of the Treasury*, 2 vols. (New York, 1846), 1:73; John Adams to Henry Knox, 19 June 1791, as cited in *"Rights of Man"* [editorial note], *TJP*, 20:278; [Smith], *The Politicks and Views of a Certain Party, Displayed*, 27–31; Adams, "Discourses on Davila," [1790], in Adams, ed., *Works of John Adams*, 6:232–34.

26. TJ to Thomas Mann Randolph, Jr., 3 July 1791, *TJP*, 20:296; TJ to John Adams, 17 July 1791, *TJP*, 20:302; TJ to George Washington, 8 May 1791, *TJP*, 20:291–92.

27. James Madison to TJ, 12 May 1791, *TJP*, 20:295; Nathaniel Hazard to Alexander Hamilton, 25 November 1791, *AHP*, 9:534; Robert Troup to Hamilton, 15 June 1791, *AHP*, 8:478.

28. For examples of this tendency, see Robert Troup to Alexander Hamilton, 15 June 1791, *AHP*, 8:478; George Washington to Hamilton, 17 October 1791, *AHP*, 9:403; Nathaniel Hazard to Hamilton, 11 November 1791, *AHP*, 534; and Hamilton to Edward Carrington, 26 May 1792, *AHP*, 11:437, 443, 444.

29. William Samuel Johnson quoted in Nathaniel Hazard to Alexander Hamilton, 25 November 1791, *AHP*, 9:532; John Beckley to James Madison, 2 September 1792, *JMP*, 14:356.

30. Alexander Hamilton to Edward Carrington, 26 May 1792, *AHP*, 11:427–29, 431–32, 435, 437–38, 440. Hamilton also surmised that Jefferson had influenced Andrew Brown, printer of the *Federal Gazette and Philadelphia Daily Advertiser*, who "was originally a zealous federalist and personally friendly to me" but whose paper now "was equally bitter and unfriendly to me & to the Government." See *AHP*, 11:431. The notion that Jefferson manipulated Madison was first suggested by Gouverneur Morris and supported by William Loughton Smith. See Morris to Hamilton, 24 December 1792, *AHP*, 13:377, and [Smith], *The Politicks and Views of a Certain Party, Displayed*, 3, 25.

31. Alexander Hamilton to Edward Carrington, 26 May 1792, *AHP*, 11:430–31, 435–36; Nathaniel Hazard to Hamilton, 25 November 1791, *AHP*, 9:533.

32. Alexander Hamilton to Edward Carrington, 26 May 1792, *AHP*, 11:429, 431, 437, 438, 439–41, 442, 444. For an analysis of this letter as a blueprint for Hamilton's subsequent attacks, see James Arthur Mumper, "The Jefferson Image in the Federalist Mind, 1801–1809: Jefferson's Administration from the Federalist Point of View" (Ph.D. diss., University of Virginia, 1966), esp. i–vii.

33. See Mumper, "The Jefferson Image in the Federalist Mind," iv–v; Elkins and McKitrick, *The Age of Federalism*, 288. For Jefferson's letter, see TJ to George Washington, 23 May 1792, *TJP*, 23:535–40. For the text that suggested Jefferson's criticisms, see Washington to Alexander Hamilton, 29 July 1792, *AHP*, 12:129–34.

34. TJ to Benjamin Franklin Bache, 22 April 1791, *TJP*, 20:246; TJ to William Short, 28 July 1791, *TJP*, 20:692–93; Donald H. Stewart, *The Opposition Press of the Federalist Period* (Albany, N.Y., 1969), 7–9, 19; Michael Lienesch, "Thomas Jefferson and the Democratic Experience: The Origins of the Partisan Press, Popular Political Parties, and Public Opinion," in Onuf, ed., *Jeffersonian Legacies*, 318–21.

35. Lienesch, "Thomas Jefferson and the Democratic Experience," 319–21; TJ to Thomas Bell, 16 March 1792, *TJP*, 20:759; TJ to Thomas Mann Randolph, Jr., 20 November 1791, *TJP*, 22:310.

36. Madison took care to preserve his anonymity as well, not only before the public but also in the view of Fenno. In 1793, as Madison prepared to submit two essays (signed Helvidius) for possible publication in the *Gazette of the United States,* he informed Jefferson that he hoped to have them "copied into another hand." See Madison to TJ, 3 August 1793, *TJP*, 26:623, 623–24n.

37. Henry Lee to James Madison, 10 September 1792, *JMP*, 14:363. See also E. Randolph to Madison, 12 August 1792, *JMP*, 349; Alexander Hamilton to Jonathan Dayton, 13 August 1792, *AHP*, 12:196; and Dayton to Hamilton, 26 August 1792, *AHP*, 275.

38. An American [Alexander Hamilton], *Gazette of the United States,* 11, 4 August 1792; John Quincy Adams to Thomas Boylston Adams, 2 September 1792, in Butterfield et al., eds., *Adams Family Correspondence*, 9:303. See also Catullus [Hamilton], *Gazette of the United States*, 15 September 1792; "T. L." [Hamilton], *Gazette of the United States*, 25, 28 July, 11 August 1792; and Detector [Hamilton?], *Gazette of the United States,* 28 July 1792. While Jefferson put Freneau on the federal payroll, the placement of public notices by Hamilton and Secretary of War Henry Knox on the pages of the *Gazette of the United States* subsidized Fenno, as Freneau pointed out. See the *National Gazette* (Philadelphia), 28 July, 15 August 1792.

39. An American [Hamilton], *Gazette of the United States,* 11 August 1792; Catullus [Hamilton], *Gazette of the United States*, 15, 19 September 1792; [Smith], *The Politicks and Views of a Certain Party, Displayed*, 22. On the adoration of Washington, see Schwartz, *George Washington*, esp. 58–69, 74–80. On Smith's relationship with Hamilton, see George C. Rogers, Jr., *Evolution of a Federalist: William Loughton Smith of Charleston (1758–1812)* (Columbia, S.C., 1962), 194, 197, 219, 237–39, 241.

40. An American [Hamilton], *Gazette of the United States,* 22 September 1792. Richard Buel observes that the Federalists' use of religion as a political issue constituted one of their most successful tactics in battles for common people's support; see Buel, *Securing the Revolution*, 138, 169–75, 231–34.

41. An American [Hamilton], *Gazette of the United States,* 15 September, 22 December, 13 June 1792; "Kibrothnataavah," *National Gazette,* 12 September 1792.

42. Joseph Priestley to Theophilus Lindsey, 17 July 1795, Original Letters from Dr. Joseph Priestley, Manuscripts Department, Dr. Williams's Library, London. Hamilton's authorship as T. L., Catullus, An American, and Metellus, is confirmed by *AHP,* where the essays are conveniently printed. While Philip Marsh ("Hamilton's Neglected Essays, 1791–1793," *New-York Historical Society Quarterly* 32 [October 1948]: 291–93) believes Hamilton also authored the attacks on Jefferson signed "Detector," Harold C. Syrett

doubts this attribution; see *AHP*, 12:123, 266. Hamilton's involvement in the production of the "Scourge" essay is suggested by the fact that a draft, in the handwriting of W. L. Smith, has been found in Hamilton's papers at the Lib. Cong.; see *AHP*, 12:411–12.

43. TJ to Thomas Pinckney, 3 December 1793, *TJP*, 24:696. See also Cunningham, *The Jeffersonian Republicans*, 29–32, 49–50.

44. Malone, 2:463, 469–70; TJ to Edmund Randolph, 17 September 1792, *TJP*, 24:387. See also "Jefferson's Alliance in 1790 with Fenno's *Gazette of the United States*" [editorial note], *TJP*, 16:247.

45. See "Enclosure: Observations on the French Debt," [ca. 17 October 1792], *TJP*, 24:496–97. For the essays that employed information contained in the letter, see [James Madison and James Monroe], *Dunlap's American Daily Advertiser* (Philadelphia), 11 November, 3 December, 31 December 1792.

46. *Dunlap's American Daily Advertiser,* 22 September 1792; TJ to George Washington, 17 October 1792, *TJP*, 24:494. Jefferson made a practice of understating to Washington the level of his political involvement. Several months later, he told the president that he kept himself "aloof from all cabal and correspondence on the subject of the government." See TJ, "Notes of a Conversation with George Washington," 7 February 1793, *TJP*, 25:154.

47. James Monroe to James Madison, 9 October 1792, *JMP*, 14:379. On the secretary of state's knowledge of Madison and Monroe's essays, see "Jefferson, Freneau, and the Founding of the *National Gazette*" [editorial note], *TJP*, 20:725. Excerpts from Jefferson's letters to Madison (20 December 1787, 3 May, 31 July, 15 August, 18 November 1788, and 28 August 1789), appeared after brief, unsigned essays by Madison and Monroe in *Dunlap's American Daily Advertiser,* 22 September, 10, 20, 30 October, 8 November, 3, 31 December 1792.

48. TJ to James Madison, 7 July 1793, *JMP*, 15:43; Madison to TJ, 11 August 1793, *TJP*, 26:655; Madison to TJ, 30 August 1793, *TJP*, 26:729; TJ to Madison, 13 March 1791, *JMP*, 13:405. See also TJ to Madison, 21 September 1795, *JMP*, 16:88–89. William Loughton Smith, Hamilton's friend, suspected that Jefferson had been instrumental in the productions of Republicans' essays; "most of them," he said, were "written either by our Hero [Jefferson] or under his influence." See [Smith], *The Politicks and Views of a Certain Party, Displayed*, 31.

49. TJ to Benjamin Franklin Bache, 22 April 1791, *TJP*, 20:246; TJ, "Notes of a Conversation with George Washington," 23 May 1793, *TJP*, 26:102.

50. Writing as Scourge, William Loughton Smith informed readers that, while Jefferson seemed "cautious and shy, wrapped up in impenetrable silence and mystery, . . . he reserves his *abhorrence* [of Federalists] for the arcana of a certain snug sanctuary, where seated on his pivot-chair, [he is] . . . involved in all the obscurity of political mystery and deception." See *Gazette of the United States*, 22 September 1792. See also [Smith], *The Politicks and Views of a Certain Party, Displayed*, 32–33.

51. See Glenn A. Phelps, *George Washington and American Constitutionalism* (Lawrence, Kans., 1993), 12–14, 60–62, 74–75, 90, 94–95, 102, 110, 116–17, 123, 144, 148, 180, 191–92; Schwartz, *George Washington*, 119–48, 202–3; Wills, *Cincinnatus*, 4–5, 87–89,

151–53, 228; and Wood, "Interests and Disinterestedness in the Making of the Constitution," 90–91.

52. For a more elaborate elucidation of the rules of political combat, see Freeman, *Affairs of Honor,* 62–104, esp. 99–101.

53. Elkins and McKitrick, *The Age of Federalism,* esp. 360–61. For Jefferson's doubts about Washington's capacity as a leader, see TJ to James Madison, [13 May 1793], *TJP,* 26:26.

54. According to John Beckley, Jefferson and his allies recognized "the attack on Mr. Jefferson . . . as the weak, insidious & contemptible efforts of Mr. Hamilton himself." See Beckley to James Madison, 10 September 1792, *JMP,* 14:361.

55. Robert R. Livingston to TJ, [February–March 1793], *TJP,* 25:304.

56. *National Gazette,* 8 September 1792; "A Republican," *National Gazette,* 19 September 1792. See also Aristides [Edmund Randolph], *National Gazette,* 26 September 1792.

57. *National Gazette,* 8 September 1792; "Columbus," *New York Journal,* reprinted in the *National Gazette,* 10 October 1792; [James Madison and James Monroe], *Dunlap's American Daily Advertiser,* reprinted in the *National Gazette,* 13 October 1792; "Justice," *National Gazette,* 24 October 1792.

58. From *Dunlap's American Daily Advertiser,* reprinted in the *National Gazette,* 26 September 1792; *National Gazette,* 8 September 1792.

59. "Kibrothnataavah," *National Gazette,* 12 September 1792; "Savannah, July 11," *Columbian Herald* (Charleston), 23 July 1793; [Smith], *The Politicks and Views of a Certain Party, Displayed,* 28.

60. *National Gazette,* 26 September 1792; "Z.," *National Gazette,* 3 October 1792, "Camillus," *National Gazette,* 24 October 1792. See also Aristides [Randolph], *National Gazette,* 26 September 1792.

61. [James Madison and James Monroe], *Dunlap's American Daily Advertiser,* 22 September 1792.

62. John Beckley to James Madison, 2 September 1792, *JMP,* 14:355; Fisher Ames to John Lowell, 6 December 1792, and Ames to Aristides, [probably 1793], in Allen, ed., *Works of Fisher Ames,* 2:955, 967, 973. Although Jefferson is not positively identified in the etching, which is dated 16 August 1793, John Catanzariti notes that the "figure . . . dominating the group bears a strong resemblance to Jefferson, whom the artist could have met or seen when the Republican leader was serving as Secretary of State in New York City in 1790." Noble Cunningham, however, leaves open the possibility that the artist meant to portray Aaron Burr as the "Antifederal Club" leader. See "A Peep into the Antifederal Club," *TJP,* 26:xliii, and James C. Kelly and B. S. Lovell, comps., "Thomas Jefferson: His Friends and Foes," *VMHB* 101 (1993): 144–45.

63. James Madison to Edmund Randolph, 13 September 1792, *JMP,* 14:364.

64. TJ to Martha Jefferson Randolph, 26 January 1793, *TJP,* 25:97–98; "Jefferson and the Giles Resolutions" [editorial note], *TJP,* 25:280–92; Robert R. Livingston to TJ, [February–March 1793], *TJP,* 25:304; TJ, "Notes of a Conversation with George Washington," 6 August 1793, *TJP,* 26:628. For a call for Jefferson's resignation, see Metellus [Hamilton], *Gazette of the United States,* 24 October 1792.

65. TJ to Horatio Gates, 3 February 1794, *TJP*, 28:14; *President II, Being Observations on the Late Official Address of George Washington: Designed to Promote the Interest of a Certain Candidate for the Executive, and to Explode the Pretensions of Others* (Newark, N.J., 1796), 15–16; William Barry Grove to James Hogg, 3 April 1794, William Barry Grove Papers, Southern Historical Collection, University of North Carolina Library, Chapel Hill.

66. Oliver Wolcott, Jr., to Oliver Wolcott, Sr., 27 January 1792, in Gibbs, ed., *Memoirs of the Administrations of Washington and John Adams,* 1:86; John Adams to John Quincy Adams, 3 January [1794], Adams Family Papers, microfilm reel 377, Massachusetts Historical Society.

2. The Election of 1796

1. Transcription from the original manuscript, William Maclay's diary, 24 May 1790, *TJP,* 16:381n.

2. James Madison to James Monroe, 26 February 1796, *JMP,* 16:232; Alexander Hamilton to unknown, [8 November 1796], *AHP,* 20:376.

3. *Aurora and General Advertiser* (Philadelphia), 4 July 1796.

4. Joseph Priestley to Theophilus Lindsey, 12 August 1795, Original Letters from Dr. Joseph Priestley, Manuscripts Department, Dr. Williams's Library. For fuller accounts of the treaty debate, see Cunningham, *The Jeffersonian Republicans,* 77–85; Elkins and McKitrick, *The Age of Federalism,* 415–49; and Sharp, *American Politics in the Early Republic,* 113–37.

5. Sharp, *American Politics in the Early Republic,* 92–112, 119 (quotation).

6. Ibid., 98–105, 108; Elkins and McKitrick, *The Age of Federalism,* 456–57, 462, 485; Thomas P. Slaughter, *The Whiskey Rebellion: Frontier Epilogue to the American Revolution* (New York, 1986), 194–95; Leland D. Baldwin, *Whiskey Rebels: The Story of a Frontier Uprising* (Pittsburgh, 1939), 260. Federalist claims that Democratic-Republican societies plotted the Whiskey Rebellion are tenuous, for a number of clubs expressed their disapproval of the armed revolt; see Baldwin, *Whiskey Rebels,* 481–82, 485; Richard H. Kohn, *Eagle and Sword: The Federalists and the Creation of the Military Establishment in America, 1783–1802* (New York, 1975), 169; and Philip S. Foner, ed., *The Democratic-Republican Societies, 1790–1800: A Documentary Sourcebook of Constitutions, Declarations, Addresses, Resolutions, and Toasts* (Westport, Conn., 1976), 59, 91–93, 147–48, 183–84, 243, 339, 378.

7. Elkins and McKitrick, *The Age of Federalism,* 441, 482–83, 484, 518; Cunningham, *The Jeffersonian Republicans,* 181; Sharp, *American Politics in the Early Republic,* 104, 123–27, 139, 150.

8. See George Washington to Alexander Hamilton, 26 June 1796, *AHP,* 20:239; Robert R. Livingston to James Madison, 16 November 1795, *JMP,* 16:126; Madison to James Monroe, 26 February 1796, *JMP,* 16:232; Madison to Monroe, 14 May 1796, *JMP,* 16:358; John Beckley to Madison, 20 June 1796, *JMP,* 16:371.

9. Fisher Ames to Oliver Wolcott, Jr., 26 September 1796, in Gibbs, ed., *Memoirs of the Administrations of Washington and John Adams,* 1:384.

10. On Adams's lamenting of his lack of popularity, see Joseph J. Ellis, *Passionate Sage: The Character and Legacy of John Adams* (New York, 1993), 57–83 *passim*.

11. TJ to James Madison, 9 June 1793, *TJP*, 26:240; Noble E. Cunningham, Jr., *In Pursuit of Reason: The Life of Thomas Jefferson* (Baton Rouge, La., 1987), 199; "Dolley, Domesticity, and the Whiskey Rebellion, 1794–1795" [editorial note], in Smith, ed., *Republic of Letters*, 847–48; Malone, 3:180.

12. Edwin Morris Betts, ed., *Thomas Jefferson's Farm Book: With Commentary and Relevant Extracts from Other Writings* (Charlottesville, Va., 1987), 47–49, 241–42, 310–11, 337–38, 426–28; Jack McLaughlin, *Jefferson and Monticello: The Biography of a Builder* (New York, 1988), 30, 109–13, 243, 257–58, 260–62; Malone, 3:194–242; Cunningham, *In Pursuit of Reason*, 196–98, 205. See also Donald Jackson, *A Year at Monticello: 1795* (Golden, Colo., 1989).

13. TJ to Maria Cosway, 8 September 179[5], *TJP*, 28:455; TJ to Philip Mazzei, 8 September 1795, *TJP*, 28:457; TJ to Thomas Pinckney, 8 September 1795, *TJP*, 28:458; TJ to Sampson Crosby, 15 September 1795, *TJP*, 28:467.

14. TJ to James Madison, 28 December 1794, *TJP*, 28:228–30; Madison to TJ, 23 March 1795, *TJP*, 28:315; TJ to Madison, 27 April 1795, *TJP*, 28:338–39. In the midst of partisan squabbling during Washington's first term, Federalist prints charged that Jefferson's opposition to John Adams's political philosophy and to Alexander Hamilton's financial program were part of his strategy to win popular backing for a bid for the presidency; see, for example, [Smith], *The Politicks and Views of a Certain Party, Displayed*, 27–31.

15. James Madison to TJ, 10 December 1796, *TJP*, 29:218. On Madison's October 1795 visit to Monticello, see *TJP*, 28:xxxvii.

16. TJ to James Madison, 27 April 1795, *TJP*, 28:339, 338; TJ to Madison, 28 December 1794, *TJP*, 28:230.

17. John Adams to Abigail Adams, 14 January 1797, Adams Family Papers, microfilm reel 383, Massachusetts Historical Society.

18. Rev. James Madison to James Madison, 25 July 1795, *JMP*, 16:41; Robert R. Livingston to Madison, 16 November 1795, *JMP*, 16:126; John C. Jones to Matthew Blair, 24 April 1796, Virginia Historical Society, Richmond; John Beckley to Madison, 20 June 1796, *JMP*, 16:371–72; Hubbard Taylor to Madison, 16 July 1796, *JMP*, 16:380. See also James Monroe to Madison, 5 July 1796, *JMP*, 16:377.

19. James Madison to James Monroe, 26 February 1796, *JMP*, 16:232–33; Madison to Monroe, 29 September 1796, *JMP*, 16:404.

20. James A. Bear, Jr., and Lucia C. Stanton, eds., *Jefferson's Memorandum Books: Accounts, with Legal Records and Miscellany, 1767–1826*, 2 vols. (Princeton, N.J., 1997), 2:935.

21. Albert Russel "to the Freeholders of the Counties of Loudoun and Fauquier," 16 September 1796, reprinted in the *Aurora*, 27 September 1796.

22. See *Aurora*, 10 February 1796: "We are happy to be informed, that Mr. Jefferson . . . is perfectly recovered from his late indisposition. May he long live, and in the moment of necessity re-appear and save his country from the unhappy effect to which it is exposed."

23. *Aurora*, 6 July 1796.

24. "A Friend to Equal Rights," *Aurora*, 1 November 1796.

25. *President II*, 13; "To the Freemen of Pennsylvania," *Aurora*, 1 November 1796; "A

Pleasant Anecdote," *Aurora,* 4 November 1796. See also [Tench Coxe], *The Federalist: Containing Some Strictures upon a Pamphlet, Entitled, "The Pretensions of Thomas Jefferson to the Presidency, Examined, and the Charges against John Adams, Refuted"* (Philadelphia, 1796), 6.

26. "To the Freemen of Pennsylvania," *Aurora,* 1 November 1796; *Aurora,* 28 October 1796. See also "An Observer," *Aurora,* 12 October 1796, reprinted from the *Independent Chronicle.*

27. Cassius, "To the People of the United States," *Aurora,* 28 October 1796, reprinted from the *Petersburg Intelligencer* (Virginia); "An Elector of Electors" (29 October letter from Pittsburgh), *Aurora,* 5 November 1796; "A Whig," *Aurora,* 18 October 1796.

28. *The Minerva, and Mercantile Evening Advertiser* (New York), 25 October 1796; "Extract of a Letter . . . Dated September 30," *Minerva,* 18 October 1796. On American reactions to the French Revolution, see Charles Downer Hazen, *Contemporary American Opinion of the French Revolution* (Baltimore, 1897), esp. 139ff.

29. *Gazette of the United States,* 1 September 1796; "Phocion," *Minerva,* 28 October 1796; John Beckley to James Madison, 15 October 1796, *JMP,* 16:409; A Correspondent in Connecticut, "Remarks on the *Aurora,* No. I," *Minerva,* 3 September 1796.

30. "Political Fanaticism," *Minerva,* 9 November 1796; *Aurora,* 1 November 1796; "A Farmer," *Gazette of the United States,* 15 October 1796, reprinted from the *Columbian Mirror and Alexandria Gazette*; "Mr. Adams's Defence of the American Constitutions," *Gazette of the United States,* 8 September 1796.

31. [Coxe], *The Federalist,* 14–15; "Elector of Electors," *Aurora,* 5 November 1796.

32. "Thomas Jefferson," *Register of the Times* (New York), 4 November 1796; Daniel C. Brent, *Virginia Herald* (Fredericksburg), 28 October 1796; [John Gardner], *A Brief Consideration of the Important Services, and Distinguished Virtues and Talents, Which Recommend Mr. Adams for the Presidency of the United States* (Boston, 1796), 8; "Amicus," *Federal Gazette and Baltimore Daily Advertiser,* 29 October 1796.

33. [William Loughton Smith], *The Pretensions of Thomas Jefferson to the Presidency Examined; and the Charges against John Adams Refuted* (Philadelphia, 1796), 4; Thomas Paine, *The Age of Reason, First Part* (1794), in Bruce Kuklick, ed., *Thomas Paine: Political Writings* (New York, 1989), 208; Florin Aftalion, *The French Revolution: An Economic Interpretation,* trans. Martin Thom (New York, 1990), 61–67; Christopher Hibbert, *The Days of the French Revolution* (New York, 1980), 230–33.

34. [Smith], *The Pretensions of Thomas Jefferson to the Presidency Examined,* 37; TJ, *Notes on the State of Virginia,* ed. Peden, 159; From a Correspondent in Connecticut, "Remarks on the *Aurora,* No. I," *Minerva,* 3 September 1796.

35. An American, "Of Religion," *Minerva,* 26 September 1796, reprinted from the *New World* (Philadelphia). On Webster's advocacy of toleration and his moderation as a Federalist, see Alan K. Snyder, *Defining Noah Webster: Mind and Morals in the Early Republic* (Lanham, Md., 1990), 148, 153, 162–63, 164, 173, 174–75.

36. "Extract," *Aurora,* 4 November 1796; "Dialogue between an Aristocrat and a Republican," *Aurora,* 12 November 1796.

37. On Jefferson's maintenance of religious privacy, see Paul K. Conkin, "The Religious Pilgrimage of Thomas Jefferson," in Onuf, ed., *Jeffersonian Legacies,* 35–36.

38. "Foul Stratagem," *Aurora,* 14 December 1796; "Extract of a Letter from a Respectable Character in Maryland, to His Friend in This City, October 5, 1796," *Gazette of the United States,* 13 October 1796.

39. "Phocion No. II," *Gazette of the United States,* 15 October 1796; Winthrop D. Jordan, *White over Black: American Attitudes toward the Negro, 1550–1812* (Chapel Hill, N.C., 1968), 271–76, 290, 292, 343, 359–60; Gary B. Nash and Jean R. Soderlund, *Freedom by Degrees: Emancipation in Pennsylvania and Its Aftermath* (New York, 1991), x–xi, xiii–xv, 8, 11, 16, 19, 26, 40–56, 61, 63, 69–70, 72–75, 78, 80, 82–83, 85–87, 89–93, 96, 98–99, 104, 108, 110, 113–15, 127, 132–33, 136–38, 153–54; Foner, ed., *The Democratic-Republican Societies, 1790–1800,* 12–13, 240.

40. Aristides [Randolph], *National Gazette,* 26 September 1792; [Coxe], *The Federalist,* 10–11.

41. "Phocion No. II," *Gazette of the United States,* 15 October 1796; [Smith], *The Pretensions of Thomas Jefferson to the Presidency Examined,* 29; Robert G. Harper to Alexander Hamilton, 4 November 1796, *AHP,* 20:371–72.

42. William Cobbett, *A Little Plain English Addressed to the People of the United States* (Philadelphia, 1795), 70, and Cobbett, "A Summary View of the Politics of the United States from the Close of the War (1783) to the Year 1794," in *Porcupine's Works* (London, 1801), 1:129n, as quoted in Foner, ed., *The Democratic-Republican Societies, 1790–1800,* 7–8; Foner, ed., *The Democratic-Republican Societies,* 8, 439–41; George Warner, *Means for the Preservation of Political Liberty: An Oration Delivered in the New Dutch Church, on the Fourth of July, 1797* (New York, 1797), 13–14, as quoted in Wood, *Radicalism of the American Revolution,* 276; Joseph Priestley to Theophilus Lindsey, 17 July 1795, Original Letters from Dr. Joseph Priestley, Manuscripts Department, Dr. Williams's Library. Supporters of the Republican Party are best described in Appleby, *Capitalism and a New Social Order, passim.*

43. David Ross to Alexander Hamilton, 16 November 1796, *AHP,* 20:397.

44. Cunningham, *The Jeffersonian Republicans,* 103–6, 110–11; *Minerva,* 3 November 1796.

45. "Letter to Mr. Fenno," *Minerva,* 28 October 1796, reprinted from the *Gazette of the United States.* Hamilton's essay appears as "Catullus No. III," [29 September 1792], *AHP,* 12:498–506.

46. [Coxe], *The Federalist,* 15–16.

47. William Cocke to TJ, 17 August 1796, *TJP,* 29:169; TJ to Cocke, 21 October 1796, *TJP,* 29:199.

48. See James Madison to TJ, 23 March 1795, *TJP,* 28:315; TJ to Madison, 27 April 1795, *TJP,* 28:338–39; TJ to Cocke, 21 October 1796, *TJP,* 29:199; Madison to James Monroe, 26 February 1796, *JMP,* 16:233.

49. George Washington, Farewell Address, 19 September 1796, in John C. Fitzpatrick, ed., *The Writings of George Washington,* 39 vols. (Washington, D.C., 1931–1944), 35:214–38.

50. TJ to Edward Rutledge, 27 December 1796, *TJP,* 29:232; TJ to George Washington, 19 June 1796, *TJP,* 29:128.

51. TJ to Edward Rutledge, 27 December 1796, *TJP,* 29:232.

52. The assertion of his cowardice appeared under the signature of Charles Simms, an Alexandria, Virginia, resident and Federalist candidate for elector, in the *Gazette of the United States,* 27 September and 6 October 1796; Jefferson was defended by Cassius, "To the People of the United States," *Aurora,* 28 October 1796, reprinted from the *Petersburg Intelligencer,* and by the letter of Gerard Banks, *Aurora,* 28 October 1796, reprinted from the *Virginia Herald.* See Malone, 1:349–51, 353, 355, 361–68, 3:279–83, and "Documents Relating to the 1796 Campaign for Electors in Virginia" [editorial note], *TJP,* 29:193–99.

53. Cassius, "To the People of the United States," *New-Jersey Journal* (Elizabethtown, N.J.), 2 November 1796. See also Daniel C. Brent, *Virginia Herald,* 28 October 1796.

54. For the full, state-by-state electoral tally, see Page Smith, "Election of 1796," in *History of American Presidential Elections, 1789–1968,* ed. Arthur M. Schlesinger, Jr., 4 vols. (New York, 1971), 1:98.

55. James Madison to TJ, 19 December 1796, *TJP,* 29:226. See also Madison to TJ, 5 December 1796, *TJP,* 29:214, and Madison to TJ, 10 December 1796, *TJP,* 29:218.

56. TJ to James Madison, 1 January 1797, *TJP,* 29:247; TJ to Madison, 17 December 1796, *TJP,* 29:223; TJ to Thomas Mann Randolph, 28 November 1796, *TJP,* 29:211; TJ to Benjamin Rush, 22 January 1797, *TJP,* 29:275.

57. TJ to James Madison, 30 January 1797, *TJP,* 29:281.

58. *Aurora,* 3 March 1797.

59. *Columbian Centinel* (Boston), 15 March 1797. See also *Minerva,* 7 March 1797.

60. Alexander Hamilton to unknown, [8 November 1796], *AHP,* 20:377; Robert Troup to Rufus King, 16 November 1796, in Charles R. King, ed., *The Life and Correspondence of Rufus King,* 6 vols. (New York, 1894–1900), 2:110. See also Sharp, *American Politics in the Early Republic,* 147–49.

61. John Adams to TJ, 12 July 1813, *TJP:RS,* 6:284; TJ, Address to the Senate, [4 March 1797], *TJP,* 29:311; Alexander Hamilton to Rufus King, [15 February 1797], *AHP,* 20:515–16. See also Hamilton to King, 16 December 1796, *AHP,* 20:445; John Adams to Abigail Adams, 12 December 1796, in Adams, ed., *Works of John Adams,* 1:495–96; Stephen Higginson to Hamilton, 12 January 1797, *AHP,* 20:465.

62. William Barry Grove to James Hogg, 4 January 1797, William Barry Grove Papers, Southern Historical Collection, University of North Carolina Library; *Gazette of the United States,* 4 March 1797; Joseph Priestley to Theophilus Lindsey, 13 January 1797, Original Letters from Dr. Joseph Priestley, Manuscripts Department, Dr. Williams's Library.

63. See, for example, "An American," *Aurora,* 9 January 1797, and Robert Goodloe Harper, Circular Letter to Constituents, 13 March 1797, in Noble E. Cunningham, Jr., ed., *Circular Letters of Congressmen to Their Constituents, 1789–1829,* 3 vols. (Chapel Hill, N.C., 1978), 1:78–79.

3. The "Nauseous Fog"

1. John Adams to Benjamin Rush, 4 January 1813, in Schutz and Adair, eds., *Spur of Fame,* 263; TJ to Elbridge Gerry, 13 May 1797, *TJP,* 29:362.

2. Col. William North to Colonel Walker, 8 May 1797, Special Collections, University of Virginia Library, Charlottesville; Fisher Ames to Christopher Gore, 17 December

1796, in Allen, ed., *Works of Fisher Ames,* 2:1208; Stephen G. Kurtz, *The Presidency of John Adams: The Collapse of Federalism, 1795–1800* (Philadelphia, 1957), 269–70, 274–79.

3. On the sedition law, see James Morton Smith, *Freedom's Fetters: The Alien and Sedition Laws and American Civil Liberties* (Ithaca, N.Y., 1956). On Jefferson's dwindling popularity, see Thomas Robbins, diary entry for 15 November 1797, in Increase N. Tarbox, ed., *Diary of Thomas Robbins, D.D., 1796–1854,* 2 vols. (Boston, 1886–87), 1:44.

4. TJ to Henry Knox, 8 April 1800, *TJP,* 31:488.

5. TJ to Philip Mazzei, 24 April 1796, *TJP,* 29:82.

6. "Jefferson's Letter to Philip Mazzei" [editorial note], *TJP,* 29:73–81; *Minerva,* 2 May 1797.

7. *Minerva,* 2 May 1797; Joseph Priestley to Theophilus Lindsey, 16 November 1797, Original Letters from Dr. Joseph Priestley, Manuscripts Department, Dr. Williams's Library.

8. "A Native American," *Gazette of the United States,* 19 May 1797; "A Fellow Citizen," *Gazette of the United States,* 31 May 1797; "Decius," *Gazette of the United States,* 11 August 1800.

9. "Z.," *Gazette of the United States,* 5 May 1797; "A Native American," *Gazette of the United States,* 19 May 1797; *Minerva,* 2 May 1797; *The Herald: A Gazette for the Country* (New York), 3 May 1797.

10. *Porcupine's Gazette,* 27 June 1798; Theodore Dwight, *An Oration Spoken at Hartford... July 4th, 1798* (Hartford, Conn., 1798), 17; "Jacobin Tricks," *Columbian Centinel,* 6 April 1799; "An unfortunate mislead Man, but a real friend to America" to John Adams, 18 April 1798, Adams Family Papers, Massachusetts Historical Society, cited in Smith, *Freedom's Fetters,* 26; TJ to Peregrine Fitzhugh, 23 February 1798, *TJP,* 30:129.

11. Abigail Adams to Mary Cranch, 13 April 1798, in Stewart Mitchell, ed., *New Letters of Abigail Adams, 1788–1801* (Boston, 1947), 156; *Gazette of the United States,* 12 April 1798. On the XYZ affair, see Cunningham, *The Jeffersonian Republicans,* 124, 133.

12. Benjamin Henry Latrobe to Dr. I. B. Scandella, 7 April 1798, Wetmore Family Papers, Manuscripts and Archives Department, Sterling Memorial Library, Yale University, New Haven, Conn.

13. Smith, *Freedom's Fetters,* 435–42; TJ to John Taylor, 4 June 1798, *TJP,* 30:389; TJ to Stevens Thomson Mason, 11 October 1798, *TJP,* 30:560; TJ's Fair Copy [of the Kentucky Resolutions], [before 4 October 1798], *TJP,* 30:543–49; Wilson Cary Nicholas to TJ, 4 October 1798, *TJP,* 30:556; Adrienne Koch and Harry Ammon, "The Virginia and Kentucky Resolutions: An Episode in Jefferson's and Madison's Defense of Civil Liberties," *WMQ,* 3rd ser., 5 (1948): 145–76; Joseph Priestley to Theophilus Lindsey, 23 December 1798, Original Letters from Dr. Joseph Priestley, Manuscripts Department, Dr. Williams's Library; Frank M. Anderson, "Contemporary Opinion of the Virginia and Kentucky Resolutions," *American Historical Review* 5 (1900): 225–52.

14. Worthington Chauncey Ford, ed., *The Spurious Letters Attributed to Washington* (New York, 1889), 81, 47, 76; George Washington to Benjamin Walker, 12 January 1797, in Fitzpatrick, ed., *Writings of George Washington,* 35:364. The forgeries first appeared in *Letters from General Washington, to Several of His Friends in the Year 1776* (London, 1777) and later as *Letters from General Washington to Several of His Friends, in June and July, 1776* (Philadelphia, 1795).

15. TJ to George Logan, 20 June 1816, *TJP:RS,* 10:176.

16. Ford, ed., *Spurious Letters Attributed to Washington,* 26; George Washington to Timothy Pickering, 3 March 1797, in Fitzpatrick, ed., *Writings of George Washington,* 35:414–16; Pickering to John Fenno, 9 March 1797, as well as Washington's statement as it appeared in print, *Gazette of the United States,* 10 March 1797.

17. TJ to James Madison, 15 February 1798, *TJP,* 30:112; TJ to Madison, 2 March 1798, *TJP,* 30:156.

18. Abigail Adams to Mary Cranch, 15 February 1798, in Mitchell, ed., *New Letters of Abigail Adams,* 133.

19. TJ's Fair Copy [of the Kentucky Resolutions], [before 4 October 1798], *TJP,* 30:548; TJ to Edward Carrington, 16 January 1787, *TJP,* 11:48–49; TJ to Carrington, 27 May 1788, *TJP,* 13:208–09; TJ to Samuel Smith, 22 August 1798, *TJP,* 30:486.

20. TJ to Martin Van Buren, 29 June 1824, Ford, 10:308.

21. *Minerva,* 21 March 1797; *Boston Gazette,* 27 March 1797.

22. Ellis, *American Sphinx,* 160–61; Burstein, *The Inner Jefferson,* 242–44; TJ to James Madison, 3 August 1797, *TJP,* 29:490.

23. "A Fellow Citizen," *Gazette of the United States,* 19, 31 May 1797. See also "A Native American," *Gazette of the United States,* 19 May 1797.

24. TJ to James Madison, 3 August 1797, *TJP,* 29:489–90.

25. James Madison to TJ, 5 August 1797, *TJP,* 29:505.

26. James Monroe to TJ, 12 July 1797, *TJP,* 29:478.

27. James Monroe, *A View of the Conduct of the Executive, in the Foreign Affairs of the United States, Connected with the Mission to the French Republic, during the Years 1794, 5, & 6* (Philadelphia, 1797), lxvi, lxii; W. P. Cresson, *James Monroe* (Chapel Hill, N.C., 1946), 148–54. For an account at variance with Monroe's, see Elkins and McKitrick, *The Age of Federalism,* 498–507, 511–13. On defense pamphlets, see Freeman, *Affairs of Honor,* chap. 2.

28. TJ to James Madison, 3 August 1797, *TJP,* 29:489. This portrayal of dueling as politics follows closely the seminal studies by Kenneth S. Greenberg, *Honor and Slavery: Lies, Duels, Noses, Masks, Dressing as a Woman, Gifts, Strangers, Humanitarianism, Death, Slave Rebellions, the Proslavery Argument, Baseball, Hunting, and Gambling in the Old South* (Princeton, N.J., 1996), esp. 1–23; W. J. Rorabaugh, "The Political Duel in the Early Republic: Burr v. Hamilton," *JER* 15 (1995): 1–23; Bertram Wyatt-Brown, "Andrew Jackson's Honor," *JER* 17 (1997): 1–36; and, especially, Freeman, *Affairs of Honor,* chap. 4. On the use of the "field" to denote the physical or metaphorical space where duels and other affairs of honor took place, see Ben C. Truman, *The Field of Honor: Being a Complete and Comprehensive History of Duelling in All Countries* (New York, 1884).

29. Chauncey Goodrich to Oliver Wolcott, Sr., 20 May 1797, in Gibbs, ed., *Memoirs of the Administrations of Washington and John Adams,* 1:535. Jefferson later reported to Madison that he "first met with" the Mazzei letter "at Bladensburgh," Maryland, en route to Philadelphia; his account books indicate that he breakfasted there on 9 May 1797. See TJ to James Madison, 3 August 1797, *TJP,* 29:489, and Bear and Stanton, eds., *Jefferson's Memorandum Books,* 2:960.

30. TJ to Alexander White, 10 September 1797, *TJP,* 29:527; "Jacobin Tricks," *Columbian Centinel,* 6 April 1799; *Philadelphia Gazette,* 11 March 1800.

31. TJ, *Notes on the State of Virginia,* ed. Peden, 61–63, 275n96; Malone, 3:346–48.

32. Luther Martin to James Fennell, 29 March 1797, printed in *Porcupine's Gazette,* 3 April 1797. On how accusations of cowardice often initiated affairs of honor, see Wyatt-Brown, "Andrew Jackson's Honor," 23, and Freeman, *Affairs of Honor,* 173.

33. On entering the "lists," see the entries in J. A. Simpson and E. S. C. Weiner et al., eds., *Oxford English Dictionary,* 20 vols., 2nd edn. (New York, 1989), 5:879, 8:1019.

34. TJ to James Madison, 7 July 1793, *TJP,* 26:444; TJ to Levi Lincoln, 1 June 1803, *TJP,* 40:464; "Fair Play," *TJP,* 40:464–69; TJ to Peregrine Fitzhugh, 4 June 1797, *TJP,* 29:417; TJ to John Gibson, 21 March 1800, *TJP,* 31:450.

35. TJ to John Page, [1] January 1798, *TJP,* 30:7; Luther Martin to TJ, 11 December 1797, *TJP,* 29:581 (printed in *Porcupine's Gazette,* 14 December 1797); TJ to Samuel Brown, 25 March 1798, *TJP,* 30:216; TJ to James Lewis, Jr., 9 May 1798, *TJP,* 340. Martin's other "abusive letters" were printed in *Porcupine's Gazette,* 17 July 1797, 4, 13, 20 January, 14 February, 3 March 1798.

36. TJ to Samuel Brown, 25 March 1798, *TJP,* 30:216; TJ to John Page, [1] January 1798, *TJP,* 30:7. Jefferson's appendix of evidence supporting his claim appears in *Notes on the State of Virginia,* ed. Peden, 226–58.

37. TJ to John Henry, 31 December 1797, *TJP,* 29:601; TJ to Samuel Brown, 25 March 1798, *TJP,* 30:216; [William Duane], *Aurora,* 31 March 1800.

38. TJ to Samuel Brown, 25 March 1798, *TJP,* 30:216; TJ to James Lewis, Jr., 9 May 1798, *TJP,* 30:340.

39. Greenberg, *Honor and Slavery,* 14; Wyatt-Brown, "Andrew Jackson's Honor," 8; TJ to John Henry, 31 December 1797, *TJP,* 29:600. On the use of holding fire—or intentionally missing an opponent—in dueling rituals, see Wyatt-Brown, "Andrew Jackson's Honor," 2, 11, and Freeman, *Affairs of Honor,* 163–64, 178–79.

40. Luther Martin to James Fennell, 29 March 1797, printed in *Porcupine's Gazette,* 3 April 1797. On Jefferson's motives for excluding Clark's testimony, see Peterson, *Thomas Jefferson and the New Nation,* 585, and Malone, 3:353–54. For appraisals of Cresap's culpability and the authenticity of the Logan speech that support Jefferson's account, see Malone, 3:354–55; Irving Brant, *James Madison,* 6 vols. (Indianapolis, 1941–61), 1:281–91; Ray H. Sandefur, "Logan's Oration—How Authentic?" *Quarterly Journal of Speech* 46 (1960): 289–96; and James H. O'Donnell III, "Logan's Oration: A Case Study in Ethnographic Authentification," *Quarterly Journal of Speech* 65 (1979): 150–56. For a critique of how Jefferson assembled, interpreted, and presented his evidence, see Paul S. Clarkson and R. Samuel Jett, *Luther Martin of Maryland* (Baltimore, 1970), 181–88.

41. TJ to James Monroe, 5 April 1798, *TJP,* 30:246–47.

42. TJ to James Monroe, 21 May 1798, *TJP,* 30:361; TJ to Samuel Smith, 22 August 1798, *TJP,* 30:485–86.

43. TJ to John Adams, 27 June 1813, *TJP:RS,* 6:233.

4. The Revolution of 1800

1. *Baltimore American,* 30 June 1800, reprinted in the *Aurora,* 3 July 1800; *Aurora,* 7 July 1800; *Connecticut Courant,* 7 July 1800; Thomas Boylston Adams to William

Smith Shaw, 3 July 1800, in Charles Grenfill Washburn, comp., "Letters of Thomas Boylston Adams to William Smith Shaw, 1799–1823," *Proceedings of the American Antiquarian Society* 27 (1917): 118. See also Thomas Robbins, diary entry for 4 July 1800, in Tarbox, ed., *Diary of Thomas Robbins*, 1:118.

2. *Gazette of the United States*, 3, 16 July 1800; [William Linn], *Serious Considerations on the Election of a President: Addressed to the Citizens of the United States* (New York, 1800), 32.

3. On Jefferson's maneuvering during the campaign, see Cunningham, *The Jeffersonian Republicans*, 129–32, 138–40, 199, 211–12, 221, and Barbara B. Oberg, "A New Republican Order, Letter by Letter," *JER* 25 (2005): 1–20.

4. *Aurora*, 3 July 1800; Caspar Wistar to William Bache, 2 July 1800, Special Collections, University of Virginia Library. On Federalist attacks on Jefferson, see Charles O. Lerche, Jr., "Jefferson and the Election of 1800: A Case Study in the Political Smear," *WMQ*, 3rd ser., 5 (1948): 466–91.

5. Gouverneur Morris, diary entry for 13 May 1800, in Anne Cary Morris, ed., *The Diary and Letters of Gouverneur Morris, Minister of the United States to France; Member of the Constitutional Convention, Etc.*, 2 vols. (New York, 1888), 2:387; John W. Steele to John Haywood, 11 March 1801, Earnest Haywood Collection, Southern Historical Collection, University of North Carolina Library; J. W. Steele to Anne Steele, [1800], Steele Papers, Southern Historical Collection, University of North Carolina Library; Elkins and McKitrick, *The Age of Federalism*, 736.

6. Joseph Priestley to Theophilus Lindsey, 21 March 1799, Original Letters from Dr. Joseph Priestley, Manuscripts Department, Dr. Williams's Library; John Marshall to James Markham Marshall, 16 December 1799, in Charles T. Cullen, ed., *The Papers of John Marshall*, 8 vols. to date (Chapel Hill, N.C., 1974–), 4:44–45; Alexander Hamilton, *Letter from Alexander Hamilton, Concerning the Public Conduct and Character of John Adams, Esq., President of the United States* (New York, 1800), reprinted in *AHP*, 25:186–234; Gouverneur Morris, diary entry for 13 May 1800, in Morris, ed., *Diary and Letters of Gouverneur Morris*, 2:387. On the plot to elect Pinckney, see Elkins and McKitrick, *The Age of Federalism*, 734–36. On rumors of an Adams-Jefferson alliance, see the account in *AHP*, 24:483–86n3.

7. David Hackett Fischer, *The Revolution of American Conservatism: The Federalist Party in the Era of Jeffersonian Democracy* (New York, 1965), 52–54, 150–52; *Address to the Federal Republicans of the State of New-Jersey* (Trenton, 1800), 6; Robert Troup to Rufus King, 1 October 1800, in King, ed., *Life and Correspondence of Rufus King*, 3:315.

8. Timothy Dwight, Vermont Travel Journal, n.d., Dwight Family Papers, Manuscripts and Archives, Sterling Memorial Library, Yale University; John Fenno, *Desultory Reflections on the New Political Aspects of Public Affairs in the United States of America, since the Commencement of the Year 1799* (New York, 1800), 52–53; *A Candid Address, to the Freemen of Rhode-Island, on the Subject of the Approaching Election* (Providence, 1800), 1; *Address to the Federal Republicans of the State of New-Jersey*, 8.

9. Dwight, *The Duty of Americans*, 20. On public opinion of Jefferson's faith, see Constance B. Schutz, "'Of Bigotry in Politics and Religion': Jefferson's Religion, the Federalist Press, and the Syllabus," *VMHB* 91 (1983): 73–91.

10. A Federal Republican [Henry William DeSaussure], *Address to the Citizens of South-Carolina on the Approaching Election of a President and Vice-President of the United States* (Charleston, 1800), 17n; [John Mason], *The Voice of Warning, to Christians, on the Ensuing Election of a President of the United States* (New York, 1800), 8, 27; Robbins, diary entry for 8 May 1800, in Tarbox, ed., *Diary of Thomas Robbins*, 1:114; *Gazette of the United States*, 10 September 1800.

11. [Linn], *Serious Considerations on the Election of a President*, 4, 5; [Mason], *The Voice of Warning*, 8, 35.

12. [Mason], *The Voice of Warning*, 9–18; [Linn], *Serious Considerations on the Election of a President*, 6–8, 13–19. See the relevant passages in TJ, *Notes on the State of Virginia*, ed. Peden, 31, 102, 138–39, 147, 159, 164–65.

13. [Linn], *Serious Considerations on the Election of a President*, 20–21, 25, 16–17; [Mason], *The Voice of Warning*, 21–23.

14. Boller, *Presidential Campaigns*, 17–18.

15. "Fabius," *Connecticut Courant*, 7 April 1800; A South-Carolina Federalist [Henry William DeSaussure], *Answer to a Dialogue between a Federalist and a Republican* (Charleston, [1800]), 7; A Federal Republican, *Address to the Citizens of South-Carolina*, 11; Theodore Dwight, Sr., to "Rev. Doctor Morse," 7 January 1800, Manuscripts Department, Beineke Rare Book Library, Yale University; *Virginia Federalist*, 22 January 1800, cited in Lerche, "Jefferson and the Election of 1800," 478.

16. A Federal Republican, *Address to the Citizens of South-Carolina*, 13. See also Fenno, *Desultory Reflections on the New Political Aspects of Public Affairs in the United States of America*, 16.

17. A Federal Republicans, *Address to the Citizens of South-Carolina*, 9–10, 15, 21; Oliver Wolcott, Jr., to Fisher Ames, 10 August 1800, in Gibbs, ed., *Memoirs of the Administrations of Washington and John Adams*, 2:401; Gouverneur Morris, diary entry for 2 December 1800, in Morris, ed., *Diary and Letters of Gouverneur Morris*, 2:396–97; [Fisher Ames], "Falkland II," [10 February 1801,] in Allen, ed., *Works of Fisher Ames*, 1:217. See also "A Layman," *The Claims of Thomas Jefferson to the Presidency, Examined at the Bar of Christianity* (Philadelphia, 1800), 49.

18. A Federal Republican, *Address to the Citizens of South-Carolina*, 13; "Fabius," *Virginia Gazette*, 10 October 1800; *Connecticut Courant*, 31 March 1800; "More Notes on Virginia," *The Gazette* (Newark), 1 July 1800; Lerche, "Jefferson and the Election of 1800," 487.

19. Joseph Priestley to Theophilus Lindsey, 21 March 1799, Original Letters from Dr. Joseph Priestley, Manuscripts Department, Dr. Williams's Library; Hugh Williamson to TJ, 6 July 1801, TJ Papers, Lib. Cong.; "Burleigh," *Connecticut Courant*, 15 September 1800; A Federal Republican, *Address to the Citizens of South-Carolina*, 10, 15, 14; Lerche, "Jefferson and the Election of 1800," 480–81. On America's rapprochement with France, see Elkins and McKitrick, *The Age of Federalism*, 618–23, 635–90.

20. Gaye Wilson, "Depictions of the Body: Images of Thomas Jefferson prior to the Election of 1800" (paper presented at the annual meeting of the Society for Historians of the Early American Republic, Philadelphia, 18 July 2014).

21. A South-Carolina Federalist, *Answer to a Dialogue between a Federalist and a Re-

publican, 21; [Noah Webster], *A Rod for the Fool's Back* (New Haven, Conn., 1800), 7; Fenno, *Desultory Reflections on the New Political Aspects of Public Affairs in the United States of America,* 9; "Burleigh," *Connecticut Courant,* 15 September 1800.

22. Richard Stanford to James Patterson, 28 February 1803, Miscellaneous Manuscripts, North Carolina State Archives, Raleigh; A Republican [Jonathan Russell], *To the Freemen of Rhode-Island, &c.* ([Providence?], 1800), 2; "A Republican," *National Intelligencer* (Washington, D.C.), 31 October 1800; *National Intelligencer,* 2 March 1801.

23. [Webster], *A Rod for the Fool's Back,* 7–8; Grotius [DeWitt Clinton], *A Vindication of Thomas Jefferson; against the Charges Contained in a Pamphlet Entitled "Serious Considerations"* (New York, 1800), 11.

24. Joseph Priestley to Theophilus Lindsey, 19 May 1800, Original Letters from Dr. Joseph Priestley, Manuscripts Department, Dr. Williams's Library; Marcus Brutus [Benjamin Pollard?], *Serious Facts, Opposed to "Serious Considerations"; or, The Voice of Warning to Religious Republicans* (N.p., 1800), 11, 12, 2; Greene [Tench Coxe], *Strictures upon the Letter Imputed to Mr. Jefferson, Addressed to Mr. Mazzei* (N.p., 1800), 3–4; Timoleon [Tunis Wortman], *A Solemn Address, to Christians and Patriots, upon the Approaching Election of a President of the United States: In Answer to a Pamphlet, Entitled "Serious Considerations," &c.* (New York, 1800), 13, 15, 34; "Civis," *National Intelligencer,* 11 November 1800.

25. Americanus, *Address to the People of the United States,* 32. On the circulation of Beckley's pamphlet, see Cunningham, *The Jeffersonian Republicans,* 198.

26. *Address to the Citizens of Kent, on the Approaching Election* (Wilmington, Del., [1800]), 4; Americanus, *Address to the People of the United States,* 7; "A Voter," *To the People of Cecil: No. I* (Wilmington, Del., [1800]), 4; Abraham Bishop, *Connecticut Republicanism: An Oration, on the Extent and Power of Political Delusion* ([New Haven, Conn.], 1800), 44.

27. Bishop, *Connecticut Republicanism,* 36.

28. Ibid., 33; Americanus, *Address to the People of the United States,* 5; Grotius, *A Vindication of Thomas Jefferson,* 3.

29. "A Republican," *National Gazette,* 31 October 1800.

30. Bishop, *Connecticut Republicanism,* 10; "A Voter," *To the People of Cecil: No. II* (Wilmington, Del., [1800]), 6–7; L, *Thoughts on the Subject of the Ensuing Election: Addressed to the Party in the State of New-York, Who Claim Exclusively the Appellation of Federalists* ([Albany], 1800), 1.

31. Richard Stanford to James Patterson, 28 February 1803, Miscellaneous Manuscripts, North Carolina State Archives; *National Intelligencer,* 17 November 1800; A Voter, *To the People of Cecil: No. II,* 1.

32. "Timoleon," *National Intelligencer,* 10 November 1800; *National Intelligencer,* 31 October 1800; Bishop, *Connecticut Republicanism,* 20; *A Test of the Religious Principles of Mr. Jefferson* (Philadelphia, 1800), ii; Timoleon, *A Solemn Address, to Christians and Patriots, upon the Approaching Election of a President of the United States,* 9.

33. Fischer, *The Revolution of American Conservatism,* 224–25; Letter of Benjamin Noves, *Aurora,* 13 August 1800.

34. Bishop, *Connecticut Republicanism,* 18–19; A Republican, *To the Freemen of Rhode*

Island, 2; Greene, *Strictures upon the Letter Imputed to Mr. Jefferson*, 9; "Washington," *A Touchstone for the Leading Partymen in the United States: Dedicated to Mr. Sedgwick* (N.p., 1800), 3–4; A Voter, *To the People of Cecil: No. I*, 4; W. W. Burrows to Jonathan Williams, 14 December 1800, Special Collections, University of Virginia Library; *Address to the Citizens of Kent*, 3.

35. Cunningham, *The Jeffersonian Republicans*, 144–47, 150, 189–90; W. Edwin Hemphill, "'In Constant Struggle': How and Why Virginians Voted for Thomas Jefferson in 1800," *Virginia Cavalcade* 2, no. 4 (Spring 1953): 8–15; Elkins and McKitrick, *The Age of Federalism*, 905.

36. W. W. Burrows to Jonathan Williams, 8 December 1800, Special Collections, University of Virginia Library; Daniel Dewey to Theodore Sedgwick, 8 December 1800, Sedgwick Papers, Massachusetts Historical Society; Robbins, diary entry for 21 December 1800, in Tarbox, ed., *Diary of Thomas Robbins*, 1:127; *The Jefferson Almanac, Calculated for Pennsylvania, Delaware, Maryland, Virginia and Kentucky* (Baltimore, 1801), i.

37. David Stone to Samuel Johnston, 24 January 1801, Johnston to Stone, 18 February 1801, Johnston Family Series, Hayes Collection, Southern Historical Collection, University of North Carolina Library; Daniel Webster to George Herbert, 7 January 1801, in Charles M. Wiltse et al., eds., *The Papers of Daniel Webster: Correspondence*, 7 vols. (Hanover, N.H., 1974–86), 1:31; [Linn], *Serious Considerations on the Election of a President*, 4; Gouverneur Morris to Alexander Hamilton, 26 January 1801, *AHP*, 25:329; Morris, diary entry for 27 December 1800, in Morris, ed., *Diary and Letters of Gouverneur Morris*, 2:397.

38. Alexander Hamilton to Gouverneur Morris, 24 December 1800, *AHP*, 25:272; Hamilton to Harrison Gray Otis, 23 December 1800, *AHP*, 25:271; Hamilton to Theodore Sedgwick, 22 December 1800, *AHP*, 25:270; Hamilton to James A. Bayard, 16 January 1801, *AHP*, 25:319–20.

39. J. M. to John Haywood, 26 February 1801, Earnest Haywood Collection, Southern Historical Collection, University of North Carolina Library; Joseph Dickson to William Lenoir, 27 January 1801, Lenior Family Papers, Southern Historical Collection, University of North Carolina Library; John Beckley to Alexander Gallatin, 15 February 1801, Gallatin Papers, Manuscripts Department, New-York Historical Society.

40. Uriah Tracy to Charles Chauncey, 12, 17 February 1801, Chauncey Family Papers, Manuscripts and Archives Department, Sterling Memorial Library, Yale University; Timothy Bloodworth to Benjamin Williams, 17 February 1801, Wetmore Family Papers, Manuscripts and Archives Department, Sterling Memorial Library, Yale University. See also Elkins and McKitrick, *The Age of Federalism*, 748–50, and Malone, 3:502–5, 4:11–14, 487–93.

41. Cato West to Andrew Jackson, 26 June 1801, in Sam B. Smith et al., eds., *The Papers of Andrew Jackson*, 9 vols. to date (Knoxville, Tenn., 1980–), 1:246; Joseph Priestley to Theophilus Lindsey, 22 July 1801, Priestley to Thomas Belsham, 15 June 1801, Original Letters from Dr. Joseph Priestley, Manuscripts Department, Dr. Williams's Library; Richard Dobbs Spaight to John Haywood, 24 February 1801, Earnest Haywood Collection, Southern Historical Collection, University of North Carolina Library; Joseph Dickson to William Lenoir, 24 February 1801, Lenoir Family Papers, Southern Histori-

cal Collection, University of North Carolina Library; David Stone to Samuel Johnston, 28 February 1801, Johnston Family Series, Hayes Collection, Southern Historical Collection, University of North Carolina Library.

42. Cato West to Andrew Jackson, 26 June 1801, in Smith et al., eds., *Papers of Andrew Jackson,* 1:246; Thomas Robbins, diary entry for 23 February 1801, in Tarbox, ed., *Diary of Thomas Robbins,* 1:132; Fischer, *The Revolution of American Conservatism,* 185; *National Intelligencer,* 3 November 1800.

43. [Linn], *Serious Considerations on the Election of a President,* 34; Grotius, *A Vindication of Thomas Jefferson,* 26. On DeWitt Clinton's penchant for dueling, see Freeman, *Affairs of Honor,* 181–87.

44. *Gazette of the United States,* 9 July 1800; *Columbian Centinel,* 19 July 1800; James Thomson to Henry M. Ridgely, 14 July 1800, quoted in Mabel Lloyd Ridgely, *What Them Befell: The Ridgelys of Delaware and Their Circle in Colonial and Federal Times* (Portland, Maine, 1949), 131; Americanus, *Address to the People of the United States,* 26.

45. TJ to John Taylor, 4 June 1798, *TJP,* 30:388–89.

46. For perceptive accounts of Jefferson's efforts in the 1800 election, from which this study benefits greatly, see Freeman, *Affairs of Honor,* 230–35, and Oberg, "A New Republican Order, Letter by Letter," 1–20.

47. Americanus, *Address to the People of the United States,* 25–28.

48. Edmund Berkeley and Dorothy Smith Berkeley, *John Beckley: Zealous Partisan in a Nation Divided* (Philadelphia, 1973), 201–2, 205–6. Jefferson remained in Philadelphia until 15 May. See TJ to Thomas Mann Randolph, 14 May 1800, *TJP,* 31:581.

49. Americanus, *Address to the People of the United States,* 4, 5; TJ to George Logan, 20 June 1816, Ford, 10:27.

50. Americanus, *Address to the People of the United States,* 32–38.

51. TJ to James Monroe, 26 March 1800, *TJP,* 31:462.

52. James Monroe to TJ, 8 April 1800, *TJP,* 31:490.

53. Ibid.

54. TJ to James Monroe, 13 April 1800, *TJP,* 31:499.

55. TJ to Archibald Stuart, 13 February 1799, *TJP,* 31:35; TJ to James Monroe, 11 February 1799, *TJP,* 31:24.

56. James Monroe to TJ, [25] May 1800, *TJP,* 31:589; Alexander Hamilton to John Jay, 7 May 1800, *AHP,* 24:464–67.

57. TJ to John Adams, 17 July 1791, *TJP,* 20:302.

58. Noble E. Cunningham, Jr., *The Inaugural Addresses of President Thomas Jefferson, 1801 and 1805* (Columbia, Mo., 2001), 1, 4, 6, 17, 19–20, 26.

59. TJ, First Inaugural Address, 4 March 1801, *TJP,* 33:148–51.

60. Ibid.; Margaret Bayard Smith, *The First Forty Years of Washington Society,* ed. Gaillard Hunt (1906; New York, 1965), 12, 29–31; *Providence Gazette,* 21 March 1801; *National Intelligencer,* 6 March 1801; Malone, 4:4; Ellis, *American Sphinx,* 169–71. For a particularly perceptive analysis of Jefferson's words, see Stephen Browne, *Jefferson's Call for Nationhood: The First Inaugural Address* (College Station, Tex., 2003).

61. *Columbian Minerva* (Salem, Mass.), 17 March 1801; John W. Steele to John Haywood, 11 March 1801, Earnest Haywood Collection, Southern Historical Collection,

University of North Carolina Library; William Barry Grove to James Hogg, 14 March 1801, William Barry Grove Papers, Southern Historical Collection, University of North Carolina Library; Gouverneur Morris, diary entry for 4 March 1801, in Morris, ed., *Diary and Letters of Gouverneur Morris*, 2:405; Edwin B. Smith to James Davenport, 6 May 1801, Special Collections, University of Virginia Library.

62. Elbridge Gerry to unknown, 1 April 1801, Elbridge Gerry Papers, Massachusetts Historical Society; Benjamin Waterhouse to unknown, 14 April 1801, Autograph Collection, Manuscripts Department, Wellcome Institute for the History of Medicine Library, London.

63. Theodore Sedgwick to Rufus King, 14 December 1801, King Papers, Manuscripts Department, New-York Historical Society; TJ, First Inaugural Address, 4 March 1801, *TJP*, 33:151.

5. President of the People

1. L. H. Butterfield, "Elder John Leland, Jeffersonian Itinerant," *Proceedings of the American Antiquarian Society* 62 (1952): esp. 219–229; "Presentation of the 'Mammoth Cheese'" [editorial note], *TJP*, 36:246–49.

2. Committee of Cheshire, Massachusetts, to TJ, [30 December 1801], *TJP*, 36:249–50. On the significance of the cheese as a medium of popular expression, see Jeffrey L. Pasley, "The Cheese and the Words: Popular Political Culture and Participatory Democracy in the Early American Republic," in Pasley, Robertson, and Waldstreicher, eds., *Beyond the Founders*, 31–56.

3. Throughout the first decade of the nineteenth century, a Federalist candidate never received more than three votes from the citizens of Cheshire. Republicans who stood for office typically won the support of around two hundred individuals. Butterfield, "Elder John Leland," 215–16.

4. TJ to the Committee of Cheshire, Massachusetts, [1 January 1802], *TJP*, 36:252; *National Intelligencer*, 20 January 1802, reprinted from the *Baltimore American*. In keeping with his practice of not accepting gifts of pecuniary value while in office, Jefferson also sent Leland home with two hundred dollars, a generous and unsolicited payment that amounted to sixteen cents per pound of cheese; see Butterfield, "Elder John Leland," 227.

5. TJ to Tadeusz Kosciuszko, 2 April 1802, *TJP*, 37:168; Robert R. Davis, Jr., "Pell-Mell: Jeffersonian Etiquette and Protocol," *The Historian* 43 (1981): 512.

6. Manasseh Cutler to Dr. Joseph Torrey, 4 January 1802, in Cutler and Cutler, comps., *Life, Journals, and Correspondence of Rev. Manasseh Cutler*, 2:66; Peterson, *Thomas Jefferson and the New Nation*, 723; Richard Sassaman, "The Original 'Big Cheese'," *American History Illustrated* 23 (January 1989): 34–35.

7. "Viator," *Western Star* (Stockbridge, Mass.), 31 August 1801; John Davis, *Travels of Four Years and a Half in the United States of America* (London, 1803), 329–30; [Thomas Kennedy], *Ode to the Mammoth Cheese, Presented to Thomas Jefferson, President of the United States, by the Inhabitants of Cheshire, Massachusetts* ([Cheshire, Mass.?], 1802); *New-York Evening Post*, 5 March 1802; *The Sun* (Pittsfield, Mass.), 16 November 1801.

8. TJ to Thomas Mann Randolph, 1 January 1802, *TJP*, 36:262.

9. Manasseh Cutler to Dr. Joseph Torrey, 4 January 1802, in Cutler and Cutler, comps., *Life, Journals, and Correspondence of Rev. Manasseh Cutler,* 2:66–67.

10. *National Intelligencer,* 20 January 1802.

11. Malone, 4:107; Michael Fry and Nathan Coleman to TJ, 17 October 1801, *TJP,* 35:457–58; TJ to Fry and Coleman, 22 October 1801, *TJP,* 35:486.

12. *City Gazette and Daily Advertiser* (Charleston), 14 March 1801; *Aurora,* 17 March 1801. Naming a child after Jefferson did not always guarantee community approval. For Johnson Cook of Marietta, Pennsylvania, a town that he described to the president as a "thicket of your sworn enemys," his intention to christen his newborn "Thomas Jefferson Cook" signified defiance of the status quo. See Cook to TJ, 17 October 1801, *TJP,* 35:455–57.

13. "Pageant," *Aurora,* 3 March 1801.

14. Benjamin Ring to TJ, 8 March 1801, *TJP,* 33:224; Willie Blount to TJ, 14 November 1801, *TJP,* 35:662; Nehemiah W. Badger to TJ, 13 February 1806, in Jack McLaughlin, ed., *To His Excellency Thomas Jefferson: Letters to a President* (New York, 1991), 301.

15. McLaughlin, ed., *To His Excellency Thomas Jefferson,* 301n; *Aurora,* 24 January, 3, 4, 11 March 1801; *The Democratic Songster: Being a Collection of New Republican Songs, Mostly Originals* (Baltimore, 1801), 10–13.

16. Joseph Chandler, *An Oration, Delivered at the Centre Meeting-House in Monmouth, Maine, on the Fourth of July, 1804, Being the Anniversary of American Independence* (Portland, Maine, 1804), 10.

17. See Noble E. Cunningham, Jr., *The Image of Thomas Jefferson in the Public Eye: Portraits for the People, 1800–1809* (Charlottesville, Va., 1981), esp. 97–109, 146–53.

18. Ibid., 55–69. Versions of Helmbold's advertisement appeared in several newspapers for more than a year. See, for example, the *Aurora,* 3 March 1801. For Helmbold's criticism of the Augustus Day print, see Charleston's *City Gazette and Daily Advertiser,* 13 July 1801. The biography distributed to purchasers, *A Concise Account of the Life of Thomas Jefferson, President of the United States* (Philadelphia, 1801), first appeared as a section of John Beckley's (as Americanus) *Address to the People of the United States.*

19. Matt. 13:42, Luke 12:31; Stanley Griswold, *Overcoming Evil with Good: A Sermon, Delivered at Wallingford, Connecticut, March 11, 1801* (Hartford, 1801), 12–13, 24–25; Abraham Bishop, *Oration, Delivered in Wallingford, on the 11th of March 1801, before the Republicans of the State of Connecticut, at Their General Thanksgiving, for the Election of Thomas Jefferson to the Presidency, and of Aaron Burr to the Vice-Presidency, of the United States of America* (Bennington, Vt., 1801), 7; Democraticus, *The Jeffersoniad; or, An Echo to the Groans of an Expiring Faction* (Fredericktown, Md., 1801), frontispiece; Tunis Wortman, *An Address, to the Republican Citizens of New-York, on the Inauguration of Thomas Jefferson President of the United States* (New York, 1801), 6.

20. On the Federalist system of interests, see Elkins and McKitrick, *The Age of Federalism,* 92–131, and Forrest McDonald, *Alexander Hamilton: A Biography* (New York, 1979), esp. chaps. 6–10. On Federalists' conflation of democracy and tyranny, see Fischer, *The Revolution of American Conservatism,* 155–63; Linda K. Kerber, *Federalists in Dissent: Imagery and Ideology in Jeffersonian America* (Ithaca, N.Y., 1970), 13–17, 174–83, 193–94, 199–200, 203–5; and Sharp, *American Politics in the Early Republic,* 73–74.

21. Mona Ozouf, "Marat," in *A Critical Dictionary of the French Revolution,* ed.

François Furet and Mona Ozouf, trans. Arthur Goldhammer (Cambridge, Mass., 1989), 248–50; Michael L. Kennedy, *The Jacobin Clubs in the French Revolution: The Middle Years* (Princeton, N.J., 1988), 180, 320.

22. [Augustus Brevoort Woodward], *Epaminondas: Originally Published in Numbers, in the New-York Gazette* (New York, 1801), 4, 6; *Columbian Centinel*, 20 June 1801; "Extract of a Letter from a Very Respectable Gentleman in Paris, to His Friend in Philadelphia," *New-York Evening Post*, 11 March 1802; Manasseh Cutler, journal entry for 2 January 1802, in Cutler and Cutler, comps., *Life, Journals, and Correspondence of Rev. Manasseh Cutler*, 2:56.

23. "More Antifederal Consistency!" *Columbian Centinel*, 13 June 1801; "A Looker On," "Kennebeck Address," *New-York Evening Post*, 3 March 1802. See also *New-York Evening Post*, 17 November 1801; "Communications," *Columbian Centinel*, 17 June 1801.

24. *New-York Evening Post*, 14 July 1802; Phocion, "To the People of Connecticut," *Connecticut Courant*, 8 March 1802, reprinted from the *Monitor* (Litchfield, Conn.).

25. [Fisher Ames], "The Republican VI," *Boston Gazette*, 13 August 1804, reprinted from the *Repertory* (Boston), in Allen, ed., *Works of Fisher Ames*, 2:331; Theodore Sedgwick to Alexander Hamilton, 10 January 1801, *AHP*, 25:311; Peterson, *The Jefferson Image in the American Mind*, 67; Everett S. Brown, ed., *William Plumer's Memorandum of Proceedings in the United States Senate, 1803–1807* (New York, 1923), 550. See also Mumper, "The Jefferson Image in the Federalist Mind," 1–59.

26. "Lavater's Aphorisms," *New York Evening Post*, 20 April 1802; Gouverneur Morris to Alexander Hamilton, 11 March 1802, *AHP*, 25:561.

27. TJ to Joseph Cabell, 26 February 1818, in Nathaniel Francis Cabell, ed., *Early History of the University of Virginia, as Contained in the Letters of Thomas Jefferson and Joseph C. Cabell* (Richmond, Va., 1856), 128; Smith, *The First Forty Years of Washington Society*, 5–8, 386.

28. Alexander Hamilton to James A. Bayard, 16 January 1801, *AHP*, 25:319, 320; William Barry Grove to James Hogg, 14 March 1801, William Barry Grove Papers, Southern Historical Collection, University of North Carolina Library; Fisher Ames to Josiah Quincy, 11 December 1806, in Allen, ed., *Works of Fisher Ames*, 2:1535; [Ames], "The Republican VI," *Boston Gazette*, 13 August 1804, reprinted from the *Repertory* (Boston), in Allen, ed., *Works of Fisher Ames*, 1:330.

29. "Pageant," *Aurora*, 3 March 1801; J. Horatio Nichols, *Jefferson and Liberty; or, Celebration of the Fourth of March* (N.p., 1801), 17.

30. *Aurora*, 4 March 1801; *A Declaration of the Principles and Views of the Democratic-Federalists, in the County of Cumberland, and the State of New Jersey* (Philadelphia, 1801), 7–8; Ebenezer Wheelock, *An Oration Delivered at Middlebury, before a Large and Respectable Collection of Republican Citizens, Assembled on the Day of the Inauguration of Thomas Jefferson, to the Chair of State* (Bennington, Vt., 1801), 8. See also *National Intelligencer*, 16 November 1801.

31. "Toasts," *Aurora*, 9 March 1801; *Connecticut Courant*, 23 March 1801; *Aurora*, 17 March 1801; *City Gazette and Daily Advertiser*, 14 March 1801.

32. *City Gazette and Daily Advertiser*, 4 March 1801; *Aurora*, 4 March 1801; *A Declaration of the Principles and Views of the Democratic-Federalists*, 8, 5.

33. Michael Fry and Nathan Coleman to TJ, 17 October 1801, *TJP,* 35:458; Abigail Adams to John Adams, 26 May 1789, in Butterfield et al., eds., *Adams Family Correspondence,* 8:360.

34. Committee of Cheshire, Massachusetts, to TJ, [30 December 1801], *TJP,* 36:249–50; TJ to Spencer Roane, 6 September 1819, *TJW,* 1425.

35. TJ, *Notes on the State of Virginia,* ed. Peden, 165. TJ's *Notes,* originally written for a select audience of a few friends, had gained great currency by the end of 1801, when it had been issued to the general public in nine separate American printings. See Charles Evans, comp., *American Bibliography, 1639–1800,* 13 vols. (Chicago, 1903–34), 7:227, 9:305, 13:156, and Ralph R. Shaw and Richard H. Shoemaker, comps., *American Bibliography, 1801–1819,* 22 vols. (New York, 1958–66), 1:79.

36. TJ to John Vanmetre, 4 September 1800, *TJP,* 32:126. Vanmetre apparently submitted Jefferson's letter for publication, for it appeared in the *Connecticut Courant,* 16 February 1801.

37. *Aurora,* 4, 12, 16 March 1801; Davis, "Pell-Mell: Jeffersonian Etiquette and Protocol," 510–14; Smith, *The First Forty Years of Washington Society,* 384, 397.

38. [Beckley], *A Concise Account of the Life of Thomas Jefferson;* Malone, 4:31; *Gazette of the United States,* 3 March 1797. See also *Connecticut Courant,* 23 March 1801, and Newman, "Principles or Men?"

39. Benjamin Rush, "Address to the People of the United States," 1787, in John P. Kaminski et al., eds., *The Documentary History of the Ratification of the Constitution,* 19 vols. to date (Madison, Wis., 1976–), 13:47. See also Gordon S. Wood, *The Creation of the American Republic, 1776–1787* (Chapel Hill, N.C., 1969), 373–74; Sharp, *American Politics in the Early Republic,* 4, 26, 64–65, 101–3; and Horst Dippel, "The Changing Idea of Popular Sovereignty in Early American Constitutionalism: Breaking away from European Patterns," *JER* 16 (1996): 21–45.

40. Seth Cotlar, *Tom Paine's America: The Rise and Fall of Transatlantic Radicalism in the Early Republic* (Charlottesville, Va., 2011), 161–70; Alexander Hamilton to James A. Bayard, 16 January 1801, *AHP,* 25:319; TJ to John Dickinson, 6 March 1801, *TJP,* 33:196; TJ to Thomas Paine, 18 March 1801, *TJP,* 33:359. Jefferson's conception of public opinion is best described in Peter S. Onuf, *Jefferson's Empire: The Language of American Nationhood* (Charlottesville, Va., 2000), 102–8, and Steele, *Thomas Jefferson and American Nationhood,* 157–68.

41. TJ to John Norvell, 14 June 1807, Ford, 9:73; TJ to William Short, 6 September 1808, L&B, 12:159; TJ to James Madison, 19 April 1809, in Smith, ed., *Republic of Letters,* 3:1582.

42. Bear and Stanton, eds., *Jefferson's Memorandum Books,* 2:1000, 1002–3, 1005–6, 1009, 1012, 1014–19, 1021, 1024, 1031, 1034–35, 1037, 1041–42, 1046, 1049, 1062, 1069, 1070, 1074, 1077, 1091–92, 1104, 1109, 1112, 1123, 1133, 1137, 1140, 1148, 1153, 1172–73, 1175, 1191, 1199, 1206, 1214–16, 1220, 1223, 1226–28, 1231, 1235, 1238–43, 1249.

43. Margaret Smith Nicholas to Dabney S. Carr, 1826, Carr-Cary Papers, Special Collections, University of Virginia Library. Nicholas, the wife of Wilson Cary Nicholas, was mother of Jane Hollins Nicholas, wife of Thomas Jefferson Randolph. See George Green Shackelford, ed., *Collected Papers of the Monticello Association of the Descendants of Thomas Jefferson,* 2 vols. (Princeton, N.J., 1965–84), 1:77.

44. Malone, 1:45; Douglas L. Wilson, ed., *Jefferson's Literary Commonplace Book* (Princeton, N.J., 1989), 6–8; Dickinson W. Adams, ed., *Jefferson's Extracts from the Gospels: "The Philosophy of Jesus" and "The Life and Morals of Jesus"* (Princeton, N.J., 1983), 30–38; Kenneth A. Lockridge, *On the Sources of Patriarchal Rage: The Commonplace Books of William Byrd and Thomas Jefferson and the Gendering of Power in the Eighteenth Century* (New York, 1992), 2–4.

45. TJ to Peregrine Fitzhugh, 23 February 1798, *TJP,* 30:129; TJ's Newspaper Commonplace Scrapbooks, 4:[12–13] (clipping sources not identified), 1:[18] (clipping source not identified but see the typographically different reprinting "INDEPENDENCE!" *The Sun* [Pittsfield, Mass.], 23 August 1806). Clippings relating to the Fourth of July appear in TJ's Newspaper Commonplace Scrapbooks, 1:[10–84] *passim.* The four scrapbooks are catalogued as "Jefferson-Randolph Family Scrapbooks, 1800–1808, Accession #5948, 5948-a, 5948-b" and are housed at the University of Virginia's Albert and Shirley Small Special Collections Library.

46. A Buckskin, *Virginia Gazette,* 10 September 1802.

47. TJ's Newspaper Commonplace Scrapbooks, 1:[11] ("RHODE-ISLAND," *Albany Register,* 26 July 1805), [30] (clipping source not identified), [21] (clipping source not identified), [28] (clipping source not identified but the Westmoreland toast also appears in the *Aurora,* 1 August 1805), [39] (clipping source not identified but the Boston toast also appears in "Selected—Toasts Drank at Boston," *Sentinel of Freedom* [Newark, N.J.], 16 July 1805).

48. Peterson, *Thomas Jefferson and the New Nation,* 703; TJ, Second Inaugural Address, 4 March 1805, *TJW,* 522. On Jefferson's presidential leadership, see Jeremy D. Bailey, "From 'Floating Ardor' to the 'Union of Sentiment': Jefferson on the Relationship between Public Opinion and the Executive," in *A Companion to Thomas Jefferson,* ed. Francis D. Cogliano (Oxford, U.K., 2011), 184–98, and Bailey, *Thomas Jefferson and Executive Power.*

49. Wills, *Cincinnatus,* 28, 32–35; Schwartz, *George Washington,* 29, 89, 116, 176–77, 237–38.

50. TJ to James Madison, 9 June 1793, *TJP,* 26:241; *Aurora,* 26 January 1793; Wills, *Cincinnatus,* xxii–xxiv; Newman, "Principles or Men?" 493–95; Edward Thornton to James Burges, 11 June 1792, in S. W. Jackman, ed., "A Young Englishman Reports on the New Nation: Edward Thornton to James Bland Burges, 1791–1793," *WMQ,* 3rd ser., 18 (1961): 111; Smith, *The First Forty Years of Washington Society,* 398; Joseph J. Ellis, "American Sphinx: The Contradictions of Thomas Jefferson," *Civilization* 1 (November–December 1994): 37.

51. On ritualistic praise for Washington, see TJ to James Madison, 9 June 1793, *TJP,* 26:241; Newman, "Principles or Men?" 493–94; and Schwartz, *George Washington,* 61–65.

6. Race, Sex, and Reputation

1. Advertisement in *National Intelligencer,* 18 August 1802.

2. A 25 August dispatch from Richmond, Va., printed in the *Columbian Centinel,* 4 September 1802.

3. *Recorder; or, Lady's and Gentleman's Miscellany* (Richmond, Va.), reprinted in the *Connecticut Courant*, 10, 27 September 1802.

4. *Gazette of the United States,* 7 September 1802. An example of the hearsay to which this paper referred can be found in the Washington, D.C., *Federalist*, which reported a year earlier "that it has long been currently reported that a man very high in office, has a number of yellow children, and that he is adicted to golden affections. It is natural to suppose it possible that personal or political enemies of Mr. J. might raise such reports, when they are wholly unfounded—and on the other side it is observed that, what everybody says must be true. . . . If they are false and malicious they ought to be contradicted." Also, in July 1802, a ballad printed in the Philadelphia *Port Folio* stated that, since "all men free alike are born," then "blackee hab De white womans" and "massa *Jefferson shall hab de black.*" See the *Federalist* (Washington, D.C.), 14 September 1801, quoted in Shultz, "'Of Bigotry in Politics and Religion'," 84, and "Asmodio," *Port Folio,* 10 July 1802.

5. *Connecticut Courant,* 10 September 1802.

6. "A Song, Supposed to Have Been Written by the Sage of Monticello," *Boston Gazette,* reprinted in the *Port Folio,* 2 October 1802.

7. TJ to Levi Lincoln, 25 October 1802, *TJP,* 38:566.

8. Noble E. Cunningham, *The Jeffersonian Republicans in Power: Party Operations, 1801–1809* (Chapel Hill, N.C., 1963), 71.

9. John Adams to Col. Joseph Ward, 8 January 1810, John Adams Letterbook, Adams Family Papers, microfilm reel 118, item 185, Massachusetts Historical Society.

10. Evidence for the relationship is described and analyzed in the Thomas Jefferson Foundation's "Report of the Research Committee on Thomas Jefferson and Sally Hemings" (January 2000), http://www.monticello.org/site/plantation-and-slavery/report -research-committee-thomas-jefferson-and-sally-hemings. The report takes into account evidence highlighted in a number of earlier studies, including Annette Gordon-Reed, *Thomas Jefferson and Sally Hemings: An American Controversy* (Charlottesville, Va., 1997), and Eugene A. Foster et al., "Jefferson Fathered Slave's Last Child," *Nature* 196 (5 November 1998): 27–28. All but one of the members of Monticello's Research Committee concurred with its conclusion that Jefferson "most likely was the father of all six of Sally Hemings's children." While the preponderance of evidence points toward a sexual relationship between Jefferson and Hemings, some who have looked closely at the issue remain unconvinced. All but one of the members of the Thomas Jefferson Heritage Society's Scholars Commission in 2001 expressed doubts ranging from "serious skepticism about the charge to the conviction that it is almost certainly false." See Robert F. Turner, ed., *The Jefferson–Hemings Controversy: Report of the Scholars Commission* (Durham, N.C., 2011), 3.

11. Like the *Recorder,* most other Federalist newspapers also made little of the immoral nature of Jefferson's alleged conduct. One journal, however, did note that if the charges were true, Jefferson "lived in the habitual violation of the seventh commandment with one of his own slaves!" See *Frederick-Town Herald,* reprinted in the *Gazette of the United States,* 27 September 1802.

12. *Recorder,* reprinted in the *Connecticut Courant,* 10 September 1802; *Lynchburg Gazette* (Virginia), reprinted in the *Recorder,* 3 November 1802; *Columbian Centinel,*

15 September 1802; Virginius Dabney, *The Jefferson Scandals: A Rebuttal* (New York, 1981), 10–11, 13 (quotations); "A Philosophic Love-Song, to Sally," *Boston Gazette*, re printed in the *Port Folio*, 6 November 1802.

13. *Recorder,* reprinted in the *Gazette of the United States*, 7, 22 September 1802.

14. John Adams to Col. Joseph Ward, 8 January 1810, John Adams Letterbook, Adams Family Papers, microfilm reel 118, item 185, Massachusetts Historical Society; Mary Chesnut, *Mary Chesnut's Civil War,* ed. C. Vann Woodward (New Haven, Conn., 1981), 29; John W. Blassingame, *The Slave Community: Plantation Life in the Antebellum South,* 2nd edn. (New York, 1979), 154–56; John D'Emilio and Estelle B. Freedman, *Intimate Matters: A History of Sexuality in America* (New York, 1988), 102–3; Eugene D. Genovese, *Roll, Jordan, Roll: The World the Slaves Made* (New York, 1972), 423; Thelma Jennings, "'Us Colored Women Had to Go through a Plenty': Sexual Exploitation of African-American Slave Women," *Journal of Women's History* 1 (1990): 60–66, 72–74; Kenneth M. Stampp, *The Peculiar Institution: Slavery in the Ante-Bellum South* (New York, 1956), 359–60; Joel Williamson, *New People: Miscegenation and Mulattoes in the United States* (New York, 1980), 42–43; Henry Bibb, *Narrative of the Life and Adventures of Henry Bibb, An American Slave* (New York, 1849), 112–18.

15. David Rice, *Slavery Inconsistent with Justice and Good Policy* (Augusta, Ky., 1792), 16, reprinted in Charles S. Hyneman and Donald S. Lutz, eds., *American Political Writing during the Founding Era, 1760–1805,* 2 vols. (Indianapolis, 1983), 2:874.

16. On the lineage of the Hemingses, see Malone, 4:495; Williamson, *New People,* 43–44; and esp. Annette Gordon-Reed, *The Hemingses of Monticello: An American Family* (New York, 2008), 41, 47–49, 55–56.

17. TJ, *Notes on the State of Virginia,* ed. Peden, 141.

18. Ibid., 138, 143; TJ to William Short, 18 January 1826, Ford, 10:362; Jordan, *White over Black,* 518 20; Ronald T. Takaki, *Iron Cages: Race and Culture in Nineteenth-Century America* (New York, 1979), 30–35.

19. David H. Fowler, "Northern Attitudes towards Interracial Marriage: Legislation and Public Opinion in the Middle Atlantic States and the States of the Old Northwest, 1780–1930" (Ph.D. diss., Yale University, 1963), 84–95; James Sullivan to Dr. Jeremy Belknap, 30 July 1795, in "Queries Relating to Slavery in Massachusetts," *Collections of the Massachusetts Historical Society,* 5th ser., 3 (1877): 414; Jordan, *White over Black,* 545.

20. *Frederick-Town Herald,* reprinted in the *Gazette of the United States,* 27 September 1802; *Federalist* (Washington, D.C.), reprinted in the *New-York Evening Post,* 30 December 1801. On Federalist criticisms of Jefferson's inconsistent stands on equality and slavery, see Kerber, *Federalists in Dissent,* 27, 39, 51–52.

21. Douglas R. Egerton, *Gabriel's Rebellion: The Virginia Slave Conspiracies of 1800 and 1802* (Chapel Hill, N.C., 1993), 141, 145, 186, 68; Michael Durey, *"With the Hammer of Truth": James Thomson Callender and America's Early National Heroes* (Charlottesville, Va., 1990), 137–39. Fear of slave revolts even affected U.S. foreign policy. See Tim Matthewson, "Jefferson and Haiti," *JSH* 61 (1995): 209–48, esp. 216–18, 222–24.

22. Jordan, *White over Black,* 470, 578–82.

23. John Quincy Adams to Rufus King, 8 October 1802, in King, ed., *Life and Correspondence of Rufus King,* 4:176–77.

24. Durey, *"With the Hammer of Truth,"* 44–47, 53–109, 129–35; *Gazette of the United States*, 27 April 1798; Smith, *Freedom's Fetters*, 342–56.

25. TJ to C. F. Volney, 20 April 1802, *TJP*, 37:296.

26. Durey, *"With the Hammer of Truth,"* 113, 117, 119–20; "Jefferson & Callender, No. 10," *New-York Evening Post*, reprinted in the *Columbian Centinel*, 21 August 1802; 28 August letter from Philadelphia, printed in the *Columbian Centinel*, 4 September 1802; TJ to James Callender, 6 October 1799, excerpt published in the *Columbian Centinel*, 16 October 1802. For the full text, see *TJP*, 31:200–201. See also the 11 August letter from "Unsettled" of Baltimore, in the *Connecticut Courant*, 16 August 1802.

27. Warner, *Letters of the Republic*, 40, 42–43, 54–55, 76, 90, 108, 141–42; John Adams to Col. Joseph Ward, 8 January 1810, John Adams Letterbook, Adams Family Papers, microfilm reel 118, item 185, Massachusetts Historical Society.

28. *Gazette of the United States*, 7 September 1802; *Connecticut Courant*, 10 September 1802; "Legislature of Massachusetts, House of Representatives: Thursday, Jan. 31, 1805, Debate on Mr. Allen's Resolution for Dismissing the Printers of the Palladium," *Columbian Centinel*, 9 February 1805.

29. *Frederick-Town Herald,* reprinted in the *Gazette of the United States*, 27 September 1802.

30. "A Friend to Good Government, from the Republican Watch Tower, for the American Citizen," *Recorder*, 29 September 1802; *Gazette of the United States*, 7 September 1802; *Frederick-Town Herald*, reprinted in the *Gazette of the United States*, 27 September 1802; *Recorder*, reprinted in the *Connecticut Courant*, 10 September 1802.

31. "Free Negroes," *Recorder*, 10 November 1802; Egerton, *Gabriel's Rebellion*, 166–67; Robert McColley, *Slavery and Jeffersonian Virginia,* 2nd edn. (Urbana, Ill., 1973), 111; John H. Russell, *The Free Negro in Virginia, 1619–1865* (Baltimore, 1913), 64–65, 69, 131, 167–68; Stampp, *Peculiar Institution*, 353; John Taylor, *Arator: Being a Series of Agricultural Essays, Practical and Political: In Sixty-Four Numbers*, ed. M. E. Bradford (1818; Indianapolis, 1977), 115. Apparently, despite his stated opposition to miscegenation, Jefferson also accepted it in practice. In addition to his own probable relationship with Sally Hemings, there is the example of Thomas Bell, a Charlottesville merchant whom Jefferson described as "a man remarkable for his integrity." Bell first leased and then purchased from Jefferson Hemings's sister Mary, with whom he admitted to having fathered two children. See Lucia C. Stanton, "'Those Who Labor for My Happiness': Thomas Jefferson and His Slaves," in Onuf, ed., *Jeffersonian Legacies*, 170, 173n15, and Gordon-Reed, *The Hemingses of Monticello*, 407–11.

32. Bertram Wyatt-Brown, *Southern Honor: Ethics and Behavior in the Old South* (New York, 1982), 307–8; Catherine Clinton, *The Plantation Mistress: Woman's World in the Old South* (New York, 1982), 211, 214.

33. *Frederick-Town Herald,* reprinted in the *Gazette of the United States*, 27 September 1802; *Recorder*, reprinted in the *Gazette of the United States*, 7 September 1802.

34. *Recorder*, 22 September 1802, reprinted in Jordan, *White over Black*, 469; Wyatt-Brown, *Southern Honor*, 307, 289; Joshua D. Rothman, "James Callender and Social Knowledge of Interracial Sex in Antebellum Virginia," in *Sally Hemings and Thomas*

Jefferson: History, Memory, and Civic Culture, ed. Jan Ellen Lewis and Peter S. Onuf (Charlottesville, Va., 1999), 89–90, 96, 104–7. In addition to the diary of Mary Chesnut, the journal of Gertrude Thomas of Georgia illustrates aristocratic women's opposition to miscegenation. See Virginia Ingraham Burr, ed., *The Secret Eye: The Journal of Ella Gertrude Clanton Thomas, 1848–1889* (Chapel Hill, N.C., 1990), 45–46, 50, 58–59, 64–65, 147, 167–69, 319–20, 321, 322, 329, 332.

35. James Callender, "A Little More Honest Mischief; or, The President Again," *Recorder,* 8 December 1802.

36. The pamphlet, *Observations on Certain Documents Contained in No. V & VI of "The History of the United States for the Year 1796," in Which the Charge of Speculation against Alexander Hamilton, Late Secretary of the Treasury, Is Fully Refuted. Written by Himself* (Philadelphia, 1797), is reprinted under the heading "Printed Version of the 'Reynolds Pamphlet'," *AHP,* 21:238–85, 243, 251, 252 (quotations). See also McDonald, *Alexander Hamilton,* 227–30, 237, 243–44, 258–59, 286, 334–36; Broadus Mitchell, *Alexander Hamilton,* 2 vols. (New York, 1957–62), 2:139, 169, 209, 217, 399–422, 457, 486, 504; and John C. Miller, *Alexander Hamilton: Portrait in Paradox* (New York, 1959), 333–40, 458–59, 462–64, 485–86.

37. "Printed Version of the 'Reynolds Pamphlet'," *AHP,* 21:243.

38. Ibid., 21:249, 244.

39. See Mitchell, *Alexander Hamilton,* 2:418, and McDonald, *Alexander Hamilton,* 336. John C. Miller maintains, however, that Hamilton's confession to an affair with Maria Reynolds did little to reverse the ill effects of Callender's attack because it "persuaded few Republicans that he was innocent of financial wrongdoing." See Miller, *Alexander Hamilton,* 464.

40. Pauline Maier, *From Resistance to Revolution: Colonial Radicals and the Development of American Opposition to Britain, 1765–1776* (New York, 1972), 33; George Roberts to Robert Crafton, 9 October 1763, extracted in Leonard W. Labaree et al., eds., *The Papers of Benjamin Franklin,* 40 vols. to date (New Haven, Conn., 1959–) 11:370–71n. For the charges against Franklin, see "Papers from the Election Campaign, 1764," in Labaree et al, eds., *Papers of Benjamin Franklin,* 11:369–72 and esp. 381–84. For the political context of the election, see J. Philip Gleason, "A Scurrilous Colonial Election and Franklin's Reputation," *WMQ,* 3rd ser., 18 (1961): esp. 68–73. On Washington, see John C. Fitzpatrick, *The George Washington Scandals* (Alexandria, Va., 1929).

41. *Columbian Centinel,* 15 September 1802; "Federal Misperceptions Detected, No. XXIV," *National Intelligencer,* 29 September 1802.

42. Malone, 1:42, 57, 59, 153–54; Anthony F. C. Wallace, *Jefferson and the Indians: The Tragic Fate of the First Americans* (Cambridge, Mass., 1999), 35–36.

43. Because slaves existed as their masters' property, it was legally impossible, for example, for a master to rape his slave. See Peter W. Bardaglio, "Rape and the Law in the Old South: 'Calculated to Excite Indignation in Every Heart,'" *JSH* 60 (1994): 756–57; D'Emilio and Freedman, *Intimate Matters,* 101; Karen A. Getman, "Sexual Control in the Slaveholding South: The Implementation and Maintenance of a Racial Caste System," *Harvard Women's Law Journal* 7 (1984): 135; Diane Miller Sommerville, "The Rape

Myth in the Old South Reconsidered," *JSH* 61 (1995): 493; Stampp, *Peculiar Institution*, 360; and Jennifer Wriggins, "Rape, Racism, and the Law," *Harvard Women's Law Journal* 6 (1983): 106.

44. "The Monarchy of Federalism," *New-England Palladium* (Boston), 18 January 1805; *New-England Palladium*, 25, 31 January 1805; [Alexander Young], *The Defence of Young and Minns, Printers to the State, before the Committee of the House of Representatives; with an Appendix, Containing the Debate, &c* (Boston, 1805), 14–15; "Legislature of Massachusetts, House of Representatives: Thursday, Jan. 31, 1805, Debate on Mr. Allen's Resolution for Dismissing the Printers of the Palladium," *Columbian Centinel*, 9 February 1805.

45. TJ to Robert Smith, 1 July 1805, in Worthington Chauncey Ford, ed., *Thomas Jefferson Correspondence, Printed from the Originals in the Collections of William K. Bixby* (Boston, 1916), 115; Malone, 1:447–51; Fawn M. Brodie, *Thomas Jefferson: An Intimate History* (New York, 1974), 368–69.

46. "Printed Version of the 'Reynolds Pamphlet'," *AHP*, 21:243.

47. Leonard W. Levy, *Jefferson and Civil Liberties: The Darker Side* (Cambridge, Mass., 1963), 61–66; Malone, 5:373, 378–79, 386–91; TJ to James Madison, 25 August 1807, in Smith, ed., *Republic of Letters*, 3:1491–92; *Connecticut Courant*, 30 September 1807.

48. Hampden [David Daggett], *A Letter to the President of the United States, Touching the Prosecutions, under His Patronage, before the Circuit Court in the District of Connecticut* (New Haven, Conn., 1808), iv, 5, 17, 18, 20, 26–27.

49. TJ to Peter Carr, 19 August 1785, in Merrill D. Peterson, ed., *The Portable Thomas Jefferson* (New York, 1977), 380–81; Durey, *"With the Hammer of Truth,"* 161–62.

50. Thomas Dwight to Hannah Dwight, 24 October 1803, Dwight-Howard Papers, Massachusetts Historical Society.

51. TJ, Autobiography, [6 January–29 July 1821], *TJW*, 45; TJ, "The Anas," 4 February 1818, *TJW*, 671; Abijah Bigelow to Hannah Gardner Bigelow, 27 December 1812, in Clarence S. Brigham, comp., "Letters of Abijah Bigelow, Member of Congress, to His Wife, 1810–1815," *Proceedings of the American Antiquarian Society* 40 (1930): 349; 2 Pet. 2:1, 14; Durey, *"With the Hammer of Truth,"* 94.

52. [Young], *Defence of Young and Minns,* preface; "Answer to the Governor's Speech, Jan. 23, 1805," *Columbian Centinel*, 26 January 1805. Jan Lewis presents an excellent discussion of this mode of thought in "The Blessings of Domestic Society," in Onuf, ed., *Jeffersonian Legacies*, esp. 121–28.

53. Newman, "Principles or Men?"

54. For a thorough and empathetic analysis of the origins and effects of the multiple connections between the Hemingses and Jeffersons, see Gordon-Reed, *The Hemingses of Monticello.*

55. Brodie, *Thomas Jefferson*, 360–61, 363–64; TJ to Levi Lincoln, 25 October 1802, *TJP*, 38:566; TJ to Robert R. Livingston, 10 October 1802, *TJP*, 38:477.

56. TJ's Newspaper Commonplace Scrapbooks, 1:[16] (clipping source not identified), [27] (clipping source not identified but the toast is also quoted in the *Balance, and Columbian Repository* [Hudson, N.Y.], 9 April 1805), [31] (clipping source not identified, but a typographically different version of the toast also appears in the *Aurora*, 8 July 1805).

57. TJ's Newspaper Commonplace Scrapbooks, 1:[56] ("Federal Dictionary," *The Democrat* [Boston], 20 August 1806, reprinted from the *Witness* [Litchfield, Conn.], 13 August 1806).

58. Sternhold [Theodore Dwight], "Song," *Connecticut Courant,* 2 March 1803. For background, see Waldstreicher, *In the Midst of Perpetual Fetes,* 198–99, and Philip Hamburger, *Separation of Church and State* (Cambridge, Mass., 2004), 140–41n21.

59. "How Nearly Is Cunning Allied to Folly," *American Mercury* (Hartford, Conn.), 24 March 1803; "To All Good People of Colour," *Connecticut Courant,* 23 February 1803, reprinted from the *Monitor* (Litchfield, Conn.).

7. Triumphs

1. *National Intelligencer,* 6 July 1803.

2. *National Intelligencer,* 6, 8 July 1803; Edward Thornton to Lord Hawkesbury, 4 July 1803, as cited in Malone, 4:301.

3. The *National Intelligencer,* 8 July 1803, for example, noted that the "very day that informed us of the recommencement of European scenes of blood, . . . announced the removal from our horizon of the only cloud that threatened our peace."

4. See Malone, 4:276–81.

5. TJ to Wilson Cary Nicholas, 7 September 1803, *TJP,* 41:346–48. Jefferson's correspondence regarding the treaty's constitutionality is more fully discussed in Smith, ed., *Republic of Letters,* 2:1287–97.

6. For even-handed but distinct discussions of Jefferson's dilemma, see Bailey, *Thomas Jefferson and Executive Power,* chap. 7; Barry J. Balleck, "When Ends Justify the Means: Thomas Jefferson and the Louisiana Purchase," *Presidential Studies Quarterly* 22 (1992): 679–96; David N. Mayer, *The Constitutional Thought of Thomas Jefferson* (Charlottesville, Va., 1994), 215–16, 244–51; Garrett Ward Sheldon, *The Political Philosophy of Thomas Jefferson* (Baltimore, 1991), 95–99; and Robert W. Tucker and David C. Hendrickson, *Empire of Liberty: The Statecraft of Thomas Jefferson* (New York, 1990), 163–71. One of the harshest, most enduring judgments remains Henry Adams, *History of the United States of America during the Administrations of Thomas Jefferson* (1903; New York, 1986), 352–90.

7. See Mumper, "The Jefferson Image in the Federalist Mind," 396–421.

8. See ibid., 36–38, 406–7.

9. Fabricius, "Louisiana Bought but Not Yet Paid For. Who Pays for It?" *Columbian Centinel,* 13 July 1803. See also Kerber, *Federalists in Dissent,* 37n, 40n, 43–45, 66, 93, 213.

10. "Extract from a Letter to a Gentleman in This City," *Gazette of the United States,* 29 November 1803; *New-York Evening Post,* 20 July 1803.

11. *An Account of Louisiana, Being an Abstract of Documents, in the Offices of the Departments of State, and of the Treasury* (Philadelphia, 1803), 11. Publishers in Albany, Philadelphia, Providence, Raleigh, Washington, and Wilmington, Delaware, issued more than a half-dozen editions of this pamphlet during 1803.

12. *Gazette of the United States,* 1 December 1803; "Extract of a Letter from a Gentleman at Washington, Dated 2d of Jan. 1804," *American Telegraphe* (Bridgeport, Conn.), 1 February 1804.

13. Samuel Brazer, *Address, Pronounced at Worcester, on May 12th, 1804, in Commemoration of the Cession of Louisiana to the United States* (Worcester, Mass., 1804), 6–7. On Brazer, see William Lincoln, *History of Worcester, Massachusetts, from Its Earliest Settlement to September, 1836* (Worcester, Mass., 1862), 205–6. On Federalist hypocrisy, see also Benjamin Rush to John Adams, 22 September 1808, in Schutz and Adair, eds., *Spur of Fame*, 121; Abraham Bishop, *Oration, in Honor of the Election of President Jefferson, and the Peaceable Acquisition of Louisiana, Delivered at the National Festival, in Hartford, on the 11th of May, 1804* ([New Haven, Conn.], 1804), 6; and Curtius [John Taylor?], *A Defence of the Measures of the Administration of Thomas Jefferson* (Washington, D.C., 1804), 130, 132. While several historians identify Taylor as the author of this pamphlet, Robert E. Shalhope questions this attribution. See Shalhope, *John Taylor of Caroline: Pastoral Republican* (Columbia, S.C., 1980), 219–20, 276n12–14.

14. Joseph Priestley to Thomas Belsham, 6 August 1803, Original Letters from Dr. Joseph Priestley, Manuscripts Department, Dr. Williams's Library.

15. Curtius, *A Defence of the Measures of the Administration of Thomas Jefferson*, 122; Brazer, *Address, Pronounced at Worcester*, 9.

16. Allan B. Magruder, *Political, Commercial and Moral Reflections, on the Late Cession of Louisiana, to the United States* (Lexington, Ky., 1803), 40, 41, 48–50; An Old Citizen, *The Pudding Proved by Eating of It; or, Fact; The Decider of Controversy, &c.* (Monroe County, Va., 1804), 11.

17. Magruder, *Political, Commercial and Moral Reflections*, 72–73.

18. *Aurora*, 3 December 1803; "Further Evidence of the Federal Valuation of Louisiana," *National Intelligencer*, 2 September 1803; William Charles White, *An Oration, Pronounced at Worcester, on the Anniversary of American Independence, July 4th, 1804* (Worcester, Mass., 1804), 10; Curtius, *A Defence of the Measures of the Administration of Thomas Jefferson*, 131.

19. *Gazette of the United States*, 1 December 1803. For assertions that Jefferson would administer—or was administering—Louisiana like a tyrant, see *Gazette of the United States*, 19 July 1803; A Native, *View of the Political and Civil Situation of Louisiana; from the Thirteenth of November, 1803, to the First of October, 1804* (Philadelphia, 1804), 14, 16; *Reflections on the Cause of the Cession of Louisiana* (Washington, D.C., 1804), 11; and *Repertory* (Boston), 6 March 1804.

20. Andrew Jackson to TJ, 7 August 1803, in Smith et al., eds., *Papers of Andrew Jackson*, 1:354; TJ's Newspaper Commonplace Scrapbooks, 1:[32–33] (*National Gazette*, 2 March 1804), [32] ("List of Toasts Drank to at the Late Celebration, Continued," *Vermont Gazette* [Bennington], 22 July 1805).

21. See the *Aurora*, 2 July 1803, as well as the *New-York Evening Post*, 11 July 1803.

22. Nathaniel Macon to TJ, 20 April 1801, *TJP*, 33:620; TJ to Macon, 14 May 1801, *TJP*, 34:110. See also Malone, 4:91–93.

23. *United States Gazette* (Philadelphia), 20 February 1805; *Aurora*, 21 February 1805.

24. TJ's Newspaper Commonplace Scrapbooks, 1:[23] (*American Mercury*, 11 July 1805); *National Intelligencer*, 21 December 1804.

25. "Republican Festival," *National Intelligencer*, 20 July 1804; "Danbury, May 16," *Republican Farmer* (Bridgeport, Conn.), 16 May 1804; TJ to Pierre Samuel du Pont de

Nemours, 18 January 1802, *TJP*, 36:391; Henry J. Knox to Samuel Thatcher, 9 February 1804, Henry Knox Papers, ser. III, Massachusetts Historical Society.

26. H. Weld Fuller, *An Oration, Pronounced in the Meeting-House at Augusta, on the Fourth of July, 1804* (Augusta, Maine, 1804), 12; *Gazette of the United States*, 3 October 1804; [Clement Clarke Moore], *Observations upon Certain Passages in Mr. Jefferson's Notes on Virginia, Which Appear to Have a Tendency to Subvert Religion, and Establish a False Philosophy* (New York, 1804), 5, 10, 15–19, 6, 30.

27. Jerry W. Knudson, *Jefferson and the Press: Crucible of Liberty* (Columbia, S.C., 2006), chap. 5; "Hume, No. XXVI: Review of Mr. Jefferson's Administration," *Columbian Centinel*, 20 October 1804; David Dzurec, "Of Salt Mountains, Prairie Dogs, and Horned Frogs: The Louisiana Purchase and the Evolution of Federalist Satire, 1803–1812," *JER* 35 (2015): 99–100.

28. *Aurora*, 5 March 1805.

29. Ibid.; *National Intelligencer*, 20 March 1804; "Richmond (Virginia): Celebration of the 4th March," *National Intelligencer*, 28 March 1804; "Pennsylvania Politicks," *Balance, and Columbian Repository* (Hudson, N.Y.), 18 June 1805.

30. See, for example, *Gazette of the United States*, 27 September 1804; *Star-Office, September 10. Annapolis, September 4. Mr. Green, as Some of the Opponents of Mr. Jefferson Have Not Yet Dropped the Charge of Inaction and Timidity against Him when Governor of Virginia, You Will Oblige Me by Publishing in Your Next Gazette a Vindication of His Conduct, Taken from a Pamphlet Sent Me by a Friend from Philadelphia* (Easton, Md., 1804); William Garrott Brown, *The Life of Oliver Ellsworth* (New York, 1905), 324 (quotation).

31. *Columbian Centinel*, 11 July 1804.

32. Curtius, *A Defence of the Measures of the Administration of Thomas Jefferson*, 38; TJ to Albert Gallatin, 18 September 1801, *TJP*, 35:314.

33. Hume, "Review of Mr. Jefferson's Administration, No. XVII," *Columbian Centinel*, 29 August 1804; "Ode to Popularity," *Port Folio*, 2 February 1805.

34. *Gazette of the United States*, 11 July 1804; TJ to James Madison, 20 December 1787, *TJP*, 12:440–41. On Jefferson's support for the rotation of the presidential office, see Mayer, *The Constitutional Thought of Thomas Jefferson*, 96–97, 225–26.

35. TJ to William Short, 30 September 1788, *TJP*, 13:619; *Gazette of the United States*, 26 September 1792.

36. Thomas Dwight to John Williams, 17 August 1803, Dwight-Howard Papers, Massachusetts Historical Society; *New-England Repertory* (Newburyport, Mass.), 16 July 1803; "Connecticut Festival," *Connecticut Courant*, 16 May 1804; *Charleston Courier*, 8 December 1803 (reprinted from the *Frederickstown Herald* [Maryland]).

37. "Measures, Not Men," *Repertory* (Boston), 22 June 1804; "President for Life!" *New-Jersey Journal*, 3 January 1804.

38. Tadahisa Kuroda, *The Origins of the Twelfth Amendment: The Electoral College in the Early Republic, 1787–1804* (Westport, Conn., 1994), chap. 15; Fischer, *The Revolution of American Conservatism*, 83–84; *Columbian Centinel*, 3 October 1804.

39. *Columbian Centinel*, 3 October 1804.

40. John P. Kaminski, *George Clinton: Yeoman Politician of the New Republic* (Mad-

ison, Wis., 1993), 274; Kuroda, *The Origins of the Twelfth Amendment,* 163; "New York Address," *National Intelligencer,* 6 April 1804.

41. TJ, Conversations with Aaron Burr, 26 January [1804], L&B, 1:448; Nancy Isenberg, *Fallen Founder: The Life of Aaron Burr* (New York, 2007), 250–69, 400–404; "TO Philip Schuyler, Esq.," *Albany Register,* 24 April 1804; Freeman, *Affairs of Honor,* 159–66, 187–98; Knudson, *Jefferson and the Press,* chap. 7.

42. TJ to Martha Jefferson Randolph, 6 November 1804, Thomas Jefferson Papers, microfilm reel 5, Special Collections, University of Virginia Library; TJ's Newspaper Commonplace Scrapbooks, 2:[41–42] ("Thoughts on Duelling," *L'Oracle and Daily Advertiser* [New York], 7 September 1808); George Tucker, *The Life of Thomas Jefferson,* 2 vols. (London, 1837), 2:200; Bailey, *Thomas Jefferson and Executive Power,* esp. 72–76, 151–70, 181, 236, 247–50.

43. TJ, First Inaugural Address, 4 March 1801, *TJP,* 33:148; Bailey, *Thomas Jefferson and Executive Power,* 137–40; Onuf, *Jefferson's Empire,* 86; TJ, Conversations with Aaron Burr, 26 January [1804], L&B, 1:445.

44. TJ to William Duane, 28 March 1811, *TJP:RS,* 3:508; TJ's Newspaper Commonplace Scrapbooks, 4:[43] (clipping source not identified but a typographically different version appears as "A Song, for the New Hampshire Election, 1805," *Political Observatory* [Walpole, N.H.], 8 June 1805).

45. *Western Star,* 4 August 1804; *Port Folio,* 17 March 1804. On the Federalist critique of democracy, see William C. Dowling, *Literary Federalism in the Age of Jefferson: Joseph Dennie and the Port Folio, 1801–1812* (Columbia, S.C., 1999), chap. 1, and Kerber, *Federalists in Dissent,* chap. 6.

46. Fisher Ames to Col. Nathaniel Dwight, 10 January 1805, Special Collections, University of Virginia Library; *Port Folio,* 16 February 1805; *Gazette of the United States,* 11 October 1804.

47. *Raleigh Register,* 9 July 1804; *Gazette of the United States,* 11 July 1804.

48. Samuel Thatcher to Thomas Dwight, 25 September 1804, Dwight-Howard Papers, Massachusetts Historical Society; "Wayne," "Alarm! Alarm! Alarm!" (New York? 1804?), Early American Imprints, ser. 2, no. 7717.

49. Malone, 4:433–34; John Rhea to his constituents, 12 February 1805, Richard Stanford [to his constituents], 1 March 1805, in Cunningham, ed., *Circular Letters of Congressmen,* 1:381, 398.

50. TJ, Second Inaugural Address, 4 March 1804, *TJW,* 518, 521–23; Bailey, *Thomas Jefferson and Executive Power,* 213–20.

51. Robert M. S. McDonald, "Partisan Views of Jefferson's Pact for a Pacific Mediterranean," *Consortium on Revolutionary Europe, 1750–1850: Selected Papers* 26 (1996): 167–73; TJ to James Madison, 15, 27 April 1804, in Smith, ed., *Republic of Letters,* 2:1308, 1324.

8. "Dignified Retirement"

1. *National Intelligencer,* 23 December 1807. On Madison's authorship of essays on the embargo, see Brant, *James Madison,* 4:397–403.

2. See Louis Martin Sears, *Jefferson and the Embargo* (Durham, N.C., 1927); Burton

Spivak, *Jefferson's English Crisis: Commerce, Embargo, and the Republican Revolution* (Charlottesville, Va., 1979), chaps. 4–7; Tucker and Hendrickson, *Empire of Liberty,* chaps. 21–23. On Jefferson's announcement of plans to retire, see Malone, 5:169–70, 549.

3. T. H. Breen, *The Marketplace of Revolution: How Consumer Politics Shaped American Independence* (New York, 2004); Sharp, *American Politics in the Early Republic,* 76, 115; Levy, *Jefferson and Civil Liberties,* 114–20, 136–39; TJ to Albert Gallatin, 11 August 1808, Ford, 9:202.

4. TJ, First Inaugural Address, 4 March 1801, *TJP,* 33:150.

5. TJ, Kentucky Resolutions of 1798: Jefferson's Fair Copy, [before 4 October 1798], *TJP,* 30:548.

6. Madison, *Political Observations,* 20 April 1795, *JMP,* 15:518.

7. TJ, "Address to Congress," 8 November 1808, *New-York Evening Post,* 11 November 1808; *National Intelligencer,* 15 February 1808; Boston Charity Subscription List, 1808–10, Massachusetts Historical Society; James Duncan Phillips, "Jefferson's 'Wicked Tyrannical Embargo'," *New England Quarterly* 18 (1945): 472; John Lambert, *Travels through Canada, and the United States of North America, in the Years 1806, 1807, & 1808,* 2 vols., 3rd edn. (London, 1816), 2:65; A Fellow Sufferer [John Park], *An Address to the Citizens of Massachusetts, on the Causes and Remedy of Our National Distresses* (Boston, 1808), 10–11.

8. Benjamin Rush to John Adams, 13 July 1808, in Schutz and Adair, eds., *Spur of Fame,* 111; Daniel Lyman to Richard Kidder Randolph, 20 August 1808, Papers of Richard Kidder Randolph, Special Collections, University of Virginia Library; John Taylor to Wilson Cary Nicholas, 10 May 1808, Edgehill-Randolph Collection, Special Collections, University of Virginia Library; *Connecticut Courant,* 10 February 1808.

9. "Diary or Narrative, by a British Subject, of a Journey from New York City to Albany by Steamboat, Thence Overland to Niagara Falls, Fort Niagara, Etc. and Return through Ballston to Hudson, Thence by Packet 'Experiment' to New York City, August 6–September 6, 1808," Manuscripts Division, New York Public Library, 4, 49–50; "Glorious Times," *Connecticut Courant,* 15 June 1808; "Evasion, of the Embargo Law," *Connecticut Courant,* 25 May 1808. See also the dispatch from Keene, N.H., *Connecticut Courant,* 25 May 1808.

10. *Connecticut Courant,* 13 January 1808; Rosalie Stier Calvert to Jean Michel van Havre, 25 April 1807, Calvert to H. J. Stier, 1 January, 12 December 1808, in Margaret Law Callcott, ed., *The Mistress of Riversdale: The Plantation Letters of Rosalie Stier Calvert, 1795–1821* (Baltimore, 1991), 164, 181, 198; John Adams to Benjamin Rush, 19 December 1808, in Schutz and Adair, eds., *Spur of Fame,* 124.

11. Peterson, *Thomas Jefferson and the New Nation,* 912–13; Connecticut General Assembly, *At a Special Session of the Gederal [sic] Assembly* (Hartford, 1809), 5; Daniel Lyman to R. K. Randolph, 31 January 1809, Papers of Richard Kidder Randolph, Special Collections, University of Virginia Library; Levi Lincoln to Albert Gallatin, 30 January 1809, Gallatin Papers, Manuscripts Department, New-York Historical Society.

12. Modern economic analysis demonstrates that smuggling did not significantly hinder the reduction of exports; see Jeffrey A. Frankel, "The 1807–1809 Embargo against Great Britain," *Journal of Economic History* 42 (1982): esp. 293–301.

13. [Daniel Webster], *Considerations on the Embargo Laws* ([Boston, 1808]), 13; Rich-

ard Saunders, "Letter I," *Republican Crisis* (Albany, N.Y.), 24 June 1808; Junius, "Letter VI: To the President of the United States," *Republican Crisis*, 29 July 1808.

14. Civis, *Remarks on the Embargo Law; in Which Its Constitutionality, as Well as Its Effects on the Foreign and Domestic Relations of the United States, Are Considered* (New York, 1808), 34; "Dignified Retirement: Parody on the House That Jack Built, Suited to the Time" (ca. 1809), Gilder Lehrman Collection, New-York Historical Society; Charles Brockden Brown, *The British Treaty of Commerce and Navigation, Concluded December 31, 1806* (Philadelphia, 1807), xiii; *Connecticut Courant*, 13 July 1808.

15. Thomas Thacher, *A Sermon Preached at the Third Parish in Dedham, April 7, 1808* (Dedham, Mass., 1808), 11.

16. Richard Saunders, "Letter V," *Connecticut Courant*, 10 August 1808, reprinted from the *Republican Crisis*; Saunders, "Letter I," *Republican Crisis*, 24 June 1808.

17. Frankel, "The 1807–1809 Embargo against Great Britain," 291–308.

18. Sears, *Jefferson and the Embargo*, 61–62, 67, 137, 164–66, 214–17, 232–36; William Jeffrey Bolster, "The Impact of Jefferson's Embargo on Coastal Commerce," *Log of Mystic Seaport* 37 (1986): 111–23; Spivak, *Jefferson's English Crisis*, 204–9; Jean M. Yarbrough, *American Virtues: Thomas Jefferson on the Character of a Free People* (Lawrence, Kans., 1998), 75–79; TJ to "Mr. Lithson," 4 January 1805, L&B, 11:55; Benjamin Rush to John Adams, 13 June 1808, in Schutz and Adair, eds., *Spur of Fame*, 109; *Aurora*, 21 November 1808. For a fascinating account of Philadelphia during this embryonic stage of the market revolution, see Laura Rigal, *American Manufactory: Art, Labor, and the World of Things in the Early Republic* (Princeton, N.J., 1998).

19. *National Intelligencer*, 6 July 1805, 16 July 1804.

20. *National Intelligencer*, 6 July 1801; Matthew Livingston Davis, *An Oration, Delivered in St. Paul's Church, on the Fourth of July, 1800* (New York, 1800), 11–12; John J. Pringle, *An Oration, Delivered in St. Philip's Church, before the Inhabitants of Charleston, South-Carolina, on the Fourth of July, 1800* (Charleston, 1800), 16; James Kennedy, *An Oration, Delivered in St. Philip's Church, before the Inhabitants of Charleston, South-Carolina, on the Fourth of July, 1801* (Charleston, 1801), 21.

21. Ebenezer French, *An Oration, Pronounced July 4th, 1805, before the Young Democratic Republicans, of the Town of Boston, in Commemoration of the Anniversary of American Independence* (Boston, 1805), 18; French, *An Oration, Pronounced before the Republican Inhabitants, of Portland, on the Fourth of July, 1806, Being the Thirtieth Anniversary of American Independence* (Portland, Maine, 1806), 6; Levi Lincoln, Jr., *An Oration, Pronounced at Brookfield, (Mass.) upon the Anniversary of American Independence, on the Fourth of July, 1807; before a Numerous Assembly of the Republicans of the County of Worcester* (Worcester, Mass., [1807]), 13.

22. John Marshall, *The Life of George Washington*, 5 vols. (Philadelphia, 1805–7), 2:377n; "A Buckskin," *Virginia Gazette*, 10 September 1802, reprinted in the *Richmond Recorder*, 29 September 1802.

23. Although Wythe's surviving correspondence with Jefferson does not reveal how he came to possess a copy of Jefferson's final draft of the Declaration, Jefferson later wrote of the "rough drafts I sent to distant friends who were anxious to know what was passing." Although "to whom" Jefferson sent his version he could "not recollect," it seems likely that

Wythe, who led Virginia's Continental Congress delegation but had absented himself to tend to business in Williamsburg while Jefferson penned the document, was one of them. See TJ to John Vaughn, 16 September 1825, Ford, 10:345. On the provenance of the Wythe copy, see Julian P. Boyd, *The Declaration of Independence: The Evolution of the Text as Shown in Facsimiles of Various Drafts by Its Author, Thomas Jefferson* (Princeton, N.J., 1945), 43–45. For a full examination of Wythe's demise, see Julian P. Boyd, "The Murder of George Wythe," *WMQ*, 3rd ser., 12 (1955): 513–74.

24. *Richmond Enquirer*, 20 June 1806, reprinted in the *National Intelligencer*, 2 July 1806. The argument that congressional editing improved the Declaration did not vanish, however; nearly two decades later, Timothy Pickering wrote that "to those 'critics' Mr. Jefferson is indebted for much of the applause which has been bestowed upon him as AUTHOR of the Declaration." See Pickering, *A Review of the Correspondence between the Hon. John Adams, Late President of the United States, and the Late William Cunningham, Esq., Beginning in 1803, and Ending in 1812*, 2nd edn. (Salem, Mass., 1824), 139.

25. *Aurora*, 28 January 1808. On the scramble to nominate Jefferson's successor, see Cunningham, *The Jeffersonian Republicans in Power*, 108–24, 140, 147, 166, 183–85, 195–96, 226–35, and Norman K. Risjord, *The Old Republicans: Southern Conservatism in the Age of Jefferson* (New York, 1965), 38–39, 86–95.

26. Thomas Thompson to Jeremiah Mason, 29 December 1806, Jeremiah Mason Papers, Manuscripts and Archives, Sterling Memorial Library, Yale University; Josiah Quincy to Timothy Bigelow, 19 January 1808, Washburn Papers, vol. 18, Massachusetts Historical Society.

27. "To the American People: A Caution," *The Democrat* (Boston), 19 December 1807; *Message from the President of the United States, Covering a Communication from the Governor of Pennsylvania, and Certain Resolutions of the Legislature of that State* (Washington, D.C., 1808), 5; *National Intelligencer*, 23 December 1807, 4 January 1808. See also *Embargo; or, The Causes Which Prompted the Measure; and the Consequences Which Must Follow Its Abrogation—Considered* (Baltimore, [1808]), 2.

28. *To the Public* (Portsmouth, N.H., [1808]), 10; *Address to the People of Massachusetts* (Boston, 1809), 4.

29. *Reasons in Justification of the Embargo; Presented to the Citizens of Washington County* (Salem, N.Y., 1808), 3; *Aurora*, 6 July 1808; Livingston, "To Candid Federalists," *Aurora*, 30 April 1808, reprinted from the *True American* (Trenton, N.J.).

30. *National Intelligencer*, 4 January 1808, 25 December 1807.

31. "Celebration of the Fourth of March," *Enquirer* (Richmond, Va.), 10 March 1809.

32. *A Report on the Present Alarming State of National Affairs* ([Schenectady, N.Y., 1808]), 7; *Connecticut Courant*, 6 April 1808; *The Constitution of the U. States, the Declaration of Rights and Constitution of Massachusetts; Together with All the Embargo Laws* (Newburyport, Mass., 1809), 1; A Citizen of Vermont, *A Free Enquiry into the Causes, Both Real and Pretended, for Laying the Embargo* (Windsor, Vt., 1808), 3; H., "To the Freemen of Connecticut," *Connecticut Courant*, 23 March 1808; *Read, Citizens of Maine, and Judge for Yourselves* (N.p., [1809]), 1; *Connecticut Courant*, 1 June 1808.

33. Senex, No. III, in *Letters under the Signatures of Senex, and of a Farmer, Comprehending and Examination of the Conduct of Our Executive, towards France and Great*

Britain, out of Which the Present Crisis Has Arisen (Baltimore, 1809), 9–10; John Rutledge, Jr., to David Humphreys, 7 January 1808, Humphreys-Marvin-Olmsted Collection, Manuscripts and Archives, Sterling Memorial Library, Yale University; Miles Standish, Jr., *The Times; a Poem, Addressed to the Inhabitants of New-England, and of the State of New-York, Particularly on the Subject of the Present Anti-Commercial System of the National Administration* (Plymouth, Mass., 1809), 15; [William Cullen Bryant], *The Embargo; or, Sketches of the Times* (Boston, 1808), 7, 8; TJ's Newspaper Commonplace Scrapbooks, 3:[64–66] ("The Embargo . . . by a Youth of Thirteen," clipping source not identified), [66] ("Presumptuous Pride," clipping source not identified but a typographically different version appears under the title "Poesy" in the *Boston Gazette*, 22 December 1803).

34. "Extract of a Letter from Washington, Dated the 19th February," *Connecticut Courant,* 8 March 1809.

35. John Adams to Benjamin Rush, 1 September 1807, Gilder Lehrman Collection, New-York Historical Society; Sharp, *American Politics in the Early Republic,* 117–20; Brown, *The British Treaty of Commerce and Navigation,* 17; *New-York Evening Post,* 29 December 1807; *Connecticut Courant,* 6 April, 30 November 1808. See also Abraham Van Vechten, *Mr. Van Vechten's Speech in the Legislature of the State of New-York, February 2, 1809* ([Albany, 1809]), 1–2, 12.

36. Nicholas Gilman to John Goddard, 1 May 1812, William Dawes Papers, Massachusetts Historical Society; Barent Gardenier, speech of 20 February 1808, in *Annals of the Congress of the United States,* 10th Congress, 1st sess., 1656.

37. TJ's Newspaper Commonplace Scrapbooks, 1:[184] ("Principles and Not Men—or, The Principles of the Old Republican Party," *Aurora,* 3 September 1806); Benjamin Rush to John Adams, 22 September 1808, Adams to Rush, 25 July 1808, in Schutz and Adair, eds., *Spur of Fame,* 121, 112, 114. The *Aurora*'s "Principles and Not Men" essay criticized not Jefferson but Postmaster General Gideon Granger and Treasury Secretary Albert Gallatin, who sided with Benjamin Franklin Bache's enemies in Pennsylvania's intraparty strife. See Andrew Shankman, "Malcontents and Tertium Quids: The Battle to Define Democracy in Jeffersonian Philadelphia," *JER* 19 (1999): 43–72, and Kim T. Phillips, "William Duane, Philadelphia's Democratic Republicans, and the Origins of Modern Politics," *Pennsylvania Magazine of History and Biography* 101 (1977): 365–87.

38. TJ's Newspaper Commonplace Scrapbooks, 4:[59–60] ("The Embargo—A Song," clipping source not identified but an early example of many typographically different versions of Henry Mellen's song appears in the *Newburyport Herald* [Massachusetts], 12 July 1808), [61] ("Parody," clipping source not identified), [60] ("'The Embargo,' Parodied by Simon Pepperpot," clipping source not identified but see the typographically different version in the *Intelligencer* [Portsmouth, N.H.], 4 August 1808).

39. Richard Saunders, "Letter II," *Connecticut Courant,* 20 July 1808, reprinted from the *Republican Crisis.*

40. "Feast of Patriotism," *Aurora,* 4 March 1808, reprinted from the *Petersburg Republican* (Virginia).

41. "Celebration of the Fourth of March," *Enquirer,* 10 March 1809.

42. "Feast of Patriotism," *Aurora,* 4 March 1807, reprinted from the *Petersburg Repub-*

lican; "The National Festival," *Aurora,* 7 July 1808; "False Colours," *Aurora,* 17 February 1808; "To the Democratic Citizens of Pennsylvania," *Aurora,* 10 March 1808; *National Intelligencer,* 18 December 1807.

43. John Adams to Benjamin Rush, 18 April 1808, in Schutz and Adair, eds., *Spur of Fame,* 107.

44. Roy J. Honeywell, "President Jefferson and His Successor," *American Historical Review* 46 (1940): 64–75.

45. *National Intelligencer,* 4 March 1809.

46. *National Intelligencer,* 4 March 1809; *Baltimore American,* 6 March 1809; *National Intelligencer,* 30 December 1807.

47. Junius, "Letter III: To the President of the United States," *Republican Crisis,* 1 April 1808; Richard Saunders, "Letter VIII," *Connecticut Courant,* 14 September 1808, reprinted from the *Republican Crisis.*

48. Lambert, *Travels through Canada, and the United States of North America,* 2:355.

49. Albert Gallatin to TJ, 18 December 1807, TJ Papers, Lib. Cong.

50. *New-York Evening Post,* 4 March 1809.

9. Light, Liberty, and Posterity

1. Randall, *The Life of Thomas Jefferson,* 3:345. Randall, whose book remains a valuable source for oral tradition, identifies the inn as "Ford's tavern." Modern research has failed to locate an inn by that name, but two taverns owned by men named Flood existed along Jefferson's route. See Lucia Stanton, *The Road to Poplar Forest* (Charlottesville, Va., 1985), a "keepsake" pamphlet published by the Thomas Jefferson Memorial Foundation.

2. Malone, 6:15, 291–92.

3. Smith, *The First Forty Years of Washington Society,* 405.

4. TJ to John Randolph, 25 August 1775, *TJP,* 1:241; TJ to William Phillips, 25 June 1779, *TJP,* 3:15; TJ to John Melish, 10 March 1811, *TJP:RS,* 3:440.

5. TJ to Alexander Gallatin, 2 August 1823, Gallatin Papers, Manuscripts Department, New-York Historical Society; *Columbian Centinel,* 12 July 1817, as cited in George Dangerfield, *The Era of Good Feelings* (New York, 1952), 95.

6. TJ to James Madison, 6 September 1789, *TJP,* 15:392–98; TJ to John Wayles Eppes, 11 September 1813, *TJP:RS,* 6:492; TJ to "Henry Tompkinson" (Samuel Kercheval), 12 July 1816, *TJP:RS,* 10:227; TJ to Spencer Roane, 6 September 1819, Ford, 10:142; TJ to John Hampden Pleasants, 19 April 1824, L&B, 16:29.

7. TJ to Thomas Jefferson Randolph, 7 December 1808, Thomas Jefferson Papers, Special Collections, University of Virginia Library.

8. "One of your readers" to "[Isaac] Collet[t]," 23 July 1810, Virginia Manuscripts Collection, Special Collections, University of Virginia Library.

9. See "Madison Takes Over, 1809" [editorial note] and TJ's Circular Letter about His Relations with President Madison, March 1809, in Smith, ed., *Republic of Letters,* 3:1563–64, 1574.

10. Jan Lewis, *The Pursuit of Happiness: Family and Values in Jefferson's Virginia* (New York, 1983); Wood, *Radicalism of the American Revolution,* 104–5, 206, 294–99, 303, 305.

11. Donald R. Hickey, *The War of 1812: A Forgotten Conflict* (Urbana, Ill., 1989), 209–13; Ward, *Andrew Jackson*, 57–64, 87–88, 188–89; Risjord, *The Old Republicans*, 188–91, 252–54; Daniel Webster, "Notes of Mr. Jefferson's Conversation 1824 at Monticello," [1825], in Wiltse et al., eds., *Papers of Daniel Webster: Correspondence*, 1:375–76.

12. Daniel Webster, "Notes of Mr. Jefferson's Conversation 1824 at Monticello," [1825], in Wiltse et al., eds., *Papers of Daniel Webster: Correspondence*, 1:375–76; Robert V. Remini, *Andrew Jackson and the Course of American Empire, 1767–1821* (New York, 1977), 128–29; Andrew Jackson to John Coffee, 28 April 1804, as quoted in Remini, *Andrew Jackson and the Course of American Empire*, 128; James Parton, *Life of Andrew Jackson*, 3 vols. (New York, 1861), 2:333; Pocahontas Bolling Cabell to Susan Hubard, 23 December 1815, Hubard Family Papers, Southern Historical Collection, University of North Carolina Library; Smith, *The First Forty Years of Washington Society*, 58–59.

13. TJ to Martha Jefferson Randolph, 8 June 1797, *TJP*, 29:424; TJ's Newspaper Commonplace Scrapbooks, 3:[193] ("My Native Home," *Vermont Gazette*, 26 August 1805), 4:[179] (clipping source not identified), [180] (clipping source not identified but a typographically different version of "Home" appears in the *Kennebec Gazette* [Augusta, Maine], 24 November 1803), [181] (clipping source not identified), [182] (clipping source not identified but a typographically different version of "The Wish" appears in the *Suffolk Gazette* [Sag Harbor, N.Y.], 29 September 1806).

14. Ward, *Andrew Jackson*, 182–90; William Fleming to TJ, 29 July 1823, TJ Papers, Lib. Cong.; Parton, *Life of Andrew Jackson*, 2:334.

15. St. George Tucker to [John] Coatler, 25 January 1816, Special Collections, University of Virginia Library; TJ to Albert Gallatin, 6 June 1817, Gallatin Papers, Manuscripts Department, New-York Historical Society; Mayer, *The Constitutional Thought of Thomas Jefferson*, 219–20.

16. TJ to George Hay, 17 June 1807, Ford, 9:59–60; TJ to Hay, 20 June 1807, Ford, 9:57.

17. Marshall, *Life of George Washington*, 5:33, 2:377n. On the Marshall biography and Jefferson's interest in propagating his version of the past, see Ellis, *American Sphinx*, 251–58.

18. TJ to John Adams, 10 August 1815, *AJL*, 2:453; TJ to William Johnson, 12 June 1823, in Smith, ed., *Republic of Letters*, 3:1864; TJ to Joel Barlow, 3 May 1802, *TJP*, 37:400–401; TJ to Barlow, 9 July 1806, TJ Papers, Lib. Cong. See also Malone, 5:356–59, and Peterson, *Thomas Jefferson and the New Nation*, 859, 949.

19. TJ, Autobiography, [6 January–29 July 1821], *TJW*, 45; John Burk, *The History of Virginia, from Its First Settlement to the Present Day*, vols. 1–3 (Petersburg, Va., 1804–1805); *The History of Virginia; Commenced by John Burk, and Continued by Skelton Jones and Louis Hue Girardin*, vol. 4 (Petersburg, Va., 1816). See also Malone, 6:218–23; Peterson, *Thomas Jefferson and the New Nation*, 949; and TJ, The 1816 Version of the Diary and Notes of 1781, *TJP*, 4:262–67.

20. TJ, The 1816 Version of the Diary and Notes of 1781, *TJP*, 4:265; TJ to James Madison, 22 June 1817, in Smith, ed., *Republic of Letters*, 3:1786; Ellis, *American Sphinx*, 253; William Johnson, *Sketches of the Life and Correspondence of Nathanael Greene, Major General of the Armies of the United States in the War of the Revolution*, 2 vols. (Charleston, 1822).

21. Charles Royster, "A Battle of Memoirs: Light-Horse Harry Lee and Thomas Jeffer-

son," *Virginia Cavalcade* 31 (1981): 120–22; TJ to William Johnson, 12 June 1823, in Smith, ed., *Republic of Letters*, 3:1862–63.

22. See Ellis, *American Sphinx,* 254–57, and Freeman, *Affairs of Honor*, esp. 62–66. Freeman dates the "Anas" to the period 1809–18; see p. 63.

23. TJ, Autobiography, [6 January–29 July 1821], *TJW*, 3.

24. Ibid., 45, 97; J. Bennett Nolan, ed., *Lafayette in America, Day by Day* (Baltimore, 1934), 257; Sarah N. Randolph, *The Domestic Life of Thomas Jefferson* (New York, 1871), 390–91. For a more skeptical view of the Jefferson-Lafayette relationship, see Conor Cruise O'Brien, *The Long Affair: Thomas Jefferson and the French Revolution, 1785–1800* (London, 1996), 31–34, 45–49.

25. Gaye Wilson, "Recording History: The Thomas Sully Portrait of Thomas Jefferson," in *Light and Liberty: Thomas Jefferson and the Power of Knowledge,* ed. Robert M. S. McDonald (Charlottesville, Va., 2012), 187–206; James Fenimore Cooper to Charles Kitchel Gardner, 24 April–17 June [?] 1823, in James Franklin Beard, ed., *The Letters and Journals of James Fenimore Cooper*, 6 vols. (Cambridge, Mass., 1960–68), 1:95–96.

26. John Adams to Timothy Pickering, 22 August 1822, in Edmund C. Burnett, ed., *Letters of Members of the Continental Congress,* 8 vols. (Gloucester, Mass., 1963), 1:516; Timothy Pickering, *Col. Pickering's Observations Introductory to Reading the Declaration of Independence, at Salem, July 4, 1823* (Salem, Mass., 1823); Lee, cited in TJ to James Madison, 30 August 1823, in Smith, ed., *Republic of Letters*, 3:1826; Fliegelman, *Declaring Independence*, 164–66, 170–75; Elizabeth M. Renker, "'Declaration-Men' and the Rhetoric of Self-Presentation," *Early American Literature* 24 (1989): 129–31.

27. TJ to John Adams, 9 July 1819, *AJL*, 2:543; TJ to James Madison, 30 August 1823, in Smith, ed., *Republic of Letters*, 3:1826; TJ, Autobiography, [6 January–29 July 1821], *TJW*, 10–24.

28. TJ, Autobiography, [6 January–29 July 1821], *TJW*, 18; Fliegelman, *Declaring Independence*, 21, 65; Charles A. Goodrich, *Lives of the Signers of the Declaration of Independence* (New York, 1829).

29. Smith, *The First Forty Years of Washington Society,* 398; TJ to John Winn, William C. Rives, Daniel M. Railey, John M. Railey, John Ormond, Horace Branham, and George W. Nichols, 25 June 1823, Thomas Jefferson Letters, 1784–1824, Southern Historical Collection, University of North Carolina Library.

30. TJ, Report of the Commissioners for the University of Virginia, 4 August 1818, *TJW,* 457–73; TJ to Thomas Cooper, 14 August 1820, L&B, 15:269; TJ to Judge Augustus B. Woodward, 3 April 1825, Ford, 10:342; Charles W. Dabney (1903), as quoted in Peterson, *The Jefferson Image in the American Mind*, 241; TJ to William Roscoe, 27 December 1820, L&B, 15:303; TJ to James Madison, 1 February 1825, Madison to TJ, 8 February 1825, TJ to Madison, 12 February 1825, in Smith, ed., *Republic of Letters*, 3:1923–26; George S. Hillard, ed., *Life, Letters, and Journals of George Ticknor,* 2 vols. (London, 1876), 1:348.

31. TJ to the Trustees of the Lottery for East Tennessee College, 6 May 1810, *TJP:RS*, 10:365; Hillard, ed., *Life, Letters, and Journals of George Ticknor*, 1:348; Frank Shuffelton, "Thomas Jefferson, Colporteur of the Enlightenment," in McDonald, ed., *Light and Liberty*, 137–57.

32. TJ to Joseph C. Cabell, 7 February 1826, Thomas Jefferson Papers, Special Collec-

tions, University of Virginia Library; Dumas Malone, *The Public Life of Thomas Cooper* (New Haven, Conn., 1926), 239–45; Ellis, *American Sphinx*, 215; TJ to Cabell, 26 February 1818, Thomas Jefferson Papers, Special Collections, University of Virginia Library; TJ to William Short, 13 April 1820, L&B, 15:245–47; TJ to Robert B. Taylor, 16 May 1820, TJ Papers, Lib. Cong.

33. Malone, 6:265; Ellis, *American Sphinx*, 282; Stuart E. Leibiger, "Thomas Jefferson and the Missouri Crisis: An Alternative Interpretation," *JER* 17 (1997): 121–30; TJ to Joseph C. Cabell, 15 February 1821, TJ to James Breckenridge, 15 February 1821, TJ Papers, Lib. Cong.

34. TJ to J. Correa de Serra, 24 October 1820, Ford, 10:163; James Madison to Samuel Harrison Smith, 4 November 1826, in Gaillard Hunt, ed., *The Writings of James Madison,* 9 vols. (New York, 1900–1910), 9:259.

35. Randall, *The Life of Thomas Jefferson,* 3:332–33; Malone, 6:309–14; TJ to James Madison, 17 February 1826, in Smith, ed., *Republic of Letters,* 3:1965–66; TJ to Edward Livingston, 25 March 1825, L&B, 16:115. On Jefferson's finances, see Sloan, *Principle and Interest,* esp. 3, 10–12, 14–26, 48–49, 55, 218–23.

36. TJ to unknown, March [1826], Bixby Collection, State Historical Society of Missouri, Columbia (photocopy, Monticello Archives, Charlottesville, Va.); P. N. Nicholas to Dabney Carr, 25 March 1827, [Hetty Carr] to Dabney Carr, February 1826, Carr-Cary Papers, Special Collections, University of Virginia Library; TJ to Thomas Jefferson Randolph, 8 February 1826, in Edwin Morris Betts and James Adam Bear, Jr., eds., *The Family Letters of Thomas Jefferson* (Columbia, Mo., 1966), 469–70; Jane Carr to Dabney Carr, 27 February 1826, Carr-Cary Papers, Special Collections, University of Virginia Library; TJ, "Thoughts on Lotteries," February 1826, L&B, 17:448–65.

37. Hetty Carr to Dabney Carr, 10, 13, 29 March 1826, Carr-Cary Papers, Special Collections, University of Virginia Library; Sloan, *Principle and Interest,* 221–23. For the lottery bill, see *Acts Passed at a General Assembly of the Commonwealth of Virginia* (Richmond, Va., 1826), 101–2. For examples of local appeals, see Nathaniel Richardson and Joseph H. Thayer, *Letter of May 23 1826 to the Citizens of Boston: A Solicitation* (Boston, 1826), and *List of Subscribers for Relief of Thomas Jefferson from Debt, May 1, 1826* ([New York, 1826]), with handwritten additions, Thomas Jefferson Papers, Special Collections, University of Virginia Library.

38. TJ to James Madison, 17 February 1826, in Smith, ed., *Republic of Letters,* 3:1964–67.

39. Remarks of Dr. Robley Dunglison, as quoted in Randall, *The Life of Thomas Jefferson,* 3:549.

40. TJ to Frances Wright, 7 August 1825, Ford, 10:344; Gordon Jones and James A. Bear, Jr., "A Medical History of Thomas Jefferson" (unpublished typescript, Monticello Archives, 1979), 131–32; TJ to Madison, 18 October 1825, 3 May 1825, in Smith, ed., *Republic of Letters,* 3:1942, 1970; Edmund Hubard to Robert Hubard, 16 June 1826, Hubard Family Papers, Southern Historical Collection, University of North Carolina Library; Samuel C. Radbill, ed., "The Autobiographical Ana of Robley Dunglison, M.D.," *Transactions of the American Philosophical Society* 63 (1963):part 8, 32.

41. TJ to Roger C. Weightman, 24 June 1826, *TJW,* 1516–17.

42. Ibid.; Elizabeth Cometti and Valeria Gennaro-Lerda, "The Presidential Tour of Carlo Vidua with Letters on Virginia," *VMHB* 77 (1969): 398. Although the note to Weightman is frequently described as Jefferson's final written words, J. Jefferson Looney, the editor of Jefferson's retirement papers, has demonstrated that he subsequently wrote at least two more letters. See Looney, "Thomas Jefferson's Last Letter," *VMHB* 112 (2004): 178–84.

43. TJ to Ellen Wayles Coolidge, 14 November 1825, in Betts and Bear, eds., *The Family Letters of Thomas Jefferson,* 461–62.

44. TJ, Epitaph, [1826], *TJW,* 706.

45. For an alternative interpretation—that Jefferson meant to commemorate his most successful attempts to undermine the power of the Virginia aristocracy—see Ronald L. Hatzenbuehler, "Growing Weary in Well-Doing: Thomas Jefferson's Life among the Virginia Gentry," *VMHB* 101 (1993): 5–36.

46. TJ to Tench Coxe, 1 June 1795, *TJP,* 28:373. Jefferson's double emphasis on light and liberty reflects nicely his longstanding ambition to earn immortal fame as a "scientist/legislator"; see Douglass Adair, "Fame and the Founding Fathers," in *Fame and the Founding Fathers: Essays by Douglass Adair,* ed. Trevor Colbourn (New York, 1974), 16–21.

47. Herodotus, *The History of Herodotus,* trans. George Rawlinson, 4 vols. (London, 1858), 2:183; Pliny, *Natural History,* trans. H. Rackham and D. E. Eicholz, 10 vols. (Cambridge, Mass., 1947–62), 10:51, 57; Vivant Denon, *Travels in Upper and Lower Egypt, during the Campaigns of General Bonaparte* (London, 1802), appendix no. II. According to E. Millicent Sowerby, Jefferson owned the edition of Denon's *Travels* cited above; he owned Herodotus's *History* in a Greek and Latin text (Herodotus, *Herodoti Halicarnassensis Historia* [Glasgow, 1761]) and Pliny's *Natural History* in Latin and French (Caius Plinius Secundus, *Histoire naturelle de Pline traduite en françois, avec le texte latin rétabli d'après les meilleures leçons manuscrites,* 12 vols. [Paris, 1771–82], and C. Plinii Secundi, *Naturalis Historiae,* 3 vols. [Rotterdam, 1668–69]); see Sowerby, comp., *Catalogue of the Library of Thomas Jefferson,* 5 vols. (Washington, D.C., 1952–59), 4:153, 1:7–8, 458–9.

48. Rudolf Wittkower, *Selected Lectures of Rudolf Wittkower: The Impact of Non-European Civilizations on the Art of the West,* comp. and ed. Donald Martin Reynolds (New York, 1989), 74, 80, 93; "Chiswick House," in *The Oxford Companion to Gardens,* ed. Sir Geoffrey Jellicoe et al. (New York, 1986), 117.

49. TJ to Charles Thomson, 20 September 1787, *TJP,* 12:161. C. F. Volney, Jefferson's friend and correspondent, expressed a similar sentiment in his *Travels through Syria and Egypt, in the Years 1783, 1784, and 1785,* 2 vols., 2nd edn. (London, 1788), 1:284, which Jefferson purchased for his library; see Sowerby, comp., *Catalogue of the Library of Thomas Jefferson,* 1:62, 4:155. On Jefferson's fascination with Egyptian antiquities, see Karl Lehmann, *Thomas Jefferson, American Humanist* (New York, 1947), 24.

50. John Zukowsky, "Monumental American Obelisks: Centennial Vistas," *Art Bulletin* 68 (December 1976): 574; R. L. Heckscher, "The Public Memorial and Godefroy's Battle Monument," *Journal of the Society of Architectural Historians* 17 (March 1958): 19–24.

51. Susan R. Stein, *The Worlds of Thomas Jefferson at Monticello* (Boston, 1993), 374; Daniel Webster, "Notes of Mr. Jefferson's Conversation 1824 at Monticello," [1825], in Wiltse et al., eds., *Papers of Daniel Webster: Correspondence*, 1:370.

52. On the use of funerary obelisks in the context of this era's Egyptian Revival architectural movement, see Richard A. Etlin, *The Architecture of Death: The Transformation of the Cemetery in Eighteenth-Century Paris* (Cambridge, Mass., 1984), esp. 44, 47, and Richard G. Carrott, *The Egyptian Revival: Its Sources, Monuments, and Meaning, 1808–1858* (Berkeley, Calif., 1978), 82–87.

53. TJ, Epitaph, [1826], *TJW,* 706; Zukowsky, "Monumental American Obelisks," 574–81. The dimensions of Jefferson's grave marker conflicted not only with Egyptian and American fashion but also with the proportions prescribed by James Gibbs, whose architectural treatises influenced Jefferson. See Gibbs, *A Book of Architecture, Containing Designs of Buildings and Ornaments* (London, 1728), xx, listed in Sowerby, comp., *Catalogue of the Library of Thomas Jefferson*, 4:381. The association of Washington with obelisks started soon after his death; see Wendy C. Wick, *George Washington: A National Icon, The Eighteenth-Century Graphic Portraits* (Washington, D.C., 1982), 141–42.

54. Robert H. Kean, "History of the Graveyard at Monticello," in Shackelford, ed., *Collected Papers of the Monticello Association*, 1:8–13; Randolph, *The Domestic Life of Thomas Jefferson*, 431–32.

55. TJ, Epitaph, [1826], *TJW,* 706; Alfred L. Bush, *The Life Portraits of Thomas Jefferson* (Charlottesville, Va., 1987), 15–17; Stein, *The Worlds of Thomas Jefferson at Monticello*, 22, 69, 219.

56. Stein, *The Worlds of Thomas Jefferson at Monticello,* 219; Randall, *The Life of Thomas Jefferson*, 3:336 (quotation).

57. Bush, *The Life Portraits of Thomas Jefferson,* 17. While Giuseppe Ceracchi presented the bust as a "gift," soon after its 1795 delivery the sculptor presented Jefferson with a bill for $1,500, which the embarrassed recipient finally settled five years later; see ibid., 15, 17.

58. "Last Scenes of Mr. Jefferson's Life, &c.," *Richmond Examiner* (Virginia), 27 October 1826; Henry Lee, *Memoirs of the War in the Southern Department of the United States,* 2 vols. (Philadelphia, 1812), 2:5–15; TJ, Diary of Arnold's Invasion and Notes on Subsequent Events in 1781, [26 July 1816], *TJP,* 4:264–65; Malone, 6:219–20; TJ to Henry Lee IV, 15 May 1826, in Henry Lee, *Memoirs of the War in the Southern Department of the United States,* 2nd edn. (Washington, D.C., 1827), 207.

59. "Last Scenes of Mr. Jefferson's Life, &c.," *Richmond Examiner,* 27 October 1826; Lee, *Memoirs of the War in the Southern Department,* 2nd edn., 190, 204–8; TJ to Henry Lee IV, 15 May 1826, in Lee, *Memoirs of the War in the Southern Department,* 2nd edn., 204–5.

60. Nicholas P. Trist to Joseph Cabell, 4 July 1826, Cabell Papers, Special Collections, University of Virginia Library; Joseph Cabell to John H. Cocke, 4 July 1826, McGregor Collection, Special Collections, University of Virginia Library; George Tucker to Messrs. Gales and Seaton, 6 July 1826, Special Collections, University of Virginia Library.

61. Radbill, ed., "The Autobiographical Ana of Robley Dunglison, M.D.," 32; Nicholas P. Trist to Joseph Cabell, 4 July 1826, Cabell Papers, Special Collections, University of

Virginia Library; Thomas Jefferson Randolph to Henry S. Randall, in Randall, *The Life of Thomas Jefferson,* 3:543–44.

62. Thomas Jefferson Randolph to Henry S. Randall, in Randall, *The Life of Thomas Jefferson,* 3:544.

Epilogue

1. Joseph C. Cabell to John H. Cocke, 4 July 1826, McGregor Collection, Special Collections, University of Virginia Library; Henry Horace Worthington to Reuben B. Hicks, 5 July 1826, Special Collections, University of Virginia Library.

2. *National Advocate* (New York), reprinted in the *National Intelligencer,* 13 July 1826; Peterson, *The Jefferson Image in the American Mind,* 4 (quotation).

3. *Independent Chronicle,* 12 July 1826; *Funereal Honors by the Town of Salem; Order of Services at the North Church in Salem on Thursday, August 10, 1826, to Commemorate the Deaths of John Adams and Thomas Jefferson* (Salem, Mass., 1826); H. W. Palvey, *The Committee of the City Council, Appointed to Make Necessary Arrangements for Testifying in a Suitable Manner, the Respect of the Citizens of New-Orleans for the Memory of the Illustrious and Venerated Thomas Jefferson and John Adams* (New Orleans, 1826); "Town Meetings on the Death of Thomas Jefferson," *Commercial Chronicle and Baltimore Advertiser,* 11 July 1826; *Nashville Republican,* 5 August 1826; Robert P. Hay, "The Glorious Departure of the American Patriarchs: Contemporary Reactions to the Deaths of Jefferson and Adams," *JSH* 35 (1969): 545n10; Sheldon Smith, "Eulogy, Pronounced at Buffalo, New-York, July 22nd, 1826," in *A Selection of Eulogies, Pronounced in the Several States, in Honor of Those, Illustrious Patriots and Statesmen, John Adams and Thomas Jefferson* (Hartford, Conn., 1826), 91–92. For the best accounts of the rituals of mourning, see L. H. Butterfield, "The Jubilee of Independence, July 4, 1826," *VMHB* 61 (1953): 135–38; Ellis, *Passionate Sage,* 210–16; Hay, "The Glorious Departure of the American Patriarchs," 543–555; and Peterson, *The Jefferson Image in the American Mind,* 3–14.

4. Smith, "Eulogy, Pronounced at Buffalo," in *A Selection of Eulogies,* 96.

5. Butterfield, "The Jubilee of Independence," 135; Hay, "The Glorious Departure of the American Patriarchs," 545.

6. John Tyler, "Eulogy, Pronounced at Richmond, Virginia, July 11, 1826," in *A Selection of Eulogies,* 2; J. L. Tillinghast, *Eulogy Pronounced in Providence, July 17, 1826, upon the Characters of John Adams and Thos. Jefferson, Late Presidents of the United States, by Request of the Municipal Authorities* (Providence, 1826), 5; Robert Little, *A Funeral Sermon on the Death of John Adams and Thomas Jefferson, Ex-Presidents of the United States, Preached on Sunday Evening, July 16, 1826, in the First Unitarian Church, Washington City* (Washington, D.C., 1826), 5.

7. Caleb Cushing, "Eulogy, Pronounced at Newburyport, Massachusetts, July 15, 1826," in *A Selection of Eulogies,* 24; *Columbian Centinel,* 12 July 1817, as cited in Dangerfield, *The Era of Good Feelings,* 95.

8. Joseph E. Sprague, *An Eulogy on John Adams and Thomas Jefferson, Pronounced August 10, 1826, at the Request of the Town of Salem* (Salem, Mass., 1826), 30; "Thomas Jefferson," *Independent Chronicle,* 12 July 1826; *Niles' Weekly Register* (Baltimore), 12 Au-

gust 1826; William Halsey, *The First Jubilee of American Independence and, Tribute of Gratitude to the Illustrious Adams and Jefferson* (Newark, N.J., 1826), 46.

9. Daniel Webster, "Eulogy, Pronounced at Boston, Massachusetts, August 2, 1826," in *A Selection of Eulogies,* 198, 194; Samuel Smith, "Eulogy, Pronounced in Baltimore, Maryland, July 20th, 1826," in *A Selection of Eulogies,* 72.

10. Edward Everett, *An Address Delivered at Charleston, August 1, 1826, in Commemoration of John Adams and Thomas Jefferson* (Boston, 1826), 30–31; John Adams to TJ, 30 June 1813, *TJP:RS,* 6:255.

11. Walter R. Johnson, *An Oration Delivered at Germantown, Pennsylvania, on the 20th of July, 1826, in Presence of the Citizens of Germantown, Roxborough, Bristol, and Penn Townships, Assembled to Commemorate the Virtues and Services of Thomas Jefferson and John Adams* (Philadelphia, 1826), 11; Sprague, *An Eulogy on John Adams and Thomas Jefferson,* 29; C. C. Cambreleng, "Eulogy, Pronounced in the City of New-York, July 17th, 1826," in *A Selection of Eulogies,* 59–70; Tyler, "Eulogy, Pronounced at Richmond," in *A Selection of Eulogies,* 2–17; William Johnson, "Eulogy, Pronounced at Charleston, South-Carolina, August 3, 1826," in *A Selection of Eulogies,* 299–328; Henry Potter, "Eulogy, Pronounced in Fayetteville, North-Carolina, July 20th, 1826," in *A Selection of Eulogies,* 129–38; John W. James, *Eulogy on Thomas Jefferson, Delivered at Columbian College, D.C., on the Fourth of October, 1826* (Washington, D.C., 1826), 3–8; Randolph, *The Domestic Life of Thomas Jefferson,* 421.

12. Sprague, *An Eulogy on John Adams and Thomas Jefferson,* 14; Charles Stewart Daveis, *An Address Delivered at Portland, on the Decease of John Adams, and Thomas Jefferson, August 9, 1826* (Portland, Me., 1826), 23, 49; Peleg Sprague, "Eulogy, Pronounced at Hallowell, Maine, July, 1826," in *A Selection of Eulogies,* 144. On Jefferson's differing views of African Americans and Indians, see John Chester Miller, *The Wolf by the Ears: Thomas Jefferson and Slavery* (New York, 1977), 64–73, 115, 145, 180.

13. *New-York Evening Post,* 30 December 1801, reprinted from the *Federalist* (Washington, D.C.); Kerber, *Federalists in Dissent,* 27–28, 54–57.

14. Kerber, *Federalists in Dissent,* 36–40, 50, 55–56. For Federalist depictions of Jefferson as an abolitionist, see "Phocion No. II," *Gazette of the United States,* 15 October 1796, and [Smith], *The Pretensions of Thomas Jefferson to the Presidency Examined,* 29. The charge that Jefferson issued inconsistent statements regarding racial issues probably best served Federalist purposes, as it stood to alienate both friends and foes of slavery from the master of Monticello while allowing them to avoid taking sides. For an example of the technique, see *Boston Gazette,* 11 November 1802.

15. Jordan, *White over Black,* 321, 430–35; Miller, *The Wolf by the Ears,* 4–5, 41–43, 145–47, 221, 225–50, 257, 258, 266–67; TJ, *Notes on the State of Virginia,* ed. Peden, 162–63; Cambreleng, "Eulogy, Pronounced in the City of New-York," in *A Selection of Eulogies,* 64. For a thoughtful discussion of Jefferson's "antislavery" credentials, see William W. Freehling, *The Road to Disunion: Secessionists at Bay, 1776–1854* (New York, 1990), 122–31.

16. Halsey, *First Jubilee of American Independence,* 23, 55.

17. TJ to Christopher Ellery, 9 May 1803, *TJP,* 40:338; TJ to James Heaton, 20 May 1826, *TJW,* 1516; TJ to Edward Coles, 25 August 1814, Ford, 9:476–79; John Adams to TJ,

3 February 1821, *AJL*, 2:571; Ellis, *Passionate Sage*, 218, 268n20. On the postmortem appropriation of Jefferson's statements by opponents of slavery, see Peterson, *The Jefferson Image in the American Mind*, 164, 172–81, and Freehling, *The Road to Disunion*, 121, 123.

18. Cushing, "Eulogy, Pronounced at Newburyport, Massachusetts," in *A Selection of Eulogies*, 28; Cambreleng, "Eulogy, Pronounced in the City of New-York," in *A Selection of Eulogies*, 63; Rev. Chester Wright, *An Address, on the Death of the Venerable and Illustrious Adams and Jefferson, Ex-Presidents of the United States, Delivered before a Large Concourse of Citizens, at Montpelier, Vermont, July 25, 1826* (Montpelier, Vt., 1826), 5.

19. Potter, "Eulogy, Pronounced in Fayetteville, North-Carolina," in *A Selection of Eulogies*, 133, 135; Smith, "Eulogy, Pronounced in Baltimore," in *A Selection of Eulogies*, 88; Tyler, "Eulogy, Pronounced at Richmond," in *A Selection of Eulogies*, 15.

20. John Stanford, *A Discourse on the Death of the Honourable Thomas Jefferson and John Adams, Delivered in the Chapel at Bellevue, N. York* (New York, 1826), 12; Potter, "Eulogy, Pronounced in Fayetteville, North-Carolina," in *A Selection of Eulogies*, 134; Alfred Johnson, Jr., *Eulogy Delivered at Belfast, August 10, 1826, on John Adams and Thomas Jefferson, at the Request of the Citizens of Belfast* (Belfast, Maine, 1826), 9–10.

21. William Wilkins, "Eulogy, Pronounced at Pittsburgh, Pennsylvania, August 24, 1826," in *A Selection of Eulogies*, 372.

22. John Adams to Benjamin Rush, 21 June 1811, in Schutz and Adair, eds., *Spur of Fame*, 182; Cambreleng, "Eulogy, Pronounced in the City of New-York," in *A Selection of Eulogies*, 60; Johnson, *Eulogy Delivered at Belfast*, 8–9.

23. Sprague, *An Eulogy on John Adams and Thomas Jefferson*, 10; Webster, "Eulogy, Pronounced at Boston," in *A Selection of Eulogies*, 208.

24. TJ to Roger Weightman, 24 June 1826, *TJW*, 1516–17.

25. Charles Francis Adams, ed., *Memoirs of John Quincy Adams, Comprising Portions of His Diary from 1795 to 1848*, 12 vols. (Philadelphia, 1874–77), 7:133. On Adams's reported last words, see Andrew Burstein, *America's Jubilee* (New York, 2001), 267–73.

Appendix

1. [Margaret Bayard Smith], "Recollections of a Visit to Monticello," *Richmond Enquirer*, 18 January 1823.

2. Through the end of the twentieth century, only a few scholars had cited the scrapbooks. See Betts and Bear, eds., *The Family Letters of Thomas Jefferson*, 203n2, 278n1, 297n1, 320–21n1; Brodie, *Thomas Jefferson*, 44, 45n35, 68–69, 69n2; TJ to John Adams, 25 February 1823, *AJL*, 2:588n64; Malone, 4:30n6, 5:10n14; Francis Coleman Rosenberger, ed., *Jefferson Reader: A Treasury of Writings about Thomas Jefferson* (New York, 1953), 97, 99, 113; William Harwood Peden, "Thomas Jefferson: Book-Collector" (Ph.D. diss., University of Virginia, 1942), 61–62, 62n1, 233; and John W. Wayland, "The Poetical Tastes of Thomas Jefferson," *Sewanee Review* 18 (1911): 283–99.

3. The University of Virginia Library describes the volumes, which appear in its online catalog as "Scrapbooks of clippings compiled by Thomas Jefferson's family, 1800–1808" and "Jefferson-Randolph Family Scrapbooks, 1800–1808," and in its card catalog

as "Scrapbooks, probably once the property of Thomas Jefferson," as containing items "clipped by Jefferson and sent to his family." See the electronic and card catalog entries for MSS 5948 and 5948-a. Since the scrapbooks are housed with the University of Virginia Library's Thomas Jefferson Papers collection, the fourth volume, which the library acquired in 1851, before the three others (see below for the circumstances surrounding acquisition of all the volumes), is listed in Constance E. Thurlow and Francis L. Berkeley, Jr., comps., *The Jefferson Papers of the University of Virginia: A Calendar* (Charlottesville, Va., 1950), as item 759: "Scrapbook of Songs and Poems. [1801 *et seq.*] 204 pp." This is the volume that provides sources for Wayland's "Poetical Tastes of Thomas Jefferson," which contains the first published assertion, albeit based on incomplete evidence, that the 1851 scrapbook was compiled by Thomas Jefferson.

4. The "discovery" of Jefferson's newspaper commonplace scrapbooks was first reported by Leef Smith, "Scrapbooks Believed to Be Work of Jefferson; Clippings, Poems Found in 4 Volumes at U.Va. Library," *Washington Post,* 30 September 1999, A9. Recent studies have made use of the scrapbooks but have assumed and not proven their connection to Jefferson. See James L. Golden and Alan L. Golden, *Thomas Jefferson and the Rhetoric of Virtue* (Lanham, Md., 2002); Jonathan Gross, ed., *Thomas Jefferson's Scrapbooks: Poems of Nation, Family, and Romantic Love* (Hanover, N.H., 2006); and Kevin J. Hayes, *The Road to Monticello: The Life and Mind of Thomas Jefferson* (New York, 2008), 504–6. Although focused on the scrapbooks' contents, information relating to their attribution to Jefferson appears in Christine E. Coalwell and Robert M. S. McDonald, *The Jefferson Scrapbooks' Story of Politics, Death, and Friendship* (Charlottesville, Va., 2000), a "keepsake" pamphlet published by the Thomas Jefferson Foundation.

5. A. T. Laird to University of Virginia librarians, 8 April 1851, enclosed in TJ's Newspaper Commonplace Scrapbooks, 4:[5–6]. This volume of the scrapbooks also contains on page [8] a dedication:

To A. T. Laird
        from E. R. Chambers.
Boydton Va.
Sept. 2, 1844.

Chambers was a judge, businessman, and civic leader in Mecklenburg, Va.; his daughter Virginia married Laird in 1853, and he was part owner, with Laird, of the 1851–54 Boydton Savings Bank. Chambers was related to Jefferson through his wife, Lucy Goode Tucker Chambers. See Susan L. Bracey, *Life by the Roaring Roanoke: A History of Mecklenburg County, Virginia* (Mecklenburg County, Va., 1977), 140, 212, 267, 275, 343, and Rose Chambers McCullough, *Yesterday When It Is Past* (Richmond, Va., 1957), 136–37, 359. Laird's reference to Jefferson's scrapbooks having been "left in his library" is consistent with an 1828 account by Joseph Coolidge, Jr., who, prior to the sale of the more valuable articles in Jefferson's collection of books, saw pamphlets scattered "in a mess upon the library floor." See Joseph Coolidge, Jr., to Thomas Jefferson Randolph, 10 February 1828, Ellen Wayles Randolph Coolidge Correspondence, Special Collections, University of Virginia Library.

6. TJ's Newspaper Commonplace Scrapbooks, 1:[2]. On the University of Virginia Li-

brary's acquisition of the three volumes, see the correspondence in the accession records for MSS #5948, Special Collections, University of Virginia Library.

7. Thomas Jefferson Randolph to TJ, 3 April 1826, in Betts and Bear, eds., *The Family Letters of Thomas Jefferson,* 476. For references to John Randolph, two of which appear in anti-Jefferson pieces dating from when Randolph was allied with Jefferson (in another, his name is toasted at a Petersburg, Va., Fourth of July banquet), see TJ's Newspaper Commonplace Scrapbooks, 1:[10], 3:[28], 4:[16]. On Randolph's library, see Hugh B. Grigsby, "The Randolph Library," *Southern Literary Messenger* 20 (1854): 76–79.

8. On Clark's relationship with John Randolph, see William Mulford, *Bannister Lodge: A History of Unbaffled Virginians* (N.p., 1982), 14–15, and Robert Alexander Lancaster, *Historic Virginia Homes and Churches* (Philadelphia, 1915), 439. (A reference to the presence of "William Clarke" at the same Petersburg, Va., Fourth of July banquet where John Randolph was toasted appears in TJ's Newspaper Commonplace Scrapbooks, 1:[10].) Clark's decision to give the scrapbooks to Sarah Randolph might have been influenced by Hugh Grigsby, who served as a delegate to the 1829–30 Virginia Constitutional Convention with John Randolph, admired his library, and encouraged Sarah Randolph's historical work. See William Cabell Bruce, *John Randolph of Roanoke, 1773–1833,* 2 vols. (New York, 1922), 2:64; Grigsby, "The Randolph Library," 76–79; and Clayton Torrence, ed., "Letters of Sarah Nicholas Randolph to Hugh Blair Grigsby," *Virginia Historical Magazine* 59 (1951): 315–36.

9. Shackelford, ed., *Collected Papers of the Monticello Association,* 2:236.

10. Thomas Jefferson Randolph to Gen. Alexander Smith, February 1830, Papers of the Randolph and Related Families, Special Collections, University of Virginia Library; TJ, "Explanation of the Three Volumes Bound in Marbled Paper," 4 February 1818, in Thomas Jefferson Randolph, ed., *Memoirs, Correspondence, and Miscellanies, from the Papers of Thomas Jefferson,* 4 vols., 2nd edn. (Boston, 1830), 4:443.

11. Nicholas P. Trist, "Backs of Letters to Thomas Jefferson," n.d., "Miscellaneous" file, Trist-Burke Family Papers, 1834–1936, Special Collections, University of Virginia Library. Trist's statement appears on the back of a letter wrapper addressed to Jefferson.

12. See, for example, the reverse side of TJ to George W. Hay, 20 April 1821, TJ Papers, Lib. Cong.

13. See "Clippings," [1803], Miscellaneous Bound Volumes, ser. 7, no. 10, TJ Papers, Lib. Cong. The existence of both the mounted and loose clippings raise intriguing questions: Why were these items not included within the newspaper commonplace scrapbooks, which also contain clippings from the same period? Were clippings mounted on scraps that were then bound together or were scraps bound together before clippings were pasted onto them? Were these clippings once bound together (as the collection title, "Miscellaneous Bound Volumes," suggests) and then unbound, as Jefferson's "Anas" was, in an attempt at conservation?

14. See Adams, ed., *Jefferson's Extracts from the Gospels,* 30–38.

15. Wilson, ed., *Jefferson's Literary Commonplace Book,* Appendix C, 219–20; TJ's Newspaper Commonplace Scrapbooks, 3:[155–57], [159–62], [167], [175–77], [182], [192–93], [199–200].

16. For recognized examples of Jefferson's numerals, see the facsimile of the "Life and

Morals of Jesus of Nazareth" in Adams, ed., *Jefferson's Extracts from the Gospels,* 127–297 *passim.* Numerals executed with a pencil appear as partial pagination in TJ's newspaper commonplace scrapbooks throughout. Note also the occasional pencil notations that guide pagination. In 3:[187], for example, is written "to follow the ode . . . [illeg.]." Pasted on the preceding page is an "Ode Sung at the Sixth Anniversary of the Newyork Belles Lettres Club."

17. TJ's Newspaper Commonplace Scrapbooks, 1:[226], [227], 2:[4], 3:[226], 4:[98], [136], [210]. (In addition, the word "and" is crossed out in 1:[224], an article is circled in 3:[97], and a printed "x" appears next to the titles of articles in 4:[147], [184], [208], [210], [212].)

18. TJ's Newspaper Commonplace Scrapbooks, 3:[49]; Wilson, ed., *Jefferson's Literary Commonplace Book,* 15, 191, 217, 218, 221, 224, 225, 226.

19. [Smith], "Recollections of a Visit to Monticello," *Richmond Enquirer,* 18 January 1823, reprinted in the *Salem Gazette,* 7 February 1823; John Adams to TJ, 10 February 1823, *AJL,* 2:587. On Adams's infirmities and his reliance on others as readers and writers, see John Ferling, *John Adams: A Life* (Knoxville, Tenn., 1992), 436, 439.

20. TJ to John Adams, 25 February 1823, *AJL,* 2:588–89. For an example of Jefferson's practice of sending poetic clippings to his granddaughters, see TJ to Ellen Wayles Randolph, 1 March 1807, in Betts and Bear, eds., *The Family Letters of Thomas Jefferson,* 297.

21. For the essay by "No Jeffersonian," see TJ's Newspaper Commonplace Scrapbooks, 3:[9]. For critiques of the embargo in that volume, see [64–66], [72–73]. For examples of other anti-Jefferson pieces, see 1:[135], [202–5], [207–9], 2:[124], 3:[7], [28–32], 4:[16], [35], [59–60].

22. [Smith], "Recollections of a Visit to Monticello," *Richmond Enquirer,* 18 January 1823. Taken "from Mrs. Smith's note book," her 1 August 1809 account appears in Smith, *The First Forty Years of Washington Society,* 65–81.

23. See Sowerby, comp., *Catalogue of the Library of Thomas Jefferson,* 3:379.

24. John Adams to TJ, 10 February 1823, *AJL,* 2:587.

25. For Jefferson's remark, which he made in an 26 April 1791 letter to Jonathan B. Smith, and a fuller description of the controversy, together with related correspondence, see *"Rights of Man"* [editorial note], *TJP,* 20:268–312.

26. TJ to Thomas Paine, 18 March 1801, *TJP,* 33:359. For the circumstances of Paine's return, see Malone, 4:192–200.

27. Thomas Paine, "To the Citizens of the United States and Particularly to the Leaders of the Federal Faction: Letter II," *National Intelligencer,* 15 November 1802.

28. Paine's 15 November 1802 anti-Adams essay appears in TJ's Newspaper Commonplace Scrapbooks, 2:[132–34]. For examples of other anti-Adams clippings, see 1:[132–34], [234–35], 2:[135–36].

INDEX

References to "Declaration" denote the Declaration of Independence, and italicized page numbers refer to illustrations.